Between Equal Rights

A Marxist Theory of International Law

Between Equal Rights

A Marxist Theory of International Law

China Miéville

AAKAR

BETWEEN EQUAL RIGHTS: A Marxist Theory of International Law
China Miéville

First Published in India 2016

ISBN 978-93-5002-446-1

Published in agreement with Koninklijke Brill NV,
Leiden, The Neatherlands for publication and sale only in the
Indian Subcontinent (India, Pakistan, Bangladesh,
Nepal, Maldives, Bhutan and Sri Lanka)

Published by
AAKAR BOOKS
28 E Pocket IV, Mayur Vihar Phase I, Delhi 110 091
Phones : 011 2279 5505, 2279 5641
aakarbooks@gmail.com; www.aakarbooks.com

Printed at
Mudrak, 30 A Patparganj, Delhi 110 091

Acknowledgements

This book is a revised version of a doctoral thesis researched at the Department of International Relations, London School of Economics and Political Science, under the supervision of Fred Halliday. Despite our many theoretical and political differences (some of them rehearsed below), he was an exemplary supervisor, and I am extremely grateful to him. The late Philip Windsor supervised during the first year of my research, and I am indebted to him for his generous input, as well as to Chris Brown and Michael Yahuda for comments during research panels.

My doctoral examination was carried out by Andrew Linklater and Peter Gowan, whose questions and criticisms were invaluable. I am fortunate to sit on the board of the journal *Historical Materialism*, and I am grateful to all those editors – Matthew Beaumont, Emma Bircham, Andrew Brown, Sebastian Budgen, Alejandro Colás, Adrian Haddock, Martin Jenkins, Alan Johnson, Esther Leslie, Martin McIvor and Greg Schwarz – from whom I have learnt during our discussions. For input, criticism, ideas and help with material, my thanks to John Game, Chris Arthur, Geoff Kay, Howard Engelskirchen, Colin Barker, Jörg Fisch, Peter Maggs and David Kennedy. The support of my mother Claudia Lightfoot and sister Jemima Miéville has been indispensable. Without the financial support of the Economic and Social Research Council I could not have started this work. My thanks to everyone at Brill, particularly Joed Elich and Regine Reincke for their patience. I owe a colossal debt to Sebastian Budgen for his suggestions and discussions.

In September 2003, I was invited to be part of the *Leiden Journal of International Law*'s symposium on 'Marxism and International Law' in the Hague. I am grateful to Miklós Redner for his organisation, and all the participants: Anthony Carty, B.P. Chimni, Martti Koskenniemi, Susan Marks (who also co-organised the event) and Brad Roth.

Finally, for detailed and often trenchant comments on an early draft of this work, I am profoundly indebted to Henry Farrell, Susan Marks, Bill Bowring, Tony Chase and Martti Koskenniemi. Though they will not be convinced by all of what follows, I have tried to rise to their challenges. Most especially my love and thanks to Emma Bircham, for her help with this book and much else. All errors and inadequacies, of course, are mine.

London, 2004

A note on terminology: in what follows, 'international relations' refers to the political environment between states, and 'IR' to the academic discipline that studies it.

Dedication

To the memory of Fred Hampton (1948–69)

Contents

Introduction 1
1. 'International law has become important' 1
2. Materialism and dialectics 4
3. The structure of the book 5

Chapter One: 'The Vanishing Point of Jurisprudence': International Law in Mainstream Theory 9
1. Beyond definition 9
2. Classic writers and debates 16
2.1. Disentangling denial 16
2.1.1. The will of the sovereign: Austin 18
2.1.2. The triumph of politics: Morgenthau 19
2.1.3. A third way? Carl Schmitt 25
2.2. Monism, dualism, positivism, naturalism 32
2.3. The high point of formalism: Kelsen 34
2.4. From rules to process: McDougal-Lasswell 37

Chapter Two: Dissident Theories: Critical Legal Studies and Historical Materialism 45
1. Beyond pragmatism 45
2. Koskenniemi and the contradictions of liberalism 48
3. Marxism and international law 60
3.1. The inadequacies of Soviet theory 60
3.2. Radicalism with rules: B.S. Chimni 64

Chapter Three: For Pashukanis: An Exposition and Defence of the Commodity-Form Theory of Law 75
1. The rise and fall of Pashukanis 75
2. *The General Theory of Law and Marxism* 77
2.1. Marxist method and the failure of alternative theories 79
2.1.1. Law as ideology 80
2.1.2. Law as iniquitous content 82
2.2. From the commodity form to the legal form 84
2.2.1. A note on history and logic 96
2.3. The withering away of law 97

3. Critiques and reconstructions 101
4. The relevance for international legal scholarship 113

Chapter Four: Coercion and the Legal Form: Politics, (International) Law and the State 117
1. The problem of politics 117
2. Pashukanis and state-derivation theory 122
3. (International) Law and the contingency of the state 128
4. (International) Law, politics and violence 133
4.1. Form, content, economics and politics in international law 137
4.2. The unlikely marriage of Pashukanis and McDougal 141
5. Problems 143
6. The violence of the legal form 150

Chapter Five: States, Markets and the Sea: Issues in the History of International Law 153
1. The invisibility of history 153
2. Origins and prehistory: an eternity of international law? 156
2.1. Pre-colonial theory: the non-Western birth of international law? 165
3. Colonialism and international law: the birth of a new order 169
3.1. Amity lines: colonialism beyond law's boundaries 179
4. The development of sovereignty: from politics to abstraction 184
4.1. Absolute ownership and Roman law 195
5. From maritime law to international law 197
5.1. Early codes: the mercantile maritime roots of international law 197
5.2. Lineages of the mercantilist state 201
5.2.1. The Navigation Acts 204
5.2.2. The East India Companies 206
5.2.3. The freedom of the seas: a dissident interpretation 208
5.3. Excursus: mercantilism and the transition to capitalism 214
5.4. Categories and dialectics 224

Chapter Six: Imperialism, Sovereignty and International Law 225
1. The nature of the relation 225
1.1. Specificity versus breadth 226

2. The crisis of mercantile colonialism 230
2.1. The imperialism of recognition 235
3. Ad-hoc legality in the nineteenth century 240
3.1. Positivism and its sources 241
3.2. 'Civilisation': a counterintuitive materialist analysis 243
3.3. Into Africa 248
4. The Berlin Conference and the 'scramble for Africa' 250
4.1. Mandates, colonies and sovereignty: tendencies and countertendencies 256
5. The empire of sovereignty 260
5.1. The international law of freedom? 268
6. New world order 271
6.1. Excursus: the Gulf War 272
6.2. The limits of legalistic opposition 275
7. The universality of legalism 281
7.1. Politics and the end of the rule 282
7.2. Force and law 286
8. Serving two masters: the imperialism of international law 289

Conclusion: Against the Rule of Law 295
1. Ideas, ideology and contestation 295
2. The rule of law's new advocates 304
2.1. From war to policing? 308
3. Against the rule of law 314
4. The future of the theory 318

Appendix: Pashukanis on International Law 321

Bibliography 337
Index 365

Introduction

1. 'International law has become important'

Debates between international lawyers do not traditionally make newspaper headlines. But on 2 March 2004, readers of *The Guardian* found a near-full-page article consisting entirely of the differing opinions of seven lawyers on the legality of the British government's war on Iraq.[1] The Labour Party's spectacularly mendacious and cack-handed management of this deeply unpopular war has given rise to enormous anger and anxiety: one of the ways this has manifested is in a surge of interest in international law, as it is widely argued that the war and subsequent occupation are illegal.[2] Though, as will become clear, I consider that an inadequate critique,[3] it is to be hoped that the new focus on international law will lead to an increase in critical approaches to the subject. This book seems to have dovetailed with a growing concern: 'International law has become important politically, intellectually, and culturally.'[4]

There is already a colossal literature on international law: it might seem cruel to add another book

[1] 'Was the War Justified? Leading Lawyers Give their Verdicts'. The legal scholars were Nick Grief, James Crawford, Malcolm Shaw, Christine Chinkin, Anthony Aust, Sir Adam Roberts and Lord Alexander, QC.

[2] Before the war, this was the 'near-unanimous view of international lawyers' ('Law Unto Themselves', The *Guardian* 14 March 2003). For an opposing viewpoint from one prominent lawyer see Roberts 2002.

[3] At worst, there is the danger that such a legalistic turn of critique 'seriously weakens the antiwar movement' (Keach 2003).

[4] Estreicher and Stephan 2003, p. 1.

to the pile. However, the bulk of this writing consists of textbooks, in which theoretical assumptions are generally unacknowledged and implicit. Many of the fundamental concepts embedded in these texts are at best highly questionable. Purporting to explain how to 'do' international law, these writings cannot get to grips with its categories or processes. The triumph of managerialism and the antipathy to theory in the field mean that these problems are not only not addressed, but are often not even perceived as problems.

There are of course books written from more explicit jurisprudential perspectives, where questions of theory and philosophy are acknowledged. Here the situation is better. However, even for many of these writers there are still certain conceptual givens, which obscure indispensable methods of analysing international law. Many of the 'debates' in international law present arguments that *mutually constitute* each other: they are recursive, and unable to examine the fundamental categories they share.

At the core of this book is an attempt to open a black box in the jurisprudence of international law – that of the *legal form* itself. It is only in grasping the specifics of that form that we can address the field's most recurring conundrum: what is the nature of a law between bodies without a superordinate authority? This question lies at the heart of many other classic debates: on the nature of obligation; monism versus dualism; the binding force of custom; and others. And yet mainstream international-law theory circles the fundamental question endlessly, never successfully engaging with it, because without a theory of legal form, the specificity of law itself is impenetrable.

In what follows, 'international law' is used in its conventional sense, to refer to public international law. The specifics of 'private' international law, 'the body of rules of municipal law which regulate legal relations with a foreign element, such as . . . contracts of sale or service between persons in different countries',[5] is beyond my scope, though there are important implications for such law in what follows.

It is my contention, as I argue below, that certain of the lacunae in the field exist because although there are writers who are sceptical about international law's impact on the international system – who claim, for example, that it is merely a moralistic gloss on power-politics – there are very few who take law seriously as a structural component of lived relations, *and who yet are fun-*

[5] Schwarzenberger 1967, p. 3.

damentally critical of it – and of those, even fewer see it as 'unreformable'. For most, it is more or less taken for granted that if one believes law has an effect, one sees it as a force for stability and order; potentially even emancipatory change. Where there is a problem of disorder or violence, it is deemed a *failure* of law: the main problem about law is that there is not enough of it. It is rare to theorise international law as an important, effective regulatory force, and yet not to defend its normative, or potentially normative, impact.

Given that the vast majority of writers on international law are lawyers or jurists, this is perhaps not surprising. Most see the law as effective and broadly positive: at a hyperbolic extreme, it has recently been claimed that '[i]t will not be an exaggeration to claim that most of the progressive ideas of contemporary humanity spring from international law.'[6] Some see international law as ineffective and wish to 'rectify' that. A few see it as effective but historically and currently of questionable socially progressive utility, perhaps because it is being 'misused' by a hegemonic power, and they wish to 'reformulate' it at the service of a radical agenda. But it would be biting the hand that feeds them for international lawyers to say that international law is an effective force, complicit in the worst of today's social problems, and yet is fundamentally unreformable. This is my conclusion.

I envisage two core audiences for this book. One is made up of international lawyers and jurists with an interest in theory, especially critical theories of the field: among them there may be some without much background in Marxism. The other consists of Marxists, who may not have much knowledge of key debates in the theory of international law. This lack of common ground means there is a risk that some sections of the book will read either as opaque or excessively introductory for one or other group. I have tried to avoid this, while keeping both readerships in mind.

I have referred to fewer cases than is usual in writing on international law. For some, especially within the field, this will count against me, but I hope it will be considered justified by my focus on the 'deep grammar' of international law, so to speak, of which specific legal cases are the surface expressions.

In the course of the analysis, I reach certain conclusions with ramifications for long-running debates within Marxism. Although I do not dwell on them,

[6] Butkevych 2003, p. 235.

the focus of this book being resolutely on international law itself, I believe that these debates are important. Above all, I have attempted some reconciliation of those traditions of Marxism which can seem quite abstract in their stress on social *form*, often taking Marx's analysis of the value-form as a starting point, and those which follow Bukharin and Lenin (among others) in stressing the concrete conjuncture of actually-existing capitalism in history.

2. Materialism and dialectics

In what follows, I regularly call to task some position or other for being 'idealist', and counterpose it to alternative 'materialist' theory. The debates around these issues are, of course, vast – this is only a brief explanatory note. By 'idealist', I mean a position that is underpinned by a notion of ideas and ideational structures (such as those of law) ontologically distinct from material circumstance – objective reality – and often understood as in some way driving it. As I try to show, such analyses (whether the theorist intends it or not) tend to notions of ideas as self-generating, and cannot give a sense of why *those* ideas at *that* time.

For the alternative, an excellent introduction to materialist jurisprudence is given by Anthony Chase. I follow him in arguing that 'materialist jurisprudence is concerned with the social and economic forces directing the course of legal development'.[7] Unlike idealism, in Trotsky's phrase, 'it does not liberate matter from its materiality'.[8]

Marxist materialism is routinely denounced as 'determinist', and as dismissing the power of 'non-economic' factors in social life. Such attacks can come from within the discipline of international law.

> Marx would have the reader believe that economic influences and material surroundings determine human perspectives, in direct contrast to culture, ideology and mentality. . . . The realm of pure human thought and idea is relegated by the Marxist to a state of jejune non-effectuality.[9]

Engels stresses the misrepresentation this involves in a response to an early version of this canard. '[I]f somebody twists this [materialist conception of history] into saying that the economic factor is the *only* determining one, he

[7] Chase 1997, p. 20, and pp. 19–36.
[8] Trotsky 1998, p. 77.
[9] Alcantara 1996, p. 42.

transforms that propositions into a meaningless, abstract, absurd phrase'. He makes clear that ideas and 'systems of dogma also exercise their influence upon the course of historical struggles and in many cases determine their *form* in particular'. Materialism inheres in the fact that 'the *ultimately* determining factor in history is the production and reproduction in real life'.[10] (One of the classic metaphors of materialism, 'base' and 'superstructure', I touch on in Chapter Three.)

As Anthony Chase puts it, '[o]ur materialist roadmap may get us on our way but we cannot advance very far without a compass.'[11] That compass is the dialectic.

Marxist materialism sees the world as a totality, and as dynamic. For there to be historical motion from within a totality, that totality must contain contradictions. In the words of two radical scientists, [s]ystems destroy the conditions that brought them about in the first place and create the possibilities of new transformations that did not previously exist.'[12] Understanding that material and social reality is total but not static is key to the Marxist dialectic, the logic of which is the logic of dynamic contradictions within a material totality – the unity of opposites.[13]

3. The structure of the book

In Chapter One, I start by offering an overview of mainstream textbook positions and jurisprudential debates, and formulating a critique of the prevalent notion that international law is a body of rules. However, though I argue that the alternative position of Myres McDougal, that law is a *process*, is much superior, I show that it leaves unanswered the question of why the process of decision-making *takes the legal form*. This recurs throughout this work as the central problem for critical scholarship of international law.

In the second chapter, I examine two streams of radical international-law scholarship: the Marxist, and that deriving from the school known as Critical Legal Studies (CLS). Most of the self-proclaimed 'Marxist' writings of Soviet jurists, I argue, shares the inadequacies of mainstream 'managerialist' writing.

---

[10] Engels letter to Joseph Bloch, 21 September 1890, reproduced in Chimni 1993, pp. 221–2 footnote 31. Emphasis in original.
[11] Chase 1997, p. 33.
[12] Levins and Lewontin 1985, p. 277.
[13] See Rees 1998 for an excellent study of the Marxist dialectic.

The best of the Marxist works available, that of B.S. Chimni, is of a different order in terms of its intellectual seriousness and insight. However, I argue that with regard to the legal form and the question of law as rules, it embeds some of the same fallacious conceptualisations as mainstream international-law jurisprudence. In contrast, the CLS approach offers a truly revelatory look at the internal contradictions of international law, and is a paradigm that gets at the *indeterminacy* of international law. However, the approach fails to ground its sometimes-brilliant analyses in material reality, and, like McDougal, cannot get to grips with the legal form itself. The CLS attempt to deploy international law at the service of a socially transformative agenda is sharply contradictory of the school's own insights.

In Chapter Three I go back to the works of the Marxist legal theorist Evgeny Pashukanis. I put forward his argument that law – and more specifically the legal form – is an expression of the relations of abstract commodity owners in commodity exchange. Given the central importance of Pashukanis to my argument, I examine his theory and those of his critics at some length, though their focus is on domestic rather than international law. There are problems and inconsistencies within Pashukanis's work, which I argue can best be answered by reference to the work itself – an immanent reformulation. This theory is a major step forward, which can not only accommodate the CLS insights about indeterminacy, but embed them in a theory of modernity for which material reality and property relations are key. I argue that the most trenchant criticisms of his theory, though answerable, are not directly germane to international law, which in some ways presents an excellent case of his model in its simplest form. There is, however, a recurring critique of Pashukanis, which is that he is unable to explain how the legal form is filled with particular norms and social content. This is the problem of politics and coercion.

In Chapter Four I argue that this criticism is misplaced. Pashukanis, without addressing specific cases, does indeed have a theory of the political, coercive determination of the content of laws. What is more, it is a theory embedded in the very categories of his supposedly 'formalistic' legal writings. Reaching it requires losing some common misconceptions about his theory, foremost among them that he 'derives' a theory of the state from juridical categories. This chapter is the theoretical heart of the book. I argue not only that the mechanisms of coercion are present in Pashukanis's commodity-form theory, but that because of its lack of an overarching sovereign, international law is uniquely suitable for illustrating and examining this. As well as being better explained by Pashukanis's theory than others, international law is an invaluable optic for developing that theory. His frequent references to international law in his major work, and his essay on the topic for the Soviet *Encyclopedia of State and Law* make clear that relations between independent agents *without* an overarching state are central to Pashukanis's work. I attempt to show that the embeddedness of violence in law, and the contingency of an arbitrating sovereign to the legal form, are key to the commodity-form theory.

In Chapter Five, I examine aspects of the early history of international law, from the late fifteenth to the eighteenth centuries. This chapter is by no means an exhaustive historical overview of the international system or international legal debates, nor do I attempt to engage with all the voluminous secondary literature. Instead, certain episodes, themes and writers are examined insofar as they illuminate the central claims of this book. I attempt to show that the categories of international law can only be understood as those of market relations slowly generalising globally, in the transition to capitalism. However, contrary to the traditions of historical materialism that rigidly counterpose politics and economics in capitalism, I argue that in these early days (and by extension now) the two were interpenetrative, most particularly at an international level. International law is especially suited to illustrating this. Seeing the categories of international law as those of commodity exchange is no contradiction to seeing it as constituted by and constituting relations of violent colonialism – indeed that that is the only way it can be understood. I try to show that maritime and merchant law, as regulators of the arenas in which market relations were first conducted across polities with any systematicity, are critical to the development of international law. As an extended coda, though I argue that disagreement on this point does not invalidate the commodity-form theory developed, I make the case that mercantilism can best be understood as a form transitional to capitalism. The main reason for developing this argument is that it illustrates a central plank of my thesis, that the separation of economics and politics – the market and coercive violence – is not constitutive of capitalism, and that the tendency toward their separation is set about by countertendencies. The economic in the political of mercantilism is the flipside of the political in the economic – the commodity – in international law.

In Chapter Six, I bring this history up to date, with a focus on the development of categories of colonialism and imperialism in nineteenth- and twentieth-century international law and relations. I argue that contrary to the traditional understanding, the epoch of 'formal imperialism' was *not* the high-point of imperialism's embedding into international law, but that imperialism predated the epoch of formal colonies, and has survived it. There has long been a tendency towards the universalisation of the sovereign state, the fundamental juridical unit of international law, and in a modern 'anticolonial' system of international law, imperialism is hidden within law, but I argue that without it, *international law could not exist*. Drawing on the insights of Chapter Four, I argue that coercive political violence – imperialism – is the very means by which international law is made actual in the modern international system. Through analysis of the Gulf War of 1990–1, I show that the indeterminacy of international law, the juridical structure of the sovereign state and the consolidation and monopolisation of capitalism in the twentieth century have combined to make an international legal system in which *the very law of self-determination* operates as imperialism.

As an afterword, I critically address notions of ideological contestation in international law, as well as recent writings on 'global governance' and 'liberal cosmopolitanism'. The former I argue is, as a radical strategy, at best severely limited, at worst legitimating of the structures it would subject to critique. I argue that the analytical claims of the latter, that the nature of international law is fundamentally changing because of a new regime of humanitarian intervention, are mistaken. The liberal-cosmopolitan writers represent a new version of the traditional call for the extension of 'the rule of law' in the international arena. I conclude by arguing that such calls, however laudable the intentions, are predicated on a misreading of the nature of law. The international rule of law is not counterposed to force and imperialism: it is an expression of it.

The title to this book comes from Marx's observation that 'between equal rights, force decides'. At first sight this might look like a cynical claim that power-politics are the only ultimately determining reality, that equal rights collapse before force. In fact, as I try to show, though it is quite true that 'force decides', the 'equal rights' it mediates are really, and remain, truly equal. This is precisely the paradox of international law: force is determining, but determining between relations which cannot be understood except as equal in fundamentally constitutive and constituting ways. The equality and the force determine each other: the equality gives determining force its shape; the force – violence – is equality's shadow.

Chapter One

'The Vanishing Point of Jurisprudence': International Law in Mainstream Theory

1. Beyond definition

Given the vast and growing literature on international law,[1] it is remarkable how few systematic attempts have been made to uncover the fundamental nature of such law as a social phenomenon.

This poverty of theory has not gone unnoticed. The 'vanishing point of jurisprudence', for example, is how T.E. Holland described international law.[2] Richard Falk has commented that 'most international lawyers, whether inside or outside of universities, profess to be anti-theoretical', often contending that 'theory is a waste of time in legal studies'.[3] In B.S. Chimni's formulation, 'the field of international legal theory still gives the appearance of a wasteland'.[4] There are encouraging signs of a growing consciousness of theoretical issues in the field.[5] The tradition of blindness, even antipathy, to theory, however, still weighs heavy in international law.

---

[1] It is estimated that 80,000 books on international law had been published by 1967, and that currently 700 books and 3,000 articles on international law are published annually (Malanczuk 1997, p. 8).

[2] Famously quoted as the epigraph to McDougal et al. 1968, p. 188.

[3] Falk 1970, p. 8.

[4] Chimni 1993, p. 15.

[5] Simpson 2000 includes evidence of this in an engaging description of the 1999 American Society of International Law Annual Meeting, with its 'distinctly different feel . . . from that of previous years', with 'less fustiness and a more self-conscious

As Koskenniemi points out, though '[d]iscussion on "theory" about international law has become a marginalized occupation', '[t]his has not always been so'.[6] It is no coincidence that the historic decline of the jurisprudential science of international law is coterminous with the spread of international law as a global system.

Early modern writers were theorising and expressing a developing system, in which new social forces were coming to the fore. International law was a function of a changing world, and it was not possible to disentangle policy from social explanation.

> [W]riters such as Vitoria, Suarez or Grotius engaged in an argument about international law in which the concrete and the abstract, description and prescription were not distinguished from each other. . . . [This fact] gives early writing its distinct flavour, its sense of being 'other' than the more methodological, or 'professional' styles of later scholarship.[7]

When this new world-system became firmly entrenched, its contradictions became – and remain – obscured. In the post-Enlightenment legal culture which separates 'theory' and 'doctrine',[8] those contradictions, reflected in social and legal theories, have for many lawyers been seen as a problem not of the world, but of 'theory' itself.

> This has made theory itself seem suspect. The endless and seemingly inconsequential character of theoretical discourse has forced modern lawyers to make a virtue out of a necessity and turn towards an unreflective pragmatism, with the implicit assumption that the problems of theory [and, we can add, history] are non-problems. . . . The modern international lawyer has assumed that frustration about theory can be overcome by becoming doctrinal, or technical.[9]

The turn to doctrine was a function of the *embedding* of 'law-ness' into the international social fabric in the nineteenth century.

---

flexing of interdisciplinary muscles' (p. 459). Though the theoretical resurgence is most clear in writers influenced by 'critical legal studies' (see Chapter Two, below), Simpson makes the interesting argument that traditional debates have also and in parallel been 'invigorated' by liberal international lawyers who have 'reached out' to International Relations scholarship, for a more interdisciplinary approach (p. 439).

[6] Koskenniemi 1989, p. XIII.

[7] Ibid.

[8] Ibid.

[9] Koskenniemi 1989, p. XIV.

> Even though in this period – and indeed throughout the century – the science of international law lost relatively in historical significance, state practice in matters of international law expanded, intensified, and accelerated to such an extent that the period clearly marks the beginning of a new era.[10]

The formulation that the theory and history of international law waned 'even though' the law itself waxed is misleading. *The very historical triumph of international law lay behind the diminution of international legal science.*

Despite – perhaps because of – the absence of international legal theory or analysis that can address the fundamental question of international law's nature, there is no lack of *definitions* of the subject matter. These definitions purport to answer the question 'What is international law?', but are generally so thin or self-recursive that they tell the reader very little. Thus for example, international law 'is the system of law which governs relations between states'[11] – and it is usually defined to include some non-state actors as well.[12] This 'rule-approach' defines a discrete and bounded arena of international law as a body of rules, thus insisting on 'a clear-cut distinction between law and non-law'.[13] This kind of classic, textbook definition represents 'a widely held perception'[14] and the 'classical view',[15] and it tells us almost nothing of the underlying nature of international law.[16]

Occasionally, hints of a more systematic theory are implicit in these definitions. Shearer, for example, defines international law as 'rules of conduct which states feel themselves bound to observe, and therefore, do commonly observe'.[17] Here the law is defined as deriving from states' practice, implying a positivist theory of the non-absolute nature of law: if a state suddenly decided it no longer felt bound to observe a particular law, then according to Shearer's definition it would cease to be law.

---

[10] Nussbaum 1947, pp. 2–3.

[11] Akehurst 1987, p. 1.

[12] Ibid., Schwarzenberger 1967, p. 3; Shearer 1994, p. 3.

[13] Koskenniemi 1989, p. 166. As Koskenniemi points out, this approach is unable 'to provide a convincing account of how law and politics can held to be so sharply distinct as assumed by it'.

[14] Higgins 1994, p. 2. Higgins herself holds an opposing view, baldly opening one book with the claim that '[i]nternational law is not rules' (Higgins 1994, p. 1).

[15] Higgins 1994, p. 5.

[16] For an attempt to provide a more carefully theorised vision of the rules-based nature of international law, though one which cannot overcome the problems laid out here, see Arend 1999.

[17] Shearer 1994, p. 3.

Malanczuk is one textbook writer who seems aware that apparently innocent definitions imply philosophical positions. He points out, for example, that the classic (pre-World War I) definition of international law as 'the law that governs the relations between states amongst each other' implies the positivist doctrine 'that only states could be subjects of international law',[18] which did not reflect reality even at the time. Without apparent censure or approval, he points out that some textbooks avoid these issues in that they 'refrain from any attempt to define international law and enter directly into the discussion of its "sources"'[19] – indeed, Malanczuk himself avoids defining his subject matter, limiting himself to observations about its scope.

Malanczuk's hesitancy about providing a definition comes in his updated version of Akehurst's classic textbook, which in contrast *opened* with a definition.[20] It is interesting that the reader learns nothing more, less or different from Malanczuk's description of the subjects and scope of international law, than from Akehurst's definition of international law itself. These definitions, in other words, generally answer the question 'What are the subjects of international law?' rather than 'What *is* international law?'

Of course, within the very textbooks that print these wan definitions are often discussions of the classic arguments in international law, between the monists and the dualists, the deniers and the utopians, the positivists and the naturalists, and so on. These are debates that do pertain to the nature of international law, and will be addressed below. But to a large extent, they leave the fundamental question unanswered.

Thus we might agree with one writer or another on these various debates – for example, picking positions at random from the classic debates, that international law is a fundamentally different phenomenon from municipal law, that it *is* law properly so-called, that it derives its obligatory nature from the practice of states – and yet still have no idea why international law takes the shape it does. Claims that international law is, say, 'composed of the principles and rules of conduct' of states,[21] are essentially claims about what international law *does* (regulates interaction), not what it *is*, as law. There is no theory of why it is *law* that does the job of regulation.

---

[18] Malanczuk 1997, p. 1.
[19] Malanczuk 1997, pp. 1–2. He cites Brownlie 1990 as an example.
[20] Akehurst 1987, p. 1.
[21] Shearer 1994, p. 3.

In this approach, as Hedley Bull puts it,

> it is not the case that international law is a necessary or essential condition of international order. The functions which international law fulfills are essential to international order, but these functions might in principle be carried out in other ways. . . . [T]he basic rules of coexistence might be stated, and a means provided for facilitating compliance with agreements, by a body of rules which has the status of moral rules or supernatural rules.[22]

Thus, the standard definitions of international law encountered in the textbooks leave the fundamental 'law-ness' of international law completely unexamined. International law is defined by its alleged regulatory effect, *which could be wrought by some other – non-legal – body of rules*. Nor should readers be misled by the mere mention of 'law' in the various definitions of international law: Schwarzenberger, for example, says that international law is 'the body of *legal* rules which apply between sovereign states'.[23] But without an analysis of law itself, mentioning the 'legal' nature of the 'rules' of international law is merely tautologous. The substantive element of the definition is its description of international law as rules of behaviour inhering between states. Bull is perspicacious on this point: 'International law may be regarded as a body of rules which binds states and other agents in world politics in their relations with one another *and is considered to have the status of law.*'[24]

Here, what makes international law something to be analysed at all – a phenomenon with social effects – is its status as a body of rules: what makes it *law* is merely the fact that it is so considered. This implies a radical contingency in the legal nature of international law. 'That modern international society includes international law as one of its institutions is a consequence of . . . historical accident'.[25] The 'law-ness' of international law is thus historically absolutely arbitrary.

---

[22] Bull 1977, pp. 136–7.

[23] Schwarzenberger 1967, p. 3. Emphasis mine.

[24] Bull 1977, p. 122. Emphasis mine. See also p. 130 for a restatement of the argument in pragmatic terms: 'If the rights and duties asserted under these rules [of international law] were believed to have the status merely of morality or of etiquette, this whole corpus of activity [of statesmen, legal advisors, international assemblies] could not exist. The fact that these rules are believed to have the status of law, whatever theoretical difficulties it might involve, makes possible a corpus of international activity that plays an important part in the working of international society.'

[25] Bull 1977, p. 137.

Inasmuch as international law is 'the vanishing point of jurisprudence', inasmuch as its nature *as law* remains opaque while its role as a regulatory mechanism is retained, this historical contingency is inevitable. International society regulates itself in various ways, it is claimed, and in the modern age we happen to call that regulation 'law'. It is to Bull's credit that unlike so many writers, he sees this implication clearly and does not shrink from it.

Most mainstream writers simply do not see the radically undermining effect of their own positions vis-à-vis the *legal* nature of international law. Even in the course of defending international law as law, for example, Malanczuk claims that

> what distinguishes the rules and principles of international law from 'mere morality' is that they are accepted in practice as legally binding by states in their intercourse because they are useful to reduce complexity and uncertainty in international relations.[26]

The 'rules' of international behaviour are taken as given, transhistorical. Inasmuch as they are law, this is simply because they are 'accepted . . . as legally binding' – they are law only because we say they are law, rather than because of their form or essence. Rules, here, are deemed central: their 'lawness' is epiphenomenal.

It should be pointed out that this thin conception of law is not confined to writers of textbooks, who are mostly concerned with the technical-regulatory rules, nor to writers such as Bull, writing from outside international law. Even writers such as Hans Kelsen and H.L.A. Hart, precisely concerned with the jurisprudence of international law, agree on the basic formulation.

Thus for Hart, as for the textbook writers, international law is law – despite its lack of centrally organised sanctions or 'secondary' rules that specify procedure for adjudication[27] – as a set of rules of conduct that are 'generally observed and regarded as valuable'[28] by states. Although it differs greatly from municipal law, what Hart sees as crucially shared is '[t]he idea of "ought" . . . the idea of law as a form of social regulation'.[29] The 'rule-ness'

[26] Malanczuk 1997, pp. 6–7.

[27] For an overview of Hart's international legal theory, see McCarthy 1998, pp. 154–6; see also Paust 1979, for a more thorough analysis.

[28] McCarthy 1998, p. 156.

[29] Ibid.

of international law is clear – he calls international laws 'social rules':[30] the 'law-ness', however, is unexamined.

Similarly, Kelsen defends the 'law-ness' of international law inasmuch as it

> is a coercive order, . . . a set of norms regulating human behavior by attaching certain coercive acts (sanctions) as consequences to certain facts, as delicts, determined by this order as conditions, and if, therefore, it can be described by sentences which . . . may be called "rules of law".[31]

Again, the substance of the definition here revolves around international law's regulatory behaviour. Its law-ness, however, is deemed distinct from this, and derives from the fact that it is called law. As one critic says, 'Kelsen provides no methodology for analysis of the difference between a moral or a legal social order'.[32]

In all of these definitions, what is evident is a failure to systematically analyse – or even take seriously – the *specificity of the legal form*. Hart makes this explicit in his claim that the analogy between international and municipal law 'is one of content not of form'[33] – the content here being the shared normative obligation contained in both sets of 'social rules'. If the legal *form* is not shared between international and municipal law, then they have no legal essence in common, and the only thing that makes them both 'law' is that they are both called law.

A belief in the historical contingency of the 'law-ness' of international regulation is the result of ahistoricism. For Bull, there is a transhistorical necessity to have 'a body of rules' 'essential to international order': international law is merely one of its forms.

It is my contention that this ahistoricism is wrong. There *is* something inescapably 'legal' about international law, and its historical emergence is part of a process of historical transformation. I will argue that the development of international law is inextricably tied to the political economy of the post-feudal world, and that such law's units of analysis are *legal* units. The framework for interaction between polities in the modern international legal system, its *modus operandi*, is fundamentally different from previous orders'.

---

30 Hart 1961, p. 231.
31 Kelsen 1968, p. 85.
32 Paust 1979, p. 41.
33 Hart 1961, p. 231.

To avoid the ahistorical contingency of Bull and others, jurisprudence must examine the fundamental nature of international law *as law*, to open up the black box at the centre of international law. As against Hart and others, I will try to show that for any systematic theory of international law, the fundamental unit of analysis must be the legal form itself.

2. Classic writers and debates

This 'fundamentalist' project does not imply a refusal to engage with the classic debates in international law – far from it. It must involve an attempt to locate oneself with reference to these, and an uncovering of the assumptions and implied theory in the various positions. I will attempt this through an examination of authors associated with some of the most important and contentious classic positions.

2.1. *Disentangling denial*

While many discussions of international law bleed it of its specifically and uniquely legal nature, a few explicitly *deny* it any law-ness. Lachs calls those of this theoretical persuasion 'deniers', for whom 'the prevailing lawlessness offered no evidence of any rule of law among nations'.[34] But this classification blurs an important distinction. Lachs includes as deniers Austin, who famously denied that international law was law 'properly so-called', asserting that it was only 'positive morality',[35] along with Morgenthau, who asserts the law will give way to politics.[36] These are, of course, two different, though related, positions. As Malanczuk puts it, '[t]he controversy . . . has often confused the question of whether international law is "law" with the problem of the effectiveness and enforcement of international law'.[37]

---

[34] Lachs 1987, p. 10.

[35] Austin 2000, p. 127.

[36] Morgenthau 1981, p. 144.

[37] Malanczuk 1997, p. 5. Oddly, Malanczuk in the very next sentence then goes on to make the mistake he is pointing out, when he claims that '[i]n foreign policy thinking, the reductionist perception of international law is still prevalent in the "realist" school', mentioning Morgenthau as exemplary (p. 5). But the dispute under discussion is 'whether international law may be properly called "law"', something that Morgenthau does not question.

Morgenthau is clear that international law does exist as a system of binding legal rules.[38] Even Lachs acknowledges this.[39] The tendency to lump together writers who deny the existence of international law as law with those who allege that it is not an ultimately determining force in international affairs is highly misleading.

A third related position is also imputed to exist within the same camp. When Lachs says that 'at the opposite end of the spectrum' from the deniers are the utopians,[40] those utopians are writers who envisage 'an ideal State or world'[41] brought about by international law. They are therefore, in fact, the 'opposite' neither of those who do not believe that international law is law, nor those who believe that international law has a negligible effect on states' actions, but of those who believe that international law can never systematically be used to *improve the world*. When Oscar Schachter considers 'the sceptics of international law' it is this third strand of denial that he focuses on: he is concerned with 'those who doubt . . . that international law can contribute significantly to international order'.[42]

It is vital to disentangle these various forms of 'denial'. One can after all imagine being a 'denier' in one, two or all three of these senses, and not in any remaining (see figure).[43]

Categories of denial		
1: The claim that international law is not law 'properly so-called'.	2: The claim that international law is not ultimately a determinant of states' policies.	3: A scepticism that international law can be used to systematically improve the world.

It is obviously true that there will be some overlap, and that some positions will tend to bleed into others: Higgins points out for example that if one holds that international law is generally ignored, 'this evidences that international

[38] Morgenthau 1967, p. 265.

[39] Lachs 1987, p. 18.

[40] Ibid.

[41] Lachs 1987, p. 19.

[42] Schachter 1991, p. 5.

[43] The variety of permutations is clear. An optimistic Austinian would agree with 1 but not 2 or 3. The 'Realists' would tend precisely to reverse this. The game of ticking or crossing next to each of the forms to classify various international legal theorists could be played almost endlessly. One striking thing is how few authors would tick all three forms of denial. Those who would disagree with all three are less rare.

law is not "real law" at all'[44] – a segue from form 2 to form 1. Denial in the second sense presumes it in the third: if international law has no systematic effect on the actions of states, it can obviously not be a force for maintaining order or improving the world. Importantly, however, the third form does *not* presume the second – it is possible to hold that law has an effect, but that it cannot maintain order.

With the exception of the second form supposing the third, these positions are distinct and do not presume each other. To lump them together thus does violence to the conceptual tools of the international legal theorist.[45] Accordingly, I will deal with representatives of the three different 'denials' in turn.

2.1.1. *The will of the sovereign: Austin*

It is important to dismiss the Austinian notion that international law is not law 'properly so-called'.[46] This position is based on the 'command' theory of law, that law is 'the command of the sovereign'.[47] If this theory of law is correct, then given the lack of superordinate authority in the international system, whatever regulatory power the system known as international law may or may not have,[48] it is not a system of law.

One of the fundamental problems with this theory is its formalism: it presumes an ideal-type definition of law – as the will of a sovereign – which is then used as a yardstick to examine reality. In other words, the concepts at work here do not analyse reality, in all its complexity, but *judge* it, and in the case of international law, find it wanting. This is a philosophically idealist approach, in which the concepts come first, and then reality is allowed in to be compared with them. A coherent theory of law (or indeed any social institution) must surely be able to explain the various forms of that institution in the real world. A theory of law which explains *away* international law as 'not-law' does not merely fail in that task – it does not attempt it.

---

[44] Higgins 1994, p. 2.

[45] For overviews of the 'deniers' see, among others, Lauterpacht 1932, pp. 301–6; Lachs 1987, pp. 13–18.

[46] Expounded in Austin 2000.

[47] Austin 2000, pp. 133–4. This theory derives ultimately from Hobbes, who states in *Leviathan* that '[w]here there is no common Power, there is no Law' (Hobbes 1981, p. 188).

[48] This is where distinguishing between various forms of denial becomes important. Austin did *not* deny that international law might have a regulatory effect on the behaviour of nations (Lachs 1987, p. 15), only that it was 'law'.

As Dinstein puts it,

> many of . . . [those who deny the legal character of international law] are captivated by a dogmatic preconception based on the incompatibility of international law with this or that technical definition of the term 'law' to which they adhere. . . . The mistake inherent in Austin's contention, like in that advanced by others, is that an arbitrary definition of the term 'law' is first prescribed as if it were obligatory, and then it is proved that international law does not fit with the Procrustean bed of that definition.[49]

Contra Austin, the object of analysis must be 'actually-existing law', which includes international law. For Austin, international law is actually 'positive morality', but his ideal-type approach leaves him totally unable to explain why we should have a system of 'positive morality' which *masquerades* as law.

Another problem with Austin's position is its circularity. In seeing the law as a function of the sovereign, there is no space for a theory of the sovereign state as a legal entity. '[I]f . . . the command of the sovereign is taken to be the unique origin of the law, then the problem arises, by what means other than legal recognition is the nature or exclusiveness of the sovereign power itself determined?'[50]

Here yet again, the legal form must be explained *away*. It is simply the form that the edicts of the state happen to take in our society. To explain the state as partly a *legal* institution, rather than just one imbued with nebulous and ahistorical *power* (here taking a historically contingent legal form), we must have a theory of the law that does not reduce itself to state or sovereign will.

To successfully theorise international law, the state, and the relation between the two, we need a jurisprudence which takes as its object international law *as it exists* in the international system: a theory which accepts that it is more than historical chance that international law is called 'law'.

2.1.2. *The triumph of politics: Morgenthau*

Morgenthau is here taken as representative of another strand of sceptic in international legal studies: 'Realism'.[51] Morgenthau did not claim that

---

[49] Dinstein 1984, p. 200.

[50] McCarthy 1998, p. 157.

[51] For brief overviews of this position and writers associated with it, see among others Slaughter Burley 1993, pp. 207–9; Boyle 1980, pp. 193–206.

international law was not law; nor did he claim that international law had *no* effect on the actions of states. Indeed, 'to deny that international law exists at all as a system of binding legal rules flies in the face of all the evidence'.[52]

However, Morgenthau's position is that there is an 'iron law of international politics, that legal obligations must yield to national interest'.[53] The rules of international law are seen as not 'as effective a legal system as the national legal systems are', and crucially, they are not 'effective in regulating and restraining the struggle for power on the international scene'.[54] Power and power-politics are the determining moment here: '[p]olitics is focal and law secondary'.[55]

According to the mainstream histories of realism, this kind of scepticism was born in reaction to the excesses of the 'legalist-moralist' or 'utopian' approaches between the First and Second World Wars.[56] The story given is that American foreign policy under Wilson and his followers, 'the high priests of the "legalist-moralist" tradition',[57] tried naively to guarantee peace through international organisations and laws, ignoring the ever-present 'struggle for power'[58] which would always undermine it. Realism about international law, and in IR more generally, then, is seen as a reaction 'against Wilsonian liberal internationalism, which presumed that the combination of democracy and international organization could vanquish war and power politics'.[59]

This juxtaposition of realism with its 'utopian' predecessors is 'pure myth'.[60] There is no doubt that Wilson expressed US foreign policy where possible in terms of liberal internationalism, national self-determination, law and the like. However, this does not mean that there was a fundamental paradigmatic difference between the putative 'idealism' of the inter-war years and a hard-nosed 'realism' afterwards. Wilson's Fourteen Points Address to Congress on 8 January 1918 is often cited as the high-minded birth of twentieth-century utopianism. However, if state practice rather than just rhetoric is taken into consideration, 'Wilson was in fact a realist'.[61]

---

52 Morgenthau 1967, p. 265.
53 Morgenthau 1981, p. 144.
54 Morgenthau 1967, p. 265.
55 Koskenniemi 1989, p. 168.
56 Boyle 1980, p. 199; Slaughter Burley 1993, pp. 207–8.
57 Slaughter Burley 1993, p. 208.
58 Morgenthau 1967, pp. 25–6.
59 Slaughter Burley 1993, p. 207.
60 Rosenberg 1994, p. 22.
61 Boyle 1980, p. 200 footnote 21.

The very Fourteen Points taken as evidence of utopianism were in fact a weapon of *realpolitik*.

> [T]he first Western reaction to the Bolsheviks' appeal to the peoples to make peace . . . had been President Wilson's Fourteen Points, which played the nationalist card against Lenin's international appeal. A zone of small nation-states was to form a sort of quarantine belt against the Red virus.[62]

Wilson's 1915 and 1916 invasions of Hispaniola (Haiti and Dominican Republic) were clearly power-political decisions, whatever the rhetoric of national self-determination. In the words of Wilson's Secretary of State, spoken with Wilson's acquiescence, '[i]n its advocacy of the Monroe Doctrine the United States considers its own interests. The integrity of other American nations is an incident, not an end'[63] – this at the high-point of talk about 'national self-determination'. It is hard not to agree that 'the significance of these Wilsonian slogans has been much overestimated in the realist literature',[64] and that the '"appeasers" of the 1930s' are 'whipping-boys of . . . realist writers'.[65]

This is not to deny that there was a change in the political mood after the Second World War, and a concomitant change in the mood of political science; only to claim that the change was more to do with presentation than substance of policy. Nor is it to deny that many of the academics and writers on international affairs after the First World War may have been naively dewy-eyed about the efficacy of international law. 'The more the facts were in contradiction to their writings, the more lyrical they grew'.[66] To this extent, it is true that realism was a reaction to the ideologues of utopianism.

Morgenthau's position that law will give way to power is predicated on a fragmentation of social sciences: 'the political realist maintains the autonomy of the political sphere'.[67] It is not only the autonomy of the political that is maintained, but its primacy, in the international arena. Therefore, Morgenthau claims that where the political scientist thinks 'in terms of interest defined as power . . . the lawyer [should think], of the conformity of action with legal rules'.[68] However, as he has already maintained that law will not restrain

[62] Hobsbawm 1994, p. 67.
[63] Robert Lansing quoted in Chomsky 1992, p. 36.
[64] Walzer 1992, p. 111.
[65] Rosenberg 1994, p. 21.
[66] Kunz 1968, p. 127.
[67] Morgenthau 1958, p. 11.
[68] Ibid.

nations from pursuing their political interest, he is essentially relegating the lawyer to a position where *as a lawyer* she cannot understand the behaviour of states: only judge them – and often judge them wanting.

There have been many critiques of Morgenthau and realism. What has come under sustained attack is his ahistoricism, particularly his claims about an eternal and abstract human nature characterised by the drive to dominate, and his refusal to contextualise the very different forms 'the struggle for power' takes in different historical epochs. These are unsustainable assertions, which leave us quite unable to get beyond a banal level of description to an analysis of the mechanisms of historical conflict and change.[69] What are of interest here are the ramifications of his realism for theories of international law.

Morgenthau holds that law will never be a fundamental determinant of politics as he sees law as defined by sanctions. As international law is 'a law among co-ordinated, not subordinated, entities',[70] there are no automatic sanctions imposed on a transgressor. The question of whether or not sanctions will be imposed is here a question of political context. As politics is primary in Morgenthau's system, even where laws *are* valid they are not binding in and of themselves, only insofar as they 'formulate in legal terms complementary interests rooted in objective social forces.'[71] Thus even where law 'works', it does so because of politics, which comes first. Conversely, '[a]n alleged rule of international law against the violation of which no state reacts, or is likely to react, is proved, by this very absence of probable reaction, not to be a valid rule of international law'.[72] In this model, law is never binding, and therefore never determining of state behaviour. It is only *valid* or not, and that validity is a function of politics.

This is political formalism, in which 'the autonomy of the political sphere' banishes law to epiphenomenality. There is a curiously double-edged attitude to legal formalism here. Morgenthau's theory *is* legally formalistic inasmuch as law is seen as a body of rules, as in the classic definition, a template by which to view and judge state behaviour. But it is unformalist in its collapsing of the distinctiveness of law.

---

[69] For example, Rosenberg 1994, pp. 15–23; Chimni 1993, pp. 36–9.
[70] Morgenthau 1967, p. 302.
[71] Chimni 1993, p. 28.
[72] Morgenthau 1958, p. 226.

> The skeptic's argument is curious because it both maintains and denies the law/politics distinction. The distinction is maintained through the assumption that law can be separated from non-law through a criterion (the likelihood of sanction) [which, we can add, takes the abstract *rules*-based nature of law as straightforward, with the underpinning or otherwise of those rules in sanctions as determinant of effectiveness]. But the distinction is denied as the question of the likelihood of sanction becomes a sociological one. Binding force emerges with factual coercion. Law is merely a division of power politics. The distinctions between law and society, legal and political disputes and legal and sociological methods vanish.[73]

The contradiction is that between rule and sanction. For Morgenthau, laws are 'not the result of the mechanics of the struggle for power but are superimposed upon that struggle in the form of norms or rules of conduct by the will of the members of the society themselves'.[74] Thus the norms are an epiphenomenal gloss to take the edge off the sharp end of power struggles. But given that the efficacy or otherwise of those rules is defined by sanctions, determined by politics, the legal formalism here is undermined by the political formalism which goes with it.

A variant of the argument levelled against Austin's formalism is pertinent here. There, the question was why this complex system of international 'positive morality' should proclaim itself *law*. At this point, the conundrum is why, given the ultimate collapse of law into politics, the edifice of international law exists at all. Morgenthau is a political *and* legal formalist, without reasons for why the abstract system of 'politics' is primary, or why the abstract system of 'law' exists. Morgenthau's 'explanation' that international law is superimposed by the members of international society tells us nothing. It is only a restatement of the mystery. International law, after all, fails in 'an attempt to exorcise social events by the infatigable repetition of magic formulae'.[75] So why does it persist?

To understand the complex interpenetration of legality and politics – and economics, and all the other supposedly separate arenas of study – we must move beyond formalism. This means moving away from abstract notions such as 'the national interest' on the one hand or 'the rule of law' as

---

[73] Koskenniemi 1989, p. 169.
[74] Morgenthau 1967, p. 220.
[75] Morgenthau 1940, p. 265.

explanations for states' behaviour. In Chimni's illuminating formulation, '[p]olitical and legal formalism join hands to deny the complex linkages which bind the sociological substratum to law'.[76]

This necessitates more than the assertion that international law does have an effect on state behaviour. Claims that 'the role of international law in international relations has always been limited, but it is rarely insignificant',[77] or that 'states do accept that international law is law; and, what is more, they usually obey it',[78] may be true. But essentially this is an attempt to criticise scepticism simply by bandying forth counter-claims, which still allows for the disaggregation of politics and law: international law is still held to be a formally distinct system, merely one that states do take note of.

To move beyond formalism altogether, we have to change the traditional approach of looking at behaviour, then comparing it to 'rules' of law. The disaggregation of law from political life is so systematically asserted, it is hard to re-embed the two: but to take law seriously as a *social phenomenon*, this re-embedding is necessary.

> By simply looking at behaviour it [scepticism] fails to answer the relevant questions of whether and to what extent legal rules worked behind that behaviour. . . . It works on the assumption that legal rules will always be overridden when important State interests are at stake – and thus ignores that such are usually given legal protection. . . . Once law is understood in a more flexible, "political" way, however, it might seem that its relevance may be safeguarded.[79]

Koskenniemi points to a more systematic sociological theory of the embeddedness of law and politics in terms of structure, as well as agency. In Chimni's words, Morgenthau's 'undialectical treatment of law and politics blinds him to the fact that international legal norms have not been superimposed on the power struggle but are a product of felt needs'.[80]

'Politics' is 'legal' from the start: to accept this is to break from formalism, be it idealistic or sceptical about law.

---

[76] Chimni 1993, p. 45.
[77] Malanczuk 1997, p. 6.
[78] Akehurst 1970, p. 2.
[79] Koskenniemi 1989, p. 170.
[80] Chimni 1993, p. 59.

2.1.3. *A third way? Carl Schmitt*

I have argued against the formalism implied in the positions that international law is not law, or that it is always, in the last instant, ineffective. Instead, the categories of 'law' and 'politics' must be problematised, in an attempt to examine the complex interpenetrations of the two.

This, however, does not close the door to the possibility of denial, or scepticism, in the third sense discussed above. It is possible to accept that international law is law, that it is always part of the international political process, *and yet argue that it cannot and will not act to further a 'just world order'*.

This is a somewhat nebulous formulation, necessarily so given the enormous range of thinkers who assert the 'normative' potential of international law, and to whom therefore this form of denial stands in opposition. For the most part these foils are liberal thinkers who hold that the basic structure of world politics is broadly acceptable, that conflict is a pathological condition, and that international law is a useful and effective (though by no means infallible) mechanism for the maintenance of order. Alternatively, there are those who hold that the structure of world politics is currently iniquitous, and that international law can have a role in improving it. These thinkers include many from the Critical Legal Studies movement, who are discussed below. The basic line of division, then, among those hopeful about the normative force of international law, is that between those for whom law is about maintenance of the status quo – that status quo conceptualised as basically just and ordered – and those for whom international law must and can be *transformative*.

Despite this fundamental distinction, we can group both schools in opposition to the 'third position' of denial, that international law is structurally incapable of acting as a transformative force for justice, or even as a maintaining force for order. Crudely, we can style these otherwise-opposed approaches as united by an 'optimism' about international law, however careful and hedged with qualification it might be.

Almost exclusively, those few writers on international law with an alternative, 'pessimistic' conception hold it as a subset of another position, usually that international law has no effect on the behaviour of states. What must be defended as at least theoretically possible is the position that the first two forms of denial are wrong, and that still the third is right: international law *is* law, *is* effective, but cannot maintain justice or order. It is perhaps not surprising that defenders of this position are so hard to find: writers who take international law seriously enough to write about it and who theorise it as an active force in politics are almost all writing because they have some stake in such law.

The optimistic view of international law arguably sees its high point in the writings of Richard Falk. His 'Grotian Quest',[81] the articulation of international law towards a transition to a more just world order deriving its premises from 'libertarian socialism, philosophical anarchism, humanism, and militant non-violence',[82] suggests both the reorientation of international law and the reorientation of society *through* international law. In the words of a reviewer, 'he believes law to be a tool of social engineering'.[83]

According to the timetable for social change Falk proposed in 1975, by the end of the 1990s the citizens of the world were due to have completed the tasks of political consciousness-raising and mobilisation, and to be reaching the final stages of 'the institutional implementation of a new global consciousness via institutional innovation'.[84] The particular inflection of international law within this political project is never systematically theorised,[85] but however that might be attempted it is hard to avoid the conclusion that the entire project was utterly utopian.[86]

There are of course writers from critical traditions who make claims that sound like support for the 'pessimistic' analysis of international law's potential to create or maintain just order, but almost all end up undercutting this aspect of their theories. For example, despite the seeming 'pessimism' of his statement that 'the realm of law was not the arena from which the struggle for radical changes could be launched',[87] B.S. Chimni also stresses that '[t]he legal system provides diverse tools to deal with the perils which face mankind'.[88] Similarly for Koskenniemi, the realisation that there is 'no coherent project

[81] Falk 1985, pp. 36–42.
[82] Falk 1983, p. 324.
[83] Higgins 1969, p. 930.
[84] Falk 1975, p. 220.
[85] According to Chimni, Falk's 'jurisprudential perspective . . . is not fully worked through . . . In fact, legal theory has never received the sustained and adequate attention of Falk' (Chimni 1993, p. 148).
[86] Bull 1975, p. 282; Stone 1984, p. 36; Michalak 1980, p. 11. It is only fair to point out that Falk accepted that his formulations in his 1975 book were excessively utopian (Falk 1980). Even with that proviso, however, his theories of international law as international law of transition have not been satisfactorily formulated, and remain more in the way of hopes than realistic proposals.
[87] Chimni 1993, p. 208.
[88] Chimni 1993, p. 210.

for a better world'[89] in international law, does not stop him arguing that progressive international lawyers *as lawyers* should be 'normative in the small' as part of an emancipatory project.[90] In Chapter Two I will return to and analyse the contradictions of these two exemplary critics as to the progressive role of international law. For now, I only point out that their allegiance to the 'third form of denial' is at best equivocal.

There is a lack in the literature of systematic developments of that pessimism regarding international law's progressive potential: I attempt to argue such a position throughout this book. If we accept the view, advanced below, that law is part of the political process of modern international relations, and also – contra the liberals – that conflict and exploitative relations are embedded in, rather than pathological too, those relations, *law itself is part of that conflictual, exploitative process.*

Perhaps the theorist who comes closest to articulating a theory of actually-existing, embedded international law as part of a political process of conflict and exploitation is the 'brilliant but sinister' Carl Schmitt.[91]

There has been a growth in interest in Schmitt in recent years,[92] but he remains a controversial figure in international law and social theory more generally, unsurprisingly given his antisemitism and close association with Nazism, during the 1930s in particular.[93] His contributions to international legal theory have been denounced as 'ideological and propagandistic Nazi bric-a-brac'.[94]

There is absolutely no doubt that Schmittiana must be viewed with caution. Ritualistic 'lip-services to the "shocking" character of Schmitt's "avowed racism and anti-Semitism"'[95] are not inoculations against the political ramifications of Schmitt's positions.[96] Nonetheless, 'even people of diametrically

---

[89] Koskenniemi 1989, p. 494.

[90] Koskenniemi 1989, p. 496.

[91] Callinicos 1989, p. 48.

[92] Among the burgeoning secondary literature, Mouffe 1999 is evidence of the uneasy interest of many on the Left in Schmitt. Balakrishnan 2000 is an indispensable recent study. From within international law, Koskenniemi reviews Schmitt's arguments in Koskenniemi 2002, pp. 413–36.

[93] For the argument that Schmitt's antisemitism was a self-serving sham (raising the question of whether a genuine antisemite or one who mums the bigotry for political advantage is the more reprehensible), see Bendersky 1987, pp. 95–6.

[94] Gattini 2002, p. 55.

[95] Ibid.

[96] Salter points out that the rise in interest in Schmitt has occurred 'precisely during a period which has coincided with the re-emergence of "the radical right" as a

opposite political allegiances can profit intellectually from taking him seriously, and not just with the intention of refuting everything he has to say'.[97] For the student of international law, Schmitt's 'many insights about law and the new political order'[98] in particular revolve around his austere analyses of the intrinsic relation between international law, political power and imperialism.

The core of Schmitt's international legal thinking is in his 1950 book *The* Nomos *of the Earth in the International Law of the* Jus Publicum Europaeum.[99] Combining history, theory and jeremiad, Schmitt examines the central importance of early colonialism in international law, and expresses anxiety about the modern 'disorientation of juridical thinking',[100] structuring his argument around his central concept of *nomos*. He is clear that it should not, as is con-

---

distinctly political force' (Salter 1999, p. 162). It is perhaps a naïveté about some of these political ramifications which underlies Carty's polite thank-you to the main conduit for recent Schmitt studies, the journal *Telos*, which he says 'continues to render a service in explaining Schmitt's views on international law' (Carty 2001, p. 25 footnote 1). However useful these translations and articles may be, they are not politically neutral 'explanations'. *Telos* and its writers have moved from critical theory 'to an embrace of conservative American populism, European radical Right theories and anti-Left movements' (Frankel 1997, p. 60), an 'obsessive hatred of welfare states' (p. 70), and 'a paradoxical commitment to a mixture of open libertarian values and narrow, sexist, ethnic, homophobic and other conservative prejudices' (p. 72). For a new example from the very heart of *Telos*'s Schmitt proselytism, see Ulmen's introduction to his translation of Schmitt's *The* Nomos *of the Earth* with its truly despicable attack on multiculturalism as an 'ideological assault on the European past in general and on "Western culture" in particular', 'anti-European propaganda' (Ulmen 2003, pp. 30, 31) (this attack was prefigured in Ulmen and Piccone's stated preference for 'European rather than Asian or African immigrants' to the US (Piccone and Ulmen 1995)). In the light of these pronouncements, it is perhaps not too far-fetched to wonder whether Ulmen's use of the antiquated and offensive term 'Negroes' without scare-quotes or apparent ironic distancing is a deliberate provocation (Ulmen 2003, p. 17). Nor are these political positions, of course, contingent to Ulmen's and *Telos*'s Schmittophilia. The degree of special pleading and bad faith with regard to The Master is evidenced by the cover copy of Telos Press's edition of *The* Nomos *of the Earth*, which describes Schmitt as someone who 'attempted to save the Weimar Republic': he was rather someone who 'did not want to save "Weimar" but only the authoritarian aspects of the Weimar constitution' and 'who opted for the authoritarian order of the Third Reich in preference to the "democratic chaos" of Weimar' (Frankel 1997, p. 73 footnote 32: see also Neocleous 1996 and Balakrishnan 2000 p. 164 and pp. 155–75). Rather than seeing *Telos* as 'left appropriation of Schmitt' (Koskenniemi 2002, p. 423 footnote 37), it looks more like Schmitt's appropriation of the Left.

[97] Balakrishnan 2001, p. 9.

[98] Koskenniemi 2002, p. 424.

[99] Schmitt 2003a.

[100] Schmitt 2003a, p. 234. See Koskenniemi 2002, pp. 415–20 for an excellent overview.

ventional, be rendered 'law . . ., regulation, norm or any similar expression'.[101] It is, rather, a slippery concept he describes thus:

> the immediate form in which the political and social order of a people becomes spatially visible . . . *Nomos* is the *measure* by which the land in a particular order is divided and situated; it is also the form of political, social, and religious order determined by this process.[102]

Nomos, then, is 'a fundamental process of apportioning space'[103] *and*, as one reviewer puts it, 'the precondition for the coming into existence of international law'.[104]

Crucial here for a radical theory of international law is Schmitt's insistence on the political violence underpinning a *nomos*. Stressing the word's relation to concepts of division,[105] Schmitt insists that the post-Medieval *nomos* was the result of *Landnahme* – land-appropriation, or colonialism. In Chapter Five I will examine specific aspects of Schmitt's theory with regard to the Americas. Here, what is important is the theory that coercive and appropriatory politics underlies international law: as one of his chapter titles has it, his is an investigation of 'Land-Appropriation as a Constitutive Process of International Law'.[106]

For Schmitt a determinant of the specific shape of a *nomon* is not 'state territory' but the concept *Grossraum* – greater space. A task of decoding must be undertaken: writing in 1940, Schmitt makes commonplace claims that his corrected theory of international law, based around that notion, would represent peace and abolish 'peace disturbing guarantees'.[107] But alongside these obligatory assurances that through 'correct' international law peace would be assured is the rather more hard-headed theory that integrating the notion of greater-space into international law can lead to 'a formation of concepts and an understanding which are more in keeping with reality';[108] and even

---

[101] Schmitt 2003a, p. 70.
[102] Ibid.
[103] Schmitt 2003a, p. 78.
[104] Doehring 2002, p. 374.
[105] With an almost Kabbalistic neurosis and precision, Schmitt repeatedly investigated the etymology of *nomos*. (Schmitt 2003a pp. 67–79; and written later, Schmitt 2003b pp. 326–7, 2003c and 2003d, p. 351.)
[106] Schmitt 2003, p. 80.
[107] Schmitt n.d., p. 14, p. 15. Page references are to an unpublished translation of Schmitt 1940, which I am grateful to Erica Benner for providing.
[108] Schmitt n.d., p. 13.

more tellingly, '[i]t avoids . . . proceeding through the character of this development into a universalistic world empire, in correspondence with the world political interests of Anglo-Saxon imperialism'.[109]

Elided to some extent with 'empire', the category of 'greater-space' is an attempt to conceptualise the non-state-bounded nature of national interest. Not so restrictively formal as to include only legal colonies, it includes also informal empires and looser conglomerates of hegemonic states and their clients: essentially, it is a frank admission of the permeable and shifting territories represented by powerful states' international claims and interests.

Schmitt claims that international law cannot be understood without *Grossraum*, a concept that 'involves a deep-seated conceptual arrangement, an historical-political process which binds all peoples and which, if not observed, would leave international law as nothing more than a succession of non-binding pseudo-norms'.[110] It is precisely a crisis of greater-space – the uncertain reconfiguring of spheres of influence – that he sees underlying the crisis of the *nomos* after Versailles.[111] This is to say that the international power dynamic is necessary to understand the actual lived reality of international law. Thus law and politics are interpenetrated.

Schmitt argues that

> out of the world market there arose of itself a world international law which could overcome state sovereignty, and *with it came a legitimacy and guarantee of the status quo* that, unlike the French effort at preserving the international status quo, had not only European but universal substance.[112]

Here, Schmitt sees law, politics and economics as linked in complex structures, economics throwing up law that is used politically to maintain the status quo. Despite his later claims for the peaceful effects of reconceptualising international law, here a particular form of international law serves as the tool of a particular hegemonic power. There is little doubt that *Grossraum* represented both a theoretical and a pragmatic political category for Schmitt: to

---

109 Schmitt n.d., p. 15. For a perspective on *grossraum* from within mainstream international law, see Vagts 1990, p. 689. Vagts unconvincingly attempts to shoehorn this essentially evasive concept into straightforward managerialist terms of the 'rights' of hegemonic versus 'subordinate' states.

110 Schmitt n.d., p. 1.

111 Schmitt 2003, pp. 234–8.

112 Schmitt n.d., p. 6. My emphasis.

some extent it aligned Schmitt with Hitlerian foreign policy.[113] However, this does not necessarily invalidate it as a theoretical tool.

Indeed, insofar as it is an acknowledgement of a rapidly shifting international reality of power politics, it may underscore it. Schmitt's desire to frankly acknowledge the central importance of *Grossraum* to international law at a time when Germany's capacity to expand its 'greater-space' was at a premium is an attempt to shift international law to a new paradigm, better suited to international realities in two ways. First, Schmitt claims that it would better reflect those realities – indeed, that the change of paradigm is 'unavoidable' given 'the irresistible development towards greater spaces and scales of space'.[114] And second, such international law would be 'in the position to allow nations organised as states to insist upon an Earth divided up into greater-spaces'.[115] It would, in other words, better serve the interests of Germany, the aspirant hegemonic power for whom Schmitt speaks.

Here we see the beginnings of a theory in which international law is understood to be an active part of conflictual international politics, used by states against each other. Schmitt's ritual claims about the increasing likelihood of peace with the new international law is easily outweighed by his stress on the way different phases and articulations of international law represent the interests of particular international powers, and that with upsets in the relative strengths of those forces, changes in the forms of international law will follow.

This is an international law which reflects and facilitates the interests of great powers in the international arena, rather than any autonomous legal sphere the careful application of which tends towards peace and justice.

Schmitt is disarming in his acknowledgement that international law will be used for imperialist purposes. So far as it goes, that analysis is persuasive.

---

[113] Kervegan 1999, pp. 58–9, pp. 62–4. Not being based on racial categories, however, that allegiance was, if not contingent, at best unstable (Koskenniemi 2002, p. 421). 'Schmitt argues that it was precisely his refusal to endorse a racially-based theory of *Grossraum*, i.e., large-scale geo-political power blocs, as distinct from his own critical, scholarly concedpt, which explains the "failure" of his work between 1933–1945 to feature within the approved lists of official Nazi publications' (Salter 1999, p. 169).

[114] Schmitt n.d., p. 15.

[115] Ibid.

To advance a theory of international relations that explains conflicting claims and exploitative relations as part of the condition of modernity, and yet to claim that law can be transformative, is to disaggregate law from politics with a notion of law's 'relative autonomy'.[116] This is to retreat into the political and legal formalism criticised throughout this chapter. To take law seriously as part of politics is necessarily to theorise it critically, to be sceptical of its claims to prevent disorder, let alone to minimise inequality and injustice.

2.2. *Monism, dualism, positivism, naturalism*

I have attempted to dispense with the formalist theories implicit in Austin's or Morgenthau's conceptions of law. Building on this critique, it is necessary briefly to situate oneself theoretically vis-à-vis the interminable debates over the basis of international law's claims to legitimacy, and to the relationship between international and municipal law.

The rejection of the abstract formalism implicit in the textbook definitions does not imply support for positivism, traditionally conceived. Positivism holds that it is the practice of states that constitutes the primary source of international law: it is counterposed to naturalism, which holds that 'the basic principles of all law . . . [are] derived, not from any deliberate human choice or decision, but from principles of justice which had a universal and eternal validity'.[117]

From the point of view of materialist theory, this is a controversy in which neither side, traditionally conceived, is persuasive.[118] Naturalism is abstract, ahistorical and idealist. Even if natural law is not seen as deriving from God,[119] it is 'universal and eternal', deriving 'not from any deliberate human choice or decision'.[120] However, positivism's claim that law is the will of the state implies an ahistorical and idealist notion of 'state will'. 'Positivism begins from certain premises, that the state is a metaphysical reality with a value

116 Chimni 1993, p. 143.

117 Malanczuk 1997, p. 15. See Malanczuk 1997, pp. 15–17 for a brief overview of the debate between naturalists and positivists.

118 'It goes without saying that the theory of natural law cannot stand the least historical or sociological criticism, for it gives an entirely inadequate picture of reality. But the main curiosity consists in the fact that the juridic theory of the state, which took its place in the name of positivism distorts reality to no less a degree.' Pashukanis 1980, p. 97.

119 Grotius claimed that 'natural law would still have existed even if God had not'. Malanczuk 1997, p. 16.

120 Malanczuk 1997, p. 15.

and significance of its own, and that endowed with such reality the state may also be regarded as having a will.'[121]

A systematic and grounded theory of (international) law must consider law and the state as the results of historical processes and social relations. Both positivism and naturalism fetishise law: one starts from abstract law, another from the abstract state. Rejecting these positions, the materialist analysis of the legal form offers a way out of this unsatisfactory dualism, with an alternative theory for the existence of effective international law.

Positivism is traditionally associated with a dualist position, which, in contradistinction to monism, considers that international law and municipal law 'represent two entirely distinct legal systems, international law having an *intrinsically* different character from that of state law'.[122] Given that the state is the vanishing point of theory in positivism, it is understandable that positivism tends towards dualism:[123] the various states have a fundamentally different relationship with the law municipally, where they are the sovereigns, and internationally, where they are also subjects. Rather than attempt a systematic theory of actually-existing law in all its variety, with the legal form opaque to them dualists can do no more than simply *note* the (profound, to be sure) differences between international and municipal law, and claim that to be a theory.[124]

Monism, however, has done little more to open up the nature of law. It is true that it is predicated on a slightly more systematic notion of law:

> Once it be accepted as a hypothesis that international law is a system of rules of a truly legal character, it was impossible according to . . . monist writers to deny that the two systems constitute part of that unity corresponding to the unity of legal science.[125]

This is persuasive. However, generally monism has simply been predicated on an alternative, no less abstract, *definition* of law. Thus Kelsen, for

---

[121] Shearer 1994, p. 21.

[122] Shearer 1994, p. 64. Emphasis in original.

[123] 'As a rule of thumb, it may be said that the ideological background to dualist doctrines is strongly coloured by an adherence to positivism and an emphasis on the theory of sovereignty, while monist schools are more inclined to follow natural law thinking and liberal ideas of a world society.' Malanczuk 1997, p. 63. See also Shearer 1994, p. 64.

[124] It is interesting that dualism is a function of a kind of monism: '[t]he "positivists" hold that the rules of international law are in final analysis of the same character as "positive" municipal law (i.e. state law) inasmuch as they also issue from the will of the state' (Shearer 1994, p. 21).

[125] Shearer 1994, p. 65.

example, is a monist only insofar as he considers law 'a coercive order'. This leaves us no clearer on the nature of the legal form, and leaves many questions unanswered, as I will argue below.

Monism is an absolute necessity insofar as the subject matter of jurisprudence is acknowledged to be law in the real world. If our project is to theorise actually-existing law, it is precisely the job of the theorist to explain why, given the disparities between international and municipal law, they are both systems *of law*. Dualism simply abdicates that responsibility. To that extent we must reject Fitzmaurice's claim that

> the entire monist-dualist controversy is unreal, artificial and strictly beside the point, because it assumes something that has to exist for there to be any controversy at all – and which in fact does not exist – namely a common field in which the two legal orders under discussion both simultaneously have their spheres of activity.[126]

This is a fallacy based on a refusal to engage with fundamental questions of jurisprudence. It is a statement of a pragmatic technical nature: essentially, it states that as the two systems generally do not collide, this is a non-issue. This is not, as Fitzmaurice claims, a 'radical view', but one based on a kind of robust 'common sense', with the theoretical poverty so often concomitant.

Having rejected dualism and 'harmonisation', and established the necessity of monism for systematic theory, the real job of analysis is still to be done. Monism is necessary for jurisprudence, but it is very far from sufficient, as a brief examination of Kelsen will show.

2.3. *The high point of formalism: Kelsen*

The most unapologetically formalist attempt to formulate a theory of international law was that of Hans Kelsen. Kelsen attempts to solve the Austinian problem of circularity described above from within Austin's formalist tradition. He remains Austinian in that he 'accepts the basic Austinian notion of law as a "coercive order"'.[127] 'Kelsen puts stress upon the coercive claims of the norms comprising international law and upon the sanctions available in the event of violations'.[128] He claims to be a positivist, in viewing law as born by the actions of the law-makers.[129]

---

[126] Fitzmaurice 1957, p. 71.
[127] Bull 1975, p. 125.
[128] Falk 1968, p. 134.
[129] 'The contents of the norms must be determined by acts of authorized individ-

In an attempt to escape Austin's circularity problem, Kelsen formulated his 'pure' theory of law.[130] This posed a highly abstract version of international law, in which that law is a coercive order of rules backed by the threat of sanctions, a system of norms determined by the law creators. He acknowledges that unlike municipal law, there is no sovereign authority to mete out sanctions, and instead that the sanctions, in the shape of reprisals and war, are executed by the wronged state.

> [I]t is the state whose rights have been violated which is authorized to react against the violator by reprisals or war as the coercive acts provided for by international law. The technique of self-help, characteristic of primitive law, prevails.[131]

In alleging that a universal sovereign is not necessary for the sanction-backed rules of international law to be law, Kelsen breaks with Austin. In so doing, he is able to break the circularity problem. For Austin, law is law inasmuch as it is the command of the sovereign: in contrast Kelsen's pure theory is internal – it attempts to be a theory of the law itself. However, the pure theory brings on its own problems.

Kelsen's theory of law as a 'normative hierarchy, in which each norm is created by a higher norm'[132] rests – and must rest – on a *Grundnorm*. This is the basic norm of a given society on which rest all the others. It is a norm that 'establishes a certain authority, which may well in turn vest norm-creating power in some other authorities'[133] – in other words, it specifies which bodies can make law.

For the system of international law, Kelsen claimed that 'the presupposed basic norm of international law must be a norm which establishes custom constituted by the mutual behavior of states as law-creating fact'.[134] Crucially, the *grundnorm* cannot be posited, but must be *presupposed*. It 'is not part of positive law – it is a hypothesis'.[135] To that extent, the edifice of the pure theory is utterly idealist. For the sake of internal rigour it sacrifices its applicability in the real world. It is the norms that are the subject of analysis (it is a

uals . . . They are valid if they are created in this way, . . . whatever their contents may be.' Kelsen 1952, pp. 410–11. We shall see, however, that Kelsen's is a peculiarly 'utopian' positivism.

130 Kelsen 1967.

131 Kelsen 1968, p. 88.

132 McCarthy 1998, p. 157.

133 Kelsen 1952, p. 410.

134 Kelsen 1968, p. 88.

135 Lachs 1987, p. 94.

'pure' theory of law), rather than the way those norms and laws pan out in actuality. Kelsen's theory, in a Kantian attempt to analyse the law as 'thing-in-itself', limits 'itself to an analysis of rules. . . . [T]he pure theory of law does not concern itself with their effectiveness, or their degree of operation'.[136]

The critique of Austin above is applicable to Kelsen here. The project of international legal theory must be to understand actually-existing international law. Kelsen's 'tendency to accept normative claims at face value, regardless of the prospect for their implementation'[137] is a product of the fact that his is an analysis of 'pure' law. 'The mistake Kelsen made was to try and derive the legal norm not from social relations but to locate it in the phenomenon of law itself.'[138] Kelsen does not see this as a failure, but as the very job of a 'pure' theory of law. But for all his claims to positivity, examining law while ignoring the lived reality of that law is a utopian and idealist project.[139]

In any case, despite his extreme formalism, Kelsen could not sustain the sharp distinction between 'law' and reality necessary for a truly 'pure' theory of law. Instead, his theory explicitly presupposed a minimum effectiveness of law in the efficacy of the legal order.[140] 'With this, however, the pure theory ceased to be pure'.[141]

Kelsen's acknowledgement that his final referent must be law in the real world vindicates the claim that it is actually-existing law which must be theorised, not some nebulous 'pure' form against which reality is but a pathologised variant. Without any attempt to theorise the relation between 'pure' law and its reality – and '[t]here is no Kelsen methodology for analysis of the intense interdependency which exists between the people and the law or between patterns of authority and patterns of control'[142] – the 'pure' theory ends up collapsing under its own contradictions: either it claims absolute divorce from reality, in which case relevance and applicability are sacrificed

136 Lachs 1987, p. 94.
137 Falk 1968, p. 134.
138 Chimni 1993, p. 220.
139 See Falk 1968, p. 135.
140 'For if we analyze our judgments concerning the validity of legal norms, we find that we presuppose the first constitution as a valid norm only under the condition that the legal order established on the basis of this constitution is, by and large, effective, that is to say, that is actually applied and obeyed' (Kelsen 1952, p. 412). See also Kelsen 1967, pp. 211–14.
141 Chimni 1993, p. 219.
142 Paust 1979, p. 38.

to formal rigour, or it admits the 'reality' of law, as Kelsen was forced to, in which case the 'pure' theory is wrong.

As Gramsci said against the ahistorical fascist idealists, his was philosophy 'not of the "pure" act, but of the real "impure" act, in the most profane and worldly sense of the word'.[143] What must be attempted, contra Kelsen and in this Gramscian sense, is a theory of impure law.

2.4. *From rules to process: McDougal-Lasswell*[144]

At the opposite end from the extreme formalism of Kelsen is the jurisprudence of Myres McDougal. Where Kelsen was interested in establishing the autonomy of the legal system, McDougal was concerned to establish its relevance as part of the political process. He claims, in fact, to achieve just the embedding of law into the structure of politics the importance of which I have stressed.

McDougal starts with a critique of rules-based international legal theory. Whether or not Koskenniemi is right that McDougal's 'assertions about the relatedness of law and politics are shared by perhaps a majority of modern international lawyers',[145] McDougal's formulation of that view – his critique of rules – sets him apart from the mainstream.

> The most fundamental obscurity in contemporary theory about international law secretes itself in over-emphasis, by most writers and many decision-makers, upon the potentialities of technical 'legal' rules, unrelated to policies, as factors and instruments in the guiding and shaping of decisions. This over-emphasis begins in the very definition of the subject-matter of international law as a system of rules.[146]

McDougal rightly sees this rules-based jurisprudence as tending towards formalism: 'it causes too many people to make sharp and unreal distinctions

---

[143] Gramsci 1971, p. 372.

[144] Myres McDougal worked in collaboration with various colleagues throughout his life, but he owed a systematic intellectual debt to Harold D. Lasswell. In response to Oran Young's speculation as to 'whether the Lasswellian conceptual apparatus is a necessary part of McDougal's jurisprudence' (Young 1972, p. 67), McDougal responded that 'the "intellectual apparatus" *is* the jurisprudence' (McDougal 1972, p. 79, emphasis in original). I follow McDougal's own convention in referring to the 'McDougal-Lasswell' approach.

[145] Koskenniemi 1989, p. 171.

[146] McDougal 1953, p. 143.

between law and policy'.[147] However, McDougal is also critical of the realists:

> At the opposite extreme from over-emphasis on technical rules, is an attitude increasingly common today which underestimates the role of rules, and of legal processes in general, and over-emphasizes the importance of naked power.[148]

Exemplary of this of course is Morgenthau, whose main flaw, claims McDougal, was 'not that he emphasizes power too much but that he doesn't emphasize certain forms of power enough'.[149] This is concomitant with the fact that Morgenthau is 'remarkably unclear about what he means by power'.[150]

McDougal's alternative conception sees law as *inextricably part of politics*. Thus, he attempts to offer a more comprehensive theory of power than the 'simple physical force' implied by Morgenthau and the realists.[151] 'In a relevant jurisprudence, international law will be explicitly conceived as the comprehensive process of authoritative decision'.[152]

Thus, law is seen as a dynamic process, rather than a static template through which to view politics. Higgins, writing from a McDougalite perspective, neatly illustrates how legal formalism, seeing international law as merely 'rules', tends to elide into political formalism, and often into legal nihilism.

> There is a widely held perception of international law as 'rules' – rules that are meant to be impartially applied but are frequently ignored. It is further suggested that these rules are ignored because of the absence of effective centralized sanctions – and, in turn, that all of this evidences that international law is not 'real law' at all. . . . [In fact,] [r]ules play a part in law, but not the only part.[153]

It is no wonder that Higgins 'remain[s] committed to the analysis of international law as *process* rather than rules.'[154]

Seeing international law as a process enables one to step outside the opposed, mutually reinforcing positions of legal and political formalism. It is a way of conceptualising law as part of politics. And if law is a process, something

---

[147] McDougal 1953, p. 144.
[148] McDougal 1953, p. 157.
[149] McDougal 1955, p. 378.
[150] McDougal 1952, p. 104.
[151] Ibid.
[152] Lasswell, McDougal & Reisman 1968, p. 202.
[153] Higgins 1994, p. 2.
[154] Ibid. Emphasis mine.

that is *done*, then legal *interpretation* becomes of paramount importance. Interpretation must be more than simply the application of static and self-explanatory rules. Contextual interpretation is the very mechanism by which law is made part of political reality: law is either static, or it is open to interpretation.

This explains McDougal's passionate defence of interpretation. 'The great defect, and tragedy, in the International Law Commission's final recommendations about the interpretation of treaties is in their insistent emphasis upon an impossible, conformity-imposing textuality.'[155] The meanings of laws cannot, in this theory, be seen as inhering simply in the words themselves in a self-explanatory way. Interpretation is not something we do to understand the law, it is part of the process that *is* law. That process contextualises the legal process as part of political history:

> If the culminating statements in a stream of assertion and counterassertion are to be properly understood, they must be put in the setting of all the preceding events that are likely to have affected the final result in any significant way.[156]

It is also interpretation which seeks to steer the political process in a particular direction: '[t]he decision-maker who engages in acts of interpretation is in search of the past and present; but the past and present are pursued as a way of accomplishing a future result.'[157]

McDougal's theory of interpretation has laid him open to fierce criticism. Interpretation, after all, is easy enough when the various participants of the process of international law have 'genuinely shared expectations',[158] but where that is not the case – when there is international legal controversy – interpretation must be directed by other factors. Given that there will be situations when 'alternative norms . . . could, in context, each be applicable',[159] the interpretation will be made in part according to the policy preferences of the lawyer.

It is to the great credit of McDougal and his associates and pupils that they acknowledge this. If law is part of politics, then politics must be part of the legal process, and political actors are not neutral. As Higgins puts it, '[b]ecause

155 McDougal 1967a, p. 992.
156 McDougal 1967b, p. xvi.
157 McDougal 1967b, p. 39.
158 McDougal 1967b, p. 40.
159 Higgins 1994, p. 6.

I believe there is no avoiding the essential relationship between law and policy, I also believe that it is desirable that the policy factors are dealt with systematically and openly'.[160] It is for this reason that McDougal-Lasswell jurisprudence is not generally known as, say, 'the process theory of law' but as the 'policy school', or 'policy-oriented jurisprudence'.

Most of his critics accuse McDougal of using categories of international law to justify whatever actions he chooses. '[W]oe to the negotiators,' says Fitzmaurice, 'if [McDougal] . . . had to be taken literally. . . . It would not be *their* treaty that would emerge from the fray, but another that someone else thought was the one they should have entered into'.[161] Stanley Anderson is harsher. 'Law is policy. Policy is human dignity. Human dignity is fostered in the long run by the success of American foreign policy. Therefore, law is the handmaiden of the national interest of the United States.'[162]

It is quite true that McDougal's 'uncritical acceptance of the views of the American "establishment"' has led him to be an 'exegete or apologist' for the US.[163] Though he often expresses his desire for a jurisprudence that furthers 'human dignity', the concept is nebulous, to say the least, and lends itself easily to more or less any approach the policy-makers decide to take. Even Higgins, a close follower of McDougal, argues that

> it is a very fine line between insisting that decisions be taken in accordance with the policy objectives of a liberal, democratic world community and asserting that *any* action taken by a liberal democracy against a totalitarian nation is lawful. . . . McDougal at times seems to step over the line.[164]

McDougal's political apologia, however, must be disentangled from his theoretical jurisprudence (much as with Schmitt). Here, a legal scepticism exclusively in the third sense above – nihilism about law as progressive 'social engineering' without doubting its political role – allows us to endorse McDougal's persuasive dynamic theory of law, without sanctioning his strategy of lending law to American power. Many of McDougal's critics are deeply sceptical of the politics behind his interpretative strategy, and they attack the

---

[160] Higgins 1994, p. 5.
[161] Fitzmaurice 1971, p. 368. Emphasis in original.
[162] Anderson 1963, p. 382.
[163] Young 1972, p. 74: this is in a far from hypercritical review. See also Chimni 1993, pp. 137–43.
[164] Higgins 1969, p. 922.

policy prescriptions embedded in his legal interpretations, believing themselves to be undermining his fundamental thesis about the nature of international law. This they have of course not done.

Underlying many of the criticisms of McDougal-Lasswell jurisprudence is the fact that it holds 'indeterminacy to be an all pervasive attribute of legal process'.[165] Those who hold that McDougal's theory of interpretation is wrong as it elides law with power are essentially claiming that, contrary to the theory of indeterminate law implied in McDougal's theory of interpretation, there is an 'ordinary language' meaning of the rules of law embedded in the 'blackletter' texts themselves. This, however, marks them out as legal formalists, open to all the criticisms levelled above. As Higgins points out,

> [i]t really carries matters no further for critics to say that this approach 'can lead to international law being used by states as a device for post facto justifying decisions without really taking international law into account'. This simply begs the question of what international law is. Such a comment merely presupposes that there is a 'real' international law that all men of good faith can recognize – that is, rules that can be neutrally applied, regardless of circumstance and context. And that is where the debate began.[166]

Having dispensed with formalism, law must be part of the political process. This means that law itself *is* a political process, and the 'meanings' and applications of legal norms cannot be pre-determined. They are constituted in interpretation, contextually.

There is another sense in which McDougal correctly holds international law to be indeterminate: 'the fact that . . . a number of fundamental concepts and rules "travel in opposites" (domestic jurisdiction and international concern, aggressive war and self-defence)'.[167] In other words, many categories of international law are mutually constituting opposites, which pull in different directions, in terms of interpretation. This is an enormously important point. However, McDougal never theorises this insight sufficiently. It is left to the Critical Legal Studies movement, most particularly and impressively Koskenniemi, to systematise the observation of these oppositional categories. This work will be examined in detail in Chapter Two.

---

[165] Falk 1968, p. 501.

[166] Higgins 1994, p. 7.

[167] Chimni 1993, p. 79. See, for example, McDougal in American Society of International Law 1954, p. 120.

There are innumerable problems underlying McDougal's paradigm. Most fundamentally, many of the categories imported from Lasswell's political theory are vacuous: crucially, the concept of 'power', which is abstract and idealist. Linked to that is a methodological individualism which cannot satisfactorily theorise the complex structures which act to restrain and enable agents in the international – and domestic – arenas.[168] 'McDougal advances a partial and reified concept of power which cloaks, on the international plane, the exploitative relation between states in the same way as it veils . . . the exploitation of the ruled by the rulers'.[169]

However, there is no reason that a systematic materialist theory of power could not be 'inserted' into McDougal's jurisprudence in place of his unsustainably abstract theory. With an alternative materialist theory of history and power, it is easy to subject McDougal's reactionary political agenda to critique, remain sceptical about the progressive, transformative application of international law, while conceptualising international law as a process as McDougal describes.

As an analysis of international law as a real force, part of a real political process, McDougal's interpenetration of law and policy through a processual theory of law is persuasive. It effectively bypasses the Scylla and Charybdis of legal and political formalism. And even if we do not *like* his application of that theory in the policy arena, it is illustrative of just how lawmakers can use international law as a political tool – how law and politics do, in fact, interpenetrate.

There is, however, a major lacuna in the theory as it applies to international law. For Young, when focusing on political decision-making as central to law, 'the concept tends to lose discriminatory power'; 'this conception encourages the inclusion of so much . . . that it often becomes difficult to identify law . . . and then to analyse the connections between law and various other aspects of a social system'.[170] Similarly, Anderson's claim that in McDougal, where '[l]aw becomes merely an increment to power',[171] 'the assimilation of law by policy'[172] means that McDougal's is 'not a juristic system'.[173]

---

168 For a very good critique of McDougal's underlying notions, see Chimni 1993, pp. 128–33.
169 Chimni 1993, p. 130.
170 Young 1972, p. 64.
171 Anderson 1963, p. 382.
172 Anderson 1963, p. 381.
173 Anderson 1963, p. 382.

The question, which McDougal's jurisprudence cannot answer, is *why law?* This, yet again, concerns the tenacity of the *legal form* itself. Without an analysis of that legal form, McDougal cannot explain why law exists as a distinct part of the political process.

We have returned to the critique levelled at so many of the mainstream writers. Without a theory of the legal form, a jurisprudential system cannot address the basic ontological question of international law. With such a theory, we might fill the gap in the processual theory of law and explain how law can be a political process, as McDougal claims, and yet how there is something in the structure of modern social relations which maintains the integrity of the peculiarly legal form of conceptualising and articulating claims. We might explain how law is political and that modern politics is a legalistic system, without collapsing law *into* politics.

A theory of the legal form is advanced in Chapters Three and Four below. First, I will examine the work of those who have gone furthest to problematise international law and international legal theory: the Critical Legal Studies movement and the historical-materialist theorists.

Chapter Two

Dissident Theories: Critical Legal Studies and Historical Materialism

1. Beyond pragmatism

The traditional canon of international legal theory has been exposed, with all its shortcomings: its endlessly recursive and fruitless counterposition of positivism and naturalism, and the intractable choice between apologetic policy-approach and utopian rules-approach theories. The modern ignoring of systematic theory can be seen as a defensive reaction to this state of affairs: international legal theorists after the Second World War 'turned to pragmatism, a modern consequentialist philosophy that emphasized institutional process, functional progress, or rule centered doctrinal specificity, while denying the relevance of coherent abstraction'[1] – that is, of jurisprudence itself.

---

[1] Purvis 1991, p. 83. Purvis sees most of those modern international legal theorists who do attempt to grapple with more fundamental questions of theory, such as McDougal, Kelsen, Schwarzenberger et al., as 'conceptual pragmatists' who reacted to the failure of 'unreflective pragmatism' and 'sought to turn abstraction into functionalism', using 'pragmatic functionalism' (p. 84). Much of Purvis's taxonomy here is questionable: he wrongly characterises Kelsen as a sceptic, for example (p. 84). His historical claim, that these more systematic theorists represented a response to the failure of 'pure' pragmatism, is also unsustainable: far from emerging 'from the efforts of the post-war scholars', Kelsen's theories were first elaborated in *Hauptprobleme der Staatsrechtslehre* in 1911 and reformulated in 1925 with the first publication of *Allgemeine Staatslehre*. Similarly, Morgenthau's scepticism was articulated in his doctoral thesis written before the 1930s (Eckstein 1981, p. 646). However, Purvis's broader point that the modern textbook writers *were* exercising a woolly pragmatism in part born of the recursive nature of classical jurisprudence of international law can be maintained.

The re-examination of fundamental questions of form is a prerequisite for the development of international legal theory. The emergence since the late 1980s of the 'New Stream'[2] of writing on international law is therefore a very welcome development. This 'New Stream' has attacked pragmatism's 'timidity' and attempted to 'dislodge the discipline of international law from its stagnation . . . and rejuvenate the field as an arena of meaningful intellectual inquiry'.[3] 'Collectively,' these writers have 'sought to wash away the idea that the discipline of international law was only a bureaucratic player in the struggle for justice in the international arena'.[4]

This 'New Stream' is the application in international law of the techniques and theoretical perspectives articulated by writers such as Roberto Unger and Duncan Kennedy, who focus – by default – on domestic law.[5] 'The New Stream . . . stands as part of a broader movement in contemporary legal theory commonly known as Critical Legal Studies (CLS) or critical jurisprudence'.[6] The CLS movement has its origins in the work of the Conference on Critical Legal Studies in the US, which first met in 1977,[7] and was internationalised in the Critical Legal Conference in Britain and the *Critique du droit* in France.[8]

The CLS movement is united in its critical attitude to mainstream legal theory and the liberal agenda and philosophy of which it is part. Its self image, as the name of the movement suggests, is negative rather than positive.

> Its roots lie in a deep sense of dissatisfaction with the existing state of legal scholarship. . . . Advocates of critical legal studies may not all share the same rank ordering of dissatisfactions but are all reacting against features of the prevailing orthodoxies in legal scholarship, against the conservatism of the law schools and against many features of the role played by law and legal institutions in modern society.[9]

These 'reactive roots'[10] explain why the movement is such a broad church, encompassing such an enormous, contradictory range of influences. The

---

[2] Kennedy 1988.
[3] Kennedy 1988, p. 6.
[4] Purvis 1991, p. 88.
[5] Unger 1983; Kennedy 1979.
[6] Purvis 1991, p. 89.
[7] For a brief description of the birth of the CLS movement in the US, see Kelman 1987, pp. 1–2.
[8] Hunt 1987, p. 5.
[9] Ibid.
[10] Ibid.

British movement has been less eclectic,[11] its main influences confined to Marxism, feminism and the Frankfurt School, with, in recent years, a turn to Derridean deconstruction and Habermas. In the US the catholicism of the movement has been extreme, where the 'New Stream' has incorporated 'normative philosophy, critical theory, structuralism, anthropology, prepositional logic, literature, sociology, politics and psychiatry',[12] as a subset of American CLS which has its own origins in 'Legal Realism, New Left anarchism, Sartrean existentialism, neo-progressive historiography, liberal sociology, radical social theory and empirical social science'[13] – along, again, with the now-ubiquitous postmodern social and linguistic theory, in both Foucauldian and Derridean variants. Given these various and sometimes contradictory influences, there is much scope for internal disagreement within CLS.[14]

The New Stream of international legal theorists is in a doubly marginal position. CLS defines itself in opposition to the mainstream – although as with postmodernism currently, that marginality is greatly exaggerated for the purposes of radical chic[15] – and within CLS, writers on international law are in a tiny minority, though the volume of international legal theory written from such a perspective has been increasing.[16]

The basic approach of the New Stream is in line with the CLS approach. Generally it includes some commitment to left/transformative politics, though emphatically not Marxism; and, crucially, a critical analysis of liberalism as 'a system of thought that is simultaneously beset by internal *contradiction* . . . and by systematic *repression* of the presence of these contradictions'.[17] This critique of liberalism and its legal system is the central shared tenet of CLS, and of the New-Stream theorists in international law.

---

[11] Fitzpatrick and Hunt 1987, p. 2.

[12] Purvis 1991, p. 88.

[13] Purvis 1991, p. 89.

[14] See Fitzpatrick and Hunt 1987, p. 2; Purvis 1991, p. 124.

[15] 'Critical legal theory is the *enfant terrible* of contemporary legal studies. It delights in shocking what it takes to be the legal establishment.' Hunt 1987, p. 5. See Kelman 1987 p. 2 for a wry comment on the spurious categorisation of CLS as an 'underground' movement. David Kennedy points out that a similar assertion of 'outsider status' is familiar not only among critical, but mainstream scholars (Kennedy 1989, p. 394, and throughout for a useful examination of the CLS approach).

[16] Kennedy and Tennant 1994 contains a comprehensive list of critical international legal sources up to 1994. Some useful introductions to the 'New Stream' are Purvis 1991; Carty 1991; Charlesworth 1992; Cass 1996; Aceves 2001, pp. 309–24.

[17] Kelman 1987, p. 3. Emphasis in original.

> The critical attack on liberalism has advanced on four principal fronts. Contemporary international law scholars have maintained (1) that the logic of liberalism in international law is internally incoherent; (2) that international legal discourse operates within a constrained structure; (3) that international legal analysis is indeterminate; and, (4) that whatever authority international law may have is self-validated.[18]

Whatever internal disagreements there are in the New Stream, this stress on the contradictions of liberalism is its most systematic and important insight. In critically evaluating the CLS/New Stream tradition, it is the most developed exposition of this insight that must be engaged with.

2. Koskenniemi and the contradictions of liberalism

Though it is awash with articles, there are few book-length works within the New Stream. Works by Anthony Carty and David Kennedy are important early formulations, but 'the most complete book-length synthesis of CLS and international law'[19] is Martti Koskenniemi's extraordinary 1989 volume, *From Apology to Utopia*.

Koskenniemi's monumental and brilliant work has justly come to be the centre of gravity for critical studies in international law.[20] More than five hundred pages of close, rigorous argument, covering an enormous number of thinkers in international law, and concluding with an extraordinarily comprehensive bibliography, Koskenniemi's book is a necessary resource.

For all the detail of his arguments, Koskenniemi's basic claim is straightforward. As Purvis puts it, international law 'pursues an unachievable resolution of the dichotomy between sovereign will and world order'.[21] He glosses Koskenniemi specifically and the CLS approach more generally as follows:

> [New Stream scholars'] basic claim is that the abstractions of liberalism are contradictory. . . . At the very highest level of abstraction . . . competing and conflicting principles operate within the law. . . . The indeterminacy thesis states that one side of the dichotomies [naturalism/positivism, normative

---

[18] Purvis 1991, p. 92.

[19] Ibid.

[20] Koskenniemi himself makes clear how much he draws from others, especially from Kennedy 1987.

[21] Purvis 1991, p. 103.

> values/concrete reality, world order/sovereign will] alone cannot survive as an adequate explanation of international law theory . . . It is impossible to find a coherent theory that can justify the rule of law in international life. . . . A theory of international law that positions naturalism over positivism, world order over sovereignty . . . must assume the existence of some natural morality independent from sovereign behavior, will, or interest. Without reference to actual sovereign practice, such scholarship would be unable to legitimate its norms . . . [I]t would be utopian. Conversely, if a theory of international law positioned positivism over naturalism, then it would necessarily lack a reflective image of sovereign behaviour. If states were paramount, international law could never impose behavioral rules against their will . . . [S]uch a theory would seem apologist. . . . International law employs a pattern of self-referential arguments that continually shift the source of its authority and origins in an effort to navigate between public order and sovereign will.[22]

As Koskenniemi puts it,

> doctrine is forced to maintain itself *in constant movement from emphasizing concreteness to emphasizing normativity and vice-versa* without ever being able to establish itself permanently in either position. . . . This . . . is ultimately explained by the *contradictory nature of the liberal doctrine of politics*.[23]

The conclusions Koskenniemi draws are severe.

> [I]nternational law is singularly useless as a means for justifying or criticizing international behaviour. Because it is based on contradictory premises it remains both over- and underlegitimizing: it is overlegitimizing as it can be ultimately invoked to justify any behavior (apologism), it is underlegitimizing because incapable of providing a convincing argument on the legitimacy of any practices (utopianism).[24]

This is a return to McDougal's untheorised assertion that 'a number of fundamental concepts and rules "travel in opposites"',[25] in 'pair[s] of opposing

---

22 Purvis 1991, pp. 106–7.

23 Koskenniemi 1989, pp. 46–7. Emphasis in original.

24 Koskenniemi 1989, p. 48. Seeing the terminology of 'apology' and 'utopia' as somewhat abstract, Callinicos suggests as alternatives 'realist' and 'cosmopolitan', thereby relating the argumentative structures Koskenniemi identifies to related state-centric and putative-international-community-based theories in IR, respectively (personal communication).

25 Chimni 1993, p. 79.

concepts'.[26] Koskenniemi has invested the assertion with considerable rigour, and illustrated it with innumerable examples of international legal discourse, to show that the content of international law is inherently indeterminate.

He describes this 'travelling in opposites' in terms of a contradiction between 'descending' and 'ascending' arguments. The former trace order and obligation 'down to justice, common interests, progress, nature of the world community or other similar ideas to which it is common that they are anterior, or superior, to State behavior, will or interest'.[27] Conversely, it is this 'State behavior, will and interest', on which ascending arguments are based.

> The two patterns – or sets of arguments – are both exhaustive and mutually exclusive.... The result... is an incoherent argument which constantly shifts between the opposing positions while remaining open to challenge from the opposite argument.[28]

This analysis not only builds on McDougal, but is reminiscent of Schmitt, who claimed that '[f]rom... one pole unforeseeable "humanitarian" interventions are permissible under international law; from the other, the smallest interference is an international law delict'.[29] Where McDougal merely notes the contradictory nature of international law, and Schmitt constructs a practical theory of legal imperialism on it, Koskenniemi *locates* this contradiction in wider social and political structures, and therefore goes furthest in analysing indeterminate law as a function of modernity.

Koskenniemi is clear that the recursive contradiction is embedded in international law *as a liberal form,* and that it is liberalism itself which is contradictory. 'The fundamental problem of the liberal vision is how to cope with

---

26 McDougal in American Society of International Law 1954, p. 120.

27 Koskenniemi 1989, pp. 40–1. The designation 'ascending' and 'descending' comes from Walter Ullman.

28 Koskenniemi 1989, pp. 41–2. For a very clear example of the ascending-descending structure of argument in action during an international legal crisis see Carothers 1984 on the Soviet shooting down of Korean Air Lines Flight 007. The dyad is particularly clear in the discussion of sovereignty: 'the question of the legality of shooting down intruding aircraft was argued not only at the level of customary norms, but also at the level of general principle. The Soviet Union and the United States made competing appeals to the meaning of the principle of sovereignty itself. The Soviet government stated bluntly that sovereignty means "sacred" borders – an absolute right to protect national airspace against any unwanted intrusion. The United States countered with its own arguments of principle. Secretary of State Shultz announced that national security concerns must be limited by "human values"' (pp. 1204–5). The opposition between the ascending argument of sovereignty and a descending argument of normativity is clear.

29 Schmitt n.d., p. 9.

what seem like mutually opposing demands for individual freedom and social order'.[30] Liberal thought, as it emerged out of the dissolution of the medieval order in which individuals were defined by social rank, posited 'that individuals are both *free* and *equal*'.[31] However, if this 'ascending' principle were all that existed, as 'individual ends differ, indeed conflict', '[i]n the absence of overriding principles civil war seems a constant threat'.[32] There are various ways to resolve this, but they all revolve around the imposition of a counterweight to these private, ascending rights, such as a 'public sphere' of government,[33] or fundamental rights[34] or 'objective interests'[35] that even ascending rights cannot breach. These are all 'descending' arguments, by which supposedly absolute rights of individuals are checked, to stop war or anarchy as rights clash.

The ascending/descending dyad is in a constant state of tension – the halves do not complement but contradict, 'continually threaten each other'.[36]

> The ascending strand legitimizes political order by reference to individual ends . . . Individuals can be constrained only to prevent 'harm to others'. But any constrains seems a violation of individual freedom as what counts as 'harm' can only be subjectively determined. The descending strand fares no better. It assumes that a set of fundamental rights or a natural distinction between private and public spheres exist to guarantee that liberty is not violated. But this blocks any collective action as the content of those freedoms . . . can be justifiably established only by reference to an individual's views thereof. . . . [U]tility conflicts with rights.[37]

The liberal theory of the 'invisible hand' is an attempt to mediate this contradiction, by claiming that ascending self-interest and descending general interest are mutually constituting. However, this is not proved, only asserted. 'The system is held together only by the . . . assumption that self-interested behaviour will ultimately be for the greatest benefit of all. To think the

---

[30] Koskenniemi 1989, p. 52. For the penetration of liberalism into international law, see pp. 55–73.

[31] Koskenniemi 1989, p. 60.

[32] Ibid.

[33] Koskenniemi 1989, p. 63.

[34] Koskenniemi 1989, p. 64.

[35] Koskenniemi 1989, p. 62.

[36] Koskenniemi 1989, p. 66.

[37] Koskenniemi 1989, pp. 66–67.

system as coherent, or workable, this is what one *has to assume*.'[38] And in fact, this supposed solution is structured with precisely the contradictory argumentative structure outlined above: it is, in other words, merely a restatement of the problem.

> It is self-interest, ultimately, which grounds the binding force of precepts of justice. I must keep my promises because otherwise I shall not be trusted. And it is in my self-interest that I shall be trusted. The argument is ascending-descending. Order is maintained by an ascending point about freedom and self-interest. It is maintained through a descending postulate about the ultimate equivalence between particular and general interest.[39]

Koskenniemi's analysis of the indeterminacy thesis, the most developed and sophisticated exposition of the CLS approach, is systematic and extremely powerful. It leads one to the conclusion that international legal doctrines are 'entirely reversible'.[40]

This can be easily illustrated. Take as an example the controversial question of reprisals activity in international law. The mainstream opinion is that reprisals are illegal.[41] The classic statement of that view, the 1964 UN Security Council resolution condemning a British reprisal against Harib Fortress in Yemen, stated that the council '[c]*ondemns* reprisals as incompatible with the purposes and principles of the United Nations'.[42] This recourse to the 'purposes and principles' of the UN represents a 'descending' (normative, moral, naturalistic) argument against unfettered state retaliation. Its authority is located in an authority superordinate to naked state will.

In response, proponents of the legality of reprisals point to Article 51 of the UN Charter, which allows the use of force in self-defence. According to Dinstein and Tucker, some reprisals are the 'functional equivalents' of self-defence, and should be legal as such.[43] Similarly, by seeing 'proportionality'

---

[38] Koskenniemi 1989, p. 67. Emphasis in original.

[39] Koskenniemi 1989, pp. 70–1.

[40] Purvis 1991, p. 113.

[41] See for example Brownlie 1963, p. 281; Schwarzenberger 1952, p. 82; Bowett 1958, pp. 13–14 (Bowett here states the majority view. His own position is ambivalent – see pp. 11–13).

[42] Cited in Falk 1969, p. 429. Emphasis in original.

[43] Dinstein 1994, p. 216; Tucker 1972, p. 586 and throughout. Describing its own actions, the US regularly makes this elision between reprisals and permissible self-defence (Reisman 1994, p. 10). Zoller distinguishes between 'law in the books' according to which reprisals are illegal, and 'law in action', where the 'back door for the use of force in peacetime' remains open (Zoller 1984, p. 39). Kalshoven, in his exhaustive

as the principle according to which a reprisal should be judged legal or illegal, the focus is on the 'wrong' of the breaching of state sovereignty, and the 'right' of the 'wronged' state to exact equivalent punishment.[44] This is to counter the descending argument with an ascending one, based on state sovereignty: any breach of that sovereignty can and must be harshly met, and it rests with the sovereign state itself to mete punishment.

However, any such ascending argument contains its own counterposition. By definition, reprisals are illegal incursions against another state's sovereignty, and if sovereignty is the basis of obligation and authority, it is hard to see how that sovereignty can legally be disrupted. This is the *ascending* version of the argument that reprisals are illegal. The counter to this is to be found in the *descending* justifications for reprisals activity, according to which reprisals can 'advance the purposes of the United Nations',[45] and are therefore legal as measures to ensure a normative order. The same descending argument is found in more abstract terms in those arguments which maintain that reprisals are the necessary homeostatic mechanism of international law, considered as a 'primitive' system: retaliation 'serves to preserve and unite a group which has been threatened by another, to fix responsibility for wrongs, and thus *to maintain a legal order*'.[46]

The debate over whether retaliation is legal resembles a children's pantomime, with ritualistic claims that 'Oh Yes It Is' countered by others that 'Oh No It Isn't'. For all the ink spilt on the subject over the last forty years, no one seems to have remarked that there is something *in the structure of the argument itself* that allows both sides to make plausible, logical claims based on fundamental legitimating concepts of international law. It is not simply due to pig-headedness or stupidity on one or other side that the argument is interminable: it is something in the process of the legal argument itself, an indeterminacy that Koskenniemi devastatingly outlines.

This analysis is highly impressive and illuminating, but Koskenniemi's idealist method means there is not much sense of the underlying political-economic dynamics that the contradictory edifice of liberalism might be

overview of reprisals activity, concludes that '[b]elligerent reprisals . . . have not so far come under a total prohibition', but that 'such a total prohibition . . . is the only tenable proposition' (Kalshoven 1971, p. 375).

44 Bowett 1972, pp. 11–13.

45 Colbert 1948, pp. 203–4. The same argument is advanced in Levenfeld 1982, at p. 35.

46 Masters 1964, p. 607. Emphasis in original. See also Kelsen 1968, pp. 87–8.

expressing. For this, we can turn instead to Marx. In *Capital,* he shows how the social relations of general commodity production are the foundation for liberalism and its contradictions.

> It is . . . the direct relationship of the owners of the conditions of production to the immediate producers . . . in which we find the innermost secret, the hidden basis of the entire social edifice, and hence also the political form of the relationship of *sovereignty and dependence,* in short, the specific form of the state in each case.[47]

At the level of individuals, as Marx suggests, the ascending and descending arguments are mediated by the state. However, this is not the case internationally, where the units are states themselves: in this instance, the relationship is still one of sovereignty and dependence, but it is no longer contained by an overarching power.

For Koskenniemi, liberalism underpins the logic of international law because of the constant application of the 'domestic analogy' by liberal writers, because without an overarching power 'the structuring power of liberal ideas in international law' was so strong.[48] There is no sense, though, of where or why these ideas are generated. Building on Marx's suggestive comments, however, we can get beyond this idealism and see that the logic of inter-state relations under capitalism is defined by the same logic that regulates individuals because in this system, and in the underlying precepts of international law, *states, like individuals, interact as property owners* – each state owns its own sovereign territory.

Grotius makes this clear.

> [T]he jurist [Ulpian] is speaking of private estates and of public law, but in speaking here of the territory of peoples and of private law the same reasoning applies, because from the point of view of the whole human race peoples are treated as individuals.[49]

This is insofar, evidently, as those individuals are owners of estates.

Despite an idealist method, Koskenniemi's exposition of liberal/legal indeterminacy is indispensible, and can easily and invaluably be marshalled as

---

[47] Marx 1981, p. 927. Emphasis mine.

[48] Koskenniemi 1989, p. 72, and more generally pp. 68–73.

[49] Grotius 2000, p. 29. See Gowan 2000, p. 145: 'Grotius . . . transferred the notion of liberty-as-property to the state in international affairs, viewing the character of state boundaries as that of a private estate.'

part of a materialist analysis. However, there are lacunae and problems with Koskenniemi and with the CLS approach in general.

One problem lies in the very eclecticism which some see as CLS's strength. This can lead to a blunting of analysis, as a plethora of conflicting influences are lumped together. For example, Koskenniemi cites Derrida to the effect that interpretation of a law will only ever offer up more words, each of which is as unstable as its fellows, maintaining a situation of radical indeterminacy in legal discourse and discourse in general.[50] However, this 'Derridean' sense of indeterminacy is *not* the same indeterminacy that Koskenniemi has outlined elsewhere in his book. That was a product of the peculiar nature of discourse reflecting the realities of the modern international system, the unstable, contradictory vacillation between sovereignty and world order. Derrida's indeterminacy is a statement of his theory of linguistic *différance* – of the endless 'chain of differential references',[51] words-as-signifiers signifying only other signifiers – and is not a restatement of the structural indeterminacy of liberal modernity.

There are many critiques of Derrida's postmodernism: this is not the place to rehearse them.[52] The point here is that Koskenniemi mis-sells his own analysis when he equates it with Derrida's linguistic essentialism. As Alcantara puts it, '[e]ven in disregard of verbal indeterminacies, Koskenniemi explains, law as a system would still be indeterminate.' This is '[m]ore significant' than the 'indeterminacy of legal texts'.[53]

---

50 'In this sense, the finding that there is no objective meaning to legal concepts, no extratextual referent which could be pointed at when disagreements arise provides the most serious threat we have hereto encountered to the possibility of delimiting law from arguments within "essentially contested" political concepts.' Koskenniemi 1989, p. 475.

51 Derrida 1976, p. 159.

52 See, for example, Norris 1992, pp. 44–7. Also Callinicos 1989, pp. 73–80 on Derrida's epistemological pessimism and idealism.

53 Alcantara 1996, p. 67, p. 66. This is a moment of rare clarity and perspicacity for Alcantara, but it is largely undermined in that he sees the systemic indeterminacy he rightly stresses as more important as a *function* of the indeterminacy of language outlined by Derrida. This he holds to be the case on the dubious grounds that 'Derrida's insight into the inadequacy of language *per se* is equally germane with regard to systems of representation generally', and that international law *is* 'one of those systems of language' (p. 66). In fact, Derrida's system can precisely be criticised for its idealist privileging of language over social being, with the concomitant 'textualist' tendency to see language as a template through which to theorise other social forms. Alcantara is right to stress the indeterminacy of the international legal form, but his reasoning for so doing is quite wrong.

Their very catholicism sometimes stands in the way of CLS writers developing rigorous, systematic analyses of international legal indeterminacy as distinguished from what are sometimes frankly theoretically contingent and far less persuasive postmodern garnishes. The sometimes indiscriminate attitude to theory comes at a price. The profusion of influences has left CLS scholars with powerful critical tools, but a poverty of systematic *theory*. As Hunt puts it, 'it is a movement in search of a theory, but at the same time it is a movement which has not agreed that such a theory is either possible or desirable'.[54]

This lack of systematicity, and its cost, can be seen most clearly in the disparity between CLS's analysis and its project – the 'alternatives' it purports to offer. As Purvis argues, 'the New Stream's ideal vision is incompatible with the movement's own premises'.[55] Koskenniemi's hard-headed critique of the 'normativity' of international law does not sit with his suggestions for action (many of the critiques of which he has latterly accepted).[56]

'Many people', he points out, 'believe that international law offers a promise of a more just society. Yet, once they enter it, they will realize that there is no coherent project for a better world embedded in the concepts which they are taught.'[57] He argues that the 'rule of law' itself must be undermined,[58] given that 'the "complete system" cannot be salvaged'.[59] However, he also maintains the possibility of a socially transformative role for international law as a tool wielded by the engaged international lawyer, who must 're-establish an identity for himself as a social actor'[60] – essentially, act as a political being with a commitment to social justice.

CLS suggests broadening the inputs to the decision-making process in international law and international legal discourse. What Koskenniemi deems necessary is the penetration of explicit (progressively framed) questions of policy and justice in legal argument – 'the inevitable movement to politics'[61] – and an attempt to see law as a process carried out by agents, 'a *practice* of attempt-

54 Hunt 1987, p. 5.
55 Purvis 1991, p. 117.
56 Personal communication.
57 Koskenniemi 1989, p. 494.
58 Koskenniemi 1989, p. 501.
59 Koskenniemi 1989, p. 495.
60 Koskenniemi 1989, p. 496.
61 Koskenniemi 1989, p. 479.

ing to reach the most acceptable solution, a conversation about what to do, here and now'.[62]

For this, Koskenniemi stresses, 'the critical lawyer must accept the reality of conflict',[63] to distance herself from utopianism. 'Critical practice', Koskenniemi explains, 'attempts to reach those conflictual views, bring them out in the open and suggest practical arrangement for dealing with conflict without denying its reality'.[64]

> The legitimacy of the CLS utopian vision of international law comes from a widened debate about international life, moving beyond mere arguments about principles and doctrines to include consideration of the full range of normative visions about a just international order. . . . The New Stream desires to save international legal discourse because as a literature about norms such discourse becomes a means to an end.[65]

Koskenniemi's move to 'critical-normative' practice is a plea to move away from reified categories in international law, and to embed the ideal of 'authentic commitment'[66] within international legal practice. Koskenniemi is clear that this move to 'normative imagination' means 'renouncing the search for a World Rule of Law which could be abstracted . . . and appear as a set of coherent principles which the layer would only have to "interpret"'.[67] However, even so critiquing the Rule of Law, 'it is possible for a critical lawyer to maintain his identity as a lawyer without giving up the (political) commitment to the criticism of objectification mistakes as illegitimate – and hence illegal – domination.'[68]

The instability – indeed self-defeating nature – of this project illustrates the flaws and inconsistencies in the theory of law that underpins it. Koskenniemi's chapter on suggested radical/critical international legal practice represents a sharp break from the rest of his book, which is consistently rigorous and persuasive. Instead, this final section is unstable in its categories, and attempts to hide the contradictory and rather wan nature of its prescriptions behind

---

62 Koskenniemi 1989, p. 486.
63 Ibid.
64 Koskenniemi 1989, p. 487.
65 Purvis 1991, pp. 117–18.
66 Koskenniemi 1989, p. 488.
67 Koskenniemi 1989, p. 501.
68 Koskenniemi 1989, p. 489.

a kind of Habermasian exuberance. One critic has described this last chapter as offering 'a tentative and rather nebulous agenda'.[69]

The claim, for example, that the critical international lawyer can recast the domination she finds normatively illegitimate as *illegal* leaves the mechanism of that judgement unclear. If the lawyer deems the domination illegal because normatively illegitimate, this is a descending argument which can be countered by an ascending assertion of state sovereignty. In other words, insofar as the 'law' laid down by Koskenniemi's transformative lawyer is in fact *law, defensible in legal terms*, and not merely a statement of opinion, it is open to the critique of contradiction and instability that Koskenniemi has spent 475 pages laying bare. If on the other hand, 'critical-normative' practice has fundamentally changed the nature of law so that this analysis is no longer valid, this 'new law' is untheorised: we are presumably describing these edicts as law insofar as they are the opinion of a lawyer, in which case their law-ness is entirely contingent. Koskenniemi's desire to rid the world of 'the Rule of Law' *using the medium of law* cannot resolve itself.

To the extent that we take seriously Koskenniemi's vision of international law as 'normative imagination', Purvis is right that the New Stream undermines its own object.

> There is nothing particularly 'legal' about this vision of international legal discourse. The New Stream has had to disavow international law's claim to an external rationality in world order solutions, and banish with it the image of the international lawyer as someone possessing unique skills for arriving at those solutions.[70]

Faced with the question of how CLS can square its analysis with its proposals, '[t]he reply lies in reflexivity'.[71] This recourse to 'reflexivity' – implicit in Koskenniemi, explicit in Alcantara – is a typical, and typically unsatisfactory, postmodern sleight of hand, a suggestion that an impossible manoeuvre can be made simply by being aware of its impossibility. This, of course, will not work, but the claim that it can is illuminating about CLS's underlying assumptions.

If to change our awareness is to change the very constraining structures around us, the implicit theory of the social world is one of constructivism.

---

[69] Byers 1999, p. 45 footnote 50.
[70] Purvis 1991, p. 117 footnote 155.
[71] Alcantara 1996, p. 72.

Alcantara makes this clear when he talks about 'how the inherited myths, concepts and models of human thought shape the manner in which we view external phenomena'.[72] This is to depict international law as an inherited, constraining myth, which is, indeed, exactly how Purvis depicts it.

> The mythical fabric of international culture permits sovereigns to assert international law without defending its rational authority. Self-validation occurs through the manipulation of cultural language, symbols and history. . . . International law's weaknesses are in some sense irrelevant; self-validation sanctions the international-law myth.[73]

According to this, the structures of everyday life, such as international law, are accretions of ideas. That is what allows for the 'transformative strategy' of reflexivity: to become aware of ideas, and to have new ones, changes the fundamental nature of things in the world.

This is a radically idealist philosophy, privileging abstract concepts over social life itself. It is ahistorical: in its enthusiastic urging to change one's conceptions, it ignores the historical conditions which make certain conceptualisations of certain social phenomena persuasive. There is no theory in Koskenniemi, for example, of precisely why the edifice of international law should be thrown up as part of liberalism.

Equally, therefore, it leaves us no way of understanding the systematic structural constraints on the 'transformative' international law prescribed. In this sense, the CLS theorists share the fundamental failure of the mainstream theorists with whom they break. For all their devastating and persuasive analysis of the failures and contradictions of liberalism and international law, they offer no theory of the legal form itself. They offer a good, 'thick description'[74] of the indeterminacy of the *content* of international law, but they cannot get to grips with i) the tenacity (or even existence) of the international legal form, ii) offer a persuasive analysis of *why* international law and liberalism are contradictory, or iii) see that 'normatively transformative law' they prefer to the 'Rule of Law' is a chimera.

---

[72] Ibid.

[73] Purvis 1991, pp. 112–13.

[74] The term is from Gilbert Ryle, and was used by Clifford Geertz in Geertz 1973 to describe a kind of deep, contextualised observational ethnology predicated on the understanding of society as fundamentally a semiotic system. I use the term here loosely.

CLS fails to make sense of international law, lacking a theory of the legal form and a historical base even for its own persuasive elements. Given their own evidence of its irredeemable instability, the CLS writers' insistence on maintaining some commitment to international law illustrates the refusal to countenance the possibility of denial in the third form described above: the possibility of taking international law seriously, while refusing to see in it hopes for transformative politics.

3. Marxism and international law

Despite elements in Marx's writings that are at least suggestive of a materialist theory of the contradictions of liberalism, the number of Marxists who have written specifically on international law is extremely small. In the remainder of this chapter, I will evaluate the most important of those Marxist works, and gauge how near we are to a systematic historical-materialist theory of international law.

3.1. *The inadequacies of Soviet theory*

One body of writing that can quickly be dispensed with are the 'official' theories of international law of the erstwhile Soviet Bloc. After 1928–30, when the era of more open theoretical debate was suppressed and theory became nothing but a tool for the exigencies of official policy,[75] the 'debates' in the USSR tended to revolve around the extent to which a new and separate sphere of 'socialist international law' was operational. The first major writer to claim that it was was Korovin, in his 1924 book *The International Law of the Transition Period*,[76] who posited 'a "pluralistic" theory of international law based on the idea of almost completely separated juridical "spheres"' including an international law of the Western 'great powers', another of the smaller capitalist states and their colonies, and another of inchoate 'socialist international law'.[77]

Korovin's work was characterised by extraordinary formalism without any fundamental jurisprudence: it tended toward questionable definition rather

[75] A second and even more crushing period of theoretical stagnation was ushered in in 1939. '[T]he imposition of A.J. Vyshinskii's legal concept on the scholarly community at the meeting of the Institute of State and Law of the Soviet Academy in 1939 meant a full stop to (and practically a deadly reprisal against) any sign of further innovation' (Varga 1993, p. xv).

[76] Korovin 1924.

[77] Cruickshank and Kubálková 1988, p. 166.

than analysis. The 'theory' of 'socialist international law' was put to bed for a while, as it sat uneasily with the official principle of 'peaceful coexistence of states of different socio-economic systems' declared by the 20th CPSU Congress.[78] According to this principle international law was precisely the institution which mediated between the nominally socialist Soviet Bloc and the West, and could not therefore be 'socialist' in itself. But the notion of 'socialist international law' resurfaced after 1960: it 'had to await political events and, in particular, the Soviet invasion of Hungary'.[79]

This new version of the theory, most systematically articulated by Grigory Tunkin, was 'a recognition of the existence of two systems of international law, the socialist law based on principles of (modified) proletarian internationalism, and the general international law of peaceful co-existence.'[80] According to Tunkin, in fact, international law constitutes both the 'general' international law, 'the result of the co-ordination of the will of *all* states',[81] and 'particular' international law, which governed the relations between local groups of states sharing socio-economic structure. This allowed him to assert the existence of socialist international law, 'created only in relations between socialist states'.[82]

This theory lacks any serious consideration of the legal form. It posits as 'law' a supposed variety of systems of regulation, one 'socialist', another capitalist, and an overarching framework of general international law that 'has no single class essence'.[83] It is surely devastating to the theory that these supposedly sharply contrasting systems share so many fundamental features. The view of general international law collapses back into an idealist view of a non-partisan structure of rules that are 'neutral' regulators, rather than reflections of any particular group interest. '[T]he Soviet conception of international law was . . . remarkably Grotian in nature'.[84]

---

[78] Cruickshank and Kubálková 1988, p. 173.
[79] Ibid.
[80] Cruickshank and Kubálková 1988, p. 175.
[81] Tunkin 1975, p. 82. Emphasis in original.
[82] Tunkin 1986, p. 250.
[83] Tunkin 1986, p. 249.
[84] Cruickshank and Kubálková 1988, p. 174. Cruickshank and Kubálková claim that the Soviet theories were Grotian only until the development of the notion of 'socialist international law'. This does not go far enough. In claiming that the overarching 'general' form of international legal regulation was a non-class form neutrally regulating interests – in Tunkin's words, 'the aggregate of norms which are created by agreement between states . . . [and] reflect the concordant wills of states' (Tunkin 1986 p. 251) – the Soviet theory in fact never broke from a traditional, classical conception

Tunkin and the Soviet writers offer nothing new: theirs is a slightly modified variant of mainstream, bourgeois international legal theory, with the addition of the peculiar and untheorised addendum of 'socialist international law'. This is asserted less because it explained anything than because 'it was unacceptable to Soviet scholars to even contemplate for a moment that the relationship between socialist countries and the outside world was regulated by bourgeois international law'.[85] Official Soviet 'Marxism' offers nothing new or helpful to international legal theory. We have to look elsewhere for serious Marxist theory.

The long dearth of Marxist and historical-materialist writings on international law has improved somewhat since the mid-1980s, as debates about globalisation and the relation between states and international markets has forced questions of international regulation onto the agenda. Some historical materialists have drawn attention to specific trans/international legal issues arising from considerations of the 'international state'.[86] However, this work has so far been somewhat tentative, and is still thin on the ground. A new generation of writers such as Claire Cutler is beginning to pick up this theoretical baton.[87] Most significant recently is the 2004 symposium on Marxism and international law in the *Leiden Journal of International Law*.[88]

Despite these developments, however, the challenge that Cain raised in 1983 remains to be fulfilled.

> [C]oncrete histories must be constructed, revealing with greater precision than hitherto the changing forms and functions of these supra-national organizations and institutions through time, and most important, also revealing both the changing social organization of capital and changes at mode of production level (often known as the balance of power) and relating these to the political/organizational changes at supra-national level which are the object of the analysis. . . . Finally, empirical investigation must consider and make public beyond the sub-specialisms which lay claim to such territories the legal forms which constitute these supra-national organizations and

of international law. For an overview of the debates among Soviet scholars, see Padjen 1975, pp. 54–100, 128–62.

[85] Chimni 1993, p. 247.

[86] In 1983 issue 11 of the *International Journal of the Sociology of Law* was devoted to this issue.

[87] See for example Cutler 1999 and 2001.

[88] The 2004 symposium comprises volume 17, issues 1 and 2.

> institutions, and examine how these are changing through time, as well as the regulatory devices which many such institutions are empowered to produce. This is nothing less than a demand for a political economy of international law.[89]

Although Cain was referring to international law in the flux of rapid globalisation, her focus on the legal forms underlying regulation points to the necessity for a political economy of international law *tout court*, not just of 'international law in globalisation'. This systematic approach has been somewhat neglected. Sol Picciotto, for example, is one of the few Marxists to have taken seriously the injunction to formulate a theory of the changing nature of international law, but his impressive work has tended to focus on the immediate interrelation between international regulation and economic neoliberalism.[90] Even his invaluable overview of international law more generally moves quickly to a focus on international law during the 'major changes and conflicts in the global system' 'often summarised [misleadingly, he stresses] by reference to the much-contested concepts of "globalisation", and the "new world order"'.[91]

Picciotto's work, with its nuanced analysis of the role of state-sponsored international legislation in bleeding 'stateness' across national boundaries, has been a powerful antidote to the widespread and simplistic assertion that globalisation is eroding the nation-state. However, it is arguable that the lack of systematic theory of the legal form articulated in his international legal writings[92] sometimes leads him to somewhat vague positions. He tends to argue for increasing international regulation – the strengthening of international law – as a progressive measure against neoliberalism. But without any analysis of the intrinsic limits of international law, he vacillates between arguing that international regulation is desirable for increasing democracy (a politically progressive move) and for 'underpin[ning] the security and confidence on which markets depend'[93] – hardly a self-explanatory good for a Marxist writer. Essentially, in the absence of a stated theory of legal form,

---

[89] Cain 1983, p. 2.

[90] See, for example, Picciotto 1983, 1988.

[91] Picciotto 1997, p. 17.

[92] There is, interestingly, no such lack in his other writings. See Holloway and Picciotto 1978b: Holloway and Picciotto 1991: Fine and Picciotto 1992.

[93] Picciotto 1998, p. 13.

it is unclear to what extent Picciotto sees international law as a force for social transformation.[94]

3.2. *Radicalism with rules: B.S. Chimni*

International Law and World Order, by B.S. Chimni, was the first serious book-length study of international law from a Marxist perspective. In this and in a shorter essay,[95] Chimni has blazed a trail. Writers in the field owe him a great debt for beginning the task of systematically theorising international law from a historical-materialist perspective.

Chimni starts with lengthy critical analysis of Morgenthau, McDougal and Falk. Two of those critiques, of Morgenthau and Richard Falk, for ignoring the role of law in international politics and for utopianism respectively, are sustained and telling. Chimni goes on to sketch the outlines of a history of international law, stressing the class politics that have informed it. He develops a theory of interpretation by which the meaning of a rule, he claims, can ultimately be ascertained – and hopefully marshalled to Chimni's progressive project. The scope and seriousness of the work are extremely impressive.

Nevertheless, there are shortcomings with the analysis. The root cause of these problems is by now a familiar refrain: Chimni fails to provide a systematic theory of the legal form. It is telling that in a book distinguished by a very wide-ranging bibliography, taking in a great number of debates in historical materialism, as well as classics of mainstream law and international law, one name is completely absent: Pashukanis.[96]

Pashukanis's theory of law is controversial among Marxists, but he is a giant of Marxist legal theory, and a dialectician who attempts over many articles and books to articulate a theory of the *legal form* itself. His theory of law will be outlined and evaluated in Chapters Three and Four below. Whatever one's view of Pashukanis's work, he is *the* central figure in Marxist legal theory, and it behoves anyone writing in that tradition to locate themselves vis-à-vis his work. It is no surprise, given this omission, that Chimni's theory of law focuses on the content of international law, rather than its structure or form.

---

[94] Picciotto 1998, pp. 11–14.

[95] Chimni 1999.

[96] It is true that Pashukanis *is* referenced in Chimni 1999, but he is quoted in passing, without attempt to evaluate or apply his theory.

Chimni is ambivalent about international law. At one point he argues that the realm of law is 'not the arena from which the struggle for radical changes could be launched',[97] and that 'international law is class law'.[98] However, he also stresses the 'relative autonomy that the legal sphere enjoys',[99] on which basis he continues to insist on the necessity of international law, even expressing cautious optimism about its progressive potential.[100]

How Chimni can square these positions is clear in his discussion of international law's 'class basis'.

> From the Marxist perspective it is this resort to principles, policies and other standards which facilitates the continuous development of the law on a class basis. For they manifest . . . the ethical-political hegemony of the ruling classes. And *if international law is class law, as it is . . ., then after peculiar features of the international context have been accommodated this understanding holds good for it as well.*[101]

Here, the *very class nature* of international law derives from 'principles' and 'policies': in other words, it is the *content* of particular legal rulings, as laid out and enforced by 'ruling classes' that makes law a class weapon, rather than anything in the structure of international law. This explains how even his stern critiques of utopian illusions over international law stop short of a fundamental – a legal-form-based – critique. In a recent article, for example, Chimni criticises the first postcolonial third-world approaches to international law ('TWAIL I') because they

> conceptualized the framework of international law as being neutral. It was perceived as an empty vessel which could be filled with any content. . . . Thus, it failed to appreciate that international law, as it had evolved, did not offer space for a transformational project. . . . It therefore overestimated the liberating potential of international law.[102]

While this reads at first as a devastating denunciation of international law, it occurs within an article the entire thrust of which is to make proposals to 'transform international law in the era of globalization from being a language

---

[97] Chimni 1993, p. 208.
[98] Chimni 1993, p. 102.
[99] Chimni 1993, p. 143.
[100] Chimni 1993, p. 205.
[101] Chimni 1993, p. 102. Emphasis mine.
[102] Chimni 2002, p. 17.

of oppression to a language of emancipation'.[103] This is possible, for Chimni, because international law has no space for a 'transformational project' only *'as it had evolved'*. This lack, in other words, is contingent to the legal form itself, on the basis of which form international law is still reformable.

Chimni sees the progressive counterpoint to 'principles' and 'policies' as manifest in 'rules'.

> [I]t is the resort to principles, policies etc., which explains the often bitter controversies in the arena of international law. Given the decentralised nature of the international system divergent ideologies invoke radically different policies and principles to arrive at decisions. In the circumstances if rules are assigned no significant place within the legal system . . . the result can only be free competition between different ideological interpretations and evaluations of particular situations and events.
>
> This state of affairs is guaranteed to ensure the collapse of the international legal system. In so far as its formal presence is yet retained it cannot but become an instrument of oppression in the hands of the more powerful states. It is important, therefore, to uphold the central place of rules within the international legal system.[104]

Having located the 'class nature' of law in specific laws' *content*, Chimni does occasionally raise the question of the separation and connection of the form and content of law: but he only does so in brief passages that do not seem to inform his analysis, and thus risk obscurity.[105] Thus his assertion that 'the content [of law] must not be wrenched away from form . . . or the content be depicted devoid of form' is admirable.[106] However, without a satisfactory theory of the legal form, this gets us nowhere. Where he discusses 'form', Chimni is in fact focusing on legal *rules*. He seems to hold that this category of 'rules' allows a nuanced middle ground between the extremes of formalism and positivism.

> The formalist approach merely absolutises this consensus through treating the legal system as a closed and autonomous system.

---

[103] Chimni 2002, p. 26.

[104] Chimni 1993, p. 102.

[105] '[T]he form and content of law are located in the matrix of the sociological basis which gives life to them, i.e., . . . the content is not without form which even while being embodied in the content itself possesses a separate identity'. Chimni 1993, p. 102. See also p. 103.

[106] Chimni 1993, p. 103.

> The result is fetishism of the law. Its opposite is rule nihilism or forms of rule skepticism. It serves the same class interests in different socio-economic conditions which require that the constraints imposed by the legal system (rules) be disregarded. A correct approach would be to avoid these twin pitfalls and recognise the significance of rules to a legal system even while emphasising the socio-economic or class basis of their origin.[107]

There is an elision here between theories of law and modes of application of law. The implication seems to be (crudely) that exploitative international class interests are served either by 'fetishistically' applying law – refusing to contextualise at all – or by disregarding rules and substituting policy. What are not explained – and cannot be, in this model – are those many cases where the *'correct' application of the 'rule' is unclear*, and where therefore there is something in that rule which *defies neutrality*. The investigation needs to take one step back to examine *the very form those legal rules take.*

Against Chimni, we can say that 'free competition' between interpretations does not ensure the destruction of the international legal system, but is in fact a pervasive feature of that system, as the arguments about indeterminacy above are intended to show. In seeing formal 'rules' as a progressive counterweight to exploitative 'policy', Chimni i) denies without any theoretical investigation the possibility that the very legal form itself – of which those 'rules' are simply expressions – is constrained and embedded with inequalities ultimately derived from class inequality, and ii) naïvely holds that 'rules' might put the brakes on the indeterminate to-and-fro of legal interpretation.

Chimni is unable to break from this model in which *rules*, rather than the legal form, are the 'fundamental particles' of international law: everything, in his model, ultimately reduces to rules. And each rule is distinct and complete: it cannot be further distilled. Thus,

> the New Haven procedure of interpretation eventually leads to, not only different interpretations of a single rule, but rather, to single interpretations of multiple rules. . . . [I]t is not interpretation at all since it is a new text which emerges from the interpretive exercise. With the result that no judgement of facts or events is possible for while an act or an omission could be unlawful if one rule (ostensibly interpretation) is adopted, it could be perfectly legal if the other rule (ostensibly interpretation) is accepted.[108]

---

[107] Chimni 1993, p. 103.
[108] Chimni 1993, p. 88.

A legal rule – for Chimni, the vanishing point of jurisprudence – being precisely a particular content in a particular form, this illustrates Chimni's methodological inability to grasp the existence of a legal form. It is a neat polemical-epistemological thrust of Chimni's to claim that the doyens of interpretation of the New Haven school in fact theorise interpretation – meaningfully construed – out of existence, but it is an unsustainable critique. It is predicated on i) Chimni's untheorised belief that interpretation must end somewhere and ii) the fact that Chimni's theoretical model is constructed on normative rather than analytical units.

It is, in fact, precisely the corollary of an analysis which accepts the indeterminacy of law that a particular act could be legal or illegal depending on interpretation. In pointing that out, Chimni seems to feel that he has undermined the theory: of course he has not.

Chimni's insistence on the progressive nature of rules is based on various factors. One is his entirely laudable attempts to differentiate himself politically from the kind of imperialist apologetics in which McDougal indulges. However, Chimni bends the stick too far in his critique of McDougal – although admittedly, McDougal himself is not always rigorous in his own formulations. Nevertheless, when for example Chimni claims that '[t]he limitless hermeneutic freedom which McDougal seeks for the interpreter is . . . subversive of the rule of law in international relations',[109] it must be pointed out that it is an exaggeration to describe McDougal's approach as 'limitless' or to say that he claims 'the text is of no great consequence'.[110] Instead, it is precisely the 'blackletter' law which provides the centre of gravity of the interpretation.

Chimni's fundamental thrust is that law that relies on interpretation cannot be a solid foundation for the 'rule of law'. The fact is that his model of the 'rule of law' is more normative than analytical. He is quite right that the necessity of interpretation undercuts any notion of the ultimate determinacy of law: but the 'rule of law' *is* the rule of indeterminate law, in which interpretation is key. (The question of what gives one particular interpretation final authority is at the core of the analysis of inter-state violence, imperialism and international law, and will be taken up below.)

[109] Chimni 1993, p. 88.
[110] Chimni 1993, p. 97.

Chimni's achievements are many and highly impressive. In dismissing the indeterminacy thesis, for example – even if wrongly, in my view – Chimni formulates a sophisticated theory of interpretation. He draws on 'ordinary language' and Wittgensteinian philosophy to claim that the fundamental unit of language is not the word but the sentence: the word in a contextual matrix. He claims that McDougal's view of legal rules starts from the separation of language and reality, the assertion of non-verbal reality.[111] He further claims that McDougal has a quasi-behaviourist view of language as a 'completely passive' reflection of reality. Words having a multiplicity of meanings, in McDougal's model they become, Chimni claims, almost Derridean, floating sets of signifiers quite decoupled from reality.

> It is now clear why McDougal traces the indeterminate characteristic of a rule to the very fact that it is formulated in words: reality is non-verbal. Furthermore, since a constitutive feature of a word is a multiplicity of meanings it is assumed that it cannot have an ordinary meaning. McDougal, therefore, finds it difficult to see how any interpretation of a rule is possible without recourse to the entire context in which those words originated.[112]

Chimni's alternative theory of language – one in which language does not passively reflect reality but is a process, part of the dynamic abstraction by which humans interact with reality, for which the sentential context is fundamental to the meaning of a word – is vastly superior to the neo-behaviourist pragmatism he criticises. To the extent that McDougal's theories are informed by that approach, Chimni is right to criticise him. However, there are two major problems with Chimni's alternative as the basis for a theory of interpretation.

First, his theory of language is constructed to counter McDougal and prove that law can be 'finally' interpreted, but this is largely tilting at windmills, as the language itself is not the source of indeterminacy for McDougal. It is perfectly possible to agree with the bulk of Chimni's linguistic philosophy, and still to hold that the legal rules, even constructed of whole sentences as they are, are indeterminate. I would claim, for example, that in the example of reprisals law given above, the indeterminate nature of the claims and counterclaims about legality is not a function of the *words* that make up the law. Chimni himself points out this weakness.

---

111 Chimni 1993, pp. 83–101.
112 Chimni 1993, p. 87.

> To all this [linguistic philosophy] McDougal would be wont to point out that the matter is not that simple in view of the contradictions which characterise legal reasoning. He lays particular emphasis on the fact that basic concepts/norms of international law come in complementary opposites making it difficult to provide even tentative answers to interpretive queries.[113]

However, Chimni expends only a little over one page of this long section on addressing this point: the other seventeen go on the linguistics, which do not undermine McDougal's theory of indeterminacy. On the dyads of mutually constituting contradictory legal concepts, the source of what Koskenniemi calls 'ascending' and 'descending' arguments, Chimni claims that these complementary opposites are not the source of indeterminacy, but are clearly delineated in most important cases.

> The collective perspective on the contradictions is translated into complementary concepts/norms with reasonably clear delineations of their spheres of application, as is certainly the case with opposites like domestic jurisdiction and international concern, aggressive war and self-defence.[114]

This is a quite extraordinary statement. The question, for example, of whether or not a particular military action is an aggressive war or self-defence is probably the source of more, and more interminable, international legal wrangling than anything else. To suggest as Chimni does that 'if scholars . . . do not find clearly etched areas of operation it is not because there are admittedly grey areas but because their analysis is ahistorical, non-system specific, and self-serving'[115] is quite inadequate. It may be true of this or that international lawyer, perhaps whole tranches of them. But it would not be a counter-argument to the observation made by Koskenniemi and others that there is something *in the very structure* of international law itself which breeds these disagreements.

Chimni cites Falk to back his claim that the boundaries of each of these dyadic terms is 'reasonably clear', but these are empty – and incorrect – propositions: no evidence or argument is offered.

> While the existence of complementary concepts/norms cannot be denied, and in fact cannot be otherwise, it may be said that 'the significance of com-

[113] Chimni 1993, p. 98.
[114] Ibid.
[115] Ibid.

> plementary norms is exaggerated'. Falk has aptly observed in this regard that 'to allege the pervasive complementarity of legal norms is to make a false allegation ...' Such contradictions as exist within the body of law reflect the internal contradictions which mark society in the process of evolution. Their resolution is a function of the self-development of the system: contradictions sharpen and eventually dissolve into one of the opposites.[116]

In fact, as I have attempted to show with reference to Koskenniemi, the significance of the existence of 'complementary norms' can hardly be exaggerated. It is quite unconvincing to denounce this as a 'false allegation'. It is undoubtedly true that these contradictions are reflections of deeper societal ones: far from being evidence that they do not riddle law, or make it indeterminate, this may, in fact, be the opposite. Chimni admits in passing that 'it is true that rules cannot uniquely determine specific facts and that an element of uncertainty will always prevail in marginal cases'.[117] This is questionable in its understatement, but is in any case a fundamental blow to Chimni's theory of discernible 'ordinary meaning'.

Of course Chimni knows that meanings are often disputed. However, his claim is that usually this is not because they are 'really' indeterminate, but because of wilful politicking by powers concerned, as for example in tendentious readings of articles 2(4) and 51 of the UN Charter during the Cuban quarantine or the Vietnam War.[118] He is plainly absolutely right that the motives behind the disagreements over content were political: however, this does not mean that they were not genuine differences of interpretation based on plausible readings of the law. Thus the only substantially *critical* part of Chimni's critique of McDougal's indeterminacy thesis is inadequate.

---

[116] Ibid. The quotes are from Falk 1970, p. 15.

[117] Chimni 1993, p. 144.

[118] Ibid.

Article 2(4) reads: 'All Members shall refrain in their international relations from the threat or use of force against the territorial integrity or political independence of any state, or in any other manner inconsistent with the Purposes of the United Nations.'

Article 51 reads: 'Nothing in the present Charter shall impair the inherent right of individual or collective self-defence if an armed attack occurs against a Member of the United Nations, until the Security Council has taken measures necessary to maintain international peace and security. Measures taken by Members in the exercise of this right of self-defence shall be immediately reported to the Security Council and shall not in any way affect the authority and responsibility of the Security Council under the present Charter to take at any time such action as it deems necessary in order to maintain or restore international peace and security'.

The second problem with Chimni's model concerns his alternative. He attempts to stress contextualisation, as McDougal does, but also to argue for a single, discoverable 'correct' interpretation to a single legal rule underpinning a law. Thus Chimni must seek a context for meaning which is more than pure linguistics, but which is not as politically broad as McDougal's, to act as basis for his 'objective theory of interpretation'. He argues that

> international law, constituted as it is by distinct activities is a language-game and the ordinary meaning of words are to be assigned in its matrix. . . . [T]he important conclusion [is] that no meaning can be affixed to words that ignores the practices which constitute international law.[119]

This is therefore necessarily a theory of interpretation with *customary behaviour* at its core. He makes this more explicit when arguing that *pacta sunt servanda* ('promises are to be kept') can be considered a 'fundamental norm' 'when depicted not as an *a priori* assumption but as a norm of customary international law'.[120] Here, *custom* underpins the fundamental building blocks of 'objective interpretation'.

This attempt at a kind of circumscribed contextualisation, however, bleeds inexorably into wider political concerns, which themselves demand analysis, and cannot be taken as given, or as *Grundnorms*: we must explain *why* states' customary international law is as it is. To suggest otherwise is an implicitly static theory of interpretation. Worse, it legitimates power politics: custom is not a stable norm or context, but can be 'used to explain the existence of any rule'.[121] What is more, it is very often a reflection of state will, as Pashukanis makes clear.

> [S]ince a) it is not always easy to decide which ideology is general and which ideology is 'legal', and b) the practice of the different states at any one time, and the practice of any one state at different times, are far from the same – in fact, therefore the source of the norms of even customary international law is drawn from the opinions of 'writers', or scholars, who

[119] Chimni 1993, p. 279.

[120] Chimni 1993, p. 269.

[121] Detter De Lupis 1987, p. 134. She excoriates customary law as 'an unacceptable fiction which obscures rather than clarifies'. While the sheer nebulousness of custom is well expressed, like so many mainstream writers, Detter De Lupis's suggested alternative of 'inter-activism' positing the existence of norms expressing 'socially necessary acts' fails to explain why law at all – again the black box is the legal form.

> usually differ decisively with each other on every question. Common, therefore, are citations to the 'majority' or to the 'overwhelming' majority of authorities. If one further notes that each of these authorities consciously or unconsciously defends those positions which are or seem beneficial to his own state, then one can imagine how hopeless will be the application of customary international law to the decision of any serious dispute.[122]

As a result of these theoretical lacunae, Chimni is equivocal, as I have argued, over the progressiveness or otherwise of international law. It is tempting to see these lacunae as stemming from his (critical) commitment to international law: he may not have illusions about it being the site for fundamentally transformative struggle, but he certainly believes, for example, that we should not be 'deprecating . . . of formal law-making . . . for it dilutes the authority of legal rules'.[123] He sees international law as positive, in that '[t]he legal system can effectively contribute [to the resolution of disputes between states] . . . if the tradition invoked has the distinctive features generally attributed to law and legal discourse'.[124] Chimni, then, sees the correct application of 'legal rules' as contributing to stability, rather than as an inextricable part of the fabric of international relations in all their conflict.

Given this commitment, it is perhaps unsurprising that Chimni would balk from the kind of analysis attempted by Pashukanis, which would throw the whole edifice into question.

The evidence of the indeterminacy of international law is persuasive, and makes sense of the innumerable, interminable arguments carried out by international lawyers on so many issues. Given that indeterminacy, there is a desperate need for a jurisprudence which can take account both of the policy orientation of states – the content of the law – and the continuing indeterminacy of a supposedly stable 'rule' – the form of the law.

Chimni points out the tendency of international legal concepts to 'travel in opposites', only to deny that it is important. The reverse is true. It is this contradiction that is at the very heart of the legal form and that has confounded most international legal scholarship since its inception. Pashukanis puts it most starkly:

122 Pashukanis 1980, p. 182.
123 Chimni 1993, p. 206.
124 Chimni 1993, p. 205.

> For the existence of international law it is necessary that states be sovereign. . . . If there are no sovereign states then there are no subjects of the international law relationship, and there is no international law. But, on the other hand, if there are sovereign states, then does this mean that the norms of international law are not legal norms?[125]

An awareness of this thread of contradiction unites writers as different as Pashukanis, McDougal and Koskenniemi, yet Chimni simply denies it meaningful existence. Instead, he quotes Engels that 'law must "be an *internally coherent* expression which does not, owing to internal conflicts, contradict itself"'.[126] This, sadly, is exactly wrong. Without a theory of the legal form, Chimni cannot address that.

For Pashukanis, without sovereign states 'there are no subjects of the international law relationship, and there is no international law'. The fundamental requirement for international law is a *relationship*. Chimni's constant focus on rules posits an international law that is outside that relationship and *applied* to it. For Pashukanis on the other hand, *out of the relationship comes the law.*

This conception of international law as process provides a link between the very different theories of Pashukanis and McDougal. It is also the beginnings of a dynamic conceptualisation of the legal form.

---

125 Pashukanis 1980, p. 178.
126 Chimni 1993, p. 269.

Chapter Three

For Pashukanis: An Exposition and Defence of the Commodity-Form Theory of Law

1. The rise and fall of Pashukanis

Pashukanis is a giant of legal theory, who was not only the dominant figure in Soviet jurisprudence in the 1920s and early 1930s, but 'has been the only Soviet Marxist legal philosopher to have achieved significant scholarly recognition outside of the USSR'.[1] Pashukanis's intellectual reputation within the USSR underwent an extreme inversion. Up to the early 1930s he was the country's pre-eminent legal philosopher:[2] from there, Pashukanis went to being denounced as a 'traitor and wrecker', an 'enemy of the people' in 1937.[3] He was arrested and disappeared in January of that year. From that point until his posthumous legal rehabilitation in 1956 – still officially wrong, but at least recognised as a thinker – Pashukanis and his theory were unmentionable in the USSR.[4]

1 Beirne and Sharlet 1990, p. 17.

2 Hazard's claims that Pashukanis's theory was 'said to be infallible' (Hazard 1979, pxiv), however, are exaggerations. While acknowledging the power and importance of his approach, Pashukanis's colleague Stuchka criticised him as early as 1927 (Head 2001).

3 Von Arx 1997, p. 3.

4 Biographical material is available in Beirne and Sharlet 1982 and Head 2004. Histories of the reception of Pashukanis's philosophy during the period are Beirne and Sharlet 1990 and Head 2004. For the rise and fall of Pashukanis's theory and its associated 'commodity exchange school of law', see Sharlet 1968, Beirne and Sharlet 1990 and Head 2004, which also contains a summary of the theory, its reception and criticisms. Head 2001 is a good overview of the legal debates in Russia to which Pashukanis's was the most important contribution.

Pashukanis's ultimate purging was a result of the inimicability of his theory to the demands of the Stalinist programme. In an attempt to trim his sails to the prevailing wind, Pashukanis revised his own work several times, and published a series of 'self-criticisms'.[5] These revisions fundamentally altered the nature of his theory, until it was 'no longer recognizable':[6] by 1931 'Pashukanis had significantly revised each of his hypotheses, including the fundamental methodological premise. The result was no longer viable as the "commodity exchange" theory of law'.[7]

For example, his 1935 work *A Course on Soviet Economic Law* and the 1936 essay 'State and Law under Socialism',[8]

> illuminate how emasculated the brilliant insights of *The General Theory of Law and Marxism* had become after the XVIth Party Congress [in June 1930] and the introduction of the second Five Year Plan. It is at this point that we no longer need to speculate on whether the intellectual revisions to the main thrust of Pashukanis' work were induced by strictly political and opportunist pressures. In the *Course on Soviet Economic Law* . . . Pashukanis offers a lengthy, simplistic and functionalist account of the nature of Soviet economic law under the transitional conditions of socialism. [It was] [c]onceived within the manifest constraints to conform with the Stalinist interpretation of Marx's and Engels' brief and unsatisfactory analyses of the period transitional between capitalism and the higher phase of communism. . . .[9]

These 'final recantations . . . are almost unreadable repetitions of Stalinist dogma'.[10] The trajectory of Pashukanis's thought ranks as an intellectual tragedy.

Pashukanis's reputation was won with his book *The General Theory of Law and Marxism* (*GTLM*), published in 1924. It is there that the core of his jurisprudence is found.[11] What follows is an exposition, development and defence of that theory, in some detail.

---

[5] For the chronology of these 'corrections', see Sharlet 1968, pp. 268–87.

[6] Sharlet 1968, p. 284.

[7] Sharlet 1968, p. 275.

[8] Beirne and Sharlet 1990, pp. 302–44 and pp. 346–61.

[9] Beirne and Sharlet 1982, p. 30. This is an earlier version of the piece subsequently published as Beirne and Sharlet 1990.

[10] Warrington 1980/81, p. 103.

[11] Peter Maggs's translation of the first edition is printed in Beirne and Sharlet 1980, pp. 40–131. *The General Theory of Law and Marxism* ran to a second edition in 1926. This second edition, though without substantial revisions, 'was a corrected and sup-

This exposition might appear abstract or arcane for the international theorist. However, the detail is necessary as the core of this book is a 'Pashukanisite' theory of international law. For this, it is necessary not only to understand his theory in general but to engage with its most trenchant critics, though none have focused on the international. If these attacks on Pashukanis's theory at a domestic level are not answered then his theory is undermined *tout court*, and the commodity-form theory of international law would be a chimera: to understand and defend his theory of international law we must understand and defend his theory of *law*.

2. The General Theory of Law and Marxism[12]

It should be emphasised that Pashukanis saw his book as only the starting point for Marxist jurisprudence. He described it as a 'sketch', 'a first draft of a Marxist critique of the fundamental juridical concepts'.[13] The fundamental thrust of his theory was, in the words of his comrade and colleague Stuchka an 'attempt to approximate the legal form to the commodity form':[14] hence the 'commodity-exchange' or 'commodity-form' theory of law.

Pashukanis saw this project as one of clarification of a theory already-existent, although not rigorously formulated, in Marx and Engels. 'The basic thesis,' he claimed, 'namely that the legal subject of juridical theories is very closely related to the commodity owner, did not, after Marx, require any further substantiation.'[15] This is modest to the point of coy. Not only are the disparate wisps of jurisprudence throughout Marx's oeuvre far from systematic, but Pashukanis claims far more than the vague 'close relation' between the commodity owner and the legal subject.

---

plemented edition', which, for example, expanded on the 'underdeveloped topic' of the state (Beirne and Sharlet 1980, p. 38). This second edition also included a useful and theoretically interesting preface (Pashukanis 1978, pp. 37–45). The second edition is available in English translated by Barbara Einhorn from the German translation of 1929 (Pashukanis 1978). I refer to both these English editions of the *General Theory* (the first English translation, Hazard 1951, pp. 111–225, is not well translated, with eccentric renderings of Marxist terminology: commodity fetishism becomes 'goods fetishism,' for example). The Einhorn translation, with Chris Arthur's 1978 introduction, has been recently republished with a new introduction by Dragan Milovanovic, Pashukanis 2001.

[12] More comprehensive expositions include Sharlet 1968; and Von Arx 1997, pp. 13–156, which offers a reading of each chapter in turn.

[13] Pashukanis 1978, p. 36.

[14] Quoted in Pashukanis 1978, p. 38.

[15] Pashukanis 1978, p. 39.

Pashukanis argues that *the logic of the commodity form is the logic of the legal form*. Chris Arthur does an excellent job of expressing this complex relation.

> Pashukanis argues that *the juridical element in the regulation of human conduct enters where the isolation and opposition of interests begins.* He goes on to tie this closely to the emergence of the commodity form in mediating material exchanges. His basic materialist strategy is to correlate commodity exchange with the time at which man becomes seen as a legal personality – the bearer of rights (as opposed to customary privileges). Furthermore, this is explicable in terms of the conceptual linkages which obtain between the sphere of commodity exchange and the form of law. The nature of the legal superstructure is a fitting one for this mode of production. For production to be carried on as production of commodities, suitable ways of conceiving social relations, and the relations of men to their products, have to be found, and *are* found in the form of law. . . .
>
> As the product of labour takes on the commodity form and becomes a bearer of value, people acquire the quality of legal subjects with rights. . . .
>
> For Pashukanis, legal forms regulate relationships between autonomous subjects – it is the subject that is the 'cell-form' of the legal system. In bringing out the specific character of such legal regulation of behaviour, he contrasts it with technical regulation by arguing that in the latter singleness of purpose can be assumed, whereas the basic element in legal regulation is contestation – two sides defending their rights. In deliberately paradoxical fashion he says that historically law starts from a law-suit.[16]

Pashukanis's argument is that in commodity exchange, each commodity must be the private property of its owner, freely given in return for the other. In their fundamental form commodities exchange at a rate determined by their exchange value, not because of some external reason or because one party to the exchange demands it. Therefore, each agent in the exchange must be i) an owner of private property, and ii) formally equal to the other agent(s). Without these conditions, what occurred would not be commodity exchange. The legal form is the *necessary form* taken by the relation between these formally equal owners of exchange values.

In the opposition and equality of legal subjects, whether exchange is peaceable or not, contestation is at least implied and is at the heart of the legal

[16] Arthur 1978, pp. 13–15. Emphasis in original.

form. Where there is even the potentiality of disputation between the *sovereign, formally equal individuals* implied by commodity exchange – as opposed to the formally unequal individuals implied by the hierarchical command relations of (say) feudalism – a specific form of social regulation is necessary. It must formalise the method of settlement of any such dispute without diminishing either party's sovereignty or equality. *That form is law*, which is characterised by its abstract quality, its being based on the equality of its subjects and its pervasive character in capitalism.

2.1. *Marxist method and the failure of alternative theories*

Pashukanis wrote in opposition to the main strands of theorising about law, both bourgeois and Marxist. I have stressed the lack of theory of legal form as the main barrier to systematic jurisprudence. That legal form was at the very heart of Pashukanis's argument.

However, the legal form which interested Pashukanis was one derived from *actually-existing law*, rather than from some abstract notion of law: it was this which distinguished Pashukanis from other 'formalists' – the neo-Kantians such as Kelsen.[17] Pashukanis's methodology was that of Marx in the *Grundrisse* and later, of 'rising from the abstract to the concrete'.[18] For Marx, the concrete 'appears in the process of thinking . . . as a process of concentration, as a result, not as a point of departure, even though it is the point of departure in reality and hence also the point of departure for observation and conception'.[19]

Thus the simplest categories of analysis – value, labour, money, etc. – are abstractions necessary for the analysis of that concrete. They constitute the building blocks of any analysis of the real world, *because of*, rather than despite, their abstraction. They are the 'determinant, abstract, general relations' from which analysis 'ascends' to more complex and concrete categories. This is 'the scientifically correct method', given that '[t]he concrete is concrete because it is the concentration of many determinations'.[20]

Pashukanis cites this passage in his opening chapter on method. He sees these observations as 'directly pertinent to the general theory of law. The

[17] Von Arx 1997, p. 14.
[18] Marx 1973, p. 101.
[19] Ibid.
[20] Marx 1973, pp. 100–1.

concrete totality – society, the population, the state – must in this case, too, be the conclusion and end result of our deliberations, but not their starting point'.[21]

As Marx pointed out, concrete reality should be the conclusion of analysis but it could not but also be the starting point of observation. This starting point distinguishes Pashukanis sharply from the neo-Kantians. Pashukanis criticised the very different kind of abstraction of 'formalists' such as Kelsen on similar grounds to those in Chapter One, above: their theory sees law as of the plane of 'ought' rather than 'is', and sacrifices applicability for systematicity.

> On the plane of the juridical *Ought,* there is nothing but a transition from one norm to another on the rung of a hierarchical ladder, at the top of which is the all-embracing, supreme norm-setting authority – a delimiting concept from which jurisprudence proceeds as from something given. . . .
>
> Such a general theory of law explains nothing, and turns its back from the outset on the facts of reality. . . .[22]

The alternative, self-styled Marxist, theories of law that were being expounded at the time were unsatisfactory in other ways.

2.1.1. *Law as ideology*

Some Marxists saw law as 'an ideological fiction, imposed on a social reality to which it has no correspondence by some organ of centralized authority'.[23] This view finds 'the origins of law in ideology, in the "heads of people", rather than in real, socioeconomic interactions or the material relationships of people'.[24]

Of course law, including international law, does have an ideological function, at the levels of fundamental structure, juridical categories and specific cases. At the broadest level, the very notion that there is a body of rules applied equally to all states has a clearly ideological and legitimating function. However inequitable the reality, for example, '[t]he principle of equity . . . is a simple formulation of part of the ideology by which it appears that international law does not operate in favour of any particular State or group of

---

[21] Pashukanis 1978, p. 66.

[22] Pashukanis 1978, p. 52.

[23] Fine 1979, p. 36.

[24] Sharlet, Maggs and Beirne 1990, p. 51. The most prominent propogator of this theory in the USSR was Reisner, a follower of Petrazhitsky's psychological school of law.

States'.[25] More concretely, 'it is a significant fact that nations are impelled to claim that their behaviour complies with international law'. The careful use of the 'rhetoric of international law'[26] illustrates that international law can serve an ideologically legitimating function.

Take, among countless other examples, NATO's claim that during the 1999 Kosovo air campaign it 'not only acted to uphold international law . . . but . . . conducted [its] air campaign in accordance with international law. In marked contrast Milosevic violated virtually every provision of international law'.[27] Peeling back this rather anxious legalist justification shows that as 'opinion began to turn against the Allies', recourse to international law was deemed necessary, in the words of Paul Virilio, if what he calls 'the *phoney war* in Kosovo was not to become a *dirty war* in the eyes of international opinion'.[28]

Ideology-critique can thus be of great importance in (international) law scholarship, as Susan Marks has persuasively argued.[29] However, there are serious limitations in focusing exclusively on law as ideology. Shirley Scott, for all the insights in her important discussion of international law as ideology,[30] is, like so many New Stream writers, idealist, seeing the power of international law as inhering in its 'ideas', which 'do seem to constitute a form of power'.[31]

One is left with no sense of *why* this 'idea' of international law should have arisen at a certain time and political-economic context. Ideology here is a posited structuring category rather than an expression of an underlying logic. The weakness of this position is visible in Scott's failure to contextualise historical change, most starkly in her depiction of decolonisation, in which the fact and the whys of self-activity of those at the sharp end of colonialism are ignored for a claim simply that there was a 'rejection of the ideology of colonialism', seemingly out of the blue.[32]

---

[25] Scott 1994, p. 321.

[26] Feinerman 1996, p. 188.

[27] Speech of 21 March 2000. <http://www.nato.int/docu/speech/2000/s000321a.htm>

[28] Virilio 2000, pp. 69, 65. Virilio goes considerably further, seeing the Kosovo crisis as overturning established norms of international law. Though he exaggerates the stability and equity of pre-existing norms he well illustrates the sense of political-legal uncertainty – near chaos, in fact – surrounding the action.

[29] Marks 2001. For an application of ideology-critique to the supposed 'norm' of 'democratic governance' in international law, see Marks 2000.

[30] Scott 1994.

[31] Scott 1994, p. 317.

[32] Ibid.

Again, at heart the limitations of the critique of law as ideology lie in the failure to theorise the legal form. Pashukanis did not deny that law can have an ideological function – he saw there to be 'no argument about this'[33] – but disputed that that is *all*, or even primarily or most interestingly what there is to it.

> Having established the ideological nature of particular concepts in no way exempts us from the obligation of seeking their objective reality, in other words the reality which exists in the outside world, that is, external, and not merely subjective reality.[34]

Here again Pashukanis's methodology of rising from the abstract to the concrete reality is driving him towards a theory of the juridical form: actually-existing law is manifestly *not* 'merely' ideological, but impinges on and regulates everyday life at all levels.

As Pashukanis points out, the afterlife exists 'in some person's minds', as does the state. But

> [u]nlike the afterlife, Pashukanis observes, the concepts of law and state reflect not only a particular ideology but the objective reality of the court system, the police and the military, the administrative and fiscal organizations of the state, and so forth. . . . Legal concepts are embodied in various forms of regulations demanding compliance rather than mere belief.[35]

Scott's claim that 'the power of international law can only be the power of the idea of international law'[36] is insufficient. The power of international law is also the armed might of powerful states enforcing their interpretation of legal rules with cluster bombs and gunships. International law's power is not only the power of ideas; it is the power of violent coercion.

2.1.2. *Law as iniquitous content*

An alternative conception of law, much-favoured by Marxists of Pashukanis's time, seemed to go some way to theorising the real, material existence of law. These were the 'sociological' theories of law, which 'treat[ed] law as the product of conflict of interest, as the manifestation of state coercion'.[37]

This position is essentially positivist, in that law is seen as the will of the state. Enforcement – coercion – is definitional to this theory. Unlike most mainstream positivists, in the hands of Marxists such as Stuchka or Plekhanov

---

[33] Pashukanis 1978, p. 74.
[34] Pashukanis 1978, p. 75.
[35] Von Arx 1997, p. 35.
[36] Scott 1994, p. 317.
[37] Pashukanis 1978, p. 53.

the state was not seen as a neutral body but an organ of ruling-class control, which was why '[m]any Marxists assumed that by simply adding in the element of class struggle to ... [positivist] theories, they would attain a genuinely materialist, Marxist theory of law'.[38] In the sphere of international law, one can see as an example of this 'content-oriented' Marxism Chimni's discussion of international law's class basis as inhering in the 'principles' and 'policies' with which the ruling class invest that law (see Chapter Two).

Compared to the 'high-sounding phrases about the "eternal idea of law"', Pashukanis was clear that this kind of left positivism was a source of 'particular satisfaction'.[39] However, it remained a source of 'disappointment' to him, because it 'exclude[d] the legal form as such from ... [the] field of observation'.[40] As has been argued, this kind of theory is unable to explain the specific *legalness* of law.

> [A] sociological approach which looks to the economic and political interests behind specific legal and penal measures appears as a significant advance over ... formalism. But here again there is a disappointment. For exclusive attention is directed towards the class interests served or the economic functions performed by one or other measure of law or punishment; in other words, exclusive to the question of content. Why these interests or functions should have been served by the *legal* form of regulation or by *penal* repression remains a question unaddressed. . . .
>
> This exclusive focus on the content of law leaves the social and historical character of its form unexamined . . .[41]

Pashukanis did not start with an *a priori* assertion of the need for a theory of the legal form, but was led to the position because of his Marxist method. Other theories failed because they did not explain actually-existing law: a theory of form was necessary because of concrete reality. That theory had to explain i) the general efficacy of law in regulating social relations, contra the neo-Kantians for whom it was a separate realm, and ii) the fact that such regulation took the form of *law*. This dual relationship was expressed in Pashukanis's stress on law's effectiveness.

38 Ibid.
39 Ibid.
40 Ibid.
41 Fine 1979, pp. 34–5.

> [T]he legal dogmatist's views on 'valid' law are not in the least binding for the historian who wishes to study law as it actually exists. Scientific, that is, theoretical study can reckon only with facts. . . . [I]f a law or decree has merely been promulgated without any corresponding relation having arisen in practice, then an attempt to create a law has indeed been made, but without success.[42]

To use Gramscian terms, Pashukanis's is a theory of real, 'impure' law. He takes as his point of departure real law in the real world, and both its reality and its 'law-ness' must be explained. For that, the legal form itself must be the starting point.

2.2. *From the commodity form to the legal form*

Pashukanis moves from a discussion of legal norms and relationships in Chapter Three of *GTLM* to the legal subject in Chapter Four. These two chapters contain the central argument of *GTLM*, wherein Pashukanis is dealing with the simplest, most abstract elements of law. It is here that the logic of the legal form is laid out.

Pashukanis's task is to relate the necessary, actually-existing, materially effective legal form to wider social relations. He takes his starting point from Marx. 'In as much as the wealth of capitalist society appears as "an immense collection of commodities", so this society itself appears as an endless chain of legal relations.'[43] Nor is this appearance illusory.

> The exchange of commodities assumes an atomized economy. A connection is maintained between private and isolated economies from transaction to transaction. The legal relationship between subjects is only the other side of the relation between the products of labour which have become commodities. The legal relationship is the primary cell of the legal tissue through which law accomplishes its only real movement. In contrast, law as a totality of norms is no more than a lifeless abstraction.[44]

It is the focus on law as a real regulatory force which explains why the legal norm – the rule – cannot be the basis of the legal form. The legal form is the form of a particular kind of *relationship*. Rules can only be derived from that

---

[42] Pashukanis 1978, p. 88.
[43] Pashukanis 1978, p. 85. The quotation is from Marx 1976, p. 125.
[44] Pashukanis 1980, p. 62.

relationship. They are thus secondary, and in fundamental jurisprudential terms, their specific content is contingent.

> In material reality a relationship has primacy over a norm. If not a single debtor repaid a debt, then the corresponding rule would have to be regarded as actually non-existent and if we wanted nevertheless to affirm its existence we would have to fetishize this norm in some way.[45]

According to the alternative, norm-driven position, in the words of one of its adherents,

> [i]t is not because creditors generally demand repayment of a debt that the right to make such a demand exists, but, on the contrary, the creditors make this claim because the norm exists; the law is not defined by abstraction from observed cases, but derives from a rule posited by someone.[46]

However, this begs the question of who it is that 'posits' the rule, and crucially, why some such 'posited' rules should be generalised and not others. It cannot merely be the case that it is when an 'authorised' body such as the state 'posits' a rule it automatically generalises. As Pashukanis points out, such an 'authorised' socially regulative force doubtless 'guarantees and safeguards the relation'[47] but it cannot be deemed to create it, not least as there are cases in which a clearly 'legal' relationship inheres between two bodies, without a 'third force' to determine a norm.

The examples he gives are of ancient inter-state contract and of feudal law, and, in a crucial footnote, of international law itself. '[M]odern international law recognises no coercion organised from without. Such non-guaranteed legal relations are unfortunately not known for their stability, but this is not yet grounds for denying their existence.'[48] *In other words, the very existence of international law as law is evidence that it is in the relationship between legal subjects rather than in any 'posited norm' that the essence of the legal form lies.*

The norm-driven paradigm cannot explain why one apparently 'valid' law is effective and another is not. For Pashukanis, given that the subject for analysis is actually-existing law, definitionally that law inheres inasmuch as

---

45 Pashukanis 1980, p. 63.
46 Shershenevich, quoted in Pashukanis 1978, p. 86.
47 Pashukanis 1978, p. 89.
48 Ibid., footnote 9.

it regulates social behaviour. If it does not, it means the attempt to create law failed.[49]

There are, of course, various different kinds of social relations that inhere under conditions of commodity exchange. In locating the legal form in the 'economic' relationships of such exchange, rather than in the superstructure of political power, as suggested by the norm-derivation theory, Pashukanis locates 'the moment of dispute' as at the basis of the legal form.[50] 'The law differentiates itself from the social relations of production in the resolution of disputes, in particular through the medium of the lawsuit.'[51] This is a corollary of the isolated, egoistical agent necessarily at the heart of commodity exchange.

> [T]he existence of a commodity and money economy is the basic precondition, without which all these concrete [legal] norms would have no meaning. Only under this condition does the legal subject have its material base in the person of the subject operating egoistically, whom the law does not create, but finds in existence. Without this base, the corresponding legal relation is *a priori* inconceivable.
>
> The problem becomes clearer still when we consider it at the dynamic and historical level. In this context, we see how the economic relation in its actual workings is the source of the legal relation, which comes into being only at the moment of dispute. It is dispute, conflict of interest, which creates the legal form, the legal superstructure.[52]

Hence for Pashukanis private law is the 'fundamental, primary level of law'.[53] The concept of public law, for example, 'can only be developed through its workings, in which it is continually repulsed by private law, so much that it attempts to define itself as the antithesis of private law, to which it returns, however, as to its centre of gravity'.[54] A complex legal system regulating all levels of social life can be thrown up which appears to differentiate itself from private law, but it ultimately derives from *the clash of private interests.*

Law is the regulatory mechanism generalised in an economy based on commodity production. The legal form is that form which regulates the legal rela-

[49] Pashukanis 1978, p. 88.
[50] Pashukanis 1978, p. 93.
[51] Von Arx 1997, p. 48.
[52] Pashukanis 1978, p. 93.
[53] Pashukanis 1978, p. 103.
[54] Pashukanis 1978, p. 106.

tionship: dispute is central, because without dispute there would be no need of regulation. The legal subject is part of this legal relationship, as '[e]very legal relation is a relation between subjects. The subject is the atom of legal theory, its simplest, irreducible element.'[55]

The commodity is, in Marx's words, 'a very strange thing',[56] an object brought to market to be exchanged, through the medium of money, for another usually very different thing. For these two things to enter into relation with each other, they must be brought to the market by their owners, who must recognise each other as such. Each human agent must recognise the relation of all others in the market to their commodities – a relation of exclusive ownership – and in so doing create a relationship of abstracted, isolated egoism between each other. The juridical relation exists in the interface between humans' relations with their commodities and concomitant relations with each other.

This, Pashukanis takes from Marx.

> Commodities cannot themselves go to market and perform exchanges in their own right. We must, therefore, have recourse to their guardians, who are the possessors of commodities. Commodities are things, and therefore lack the power to resist man. . . . In order that these objects may enter into relation with each other as commodities, their guardians must place themselves in relation to one another as person whose will resides in those objects, and must behave in such a way that each does not appropriate the commodity of the other, and alienate his own, except through an act to which both parties consent. The guardians must therefore recognize each other as owners of private property. This juridical relation, whose form is the contract, whether as part of a developed legal system or not, is a relation between two wills which mirrors the economic relation. *The content of this juridical relation . . . is itself determined by the economic relation.*[57]

The importance of this passage to Pashukanis's theory can hardly be overstressed. 'By asserting that exchange requires mutual recognition of private property rights, Marx clearly acknowledges that the legal relation between subjects is intrinsic to the value relation.'[58] The legal subject is defined by

---

55 Pashukanis 1978, p. 109.
56 Marx 1976, p. 163.
57 Marx 1976, p. 178. Emphasis mine.
58 Von Arx 1997, p. 66.

virtue of possessing various abstract rights – '[t]he isolated, abstract, impersonal legal subject . . . cannot be identified with the specific attributes or roles of any particular social actor'.[59] This formal equality of distinct and different individuals is in exact homology with the equalisation of qualitatively different commodities in commodity exchange, through the medium of abstract labour (the stuff of value). Thus with the generalising of legal relations, '[l]egal fetishism complements commodity fetishism'.[60]

Whereas under feudalism 'every right was a privilege',[61] every right was identified with a specific social position vis-à-vis others, capitalist exchange is characterised by the generalisation of 'Freedom, Equality, Property and Bentham'.[62] The historically progressive generalisation of 'equal rights' is the generalisation of the abstract legal subject, 'an abstract owner of commodities raised to the heavens'.[63] This is why contract is so vital to Pashukanis's theory of law. Abstract and equal subjects, the atoms of the legal relationship, cannot relate to each other according to principles of 'traditional' privilege, but do so by means of *contract*, which is the *formalisation of mutual recognition of equal subjects.*

This mutual recognition is a rationalisation of 'the organic forms of appropriation based on labour, occupation and so on, which the society of commodity producers finds in existence at its inception'.[64] Without a contract, Pashukanis writes, 'the concepts of subject and of will only exist, in the legal sense, as lifeless abstractions. These concepts first come to life in the contract'.[65]

It is clear that according to Pashukanis, law cannot be relegated to the superstructure. In terms of Marx's base-superstructure analogy, the *legal form* under capitalism is an integral part of the relations that constitute the 'base'.

Marx's model has been subject to almost unending criticism since its formulation. A detailed defence of *a* base-superstructure model (because depending which quotations from Marx one takes, various different models can be envisioned) is beyond the scope of this discussion.[66] Here, I will only say

---

[59] Von Arx 1997, p. 69.
[60] Pashukanis 1978, p. 117.
[61] Pashukanis 1978, p. 119.
[62] Marx 1976, p. 280.
[63] Pashukanis 1978, p. 121.
[64] Pashukanis 1978, p. 122.
[65] Pashukanis 1978, p. 121.
[66] For defences of the model see (among many others) Harman 1998; Callinicos

that the base-superstructure metaphor is no more than a statement of materialism.

It does not necessitate any simplistic 'reflection' of the economic in the realm of ideas – to think so is to misunderstand the metaphor as static. 'It is the economy as a source of change . . . rather than as an unmediated cause . . . that should draw our attention'.[67] Rather than a 'deterministic Marxist dialectic between an economic base and its ideological superstructure',[68] then, this dialectical analysis of a contradictory totality, '*necessarily* requires that [Marx] . . . reject[s] reductionist formulations'.[69]

For example, he accepts although it is true on one level that whereas 'material interests are preponderant' for modernity, they are 'not for the Middle Ages, dominated by Catholicism, nor for Athens and Rome, dominated by politics'. However, his model – his philosophical materialism – holds, as

> [o]ne thing is clear: the Middle Ages could not live on Catholicism, nor could the ancient world on politics. On the contrary, it is the manner in which they gained their livelihood which explains why in one case politics, in the other case Catholicism, played the chief part.[70]

The base-superstructure model, then, as philosophical materialism, does not consign one form of social institution or another to 'non-effectuality'.[71]

> The distinction between base and superstructure is not a distinction between one set of institutions and another, with economic institutions on one side and political, judicial, ideological etc institutions on the other. It is a distinction between relations that are directly connected with production and those that are not. Many particular institutions include both.[72]

Pashukanis's theory of law is a perfect illustration of this double penetration of 'base' and 'superstructure' in the same institution. There has been confusion over whether or not Pashukanis sees law as part of the base. On the one hand, Binns, for example, criticises him for asserting that 'law is part of the

---

1988, pp. 172–7; Callinicos 1996, pp. 112–21. For a lively and brilliant investigation of its application to jurisprudence, in which the dialectic is key to overcoming any determinism, see Chase 1997, pp. 32–49.

[67] Chase 1997, p. 45.
[68] Purvis 1991, p. 99.
[69] Rees 1998, p. 107.
[70] Marx 1976, p. 176 footnote 35.
[71] Alcantara 1996, p. 42.
[72] Harman 1998, pp. 28–9.

base of society'.[73] Warrington, on the other hand, disputes this, claiming that Pashukanis was concerned with circulation, rather than production, and 'he did not consider that commodities had anything to do with the base'.[74] 'The law for Pashukanis is merely a *product* of the base'.[75]

Warrington is correct to point out that the relationship between commodities and the material base is not investigated in Pashukanis. Because of this, a contradiction arises. It is quite true that the base consists of production, or more exactly 'relations . . . directly connected with production',[76] and that therefore, it seems to make little sense that a legal form which is homologous to the commodity form actualised in *exchange* would be part of that base. However, contra Warrington, Pashukanis does seem to assert this.

> Marx himself emphasizes the fact that the basic and most deeply set stratum of the legal superstructure – property relations – is so closely contiguous with the base that they are 'the same relationships of production expressed in legal language'. . . . The political superstructure . . . is a secondary, derivative element.[77]

> [A]t a particular stage of development, the social relations of production assume a doubly mysterious form. On the one hand they appear as relations between things (commodities), and on the other, as relations between the wills of autonomous entities equal to each other – of legal subjects. In addition to the mystical quality of value, there appears a no less enigmatic phenomenon: law. A homogeneously integrated relation assumes two fundamental abstract aspects at the same time: an economic and a legal aspect.[78]

---

[73] Binns 1980, p. 104. Binns argues against him that 'the crucial element of law is not the identification of the interest of one individual *against another* . . . but the identification of all citizens *with their state*' (Binns 1980, p. 109) and that law is hence superstructural. In locating the state as central to law, Binns's theory is open to all the criticisms of the norm-driven theory of law outlined above. Walicki also argues that for Pashukanis the source of law 'should be seen in the economic base rather than in the ideological superstructure' (Walicki 1995, p. 356), and interestingly argues that this puts Pashukanis's theory at odds with Lenin's aims during the Russian NEP (New Economic Policy) that restored some market relations in 1921.

[74] Warrington 1980/81, p. 104. Emphasis in original.

[75] Warrington 1980/81, p. 105. A more explicit claim is Eldred's who simply states that Pashukanis 'attempt[s] to derive superstructural relations of property and right on the basis of Marx's capital-analysis' (Eldred 1984, p. 35). Another such claim – and critique, on the basis of Pashukanis's putative superstructural derivation of law – is in Taiwo 1996, pp. 81–3.

[76] Harman 1998, p. 28.

[77] Pashukanis 1980, p. 66.

[78] Pashukanis 1978, p. 117.

Although the language is slightly evasive, in claiming that 'relations of production' (part of the base) assume both economic and legal aspects 'at the same time', Pashukanis clearly suggests that the legal form is no less fundamental to the base than the economic form. In distinguishing this legal form from 'the political superstructure', which is 'secondary', he implies that the legal form is not of the superstructure.

Warrington's criticism seems to hold: how can an *exchange* relation be part of a base, which consists of relations and forces of *production*? Given that Pashukanis derives his legal form from exchange rather than production, there is a related broader methodological point, first raised by Korsch in 1930, who criticised Pashukanis's 'extremely strange – for a "Marxist" – overestimation of "circulation"'.[79]

Chris Arthur explains what is at stake.

> Pashukanis makes reference to commodity exchange without taking account of the various forms of production that might involve production for a market. . . . The suspicion arises that he has failed to correlate the form of law with a definite system of relations of production because reference to the level of market exchange is insufficiently precise. He does not say anything about that essential indicator of bourgeois relations – the extraction of surplus value by the class owning the means of production.[80]

Fine has made this central to his critique of Pashukanis. Pashukanis's excessively '"negative" critique of law which ignored its egalitarian and democratic aspects' was, he claims, a product of looking 'only at the surface of society',[81] rather than deriving law 'from social relations of *production*'.[82]

However, as Von Arx points out, Pashukanis's project is precisely to analyse the legal *form* 'independent of the content of legal norms':[83] it is that content, the specific norms *constructed* on the legal form, which we might expect to reflect class relations of production. The complaints about Pashukanis focusing on exchange to examine the legal form are 'misplaced', says Arthur,

> for it is precisely one of the interesting features of bourgeois exploitation that it inheres in economic relations that *do not* achieve formal legal

---

[79] Korsch in Pashukanis 1978, p. 195.
[80] Arthur 1978, pp. 29–30.
[81] Fine 1984, p. 158. Other writers who criticise Pashukanis for emphasising exchange at the expense of production include Cotterrell 1980; and Young 1978.
[82] Fine 1979, p. 43.
[83] Von Arx 1997, p. 170.

> expression. Formally speaking, Pashukanis is *correct* to refer law only to social relationships based on commodity exchange. . . . The monopolisation of the means of production by the capitalist class is an *extra*-legal fact (quite unlike the political-economic domination of the feudal lord). The bourgeois legal order contents itself with safeguarding the right of a property owner to do as he wishes with his own property – whether it be the right of a worker to sell his labour power because that is all he owns, or that of the capitalist to purchase it and retain the product.[84]

The same point can be made in value-theoretical terms.

> The whole point about the value form is that nothing changes when the form of simple circulation becomes the bearer of a capital circuit, so although a new relation is expressed in the value form this does not register, and on the surface the same legal subjects obtain.[85]

The maintenance of the value form (and we can add, the concomitant legal form) across different modes of production based on different class relations is explicitly argued by Marx.

> Whatever mode of production is the basis on which the products circulating are produced – whether the primitive community, slave production, small peasant and petty-bourgeois production, or capitalist production – this in no way alters their character as commodities, and as commodities they have to go through the exchange process and the changes of form that accompany it.[86]

The point is that for Pashukanis, the legal form is the form of the relations that inhere between the necessarily abstract and isolated bearers of commodities. Those bearers are derived from the commodity form itself, and are an intrinsic part of the commodity relation. The legal form is intrinsic to any system of commodity exchange. While commodity exchange under capitalism is different from simple commodity exchange, in that it is based on and reproductive of exploitative class relations of production, it is also true that as commodity exchange it is *also* a free and equal exchange of equivalents, borne by abstract, isolated social agents. Relations of production must be analysed to make sense of the particular class relations under capitalism, but the *legal*

[84] Arthur 1978, p. 30.
[85] Arthur, personal communication.
[86] Marx 1981, p. 442.

relations remain an expression of the relations of circulation. That is precisely why formal freedom and substantive unfreedom coexist under capitalism.

Thus we have answered the methodological critique that Pashukanis's focus on circulation at the expense of production undercuts his analysis of the legal form itself. It is precisely '[t]he sphere of circulation or commodity exchange . . . [that] is in fact a very Eden of the innate rights of man',[87] and it is this sphere 'with its exchange of equivalents by free persons, that is expressed in juridical relations'.[88]

However, this leaves unanswered Warrington's original critique. Even if we accept that the sphere of circulation is the locus of the legal form, how, in the Marxist model, can that be part of the base? Certainly Pashukanis does not clarify this point. However, an answer is present in his text. He claims that social relations of production only 'assume a doubly mysterious form' – only become penetrated by economic and juridical aspects – 'at a particular stage of development'.

> Only in the conditions of a commodity economy is the abstract form of a right created, i.e. the capacity to have a right in general is separated from specific legal claims. Only the constant transfer of rights taking place in the market creates the idea of their immobile bearer.[89]

In other words, where there are legal relations in a society *not* composed of generalised commodity production, they will be context-specific. But the *generalising* of the legal form can only occur under conditions of generalised commodity exchange. The final universalisation of a commodity economy is, of course, capitalism. And, crucially and uniquely under capitalism, all social production is production *for exchange*.

In other social formations, the bulk of production would be for subsistence, with the surplus or the product of a specialised minority being exchanged as commodities. In capitalism, however, the economic motor of society – production itself – is directly dependent on exchange: '[t]he transformation of the elements of production into the commodity product, *P* into *C′*, proceeds in the sphere of production, while the transformation of *C′* back into *P* takes place in the circulation sphere.'[90] Indeed,

---

[87] Marx 1976, p. 280.
[88] Arthur 1978, p. 30.
[89] Pashukanis 1980, p. 79.
[90] Marx 1978, p. 153.

> [i]t is precisely because the money form of value is its independent and palpable form of appearance that *the circulation form* M . . . M′, which starts and finishes with actual money, expresses money-making, *the driving motive of capitalist production*, most palpably. The production process appears simply as an unavoidable middle term, a necessary evil for the purpose of money-making.[91]

Marx is clear that the focus on circulation under capitalism 'bears an illusory character',[92] in that the capitalist *production* process based on the exploitation of wage-labour is presupposed but invisible. However, this illusory character does not mean that circulation is *not* central to the capitalist economy and production: the very 'illusory significance' of circulation is an inevitable product of seeing the self-expansion of value in the form of money as 'the exclusive form' of the circuit of capital.[93]

In other words, capitalist production is dependent on circulation like no other mode of production in history. Not only is all production *for* exchange, but the producers only avail themselves of production *by* exchange: that is the nature of wage-labour as opposed to other forms of surplus-extracting relations. The wage-labourer sells her labour-power to the capitalist for its value, in an act of exchange without which capital would be paralysed.[94] It

[91] Marx 1978, p. 137. Emphases mine.

[92] Marx 1978, p. 141.

[93] Marx 1978, p. 142.

[94] There is great debate among Marxists as to the extent to which 'free' labour is necessary for the capital relation to inhere, and whether for example plantation slavery can be considered part of capitalism. This is way beyond the scope of this essay. Suffice to say here that as I consider plantation slavery to be what Marx called 'capital-positing' labour, which produces a surplus for capitalism, it, indentured labour and various other 'non-free' forms can and do exist under, and as part of, capitalism. However, Marx's continued insistence that wage-labour is a defining feature of capitalism is true, and in its generalisation and the concomitant mutual reinforcing of capitalist production by capitalist exchange the argument above holds. I would argue that there is a tendency towards juridically free wage-labour in capitalism, but that countervailing tendencies come into play to negate it at certain conjunctures of actually-existing capitalism. I would therefore agree with those theorists who claim that the 'freedom' from material goods, ie. the necessity of selling labour-power, is fundamental in capitalism in a way that the juridical freedom of bourgeois liberal democracy is not. This would suggest that liberal-democratic forms of capitalism represent, as it were, centres of gravity towards which more despotic political forms of capitalism tend, and thus it does not render the discussion of such juridical freedoms 'contingent' to the study of capitalism, any more than the countervailing tendencies from the tendency of the rate of profit to fall render discussions of capitalist crisis unnecessary. See among others Binns and Haynes 1980; Banaji 1977 and 2003; Bakan 1987; Miles 1987.

is, after all in the sphere of commodity exchange 'within whose boundaries the sale and purchase of labour-power goes on'.[95]

Given that the market is the driving mechanism for production itself it is no paradox simultaneously to claim that 'the capitalist production process is the basic pre-condition' of the circuit of capital,[96] *and* that therefore exchange relations *under capitalism* cannot be relegated to the superstructure. They have to be seen as part of the determining economic base of a society. Given that for Pashukanis simultaneously with these exchange relations the legal subject is thrown up, it makes sense to see *the legal form itself* as part of the base.

However, in discussing the historical emergence of law, Pashukanis seems to allege the opposite, that law is in fact superstructural.

> It is dispute, conflict of interest, which creates the legal form, the legal superstructure. In the lawsuit, in court proceedings, the economically active subjects first appear in their capacity as parties, that is, as participants in the legal superstructure. Even in its most primitive form, the court is legal superstructure par excellence. The legal differentiates itself from the economic and appears as an autonomous element through legal proceedings.[97]

At first glance, the law here seems to be defined as superstructure. *But 'the legal form, the legal superstructure' are two different things.*

We have already seen that Pashukanis argues, with Marx, that the legal subject is the juridical expression of the commodity owner, as the property relation 'stands in such close contact "with the existing relations of production" that it "is but a legal expression for the same thing"'.[98] At the level of the legal subject existing in relation to other legal subjects, the legal relationship, the legal form itself is part of the economic base.[99]

---

95 Marx 1978, p. 280.

96 Marx 1978, p. 143.

97 Pashukanis 1978, p. 93.

98 Pashukanis 1978, p. 91, quoting Marx from the 1859 'Preface to the Critique of Political Economy'.

99 It is true that at times Pashukanis seems to imply that the legal relations comes *after* the economic relation, describing the economic relation as the '*source* of the legal relation, which comes into being only at the moment of dispute' (Pashukanis 1978, p. 93. Emphasis mine). But this is an undialectical slip. For in the commodity form itself, dispute, coercion and violence are inherently implied. The notion of 'mine' necessary to ownership and commodity exchange is only meaningful inasmuch as it is 'mine-*not-yours*'. The fact that something is 'mine' necessarily defines it in opposition to a counterclaim, whether or not that counterclaim is in fact made. Disputation, and hence the legal form itelf, lurks at the heart of the most peaceful private property

But '[t]he legal differentiates itself from the economic and appears as an autonomous element through legal proceedings'.[100] The juridical relation is partly constitutive of the fundamental social relation, but it can only become visible as itself, ie., as a *legal* form, through the medium of *actually-existing law*. 'In the lawsuit, in court proceedings, the economically active subjects first appear in their capacity as parties, that is, as participants in the legal superstructure.'[101] The various particular mechanisms by which the legal form is actualised in various historical conjunctures are superstructural.

In Artous's words, by this 'double determination' Pashukanis explains how 'the juridical relation implants itself in the relations of production, but [that] the juridical form could not exist without the institution which is the [legal] process'.[102] A particular legal superstructure allows the *legality* of the legal form to become visible – and is necessarily thrown up by it. So the legal form is of the base, and it actualises through the necessary particularities of the legal superstructure. In other words, law is precisely one of those social institutions Harman describes which contain both relations directly connected with production (the base – here the *legal form*) and those not (the superstructure – here the *particular legal proceedings*, the specific court and so on).

It is thus misleading to claim that Pashukanis sees 'law' as part of the base, or part of the superstructure.[103] 'Law' is a complex of social relations, norms, rules and formal proceedings which, under capitalism, straddles both levels of society.

2.2.1. *A note on history and logic*

There is an important distinction between the *logical* movement from simple commodity exchange to commodity exchange based on capitalist relations of production and the *historical* movement from exchange of commodities under

---

relation. Accordingly, and against some of Pashukanis's own assertions, as an expression of relations of exchange which under capitalism inhere in the base, the legal form itself must also be so located.

[100] Pashukanis 1978, p. 93.

[101] Ibid.

[102] Artous 1999, p. 139. Translation mine.

[103] Unlike Binns or Warrington, Von Arx sees that at different points Pashukanis makes contradictory claims about the status of law, although she apparently sees the 'superstructural' claims as simply inconsistent (Von Arx 1997, p. 66 footnote 181). Pashukanis's own formulations were sometimes contradictory. At one point, for example, he seems to imply that the very *legal subject* is in fact superstructural (Pashukanis 1978, p. 93). This stands in contrast to the thrust of his theory.

pre-capitalist societies to that in capitalism itself.[104] Pashukanis elides this distinction.

> [T]he dialectical development of the fundamental juridical concepts not only provides us with the legal form as a fully developed and articulated structure, but also reflects the actual process of historical development, a process which is synonymous with the process of development of bourgeois society itself.[105]

But despite his claim to derive the historical development of legal forms from their systematic derivation, Pashukanis 'offers no detailed account of the historical process underlying the maturation of these [pre-capitalist] "embryonic legal forms" into bourgeois law'.[106] His theory is a dialectical-logical theory of the legal form, and any implications for a historical narrative or theory are inchoate.

A history of the development of the legal form *can* be developed using Pashukanis's theory. In *Capital* Volume 3 Marx's chapter on 'Historical Material on Merchant's Capital'[107] offers a fascinating account of the transition from pre-capitalist forms of commodity exchange based on mercantile activity, in which well-developed commercial capital (and hence market activity) is necessary but not sufficient for a move to industrial capitalism, and he claims that *given certain other social conditions* trade will move from existing in the interstices of society/societies to become the basis for industrial capitalist production. Given that the legal form is a function of exchange relations, this paradigm is suggestive about law's transition from a superstructural phenomenon occurring in the 'pores' of society, inhering in the special realm of the exchange sphere (such as the 'law merchant' of the thirteenth century, which held in certain regularised market places),[108] to a generalised form that permeates every level of society given the universalisation of market relations.

2.3. *The withering away of law*

Among the various criticisms levelled at Pashukanis, one is the accusation that his theory 'is ultimately a theory against law'.[109] Now, one could point

---

104 Arthur 1999 is an excellent introduction to this vital distinction.
105 Pashukanis 1978, p. 59.
106 Von Arx 1997, p. 79.
107 Marx 1981, pp. 440–55.
108 Morton 1989, p. 74. See more generally Trakman 1983.
109 Von Arx 1997, p. 8.

out that Pashukanis stressed that the legal form would continue to inhere in the USSR for some time after the revolution of 1917, that he did not advocate the active destruction of law, that his work as a jurist showed his commitment to the progressive application of law, and so on. All this is true, but it rather misses the point. Pashukanis was, absolutely, hostile to law, inasmuch as he understood it to be a reflection of capitalist property relations, an integral part of a class society where the market had a commanding role, and he did not believe that it would last as communism flowered. To criticise Pashukanis for this view is to decide in advance that law is to be defended.

I have repeatedly argued that we must allow the possibility of a theory which posits the legal form as a real and active factor in social relations, yet denies that it can be a force for progressive change, or even the maintenance of order (itself only self-evidently a good for conservative critics). In Pashukanis's theory, we have precisely such a theory.

Although Pashukanis attempted to make theoretical peace with Stalinist entrenchment, it was ultimately his theory's hostility to law, and his insistence on its ultimate withering away, that led to Pashukanis's murder.

> The demand for greater contractual discipline within the planned economy, the revival and strengthening of Soviet family law . . . and, above all, the publication of the draft of a new constitution in June 1936, all clearly foreshadowed an impending major change in Soviet legal policy. The new constitutional right of ownership of personal property and the provisions for the first all-union civil and criminal codes implied the reinforcement rather than the withering away of the law. Stalin's famous remark later that year that 'stability of the laws is necessary for us now more than ever' signaled the new legal policy. . . .[110]

Pashukanis had argued in 1929 that '[t]he problem of the withering away of law is the cornerstone by which we measure the degree of proximity of a jurist to Marxism'.[111] Stalin could not allow the argument that law would wither away under socialism, as under Stalinism law was manifestly still required.[112]

---

110 Beirne and Sharlet 1990, pp. 37–8.

111 Pashukanis 1980, p. 268.

112 The question of what type of society was the USSR if not socialist has given forth a vast literature, and is way beyond the scope of this book. My research leads me to identify with that body of theory which holds that the dynamic of competitive accumulation in the USSR and its satellites (originally a competition with the West

Even as he attempted to recant, Pashukanis was unable 'totally to deny his major premise. *The General Theory* proclaimed loud and clear that there is no such thing as proletarian law and that the law of the Soviet State was simply a form of bourgeois law frozen into immobility'.[113] Even in his abject 'State and Law under Socialism', written as late as 1936, Pashukanis can still only go so far as to quote Lenin saying that 'it is inconceivable that people will immediately learn to work *without any legal norms* after the overthrow of capitalism'.[114] This is doubtless true, and did not contradict what Pashukanis had always claimed, which was that law would *wither away* under socialism – no time limit was specified. Even on the eve of his death he could not accommodate the notion of proletarian law into his theory. It is no wonder that '[t]he self-criticisms remained unsatisfactory'.[115]

Pashukanis's vision of an alternative to law was problematic. He counterposed legal regulation with technical regulation which does not abstract from context. The move from capitalism to socialism would entail a move from economic relations driven by the anarchy of the market to democratic planning. As this generalises, and resources become allocated according to need, the opposition of private interests that characterise a commodity economy would dissolve. Technical regulation, which Pashukanis saw as based on the premise of '[u]nity of purpose',[116] 'is undoubtedly strengthened over time through being subjected to a general plan of the economy'.[117]

It is wrong to allege that this theory 'cut with the grain of Stalinism' by 'supporting the supposedly "technical" nature of regulation under socialism'.[118] It was, after all, the strengthening of *law*, rather than technical regulation, which characterised Stalinism, and made the commodity-form theory of law inimical to it. However, it is true that Pashukanis's vision of generalised technical regulation is excessively bureaucratic, and has no

---

over the means of destruction – military hardware – as well as means of production – the heavy industry needed to produce them) subordinated the inchoate movement toward grass-roots democracy and workers' control of the state, and that therefore far from being 'socialist' or even a 'degenerated workers' state', the USSR can best be described, certainly after 1928, as 'bureaucratic state capitalism', whatever its propaganda claimed. See among many expositions of this theory especially Cliff 1996 and Callinicos 1990 at section 5.1.

[113] Warrington 1980/81, p. 103.

[114] Lenin, quoted in Pashukanis 1980, p. 349. Emphasis in Pashukanis.

[115] Redhead 1978, p. 116.

[116] Pashukanis 1980, p. 60.

[117] Pashukanis 1978, p. 131.

[118] Binns 1980, p. 111.

mechanism for dealing with continued conflict under socialism. We can question Pashukanis's suggested post-revolutionary alternative to law (which is in any case entirely suggestive, rather than worked out), but this does not invalidate his thesis about the ultimate withering away of law.

It is true, as Von Arx argues, that law predated capitalism – a point Pashukanis is well aware of, and makes several times, in his discussions of Roman law, feudal law, law merchant and so on. However, she concludes therefore that 'there is no reason to believe that it will not survive capitalism'.[119] This does not follow. The existence of law before capitalism was, for Pashukanis, a function of the pre-capitalist market. Market relations were not generalised, and nor were legal relations. Inasmuch as it would be extremely unlikely for market mechanisms to disappear overnight in the case of a socialist revolution, law would undoubtedly continue to exist in some form (probably losing its general and abstract character over time) and therefore would 'survive capitalism'. But Von Arx means more than this. She asserts, without argument, that under socialism 'certain interests will require protection, by means of rights', that Pashukanis 'does not recognize that there is reason to value procedural and substantive justice', and 'does not grasp law's progressive potential'.[120]

First, it is absurd to claim that because he does not see law surviving beyond capitalism, Pashukanis does not value justice. The equation of law and justice is ideological: law deals only with an abstract 'justice' between juridical subjects, rather than concrete human agents, as Pashukanis makes clear. Particularly if one sees modern social ills as entirely compatible with legal 'equality' and hence 'justice', then it is precisely one's concern for social justice that *undermines* one's respect for law. The 'progressive potential' that Von Arx sees in law is not argued for, but merely asserted in an untheorised way. It is true that Pashukanis cannot suggest a satisfactory alternative system for regulating social conflict in socialism, but his inability to do so has, frankly, no impact on his analysis of the legal form and its ultimate disappearance.

According to Von Arx, Pashukanis's 'answer to the conflict between substantive inequality and formal equality is the elimination of formal equality'.[121] This is, however, not true. Pashukanis does not see the *elimination* of law as an answer to anything: instead, he sees its eventual *withering away* as

119 Von Arx 1997, p. 213.
120 Von Arx 1997, pp. 213–14.
121 Von Arx 1997, p. 214.

an inevitable *result* of the generalisation of substantive equality and the marginalisation of social relations mediated by the market.

It is interesting that what Fine sees as Pashukanis's 'excessive' hostility to law, that supposedly leads him to ignore 'its egalitarian and democratic aspects',[122] is for Fine a product of Pashukanis's privileging of exchange over production. It is hard to see how it could be said that Pashukanis 'did not appear to learn . . . that equality before the law provides a measure – albeit limited and formal, but not illusory – of equality'.[123] Certainly Pashukanis does not stress this element of law in his analysis, but he does clearly counterpose law and feudal relations in which

> '[t]he content of individuality was not one and the same. The estate, property position, profession, belief, age, sex and physical strength led to deep inequality in legal capacity.' Equality between subjects was assumed only for closed relationships in a definite narrow sphere.[124]

For Pashukanis, law did precisely lead to a 'measure of equality'. However, he was concerned to stress the limits to the progressive nature of the legal form.

Against Fine, in fact, it is precisely Pashukanis's focus on exchange relations to derive the legal form that *vindicates* his refusal to countenance a progressive continuation of law under socialism.

> No amount of reformist factory legislation can overcome the basic presupposition of the law: that a property freely alienated *belongs* to the purchaser, and hence that the living labour of the worker becomes, through exchange, available for exploitation by capital.[125]

In its very neutrality, law maintains capitalist relations. Law is class law, and cannot but be so.

3. Critiques and reconstructions

One important and salient critique is that Pashukanis's quite abstract model 'cannot account for twentieth-century developments in law'.[126] Some suggest

---

[122] Fine 1984, p. 158.
[123] Fine 1984, p. 161.
[124] Pashukanis 1980, p. 80 (the quotation is from Gierke).
[125] Arthur 1978, p. 31.
[126] Von Arx 1997, p. 8.

that changes in law have fundamentally undermined the commodity-form theory.

> Even critics who are generally sympathetic to Pashukanis question the continuing vitality of his commodity exchange theory of law in the era of monopoly capitalism. While Pashukanis is credited with presenting an adequate account of the legal form for competitive, *laissez-faire* capitalism, the *General Theory*'s market model is perceived to operate uneasily within late capitalism.[127]

The claim is that 'changes in private law signal a *fundamental* alteration of the legal subject';[128] 'critics charge that *General Theory*'s form of law . . . is incapable of accommodating the new content and role being demanded of law'.[129] The commodity-form theory of law, it is implied, used to be correct, but no longer is.

If this is true, it is extremely strange. This would be to say that the fundamental particles of law, the legal subject, the legal form, the juridical relation itself, so central to the development of market economy and capitalism, *were* at one point derived from the commodity relation, as Pashukanis explains. But that at some point in the late nineteenth or early twentieth century, the *basic ontological structure* of law underwent a change. What we now call law must be fundamentally different from what was previously called law.

Put so baldly, most writers would probably balk at this position. It is, however, immanent in any notion of basic changes in the legal form. Take, for example, Von Arx's claim that

> the form of law described by Pashukanis has simply not survived the transition to monopoly capitalism wholly intact. The *General Theory*'s fixation on the form and principles of 19th century law causes Pashukanis to overlook . . . the transformation of the legal subject in private law, . . . [and] equally remarkable developments . . . [in] public law.[130]

The claim is made in the context of the apparently growing importance of 'status' to the legal form, undermining its basis in formal equality, a change the commodity-form theory is deemed unable to explain. In this model the legal form *did* derive from the commodity relationship, but now no longer

[127] Von Arx 1997, p. 198.
[128] Von Arx 1997, p. 202. Emphasis mine.
[129] Von Arx 1997, p. 204.
[130] Von Arx 1997, p. 203.

does. Whether the claim is that there is a totally different basis for the legal form, or that the form is now based on some other relationship *in addition* to the commodity relationship, this is a fundamental break with Pashukanis, whose whole theory revolved around the logical derivation of the legal form from the commodity form.

In its rigorous and systematic derivation of law, the commodity-form theory cannot accommodate dilution: if law is still law, but is derived from the commodity-form *along with something else*, then the commodity-form theory, which explained the very existence and 'law-ness' of law from the heart of the commodity, is invalidated.

Theories claiming that Pashukanis is 'no longer' right elide with more fundamental critiques of his approach *tout court*. The former tend to focus on what is different about modern and earlier forms of law, but they leave untheorised that which is shared – and if we believe that they are both law, they must share some form from which to derive a common 'law-ness'. As Pashukanis's theory has been judged inadequate in this model, that shared legal form must derive from something other than the commodity-form. To say that Pashukanis was once right but is no longer, in other words, is to say that he was never right.

There is, however, a way of taking seriously changes in the law without undermining the commodity-form theory of law. Rather than the revision of Pashukanis's theory, the twentieth century's legal changes, developments in contract, administration and law necessitate the development of that theory on the basis of the theory itself.[131]

The focus on status is based on modern law's tendency toward '[l]egal recognition of entities such as private corporations, associations, funds, unions, utilities and public corporations'[132] – the fact is that '[t]he rights of Pashukanis's isolated legal subject are no longer regarded as absolute'.[133] There has been a move away from the notion of the isolated and abstract individual as the unit of contract.[134]

A second, linked, tendency, is the extension of 'administration'.

> When public authority routinely uses law to intrude into economic life, the function of the legal order undergoes a fundamental transformation. In the

---

131 In a personal communication, Chris Arthur has written, for example, that 'with the development of the economy to joint stock enterprises etc. the notion of legal person has to be *developed*.' (Emphasis mine.)

132 Von Arx 1997, pp. 202–3.

133 Von Arx 1997, p. 204.

134 See also Feinman and Gabel 1990, pp. 379–81.

> era of the interventionist state, law's role can no longer be conceived solely as the protection of equivalent exchange, free will, private ownership and individual autonomy.[135]

Administrative law is indeed fundamentally important to the modern state. It is also true that Pashukanis's perspective, with his excessively sharp distinction between administration and law, militates against his being able to conceptualise this as a *legal* movement.[136] Some conclude on this basis that the 'far reaching changes in administrative law within capitalist societies serve to undermine his basic thesis'.[137]

Theorists who stress this double movement – the extension of contractual relations to include legal personalities other than abstract individuals, and the extension of administrative law – to undermine Pashukanis's thesis have seemed unable to offer convincing *general* theories of law on the basis of their observations. I contend that it is possible to develop the commodity-form theory of law to take account of these changes. Not only that, but that such a historicised commodity-form theory is the only paradigm able to explain not only the differences between laws in different epochs, but their shared feature, the legal form itself, that which makes them all law. For this reason it remains by far the most compelling theory of the legal form.

Much of what follows is based on a 'Pashukanisite' reading of the invaluable historical work of Kay and Mott.[138] Although a development of Pashukanis's theory is not at all the authors' aim – their only mention of Pashukanis is a brief and convincing criticism of his flawed theory of the labour contract,[139] on which more below – there is nothing in their theory that cannot be invaluably assimilated into the commodity-form theory. Indeed, their observation that '[l]aw is not a set of coercive rules, but a tangible expression of a social form with a predetermined historical content, namely the

---

[135] Von Arx 1997, p. 205. The formulation that the legal relation is about the 'protection' of the commodity relation, rather than another way of seeing that relation itself, is misleading.

[136] 'By insisting on a clean break between law and administration, Pashukanis both distorts the relationship between these two realms and ignores the overwhelming importance of administrative law in the twentieth century legal order.' Von Arx 1997, pp. 206–7.

[137] Gregory 1979, p. 141.

[138] Kay and Mott 1982.

[139] Kay and Mott 1982, p. 111.

commodity nature of the products of labour under a regime of absolute property'[140] neatly dovetails with Pashukanis's.

I have argued that given the fundamental ontogeny of the legal form in contract, it is methodologically correct to see exchange relations as the realm of the legal form. However, I have also argued that uniquely under capitalism, the exchange of commodities cannot be considered 'merely' superstructural. In capitalism's economy of generalised production *for* and *on the basis* of commodity exchange, those exchange relations are fundamentally tied to production itself. For Marx, this is nowhere more clear than in the fact of 'free' wage-labour. It is in the generalisation of this form that capitalism's exploitative productive relations become mutually constitutive with its 'free' commodity-exchange distributive system.[141]

It is at this point of intersection that the difficulty arises for contract theory. 'Labour law is the most complex and equivocal of the laws of property for fundamental reasons. . . . The buying and selling of labour-power summarises the contradictions of capitalist society in a single moment.'[142] The problem is to reconcile the necessary and contradictory poles of the wage contract – formal equivalence of the parties, and real subsumption of labour to capital.

> A simple contrast of the buying and selling of labour-power with other commodities reveals the difficulty facing the legislator. When an individual sells a commodity other than labour-power, the act of sale is a final alienation. . . . This is not the case with labour-power, which is an attribute of the subject and cannot be consumed without his presence, participation and cooperation. Unlike other objects which are external to the seller, labour-power cannot be definitively alienated. Thus the first difficulty is to formulate a labour contract which provides for the alienation of an object – which by its very nature cannot be alienated. . . . [T]he difficulty is one of including labour-power within the general law of property, while at the same time being forced to acknowledge that labour-power is not an object of property like others.
>
> The second difficulty of labour law, and a consequence of the first, is that the alienation of labour-power which actually occurs, and which the labour contract is there to effect, must in fact be denied by the contract, since it is

---

140 Kay and Mott 1982, p. 94.
141 Marx 1973, p. 225; see also Marx 1976 p. 274.
142 Kay and Mott 1982, p. 111.

> incompatible with the general supposition of private property. If the labour contract were formulated in such a way as to recognise that the worker was actually alienating his capacities, it would be inconsistent with the general principles of the formation of contracts . . . [ie.] the definition of the worker as a universal subject in full possession of himself at all times.[143]

Though Pashukanis was not wrong to derive law from exchange, he fails to address the unprecedented historical relation between circulation and production *under capitalism,* and is thus unable to theorise the labour contract necessary for developed monopoly capitalism, or even for industrial capitalism *tout court* (critics who claim that his theory cannot take account of twentieth-century developments in fact do not set their criticisms early enough). That failure underpins his inability to historicise the legal form and make sense of later developments.[144]

Pashukanis rightly saw that the wage relationship necessitated 'despotism in the manufacturing division of labour',[145] the alienation to the employer of the worker's 'will and its rational use'.[146] Focusing as he did on law's contractual basis between supposedly free and equal individuals, he became unstuck by precisely the paradox that Kay and Mott outline, and could not conceive of labour legislation as law. His alternative formulation was quite unsatisfactory.

> [C]ontrol within the enterprise remains the private affair of each individual capitalist. The establishment of labour regulations is an act of private legislation; in other words, it is a piece of pure feudalism. This remains true despite the lengths to which bourgeois jurists go in order to tart it up in a modern fashion by creating the fiction of the so-called *contrat d'adhésion*. . . .[147]

The notion that the relation at the heart of capitalist exploitation is a feudal atavism is clearly quite untenable. However, despite this rather cursory claim,

---

143 Kay and Mott 1982, p. 113.

144 Howard Engelskirchen makes this key to his critique of Pashukanis, and dovetails it with the critique that the commodity-form theory cannot account for administration: 'forms of administrative law generally, such a characteristic feature of the modern state, owe their development in substantial part to advances in labor legislation, and the problem of the legal form is misperceived if it is reduced to what we could characterize in the Anglo-American tradition as the forms of common-law legal development – tort, contract, real property, and the like.' (Engelskirchen 1992, p. 111.)

145 Marx 1976, p. 477.

146 Kay and Mott 1982, p. 113.

147 Pashukanis 1978, pp. 141–2.

an awareness that labour legislation – the regulatory framework for the contractual relationship between labour and capital – must be subsumed under the general legal form was implicit in Pashukanis's theory. When he notes, for example, that '[e]very buyer and seller is . . . a legal subject par excellence',[148] it is impossible to conceive of the buyers and sellers of labour-power in any other way.

As Kay and Mott point out, the labour contract is an unstable form that attempts to mediate contradictions.

> The solution that the law has developed combines two elements:
>
> 1) The episodic nature of the transaction: so that the worker only submits himself to capital period by period, and never finally alienates his will. This permits the illusion that he remains in ultimate possession of himself. . . .
>
> 2) In the contract itself the object that is formally alienated does not appear as labour-power, i.e. a capacity which is an immediate attribute of the subject, but as labour, i.e. expended labour-power, or labour which has become external to the worker.[149]

The subordination of the labouring population to industrial capital necessitated a development of the categories of individual property which had been adequate to mercantile and artisan-based capitalism 'when the process of accumulation was realised through the will of individual entrepreneurs'.[150] The move to joint-stock companies provided the germ-seed of the modern corporation. This meant, in Marx's words, then Kay and Mott's,

> [c]apital, which is inherently based on a social mode of production and presupposes a social concentration of means of production and labour-power, now receives the form of social capital (capital of directly associated individuals) in contrast to private capital, and its enterprises appear as social

[148] Pashukanis 1978, p. 143.

[149] Kay and Mott 1982, p. 114. The appearance that what is bought is labour, rather than labour-power – actual work, rather than the capacity to work – is illusory. The very fact of 'despotism' within the workplace means that the capitalist must have power to decide what work is done, and therefore his/her employees alienate not a specific outlay of labour (which would imply that the capitalist did not have control over that outlay at the point of production) but their *ability so to do*. Nevertheless, the *appearance* is that it is a specific job which is bought.

[150] Kay and Mott 1982, p. 101. What follows is a truncated version of the historico-logical sequence they outline throughout the second half of their book.

> enterprises as opposed to private ones. This is the abolition of capital as private property within the confines of the capitalist mode of production itself.[151]

> Legislation in 1855 and 1862 established the principle of limited liability. . . . [T]his new legal form. . . . established a clear distinction between the private property of the capitalist (subject to consumption) and the property of the capitalist project (subject to accumulation).[152]

It is now the capitalist *project* which must use wage-labour to accumulate, as opposed to the individual capitalist. A necessary corollary of this was the development of the juridical form to allow for a corporate body to be the owner of a commodity and therefore to retain legal personality. This was not a 'new' legal form but a development of the legal form Pashukanis outlines *on the basis of that form itself.*

With the move to the juridical acknowledgement of the agency of abstract entities of accumulation, the same tendency manifested on the side of the working class, where abstract entities of production were necessarily legally recognised. It would be nonsensical for the company to engage in a vast number of contracts, each with its own set of negotiations, one with each of its workers, and it would diminish the formal power of the corporation vis-à-vis its workers if each of them was its formal equal. The legal formalisation of capital's agent, the company, had its flipside in the formalisation of labour's agent, the collective organisation of workers, the trade union. 'In composing the fully developed wage contract, it is necessary for the state to establish the subjectivities of *both* parties, since neither capital nor labour are spontaneous economic entities.'[153]

Marx himself points out the extent to which such double-sided legalisation of capital and labour as collectives is a result of the peculiar nature of labour-power as a commodity, for similar reasons as those laid out by Kay and Mott.

> The capitalist maintains his right as a purchaser when he tries to make the working day as long as possible . . . On the other hand, the peculiar nature of the commodity sold implies a limit to its consumption by the purchaser, and the worker maintains his right as a seller when he wishes to reduce the

151 Marx 1981, p. 567.
152 Kay and Mott 1982, p. 102.
153 Kay and Mott 1982, p. 115.

> working day to a particular normal length. . . . [I]n the history of capitalist production, the establishment of a norm for the working day presents itself as a struggle over the limits of that day, a struggle between collective capital . . . and collective labour. . . .[154]

As Kay and Mott point out, 'trades unions have from 1871 been the legally constituted subjectivity of the working class'.[155] There was a sequence of legal reforms and judgements extending the legal personality of the trade unions from 1841 to 1918. 'This sequence of legislation defining both labour organisations and their space in law, was the formation of the legal subjectivity of labour by the state.'[156]

What we have here is a theory of the legal recognition of corporations and unions, one of the fundamental changes in contract sometimes deemed to undermine Pashukanis's theory, understood as a shift in the atoms of the juridical relationship *on the basis of the commodity relationship under changing conditions of mass industrialisation and the commodification of labour-power itself.* In other words, this does not represent a move *away* from the commodity-form theory, but a *vindication* of it.

At the heart of the capitalist economy is the extraordinary commodity of labour-power, which is a commodity simultaneously like and utterly unlike any other. Pashukanis failed to apply his own theory with sufficient systematicity. But it is only through the application of the commodity-form theory of law itself to that unique commodity that we can see how the form of law itself must develop, *on the basis of its own fundamental form*, as capitalism ages.

As to the extension of administration, it might look as if Kay and Mott share the simplistic notion of Pashukanis's critics, that it represents a move away from the commodity-form theory of law, as it represents a move away from *laissez-faire* capitalism. 'Contemporary administration of economic and social life contrasts with earlier forms of control through the law, along the same lines that a system of regulated prices differs from a free-market mechanism.'[157]

---

[154] Marx 1976, p. 344.

[155] Kay and Mott 1982, p. 115.

[156] Kay and Mott 1982, p. 117. At the time of writing, Kay and Mott were keen to point out that there was some move back toward individual employment contracts: nonetheless, this is still on the basis of a broadly conceived labour contract, and remains relatively epiphenomenal to the huge shift represented by the move to collective bargaining.

[157] Kay and Mott 1982, p. 94.

Administration and law are not so sharply counterposed as Pashukanis suggests. But where most critics simply (if rightly) assert that administration must be seen as law, and perhaps that this therefore undermines the commodity-form theory,[158] Kay and Mott historicise that insight, and open for investigation the precise dynamics of 'administration' and 'law'. Their analysis shows (contradicting Pashukanis's own distinctions) that it is only the full application of the commodity-form of law in given historical conjunctures that allows us to understand the spread of administration. The commodity-form theory is vindicated by the very changes which Von Arx and others see undermining it.

The same process of formal recognition of capital and labour in the nineteenth century pulled the atoms of contract theory away from abstracted individuals, and necessitated a growth in particularistic administration.

> By 1870 the wider law of labour was faced with the task of recognising the labour-power of the proletariat as a general force, but was no longer adequate to this task, and the gaps between legal forms had to be filled, in order to create a continuum of order. This process is administration, which addresses itself to particulars . . . and from these particulars creates schematised or partial objects, which although abstracted from the social matrix, leave traces of their concrete origins within the procedures of administration itself. Thus the law-and-administration continuum came into being. . . . The . . . continuum is founded in order, itself the state's apprehension of its task of maintaining private property as a universal form.[159]

Thus it is the continuing and inevitable failure of existing laws to patch up all the holes in the social fabric that necessitates the extension of administration. Administration *is law*: it is somewhat removed from private law, where the legal form exists in its 'purest' form, but administration – public law – is directly derived from that form. Only in the context of generalised

---

[158] Administrative law 'resist[s] the application of conventional legal doctrines drawn from the commodity exchange model of private law. Because they are oriented primarily towards substantive social purposes rather than the protection of private autonomy or the resolution of private conflicts, the *General Theory* would place them in the realm of extra-legal, administrative regulation. For Pashukanis the form of bourgeois law is articulated in neutral, nonpolitical terms and operates through the use of formal, objective, impartial rules and procedures. Consequently, regulations directed at substantive, particularistic ends which employ instrumental, purposive processes are outside the legal form' (Von Arx 1997, p. 206).

[159] Kay and Mott 1982, p. 133.

commodification and juridical relations does administration manifest through the specific form of 'administrative law'.

Administration is the necessary 'particularistic', 'political' corollary of the legal form's abstract formality, and it is continually thrown up. The attempt to apply abstract laws in particular conjunctures, in a developing history of class conflict, will always leave gaps that must be plugged by the capitalist state, the guarantor of law within national boundaries.

> Legal and administrative forms . . . always arise from the movements of labour and the efforts of the state to contain them in formal terms, so that the study of law and administration over time can be taken as an archaeology of decayed bodies politic, the corpses of organised working-class oppositions. . . . Administration is working-class power *post festum;* working-class political victories captured and formalised at their moment of triumph.[160]

Those administrative rules are *law*, in that they take the legal form. They attempt, in their very particularity, to approximate the abstraction of the legal form. This can be seen in the peculiar dialectic between 'particularism' and 'abstraction' in anti-discrimination legislation – public, administrative, law.

> Even when it is apparently providing real or specific justice for deprived groups in society, the state always maintains the legal form, and its justice is always formal. A clear example is the legislation to promote equal pay for women. . . . The tribunals . . . treat women as a series of individuals, each the subject of a formal right to equal pay. But the concrete means for establishing the equality of female to male labour, a comparison required by the law, are conspicuously absent, and there is no provision for dealing with concentrations of female labour in a limited range of low-pay occupations.[161]

Administration addresses a specific inequality through an attempt to formalise the marginalised group as equal. The attempt is therefore to solve a particular problem through the subsumption of a particular category – here women – into a formal, abstract, juridical one, to *insist upon its abstract equality*.

With a similar reaggregation of the particular and the abstract, the Marxist legal theorist Howard Engelskirchen has criticised the argument that anti-discrimination legislation represents a curtailment of freedom of contract.

---

[160] Kay and Mott 1982, p. 96.
[161] Kay and Mott 1982, p. 95.

Instead, he argues that it is 'an expansion of bargain disembarrassed by historical baggage in no way intrinsic to its functioning'.[162]

The movement is therefore a constant spiral – or, better, a vast proliferation of spirals, a fractal: administration picks at specific problems, abstracts them within the legal form, thus inevitably leaving particular lacunae or creating new problems that cannot be solved by those moments of abstraction, to be dealt with by the next wave of administration, in response to class conflict.

What is clear is that although it is true that Pashukanis is wrong to counterpose administration and the legal form, it is *not* true that the growth of administration undermines the commodity-exchange theory. On the contrary, the growth of administration, particularly public law, can only be explained through the historicising of the commodity-form theory.

Interestingly, though she later contradicts herself by implying that the growth of administration in the twentieth century undermines law, drawing very explicitly on Marx, Von Arx is clear that 'these legislative modifications of the wage relation represent a development in contract law, not its demise'.[163]

---

[162] Engelskirchen 1997, pp. 572–3: 'the autonomy presupposed by contractual relationships is relational, and in the reproduction of interdependent autonomy resort to exchange is presupposed. Nothing in the reproduction of the social relations that gives rise to contractual consent, reflects or depends upon a unilateral exercise of arbitrary caprice extended to race or gender. Instead, it is exclusion from exchange that compromises the social function of bargain. . . . To blunt their [racism's and sexism's] reproduction does not in any way compromise the consent constituted and reproduced by bargain or exchange or interdependent autonomy. No formal autonomy presupposed by contract is undermined. . . . Free choice is liberated, not overridden, by legal action taken to foreclose such exclusions from exchange.'

[163] Von Arx 1997, p. 190. See pp. 180–90: '"The revolutions effected by machinery in the juridical relations between the buyer and seller of labour-power, causing the transaction as a whole to lose the appearance of a contract between free persons, afforded the English Parliament an excuse, *founded on juridical principles*, for the interference of the state with factories."

'The history of the Factory Acts confirms Marx's position. Classical contract doctrine itself provided the initial "excuse" for legislative intervention into the wage relation. The statutes discussed in *Capital* apply almost exclusively to minors and women, who were incapable of contracting at common law. Consequently, the state could justify its intrusion into the workplace on paternalistic grounds, consistent with the law of contract. . . . The economic and political movement of the working class . . . ultimately compelled parliament to recognize that the wage exchange generally fails to satisfy the underlying assumptions of classical contract doctrine regarding the freedom and equality of the parties. To compensate for the inequality in bargaining position between worker and capitalist, the Factory Acts simply remove certain terms and conditions from the realm of private decision-making. A similar result was achieved . . . in the United States . . . to ensure equality in bargaining power by recognizing the

Against Von Arx's assertion that '[t]he *General Theory* . . . cannot account for such developments in the legal form',[164] the germ-seed of this understanding is clearly present in Pashukanis himself, in his claim that public law 'can only be developed through its workings, in which it is continually repulsed by private law, so much that it attempts to define itself as the antithesis of private law, to which it returns, however, as to its centre of gravity'.[165]

Many of Pashukanis's shortcomings stem from his occasional failure to fully appreciate the contradictory, dialectical moments present in the commodity or legal relations. For example, I have tried to show that the particularism of administration is not sharply counterposed to the abstraction of the legal form when the legal form is considered in development through the particularities of social relations.

The commodity form and the legal form are formal, abstract, contractual in their essences, but they inevitably throw up particularities and the fact of coercion, and those dialectical others, the bad consciences of formal abstraction, cannot be considered in isolation from the commodity or legal forms themselves. That was Pashukanis's error. But the error was one of undialectical application of the commodity-form theory itself. I have tried to illustrate that a nuanced and historical application of that theory remains the only approach to law which even comes close to taking seriously the existence and historical development of the legal form.

4. The relevance for international legal scholarship

The response to Pashukanis's critics and the attempt to develop the commodity-form theory has been driven by problems in domestic law. The exposition may seem arcane for the international legal scholar, given that the basis for the development of the theory has been the relation between circulation and production in wage-labour – the legal relation perhaps least like relations between states.

---

rights of workers to act collectively.' The initial quote is from Marx, *Capital* Volume 1, the 1967 Aveling translation, p. 397. The emphasis is Von Arx's. This expresses with excellent clarity the movement of contract theory on the basis of its own foundations and the concomitant spread of administration, as well as the granting of legal personality to a collectivity of the working class.

[164] Von Arx 1997, p. 190.

[165] Pashukanis 1978, p. 106.

This raises the question, though, of whether in the international realm, where relations between the juridical units are relations either of exchange or administration rather than of wage-labour, a *simpler* form of Pashukanis's theory might hold. With the above analysis we can evaluate the differences and shared elements of international and domestic law. Both are moments of the same form: it is the fact of generalised wage-labour which universalises that form as the regulatory framework of capitalism, but the constant presence and permeation of wage-labour in domestic law complicates it for the commodity-form theory – unlike international law.

The most tenacious criticism of Pashukanis remains that he is unable to address questions of politics; that he cannot satisfactorily explain the relation of the state to the law, that he does not explain or take seriously the *content* of his legal form. I reject this, and will argue that the theory can perfectly successfully deal with these questions, although it does sometimes necessitate a more nuanced dialectical development of his own units than Pashukanis offered.

This question of politics and the state, the substantive content of laws and their coercive application, is directly relevant to international law: in fact, it represents the conceptual bridge linking Pashukanis's theory of law at the domestic and international levels. The argument and exposition above is intended as introduction to the commodity-form theory of international law developed below.

Pashukanis's theory is of the deep grammar of law – what has been described as 'timeless structures'.[166] Levels of mediation are necessary to rise from this abstract to concrete moments, as the discussion of administration above makes clear. This is no less true for international law. Pashukanis's essay on the subject was written before the era of the UN and the chaotic multilateral developments of decolonisation:[167] it is an invaluable starting point not because it can be read straightforwardly as 'about' today's international arena, but for its historical perspective, and precisely as an application of the commodity-form theory to a concrete historical moment. Pashukanis's contribution to international law theory, however, is based on much more than this one piece.

Pashukanis provides the indispensable optic to understand international law, but a focus on international law in turn allows us to clarify some of his

[166] Cotterrell 1996, p. 115.
[167] Pashukanis 1980b. Appendix below, pp. 321–335.

ambiguous, unclear or mistaken formulations. A careful application of the commodity-form theory of law to international law can thus contribute to a more complete and nuanced development of that theory itself.

We need Pashukanis to make sense of international law and the legal form: and we need international law to make better sense of Pashukanis.

Chapter Four

Coercion and the Legal Form: Politics, (International) Law and the State

1. The problem of politics

Many critics claim that there is no space for politics in Pashukanis's theory: this is apparently its most intransigent problem. To the extent that 'administration' is seen as political, the argument above that such administration is still derived from the legal form itself is a response to this. However, this is not sufficient. Such an integration of administration into the commodity-form theory goes some way to showing how particular political practices can go hand in hand with the legal form, but there remains the problem of systematically mapping the relation between form and content of law.

Pashukanis himself was concerned to stress the importance of *not* fetishising the politics, the content of law, as the source of class inequality. '[T]he fundamental juridical categories cited above are not dependent on the concrete content of its legal norms, in the sense that they retain their meaning irrespective of any change in this concrete material content'.[1] He describes those Marxists who focus on 'the concrete content of the legal norms and the historical development of legal institutions' as having 'no responsibility towards jurisprudence'.[2]

---

[1] Pashukanis 1978, p. 47.
[2] Pashukanis 1978, p. 54.

However, Pashukanis considered his work a corrective to the tendency to analyse legal content *in isolation*. This does not mean such content is unimportant – only that it must proceed on the right basis. He accepts that 'it is legitimate, up to a point',[3] to focus on the content. By doing so, Pashukanis explains that 'all we get is a theory which explains the emergence of legal regulation from the material needs of society, and thus provides an explanation of the fact that legal norms conform to the material needs of particular social classes'.[4] This is not a bad start. But to proceed beyond a nebulous left functionalism, the content of law must be considered a content of a particular form.

Pashukanis's is a theory of the legal form, but it does not follow that it is *inimical* to examinations of particular legal contents.[5] Even one of his critics observes that '[t]he theoretical achievement of Pashukanis . . . has been to steer a course between the fetishism of form and the fetishism of content'.[6] He left the mechanisms of the relation between form and content, however, unexamined. It is this which lays him open to the criticism that there is no space for the politics of law – the politics of legal content – in his work.

This lacuna can best be addressed from within the theory itself. After all, while politicising laws does not undermine the understanding of the legal form, only with a correct understanding of the legal form can the processes of legal 'politicking' be made sense of.

One of Pashukanis's modern followers puts the case succinctly.

> Pashukanis is criticized for overlooking the role of the law as an instrument of class domination in the hands of the capitalist class. Against this, two things should be noted. The main form of class domination in capitalism, according to Marx, is that which results from exclusive ownership of means of production by some while the rest effectively own nothing but their labor-power. Pashukanis's theory shows nicely how the law serves this form of domination all the while appearing to protect naturally the property right of worker and capitalist alike. As for the further uses or abuses of the law by the holders of power, Pashukanis aims to give us only the general structure the law will have. It [sic] does not deny that within that structure those with the power to do so will use the law to serve their own ends.[7]

---

[3] Pashukanis 1978, p. 55.
[4] Ibid.
[5] As implied, for example, in Warrington 1984.
[6] Fine 1979, p. 34.
[7] Reiman 1995, pp. 134–135.

Jessop is more forthright.

> Pashukanis has . . . been charged with ignoring the major part played by repression in the legal order and the bourgeois state. This charge is . . . unjustified. For, not only does Pashukanis fully subscribe (whether rightly or wrongly) to the Marxist-Leninist view of the state as a machine for class-repression and emphasize the role of *raison d'état* and naked expediency in certain areas of its operation . . ., he also provides an explicit account of the self-contradictory appearance of law as subjective freedom coupled with external regulation and, indeed, tends to give greater weight to the role of organized violence than to individual will in the sphere of public law. . . .[8]

It would be excessively simplistic to consider Pashukanis's a theory of law as an empty bottle into which any content can be poured. That would be to conceptualise content and form as separate, isolated qualities of a social formation, and to fail to understand the dialectical interrelation between the two. As Chris Arthur puts it,

> [f]rom a dialectical point of view a form is the form of its content, and one may be alarmed at the outset if one imagines that Pashukanis proposes to write a treatise on legal forms in abstraction from content. However this would be a misunderstanding. In characterising law as a *bourgeois* form he clearly *is* relating law to a definite material content – the social relations founded on commodity exchange.[9]

However, two more steps must be taken. One is to remember that the social relations of capitalism are not simply the 'social relations founded on commodity exchange', but are *also* social relations of exploitative inequality embedded in the wage relation. The development of the legal form to take account of the wage-form is germane here. I have argued that the commodity-form of labour-power under capitalism allows that commodity – contra Pashukanis – to be subsumed within the legal form itself. Therefore, as the legal form embodies the concrete content of social relations founded on commodity exchange, where labour-power itself is universally commodified, under capitalism, the legal form will also embed the particular exploitative class relations of capitalist exploitation. This is not *in addition* to embodying the

[8] Jessop 1990, p. 60.
[9] Arthur 1978, p. 29.

abstract formal equality of simple commodity exchange. It is *in so doing* under the particular conditions of capitalism, in that the wage-form, the seat of exploitation, is brought into the realm of the juridical as a commodity-form.

However, these derivations remain at a very abstract level: there are many different ways the social relations of capitalism can be made manifest in laws. And that manifestation may not be one-sidedly in the interests of capital: class struggle is intrinsic to capitalism, and the attempt to 'domesticate' resistance means that 'progressive' laws may be passed at times of working-class strength – although those laws may may be turned to the advantage of capital. Marx's discussion of legislation to limit the working day, for example, shows how although the laws were driven by working-class pressure, they also drove capital to improve its productive capacities.[10]

Marx's discussion of factory legislation is important not only in his discussion of how laws are rarely straightforwardly 'for' or 'against' a particular class. More crucially, he lays out in inchoate form a theory of the imposition of particular contents into the legal form.

> The capitalist maintains his right as a purchaser when he tries to make the working day as long as possible. . . . On the other hand . . . the worker maintains his right as a seller when he wishes to reduce the working day to a particular normal length. There is here, therefore, an antinomy, of right against right, both equally bearing the seal of the law of exchange. *Between equal rights, force decides.*[11]

Marx has disentangled Reiman's point that 'those with the power to do so will use the law to serve their own ends'[12] into two separate arguments. One is that it is very likely that the powerful will be able to accommodate or co-opt whatever progressive intentions are embedded in a particular law. The other, more fundamental point, is that it is usually the representatives of the powerful who actually make the laws, who force particular political contents into the abstract legal form. If 'force decides', after all, then it is not an equal battle between capital and labour. Within the boundaries of a nation-state,

---

[10] Marx 1976, pp. 604–607. 'The inconveniences we expected to arise from the introduction of the Factory acts into our branch of manufacture, I am happy to say, have not arisen,' he quotes one industrialist as saying. 'We do not find the production at all interfered with; in short we produce more in the same time.' (Marx 1976, p. 606.)

[11] Marx 1976, p. 344. Emphasis mine.

[12] Reiman 1995, p. 135.

capital has on its side the legislature, an arm of the bourgeois state. It is the judicial wing of the state that is, institutionally, given the power to force a particular content into the legal form.

Why does the state and law take the side of capital? One obvious reason, stressed by Miliband, might be the class position of the judiciary.

> [J]udicial elites, like other elites of the state system, are mainly drawn from the upper and middle layers of society: and those judges who are not have clearly come to belong to these layers by the time they reach the bench. Moreover, the conservative bias which their class situation is thus likely to create is here strongly reinforced by the fact that judges are . . . also recruited from the legal profession, whose ideological dispositions are traditionally cast in a highly conservative mould. . . . Moreover, governments which are generally in charge of the appointment and promotion of judges are most likely to favour men of precisely such conservative dispositions. . . . The reason why these ideological dispositions are important is obvious – they greatly affect the manner in which the judicial function is discharged. Judges, it is generally accepted, are not 'law-vending machines', or the helpless prisoners of a set legal framework or the mere exponents of the law as they find it. . . . [T]here is room, inevitably, for judicial discretion in the application of the law and for judicial creativity in actually making law. . . . In thus interpreting and making law, judges cannot fail to be deeply affected by their view of the world. . . .[13]

There is little to disagree with there, so far as it goes. The problem with Miliband's position is his unconvincing implication that the capitalist nature of the bourgeois state (and judiciary) is essentially contingent to its structure, and inheres solely or even primarily in the attitudes of its agents.

However, Miliband's point that the judiciary is in a position to *make* law is absolutely right, and dovetails perfectly with McDougal's stress on the creative role of interpretation of statute in international law. Within the confines of a nation, it is the state as superordinate authority and its agents that have final authority over the interpretation – and hence creation – of law. *This is not the case with international law*, and the implications of that difference will become clear.

If we reject Miliband's theory of the state, while acknowledging that state's monopoly on authoritative legal interpretation domestically, the question of

---

[13] Miliband 1969, pp. 124–6.

how to understand the capitalist state becomes very important, to make sense of the final arbiter of law domestically and the very *unit* of law internationally. The scope of this enormous debate can only be touched on here. One aspect of this state debate, though, is centrally important to this chapter: Pashukanis himself is often seen as a founding figure of a particular theory of the state.

2. Pashukanis and state-derivation theory

The claim is that as part of his theory of law, Pashukanis articulated a theory of the bourgeois state. Writers associated with what is understood as his position are sometimes known as the 'capital logic' or 'state derivation' school – although those so gathered disagree on many issues, they are united by an abstract methodological starting point.

> The principal concern of the so-called 'capital logic' school is to derive the *form* of the capitalist state from the nature of capital and/or to establish those *functional prerequisites* of accumulation whose satisfaction must be mediated through state activity.[14]

Pashukanis's status as a patron saint of this school is widely accepted, whatever one thinks of the school itself,[15] because it is claimed that he 'tried to derive the specific historical form of bourgeois law *and its associated state* from the essential qualities of commodity circulation under capitalism'.[16]

If this is correct, then there is in the heart of Pashukanis's own theory a model of that coercive body with monopoly power over domestic legal regulation. If the legal form is made concrete through the coercive powers of the bourgeois state, and if the bourgeois state is derived through the same social relations as law, a neat circularity emerges. This would clearly answer the charge that Pashukanis fails to theorise the political – that is, the coercive aspects of law.

---

[14] Jessop 1990, p. 52.

[15] Von Arx 1997, p. 6. 'The "capital logic" school in Germany is perhaps most directly indebted to Pashukanis's work'. For essential overviews see Holloway and Picciotto 1978a; Clarke 1991. For a brief summary see (for example) Barrow 2000, pp. 93–100.

[16] Jessop 1990, p. 52, emphasis mine. Holloway and Picciotto 1978b, p. 18: 'Pashukanis ... was concerned to derive the form of law and the closely related form of the state from the nature of capitalist commodity production'. Barrow repeats the claim (2000, p. 99).

The starting point for many of the state-derivationists is Pashukanis's formulation of the question:

> [W]hy does class rule not remain what it is, the factual subjugation of one section of the population by the other? Why does it assume the form of official state rule, or – which is the same thing – why does the machinery of state coercion not come into being as the private machinery of the ruling class; why does it detach itself from the ruling class and take on the form of an impersonal apparatus of public power, separate from society?[17]

The argument is that Pashukanis derives the bourgeois state, with its apparent neutrality, its irreducibility to a set of particularistic interests, from the necessities of generalised commodification. Given the universalisation of abstract legal individuals, only an abstract arbiter of competing claims – the bourgeois state – can maintain their formal equality. Jessop summarises the position admirably. In the context of his theory of the legal subject,

> Pashukanis tried to derive the form of the bourgeois state as an impersonal apparatus of public power distinct from the private sphere of civil society. He argued that the legal form of the *Rechtstaat* (or constitutional state based on the rule of law) characteristic of bourgeois societies is required by the nature of market relations among free, equal individuals. These must be mediated, supervised and guaranteed by an abstract collective subject endowed with the authority to enforce rights in the interests of all parties to legal transactions.[18]

Much of the 'derivationist' theory is fascinating and theoretically fecund.[19] The question, however, is whether Pashukanis's theory of law and his apparent theory of the state are truly inextricable. We should start by examining those statements where Pashukanis appears to 'derive' the state most clearly.

> Effective power acquires a markedly juridical, public character, as soon as relations arise in addition to and independently of it, in connection with the act of exchange, that is to say, private relations par excellence. By appearing as a guarantor, authority becomes social and public, an authority representing the impersonal interest of the system.[20]

---

[17] Pashukanis 1978, p. 139.
[18] Jessop 1990, p. 53.
[19] Particularly the essays in Halloway and Picciotto 1978a, especially Hirsch 1978, Blanke, Jürgens and Kastendiek 1978, and von Braunmühl 1978.
[20] Pashukanis 1978, p. 137.

> To the extent that society represents a market, the machinery of state is actually manifested as an impersonal collective will, as the rule of law, and so on. Every buyer and seller is, as we have already seen, a legal subject par excellence. The autonomous will of those engaged in exchange is an indispensable precondition wherever the categories of value and exchange value come into play. . . . Coercion as the imperative addressed by one person to another, and backed up by force, contradicts the fundamental precondition for dealings between the owners of commodities. In a society of commodity owners, and within the limits of the act of exchange, coercion is neither abstract nor impersonal – hence it cannot figure as a social function. For in the society based on commodity production, subjection to one person, as a concrete individual, implies subjection to an arbitrary force, since it is the same thing, for this society, as the subjection of one owner of commodities to another. That is also why coercion cannot appear here in undisguised form as a simple act of expediency. It has to appear rather as coercion emanating from an abstract collective person, exercised not in the interest of the individual from whom it emanates . . . but in the interest of all parties to legal transactions.[21]

The theory as outlined is intuitively appealing. It makes sense as an explanation for why it is functional for capitalism to have an abstract state authority guaranteeing the legal form, and in so doing, giving that form concrete content. However, Pashukanis does not see the state itself as *logically necessary* for capitalism.

Most of the claims made in his chapter on 'Law and the State'[22] are historical and more or less contingent, rather than rigorously logical and necessary. For example: 'thanks to its new role as guarantor of the peace indispensable to the exchange transaction, feudal authority took on a hue which had hitherto been alien to it: it went *public*'.[23] This may be so, just as it may be that feudal power's new role as an abstract state made it peculiarly suited to be the arbiter of laws, but this is not a statement about the necessity or derivation of the bourgeois state form.

There are other formulations like this: '[t]he "modern" state (in the bourgeois sense) comes into being at that point in time when the organisation of

[21] Pashukanis 1978, p. 143.
[22] Pashukanis 1978, pp. 134–50.
[23] Pashukanis 1978, p. 136. Emphasis in original.

power by groups or classes encompasses a sufficiently expanded activity in market transactions'.[24] 'Thus there arises, besides direct, unmediated class rule, indirect, reflected rule in the shape of official state power as a distinct authority, detached from society'.[25] These claims may be true. But they are historical and suggestive, rather than a systematic theory of state derivation.

And nor were they intended to be. At the very heart of his supposed derivation, after he has asked the 'classical question'[26] as to why class dominance takes on the form of an impersonal mechanism, Pashukanis takes inadequate theories to task:

> It is not enough to confine ourselves to pointing out that it is *advantageous* to the ruling class to erect an ideological smokescreen, and to conceal its hegemony beneath the umbrella of the state. For although such an elucidation is undoubtedly correct, it still does not explain how such an ideology *could* arise, nor, therefore, does it explain why the ruling class *has access* to it.[27]

Thus at the very point when he is demanding rigour in theorising the state, what he insists must be explained is how the abstract bourgeois state *could*, not 'did' or 'must', arise. He is thus demanding a *sufficient*, not a necessary, theory of the bourgeois state. Thus despite his own use of the term 'derivation', this is not a strong 'derivationist' theory.

None of this is to deny that there is a powerful functional role to the abstract bourgeois state, nor to deny that Pashukanis's theory does an excellent job of outlining why. But it is to say that there is no theory of *the* form of *the* bourgeois state to be 'derived' from Pashukanis's theory, and nor did he think there was.

Consider a revealing aside. Again, at the heart of his apparently most 'derivationist' moment, as Pashukanis asks why the state apparatus is not 'a private apparatus of the ruling class' but 'an impersonal apparatus of public power distinct from society',[28] a footnote draws attention.

> In our time of intensified revolutionary struggle we can observe how the official apparatus of the bourgeois state recedes into the background in

[24] Ibid.
[25] Pashukanis 1978, p. 138.
[26] Blanke, Jürgens and Kastendiek 1978, p. 121.
[27] Pashukanis 1978, pp. 139–40. Emphases mine.
[28] Pashukanis 1980a, p. 94.

> comparison with the 'voluntary guards' of the fascists and their ilk. This once more shows that when social equilibrium is disrupted it then 'seeks salvation', not by creation of 'an authority standing above classes', but by the maximum pressure of the forces of the struggling classes.[29]

Thus there is nothing inevitable about the particular form of the bourgeois state. Even as he stresses the importance of the 'abstract' bourgeois state, Pashukanis reminds the reader that in particular historical conjunctures *that very state* will seek alternative, altogether less abstract methods to achieve its ends, without ceasing to be a capitalist state: it is the 'official apparatus' that recedes, not the state itself, which in this instance is the very body 'seeking salvation' through recourse to fascism.

There are admittedly times when Pashukanis makes stronger claims for the derivation taking place. The long passage above where he talks about the coercion necessary under capitalism and why it must take the bourgeois state form more than any other represents his attempt logically and systematically to derive the necessity for an abstract state. But it is based on a false premise.

'Coercion', he writes, 'as the imperative addressed by one person to another, and backed up by force, contradicts the fundamental precondition for dealings between the owners of commodities.'[30] This is *absolutely untrue,* and is a characteristic slip – sometimes Pashukanis's excessive formalism lead him to neglect the 'succulence' of dialectical contradictions inherent in seemingly stable categories.

I have argued that contrary to some of Pashukanis's claims, disputation and contestation is intrinsic to the commodity, in the fact that its private ownership implies the exclusion of others. Similarly, violence – coercion – is at the heart of the commodity form, and thus the contract. For a commodity meaningfully to be 'mine-not-yours' – which is, after all, central to the fact that it is a commodity to be exchanged – some forceful capabilities are implied. If there were nothing to defend its 'mine-ness', there would be nothing to stop it becoming 'yours', and then it would no longer be a commodity, as I would not be exchanging it. Coercion is implicit. 'If the category of contract, a joint act of will founded on mutual recognition, is considered to be the

29 Pashukanis 1980a, p. 130 footnote 47.
30 Pashukanis 1978, p. 143.

original modus of law, then it is clearly a form that cannot exist without constraint.'[31]

And at a slightly higher level of concreteness, taking the analysis from the individual to the societal level, force must be a general condition for the maintenance of commodity relations.

> The reason is plain enough. Existing property relations [ie., *not yet* productive relations] systematically *separate producers from the objects of their need*, on an everyday and continuous basis. In commodity production, 'need' and 'right' stand opposed. The organisation of existing society constantly *impels* individuals, groups, classes and other collectivities towards . . . the 'invasion of the rights of others'. The motive to trespass, steal, invade, oppress, rob and generally transgress property right is continually recreated through the pressure of material need.
>
> Hence this system of social production relations generates a permanent and general requirement for means of 'defence', i.e. for means of violence and its organization. Without a constant threat and/or application of force, commodity production would stand in danger of rapid subversion and breakdown.[32]

In other words, and contrary to a claim Pashukanis makes, coercion backed by force is implied in a generalised form *and* 'addressed by one person to another' – ie. by all owners of commodities to all other owners of commodities – *in the very nature of commodity exchange and production*. For Barker, as the violence itself appears more fundamental – at the heart of the commodity – '[t]he *social organisation* of necessary force and the specific matter of the *state* still await further development'.[33]

In other words, the anomalous passage where Pashukanis does appear to see the abstract state as necessary is only a function of his occasional

---

[31] Blanke, Jürgens and Kastendiek 1978, p. 123. See Banaji 2003, p. 69: 'When is a contract "voluntary"? The answer is, probably never.' At its most extreme, such 'coercive contract' underlies the nineteenth-century notion of a 'large group of slavery defenders' in the American south that slavery itself 'had a quasi-contractual character' (Jenkins 1935, p. 112). These writers such as Samuel Seabury, Edmund Bellinger and others problematise these apparently peaceful categories (moved, of course, by appalling political motivations. Not that it is new for Marxists to turn the theories of pro-slavery writers against bourgeois categories – see Negri's invocation of John Caldwell Calhoun (Negri 1999, pp. 184–5)).

[32] Barker 1998, p. 27.

[33] Barker 1998, p. 28.

erroneous claims that violence is not at the heart of the commodity (I shall show that elsewhere in his writing, he maintains a far more persuasive awareness of embedded violence). In the realisation that violence *is* integral to commodity exchange, 'politics' – coercive force, violence – is brought *closer*, but its *specific form* – here the bourgeois state – is not so fundamental, and certainly not 'necessary'.

For the most part, then, Pashukanis explicitly lays out that his is not a systematic derivationist position, but only one of sufficiency. What is more, at the point where he does attempt to derive the state's necessity, his analysis breaks down because his categories are insufficiently nuanced. Some of the most interesting state-derivationist theorists acknowledge that Pashukanis's theory asserts the necessity of politics but does not imply the bourgeois state form. His focus on the freedom and equality of the subjects of exchange, they claim

> lead . . . to the category of the *form of law* and to the necessity of a force to guarantee the law, a force which we will call *extra-economic (coercive) force*. By this we mean not so much the organized apparatus (or an instrument) but essentially only a basic function which can be derived on the conceptual level of form analysis. With that we have by no means arrived at 'the state', but at different forms of social relations, namely economic and political relations, which are peculiar to the bourgeois mode of production.[34]

Pashukanis's theory does imply coercion and politics, but does not imply the necessity of a particular form of organisation of that coercion. The state certainly 'injects clarity and stability into the legal structure',[35] but that is a secondary function.

This rejection of the capital-logic theory of the state is important: it emerges that the very *lack* of a state-derivation theory in Pashukanis *key to understanding the nature of law and international law.*

3. (International) Law and the contingency of the state

Far from deriving the state, for Pashukanis the state as an abstract arbiter, a public authority, is in fact *contingent to the legal form.*[35] It is this that makes

[34] Blanke, Jürgens and Kastendiek 1978, p. 121.
[35] Pashukanis 1980a, p. 68.

him such a vital theorist for international law: he makes clear time and again that the lack of a sovereign does not make international law any less 'law'. Pashukanis does not deny the need for coercion, but is clear that *overarching* and *abstract* coercion, while it does 'inject stability' and is functional to capitalism that is not in crisis, is extrinsic to the legal form itself.

> It is obvious that the idea of external coercion, both in its idea and organization, constitutes an essential aspect of the legal form. When no coercive mechanism has been organized, and it is not found within the jurisdiction of a special apparatus which stands above the parties, it appears in the form of so-called 'inter-dependence'. The principle of inter-dependence, under the conditions of balance of power, represents the single, and it can be said, the most unstable basis of international law.[36]

In his neglected essay on international law (reproduced as appendix to this book), Pashukanis excoriates bourgeois jurisprudence for the amount of ink spilt on the question of whether the lack of a superordinate authority means international law is not law. He makes clear that such authority is not necessary or immanent to law.

> No matter how eloquently the existence of international law is proved, the fact of the absence of an organizational force, which could coerce a state with the same ease as a state coerces an individual person, remains a fact. The only real guarantee that the relationships between bourgeois states . . . will remain on the basis of equivalent exchange, i.e. on a legal basis (on the basis of the mutual recognition of subjects), is the real balance of forces.[37]

Unsurprisingly, each time Pashukanis points out the contingency of organised external coercion to law, international law is exemplary. Take the discussion in his chapter on 'Norm and Relation', which is probably the most lengthy and careful exposition of the case.

> [O]ne can modify the thesis (that norm and law can be equated) and emphasise, not the norm as such, but rather the objective regulative forces operating in society. . . . [I]f under that heading one means a particular, consciously

---

[36] Pashukanis 1980a, p. 108.

[37] Pashukanis 1980b, p. 179: below p. 331. This essay gives the lie to McWhinney's somewhat garbled argument concluding that 'Pashukanis . . . concluded that it was purely scholastic . . . to attempt to define the "nature" of international law' (McWhinney 1984, p. 14).

> organised system which guarantees and safeguards these relations, then the fallacy becomes absolutely clear. Of course one cannot assert that the relation between creditor and debtor is *generated* by the system of compulsory debt collection operating in the state in question. The objective existence of this system certainly *guarantees* and *safeguards* the relation, but it in no way creates it. . . . [O]ne can conceive of very different degrees of perfection in the functioning of this external coercive social regulation and consequently of the most varying degrees of guarantee of certain regulations . . ., without these relations themselves suffering the smallest variation in their substance. We can conceive of a borderline case in which, *apart from the two parties relating to one another, no other third force can determine a norm and guarantee its observance*: for example, any contract of the Varangians and the Greeks. Even in this case the relationship still remains in existence.[38]

From there Pashukanis goes into a revealing footnote.

> The entire feudal legal system rested on such contractual relations, guaranteed by no 'third force'. In just the same way, modern international law recognises no coercion organised from without. Such non-guaranteed legal relations are unfortunately not known for their stability, but this is not yet grounds for denying their existence.[39]

It is clear that Pashukanis sees overarching authority or any particular state form as contingent to the legal relationship inhering between two formally equal partners in the context of an exchange relationship. However, he goes further than this. For Pashukanis, law itself – in its earliest, embryonic form – is a product precisely of the *lack* of such an authority.

> The development of law as a system was evoked not by the requirements of the state, *but by the necessary conditions for commercial relations between those tribes which were not under a single sphere of authority*. . . . Commercial relations with foreign tribes, with nomads, and plebeians [in Rome] . . . ushered in the *ius gentium*, which was the prototype of the legal superstructure in its pure form. In contrast to the *ius civile*, with its undeviating and ponderous forms, the *ius gentium* discards all that is not connected with the goal – with the natural basis of the economic relation. . . . Gumplowicz . . .

[38] Pashukanis 1978, pp. 88–9. Initial three emphasese in original, final mine.
[39] Pashukanis 1978, p. 89 footnote 9.

> is mistaken in thinking that the system of private law could have developed . . . in a derivative fashion from public power.[40]

For the international legal scholar, this is a stunning theoretical illumination. The debate Pashukanis considers in his essay on international law has not, after all, gone away. '[T]he central preoccupation' for the discipline, and one to which the possibility of a 'theoretical response' has been 'rejected' by much modern legal theory,[41] is how, with the lack of a superordinate authority, international law can be law. *Pashukanis has here, in passing, solved the most tenacious problem of the legality of a decentralised legal system.*

For the commodity-form theory, international and domestic law are two moments of the same form. Pashukanis's claims that (proto-)international law historically predates domestic law have nothing to do with any putative ontological primacy of the international sphere: it is, rather, because law is thrown up by and necessary to a systematic commodity-exchange relationship, and it was between organised but disparate groups without superordinate authorities rather than between individuals that such relationships sprang up.[42]

---

[40] Pashukanis 1980a, p. 69. Emphasis mine.

[41] Kennedy 1996, p. 400. He goes on to explain that for most twentieth-century legal theory questions around this 'might be addressed doctrinally . . . or procedurally . . . or, more recently, institutionally, professionally, practically, ultimately by attention to the behavior of states, by pragmatic observation, but not theoretically'.

[42] This dovetails intriguingly with Richard Tuck's claim that for the early writers in international law and sovereignty, particularly Grotius and Hobbes, 'individuals heuristically took on the characteristics of sovereign states' (Tuck 1999, p. 129), and that for those writers 'we can best understand the rights which individuals possess *vis-à-vis* one another . . . by looking at the rights which sovereign states seem to possess against one another' (Tuck 1999, p. 85). For one sympathetic reviewer, '[t]his seems a far-fetched proposition', and '[i]t is one matter to establish a linkage between the notion of a sovereign, unsociable property owner within early modern societies and the sovereign, unsociable states under construction in this period . . . [b]ut it is another matter to give priority to the external rivalry of states. . . . This seems a perverse move' (Gowan 2001, p. 154). However, the cross-reference here with Pashukanis is at least suggestive. If it is agreed that the juridical conceptualisation of the individual is an indispensable element in the construction of the sovereign, unsociable individual, then Pashukanis's claim that the juridical unit first inheres between polities makes Tuck's proposition look less 'perverse': the juridical individual would indeed follow (from?) the juridical polity – by the time of these writers, crucially, the state (though questions of 'derivation' need to be nuanced: without a sense of the underlying marketisation of which these forms would be expressions, there is a danger (even in Tuck) of the process appearing to come about through a kind of autopoietic domestic-analogy-in-reverse). In this way, counterintuitively looking *first* at the international level before narrowing focus to the individual, we might make some headway with the project that Adorno literally dreamed of – understanding 'The Transition From the Living Human Being to the Legal Entity' (Halley 1997, p. 72).

Of course, this is only the germ-seed of international law. For Pashukanis, '[t]he Treaty of Westphalia [in 1648] . . . is considered the basic fact in the historical development of modern (i.e. bourgeois) international law'.[43] Pashukanis does not provide a theoretically informed history of international law – his historical pronouncements are useful but schematic. He makes it clear, though, that 'the state only fully becomes the subject of international law as the bourgeois state'.[44]

On one level this is tautologous: the modern notion of the 'international' is inextricable from the development of the nation-state, an essentially modern (capitalist) form. To that extent international law is definitionally a capitalist form. However, what Pashukanis is stressing is that with this epoch lie the changes that underly 'the theory of the state as the sole subject of the international legal community'.[45] In other words, what we might call *proto*-international law, the legal form regulating relationships between organised social groups, predates capitalism and the bourgeois state. Only when the bourgeois state becomes the central subject of those relations can we with full justification call them international law: that is when the 'international' is born. But *the form of the relations* already existed.

> As a separate force which set itself off from society, the state only finally emerged in the modern bourgeois capitalist period. But it by no means follows from this that the contemporary forms of international legal intercourse, and the individual institutions of international law, only arose in the most recent times. On the contrary, they trace their history to the most ancient periods of class and even pre-class society. To the extent that exchange was not initially made between individuals, but among tribes and communities, it may be affirmed that the institutions of international law are the most ancient of legal institutions in general.[46]

Thus the state is central to the *development* of law, both domestic and international, but not to the legal form itself.[47]

---

[43] Pashukanis 1980b, p. 174. Page 326 below

[44] Pashukanis 1980b, p. 174. Page 327 below.

[45] Pashukanis 1980b, pp. 173–4. Page 326 below.

[46] Pashukanis 1980b, p. 175. Page 327 below.

[47] Though arguing from a perspective of radical 'libertarianism' wildly antipathetic to Pashukanis's Marxism, suffering philosophical deficiencies (such as the apparent equation of 'justice' and 'law'), and marshalling his evidence to support an indefensible and utopian position of anarcho-capitalism space precludes me from critiquing here, Benson 1991 contains several interesting examples of legal systems without over-

4. (International) Law, politics and violence

There is a conundrum for Pashukanis. On the one hand he stresses the 'lawness' of legal relationships without superordinate authorities. On the other, we have seen that at one point he alleges that coercion 'as the imperative addressed by one person to another, and backed up by force' is inimicable to commodity relations.[48] *Law*, on the other hand, clearly requires force, as Pashukanis makes clear.[49] Where, then, does the coercive violence in law without an abstract state come from?

I have argued against Pashukanis that violence and coercion *are* immanent in the commodity relationship itself. If this is accepted, the conundrum disappears as it is clear that in legal systems without superordinate authorities self-help – the coercive violence of the legal subjects themselves – regulates the legal relation. The importance of this solution to Pashukanis's paradox cannot be overstated. It is key to understanding the mechanisms of international law and the legal form, and is at the heart of the analysis of international law and imperialism in Chapter Six below.

It is also clear that notwithstanding his own occasional comments to the contrary, Pashukanis throughout his work – particularly when discussing international law – understood that this was the nature of legal coercion without a superordinate force. He cites 'inter-dependence' or 'reciprocity' 'under the conditions of the balance of power'[50] or 'the real balance of forces'[51] – a backdrop of force-mediated relations – as at the basis of international legal regulation.

In fact, Pashukanis's understanding of the interpenetration of coercive force and the legal form is deep and systematic, and is not isolated to his discussions of international law. Contradicting his own assertion that coercion is antipathetic to the commodity relationship, for example, he claims that

> [l]egal intercourse does not 'naturally' presuppose a state of peace just as trade does not . . . preclude armed robbery, but *goes hand in hand with it*. Law

---

arching (state) authority, which dovetail suggestively with Pashukanis's analysis of state-contingency.

[48] Pashukanis 1978, p. 143.

[49] Pashukanis 1980a, p. 108 and elsewhere. '[T]he idea of external coercion . . . constitutes an essential aspect of the legal form'.

[50] Pashukanis 1980a, p. 108.

[51] Pashukanis 1980b, p. 179. Page 331 below.

> and self-help, those seemingly contradictory concepts are, in reality, extremely closely linked.[52]

To understand, as Pashukanis clearly does, that robbery (non-consensual possession of another's commodity) goes 'hand in hand' with trade (consensual exchange of commodities), is to understand that violence is implicit in the commodity, and therefore legal, form. If 'mine' implies force to keep it from becoming 'yours', then robbery is the failure of that force, and the success of someone else's. For Pashukanis 'order is actually a mere tendency and end result (by no means perfected at that), but never the point of departure and prerequisite of legal intercourse'.[53]

Compared to this, and mindful that an awareness of the centrality of coercion to the law is not restricted to radical theorists but has been part of some 'mainstream' legal philosophy since at least the late nineteenth century,[54] the signal failure of much mainstream international law to make sense of sanctions and violence is marked. Though there are of course exceptions, scholars for whom '[c]oercion accompanies law like a shadow',[55] one senses in much writing on this topic a petulance at the very tenacity of this problem, and a concomitant evasion of analysis dressed up as a high-minded refusal to be bogged down in vulgar details. 'It is clear . . .' says Shearer, for example,

> that a complete explanation of . . . [international law's] binding force, embracing all cases and conditions, is hardly practicable. Indeed, there is something pedantic in the very notion that such a comprehensive explanation is necessary or desirable.[56]

This collapse of analysis reaches astonishing levels of crudity.

> Apart from the sanctions and pressures . . . the main elements reinforcing the obligatory character of the rules of international law are the empirical facts that states will insist on their rights under such rules against states which they consider should observe them, and that states recognise international law as binding upon them. . . . The ultimate reasons that impel states to uphold the observance of international law belong to the domain of political science, and cannot be explained by a strictly legal analysis.[57]

---

[52] Pashukanis 1978, p. 134. Emphasis mine.
[53] Pashukanis 1978, p. 135.
[54] See Jhering 1924, pp. 176–218 and elsewhere.
[55] Zoller 1984, p. xi.
[56] Shearer 1994, p. 27.
[57] Ibid.

Shearer alleges that the binding force of international law inheres in the fact that states observe it. This statement of the fact to be explained as its own explanational is clearly nonsensical. As if aware that this is unsatisfactory, Shearer wanly dismisses this question as one for political science *rather than* law. He is quite right to conclude his chapter by observing that 'the problem of the binding force of international law ultimately resolves itself into a problem no different from that of the obligatory character of law in general',[58] but as he has precluded any examination of the systematicity of violence in law or international law, he cannot even approach an answer.

Similarly, Akehurst claims that

> [i]t is unsound to study any legal system in terms of sanctions. It is better to study law as a body of rules which are usually obeyed, not to concentrate exclusively on what happens when the rules are broken. *We must not confuse the pathology of law with law itself.*[59]

Here the failure of analysis is stark. The notion that breaches of law, disputes moderated by coercion, are pathological to law, rather than fundamental elements of the legal fabric, is remarkable. In contrast, Pashukanis casually makes this clear.

> *Russkaya Pravda* . . . consists of 43 articles. . . . Only two articles do not relate to violations of criminal or civil law. The remaining articles either determine a sanction, or else contain the procedural rules applicable when a rule has been violated. Accordingly, *deviation from a norm always constitutes their premise.*[60]

Law and violence are inextricably linked *as regulators of sovereign claims.* Pashukanis can therefore square two seemingly opposed points of view in Marx. One is the stress on juridical equality and exchange of equivalents. The other is Marx's claim '[e]ven club law is law'.[61] Mediating these two conceptions, and a solution to Pashukanis's paradox outlined above, is that other remark of Marx's: *'between equal rights, force decides'*.[62]

---

[58] Ibid.

[59] Akehurst 1987, p. 7. Emphasis mine.

[60] Pashukanis 1980a, p. 110. Emphasis mine.

[61] Marx quoted in Pashukanis 1978, p. 134. The original is in Marx 1973, p. 88. In this translation, it reads '[t]he principle of might makes right . . . is also a legal relation'. I have chosen the former as the starker formulation.

[62] Marx 1976, p. 344. Emphasis mine.

On the one hand law is an abstract relationship between two equals, on the other Marx claims the naked imposition of power as a legal form. 'This is not a paradox', Pashukanis makes clear as 'law, like exchange, is an expedient resorted to by isolated social elements in their intercourse with one another'[63] – as is violence. In the absence of an abstract 'third force', the only regulatory violence capable of upholding the legal form, and of filling it with particular content, *is the violence of one of the participants.*

This is why '[l]aw and self-help . . . are, in reality, extremely closely linked'.[64] And that is why, Pashukanis points out, in the absence of a sovereign, '[m]odern international law includes a very considerable degree of self-help (retaliatory measures, reprisals, war and so on)'.[65]

Violence is intrinsic to law, but it is in the absence of a sovereign that the violence retains its *particularistic,* rather than abstract impersonal (state) character. Pashukanis expresses this in an extremely important passage.

> [T]he armed individual, (or, more often, group of people, a family group, a clan, a tribe, capable of defending their conditions of existence in armed struggle), is the morphological precursor of the legal subject with his sphere of legal power extending around him. This close morphological link establishes a clear connection between the lawcourt and the duel, between the parties to a lawsuit and the combatants in an armed conflict. But as socially regulative forces become more powerful, so the subject loses material tangibility. His personal energy is supplanted by the power of social, that is, of class organisation, whose highest form of expression is the state.[66]

Where there are no such 'socially regulative forces', that coercion *remains embedded in the participants.* International legal theory stresses self-help as the medium of sanction in international law.[67] The morphological proximity of the legal subject and the armed unit is nowhere more clear than in international law.

Unsurprisingly given this proximity of law and force, 'the better part' of international law's 'norms refer to . . . warfare. . . . [I]t directly assumes a condition of open and armed struggle'.[68] These laws, concerned with regulating

---

[63] Pashukanis 1978, p. 134.
[64] Ibid.
[65] Ibid.
[66] Pashukanis 1978, p. 118.
[67] Akehurst 1970, p. 6; Kelsen 1968, p. 88; et al.
[68] Pashukanis 1980b, p. 169. Page 322 below.

the political violence of states, are surely 'public' law: indeed, what is usually meant by 'international law' is precisely 'public international law'.[69] I have shown that for the commodity-form theory international law represents in some ways a simpler form of the legal relationship , and yet it consists of 'public' law which Pashukanis claims is secondary and derived from 'private' law. This may look like a paradox for the commodity-form theory.

However, for Pashukanis, in the absence of a sovereign authority, *precisely because* the coercive violence inherent in the commodity/legal relationship between abstract equals must inhere in the participants themselves, 'public' political relations *are* exchange relations. The public and the private are inextricable here. Inasmuch as the units of the legal relationship are formally equal, 'the struggle between imperialist states must include an exchange as one of its components. And if exchanges are concluded then forms must also exist for their conclusion'[70] – which means violence.

For international law, then, the question of the 'derivation' of public from private law is nonsensical. This interpenetration is why '[t]he development of the law of war is nothing other than the gradual consolidation of the principle of the inviolability of bourgeois property'.[71]

Without a third force – ie., precisely in its simpler form – the legal form could not actualise the coercion necessary for its existence outside of the coercive capabilities of the participants. It is true, in other words, that private law is the basis of public law, as we now perceive them from within a state, separated from each other, but that very distinction is only meaningful as a result of that state's superimposition onto the legal form. In its root form – and in international law – the law was *simultaneously abstract and particularistic* – 'public' and 'private'. 'There was no distinction', Pashukanis says of early law without a third force, and thus of international law, 'between law as an objective norm and law as a power'.[72]

4.1. *Form, content, economics and politics in international law*

I have tried to show how the legal form inheres between the subjects of international law. What of the content of international law?

---

[69] See for example Akehurst 1970, p. 1: 'International law (otherwise known as public international law or the law of nations) . . .'

[70] Pashukanis 1980b, p. 169. Page 322 below.

[71] Pashukanis 1980a, p. 128 footnote 30.

[72] Pashukanis 1980a, p. 44.

Chris Arthur's assertion that the form is the form of its content implies that the content of domestic law under capitalism is – at an abstract level – that of class exploitation based on surplus extraction in production, and the concomitant class struggle. These, however, are not the relations between the units of international law, states themselves.

In his essay on international law, Pashukanis makes clear what these relations are, and therefore what is the social content of international law. 'The historical examples adduced in any textbook of international law loudly proclaim that *modern international law is the legal form of the struggle of the capitalist states among themselves for domination over the rest of the world*.'[73] It is that 'struggle of capitalist states among themselves' that is the 'real historical content hidden behind' the legal form.[74]

The 'real content' of law at this level is still very abstract. There are various methods by which that 'real content' could be fleshed out through the legal form into particular laws. We must take the analysis nearer the concrete.

For Pashukanis the formalisation of the state as the subject of international law was the flipside of the process by which the state finally consolidated its role as the abstract 'third force' for regulating the legal form internally. Although on the one hand the bourgeoisie 'subordinated itself to the state machine',[75] at the same time that very state machine acts *for* its 'national-capital'.

On the interests being pursued by the capitalist states, Pashukanis quotes Lenin's *Imperialism* approvingly[76] (although unaccountably ending his quote just before the nub of the matter):

> The epoch of modern capitalism shows us that certain relations are established between capitalist alliances, *based* on the economic division of the world; while parallel with this fact and in connection with it, certain relations are established between political alliances, between states, on the basis of the territorial division of the world, of the struggle for colonies, of the 'struggle for economic territory'.[77]

Now for Lenin, it is the particular interpenetration of *late, cartelised* and *monopoly* capital with the state that leads to the twentieth century's direct

---

[73] Pashukanis 1980b, p. 169. Emphasis in original. Page 322 below.
[74] Pashukanis 1980b, p. 169. Page 322 below.
[75] Pashukanis 1980b, p. 174. Page 327 below.
[76] Pashukanis 1980b, pp. 169–170. Pages 322–3 below.
[77] Lenin 1939, p. 75.

expropriation of territory in colonialism and war. The ramifications of this analysis for international law are developed in Chapter Six below. Here I will only briefly point out that despite the historical particularity of Lenin's theory, it is more generally true that the struggle between capitalists is based on the economic division of the world, and the fact that that economic division will be brought about politically by the state, which relies in turn on the capitalist economic system.

This is of course not a systematic theory of the capitalist state, but it is a preliminary theoretical justification for the intuition that the struggle between capitalist states is more than a struggle between states that happen to have capitalist economies. It is a struggle *for* resources *for capital*. That is what makes the state a capitalist state. This is not a return to 'capital logic', but nor is it to imply that what limited 'autonomy' the state has allows it to forget the needs of its capitals – the 'structural interdependence' means that the state's 'own revenues and its own ability to defend itself against other states depend . . . on the continuation of capital accumulation'.[78]

If we agree with Pashukanis, therefore, that the 'real historical content of international law . . . is the struggle between capitalist states',[79] that content is an ongoing and remorseless struggle for control over the resources of capitalism, that will often *as part of that capitalist ('economic') competitive process* spill into 'political' violence.

> [E]ven those agreements between capitalist states which appear to be directed to the general interests are, in fact, for each of the participants a means for jealously protecting their particular interests, preventing the expansion of their rivals' influence, thwarting unilateral conquest, i.e. in another form continuing the same struggle which will exist for as long as capitalist competition exists.[80]

What has emerged is a fascinating circularity. Capitalism is based on commodity exchange, and I have tried to show that such exchange contains violence immanently. However, the universalisation of such exchange has tended to lead to the abstraction of the state as a 'third force' to stabilise the relations. Thus politics and economics have been separated. *In the same moment,*

---

[78] Harman 1991, pp. 13, 15.
[79] Pashukanis 1980b, p. 172. Page 325 below.
[80] Pashukanis 1980b, p. 170. Page 323 below.

the flipside of that separation and the creation of a public political body was the investiture of that body – the state – as the *subject* of those legal relations which had long inhered between political entities, and which now became bourgeois international law. But that process itself necessitated the self-regulation of the legal relation internationally by its subjects; this self-help was a simultaneously 'political' and 'economic' function. This is, then, a manifestation of *the collapse of the distinction between politics and economics inherent in the very dynamic which had separated them.*

We have identified the social relations which make up the content of international law as the competition between capitalist states. We have also seen that might makes right, that the necessary coercive force will be held by the participants to the legal relations. And, of course, it will not be held equally.

> [B]ourgeois international law in principle recognizes that states have equal rights yet in reality they are unequal in their significance and their power. For instance, each state is formally free to select the means which it deems necessary to apply in the case of infringements of its right: 'however, *when a major state lets it be known that it will meet injury with the threat of, or the direct use of force, a small state merely offers passive resistance or is compelled to concede.*' These dubious benefits of formal equality are not enjoyed by those nations which have not developed capitalist civilization and which engage in international intercourse not as subjects, but as objects of the imperialist states' colonial policy.[81]

Although here talking about formal colonialism, a topic developed below, we can easily translate Pashukanis's observation into a more general one about the behaviour of capitalist states in their interactions. The fact is that although both parties are formally equal, they have unequal access to the means of coercion, and are not therefore equally able to determine either the *policing* or the *content* of the law.

Given that the legal form is the same in international and domestic law, it is clear that the indeterminacy previously outlined is inherent in that form *tout court*, something about which Pashukanis is clear.[82] The apparent 'deter-

[81] Pashukanis 1980b, p. 178. Pages 330–1 below. The quote (in italics – emphasis mine) is from V.E. Grabar 1912, *The Basis of Equality between States in Modern International Law*, Moscow: Publishing House of the Ministry of Foreign Affairs.

[82] Pashukanis 1980a, p. 59. 'The dogma of private law is nothing more than an endless chain of arguments *pro* and *contra* imaginary claims and potential suits.'

minacy' of legal content in domestic law is solely a product of the fact that internally the state has a monopoly on legitimate violence. As it is only effective law that can meaningfully be considered law in materialist terms, the policing of the law in accordance with the state judiciary's edicts as to content grants that state a monopoly on legitimate interpretation.

Without that third force the policing of the form and therefore its interpretation – its investiture with particular content – is down to the subjects themselves. This is why a less powerful state either 'offers passive resistance or is compelled to concede'. And that is how the *particular* contents and norms that actualise the *general* content of competitive social relations are invested into the legal form.

4.2. *The unlikely marriage of Pashukanis and McDougal*

The theories of Myres McDougal – reactionary US apologist and professional jurist – and Evgeny Pashukanis – revolutionary (in his early period) Bolshevik and critic of law – have fascinating points of connection. To an extent, each complements and fills in lacunae in the other.

I do not wish to suggest theoretical equivalence. Pashukanis's work is based on a historical and dialectical method, and is a contribution to a total theory, a detailed, rigorous conceptualisation of the world: McDougal's is based on idealist and nebulous notions of power and politics, a reductionist, untheoretical individualism. However, McDougal's theory of international law as process is compelling, and towers over the textbook formalism of most international legal theorists. I have suggested that many of the failings of his conceptions of 'national interest' and 'power', for example, could be solved from within an alternative materialist paradigm, while retaining the processual theory itself. The big problem in McDougal's theory, however, remains the question of why certain avowedly political processes become law – in other words, where does the legal form come from?

With the commodity-form theory of law, the provenance, generalisation and tenacity of the legal form is directly rooted in exchange relations. Given that relations between sovereign states are those very relationships of abstract equality inhering between owners of private property – a fact recognised by mainstream international law since Grotius[83] – we have here an answer to

---

[83] Pashukanis 1980b, p. 176. Page 329 below. '[Grotius's] whole system depends on the fact that he considers relations between states to be relations between the

McDougal's conundrum. *The legal form will be the form taken by the political process of struggle between states where relationships between those states are based on sovereignty, which is itself private property, ownership of their own territory.*[84] Those, after all, are the conditions necessary for exchange of equivalents.

As to what McDougal can offer commodity-form theory, his frank description of how particular political processes become law is invaluable to understand the changing political contents of the abstract legal form. 'In a relevant jurisprudence,' he says, 'international law will be explicitly conceived as the comprehensive process of authoritative decision'.[85] For a decision to be authoritative – for a particular interpretation to defeat rivals – it must be backed up by the more powerful coercive force in a particular legal relationship.

This is why international law is a paradoxical form. It is simultaneously a *genuine relation between equals*, and a form that the weaker states *cannot hope to win*.[86] That, rather than any simple collapse into power politics, is the meaning of Marx's words that '[b]etween equal rights, force decides'.

Of course, because there is no superordinate state, the stronger participant in a legal relationship may declare the content of the legal form to be a particular interpretation, and – with their greater coercive force – may act as if it is so and make the facts on the ground, but that does not mean that their *interpretation* is universally accepted. Where there is a monopoly of interpretation, where the legal form is made manifest in statutes issued by the state, it is much harder to question the interpretation decided on for particular laws.

Broadly, there are two levels of politics, of coercion, involved in fleshing out the legal form. The first is to give that form content by deciding *in the abstract* what kind of action will and will not be legitimate: the second is to decide, on that basis, whether a particular concrete act is therefore legitimate.

---

owners of private property; he declares that the necessary conditions for the execution of exchange, i.e. equivalent exchange between private owners, are the conditions for legal interaction between states. Sovereign states co-exist and are counterposed to one another in exactly the same way as are individual property owners with equal rights.'

[84] It should be pointed out that *actual exchange* may or may not exist between states. All that is needed for their relations to take the legal form is that the relations be those *necessary* for exchange. Without a recognition of private property any relations that might take place would not be *exchange*.

[85] Lasswell, McDougal & Preisner 1968, p. 202.

[86] This is neatly summarised in Pashukanis's point, made previously, that without a superordinate authority there is no distinction 'between law as an objective norm and law as a power' (Pashukanis 1980a, p. 44).

Domestically, lawyers may well argue with the state that their client is not guilty of a particular crime, but it is virtually impossible for them to argue that the *category of action itself* is not in fact a crime. This, however, is not so for international law, where there is no monopoly even on that primary level of interpretation.

Take the example of reprisals, discussed in Chapter Two. The debate between jurists is not whether this or that action is a reprisal and therefore illegal, but whether reprisals *as a category* are illegal. Here, the importance of 'authoritative' decision is key. After all, the majority of writers agree that reprisals are illegal. However, as long as Israel, for example, is able to interpret reprisals as legal,[87] openly to claim its activities *as* reprisals, and to be a strong enough power (with the US's support) to defeat or silence any dissenters, then it is nonsensical to claim that reprisals are functionally illegal.[88]

Neither, of course, does this mean that they are 'legal': the law is indeterminate, and the question of their legality is unanswerable in the abstract. All that can be decided is whether, in a particular concrete conjuncture, reprisals (or any other activity) are being treated as illegal.[89] It is therefore perfectly possible for reprisals to be functionally 'legal' in one conflict and 'illegal' in another, simultaneously.

5. Problems

Critics might claim that here, the entire theory of law founders. In acknowledging that the same action might be simultaneously legal and illegal, are we not making a mockery of the very notion of law?

This claim, however, rests on the discredited view that law is a system of norms or rules. It is the critique of this position that is the shared starting

---

[87] See for example Blum 1970; Dinstein 1994.

[88] This dovetails with the argument made by Bowett, that there is a 'credibility gap' created by 'the divergence between the norm [which condemns reprisals as illegal] and the actual practice of states' (Bowett 1972, p. 1).

[89] Those writers who characterise international law as a 'primitive' system, and see reprisals as a central sanction of that law, are missing the point. It is true that 'self-help' is the only serious coercive mechanism in the international system, and reprisals are an example of such self-help. However, it is also true that not all states can retaliate against a breach of law – Grenada might have had a strong case that the US invasion against its sovereignty in 1983 was illegal, but it was quite unable to retaliate. What is central to international law is coercive self-help, rather than some abstract category of 'reprisals'.

point of McDougal and Pashukanis. McDougal says '[t]he fundamental obscurity in contemporary theory about international law . . . begins in the very definition of the subject-matter of international law as a system of rules':[90] Pashukanis that '[t]he standard view posits objective law or a norm as the base of the legal relationship' but that 'law as a totality of norms is no more than a lifeless abstraction'.[91]

From here the two go in different directions, McDougal stressing process in the abstract, Pashukanis grounding that process as inhering between legal subjects, and theorising it as a *relationship*. However, in stressing the dynamic as opposed to the static, they share an understanding that particular norms are historically contingent. The simple fact of the historical change or repeal of certain legal norms illustrates this.

A legal order is not defined by the content of its norms but by the kind of relations it regulates – ie., those between abstract equal units. We have seen that law is indeterminate, that it is a process, that its content is determined according to political context. The coexistence of contradictory norms in the international arena is merely unusually clear evidence that different contents can flesh out the legal form.

The content of a norm is the product of what is usually, especially in policy-oriented jurisprudence, called 'authoritative decision',[92] and would better be termed *coercive interpretation*. It is therefore up for grabs. Where there is no monopoly of interpretation there is no reason at all that for two sets of claims, contradictory interpretations might not be backed up by stronger coercive force in each case. This is why, as Pashukanis points out, 'the practice of the different states at any one time, and the practice of the same state at different times, are far from the same'.[93]

Used as we are to living in superordinate states, contradictory interpretations of legal norms makes us somewhat uneasy: but they are an inevitable corollary of the theory of the legal form and legal process. What is more, the international legal arena is riddled with such disputes between jurists and states. '[T]he source of the norms of even customary international law is drawn from the opinions of "writers", or scholars,' Pashukanis tartly notes,

[90] McDougal 1953, p. 143.
[91] Pashukanis 1980, p. 62. See also pp. 62–74.
[92] See McDougal, Lasswell and Reisman 1981.
[93] Pashukanis 1980b, p. 182.

'who usually differ decisively with each other on every question.'[94] Consensus *may* emerge, of course,[95] but its absence is not any collapse of law.

There is a second, and more serious, criticism to be levelled at this kind of interpretation-centred theory. It is clear in Young's critique of McDougal.

> [W]hen law is defined in terms of the making of effective and authoritative decisions . . . the concept tends to lose discriminatory power for many purposes. . . . [T]his conception encourages the inclusion of so much under the heading of law . . . that it often becomes difficult to identify law . . . and then to analyze the connections between law and various other aspects of a social system. . . .[96]

In essence the question is how, in this theory, does one distinguish legal and non-legal relations? The thrust of the analysis so far has certainly been to collapse sharp distinctions between politics and an abstract arena of 'law'.

In Chapter One I argued that McDougal could not make sense of why social relations should take the form of law, and that this was because he has has no theory of the legal form. By bringing in.Pashukanis therefore we have addressed this lacuna and perhaps solved the problem. Those relations are legal which are about the regulation of claims between sovereign individuals based on private property.

However, in a society of universal commodity production and exchange relations, the fact is that almost *all* relations (including all those inhering between states) could be seen as constructed on that foundation of abstract equivalence. Young's critique, then, comes back from the opposite side. Originally it said that McDougal could not explain where law starts: now it can be turned against Pashukanis, to say that he cannot explain where law *stops*. With no understanding of the legal form, McDougal's processual theory could not explain why any relation would take the shape of law: with the commodity-form theory in place, have we instead become unable to explain why any relation would *not* take that shape?

Pashukanis makes a few remarks that bear on this question. He talks about the unstable nature of international law, and raises the question of its limits.

---

94 Pashukanis 1980b, p. 182.
95 Ibid. 'There are . . . few generally recognized written norms of international law'.
96 Young 1972, p. 64.

> In critical periods, when the balance of forces has fluctuated seriously, when 'vital interests' or even the very existence of a state are on the agenda, the fate of the norms of international law becomes extremely problematic. . . . The best illustration of this is afforded by the last war, of 1914–1918, during which both sides continuously violated international law. With international law in such a lamentable condition, bourgeois jurists can be consoled only with the hope that, however deeply the balance was disturbed, it will nevertheless be re-established: the most violent of wars must sometime be ended with peace . . . the governments will return to objectivity and compromise, and the norms of international law will once again find their force.[97]

The claim that international law was 'continuously violated' during the war needs closer examination. Given that in the analysis developed, the same act can be functionally 'legal' and 'illegal' simultaneously, it is hard to see how these actions – or any – can be defined as violations of law.

First, however, it should be remembered that Pashukanis does not deny that there are *some* norms of international law which are shared, ie. the interpretation of which is not controversial, although it is worth pointing out how very small their number is. In addition to illustrating how interpretation is generally driven by political expediency, a 1940 examination of the record of the Permanent Court of Arbitration of the League of Nations gives some idea of just how few 'uncontroversial' cases there are.

> Judges who were the nationals of parties before the Court voted in favour of their country in ninety-five out of 100 cases. In the four cases where a judge voted against his own country, three of them were unanimously decided. In other words, the legal situation was so obvious that it would have been very difficult to deviate from the decision of the Court.[98]

In this example, in only three per cent of cases did the application of the norm seem self-evident.[99] Of course, holding that law is indeterminate means that even in these 'uncontroversial' cases, it is not that the law has actually reached some limit of 'interpretability', that this is the 'actual' meaning of the law. It is only an admission that the facts of particular cases vary the ease with which

[97] Pashukanis 1980b, p. 179.
[98] Grewe 2000, pp. 614–15.
[99] Even something so near-universally legally condemned as the Israeli settlements in the West Bank and Gaza Strip can be and have been defended in international law (see the Israeli Government's policy guidelines, issued March 2001).

arguments can be made, and in these examples, no counter-argument was put – not that no such argument *could be put*. But Pashukanis's point is that in a state of political crisis like war, states will be willing to break *even those* shared and generally agreed norms. Therefore when there are political actions which are in contravention of an *uncontroversial* norm, we can reasonably say that actions are 'purely' political, rather than legal – are in fact functionally illegal.

The focus on the materiality of law means that if no state anywhere is obeying a particular norm, a very strong case can be made that the norm has collapsed, as it is no longer meaningfully regulating anything.[100] But although the ignoring of norms is common in war, it differs from the obsolescence of a norm during peacetime in that i) the political context is *defined* by the participants as pathological (even if analysis points to the immanence of war in capitalist peace), and concomitantly ii) the states generally claim to uphold the laws they are breaking, through special pleading that the delict of the law was due to the unusual circumstances and should not be seen as normalised.

In this situation, it can be meaningful to talk of the breaking of international laws. After all, even a materialist focus on effective law would have to take *patterns* of behaviour over time as evidence that a law was meaningless: if by coincidence large numbers of people contravened a particular law for one day then began obeying it again, it would seem very odd to define the situation as one in which the law had ceased to hold, then re-established itself, rather than one in which the law had been broken. Such an approach would be to fetishise the focus on 'effective' law and abstract it: 'effectiveness' must be judged in political context, over time.

During war, large numbers of violators loudly proclaim the very law they violate. Even its widespread breaking cannot immediately, then, be seen as rendering it obsolete. Therefore the (relatively rare) situation of widespread abuse of more or less universally shared norms can be seen as 'pure politics'.

However, while a war represents a situation of widespread law-breaking, then, it is also one of law-*assertion*. The spirals of reprisal and counter-reprisal which tend to characterise law are very often described and justified

---

[100] If the normative were always negated by contrary practice, either it could not exist or its existence would be pointless, since the normative subsists in and even thrives on the transgression of it. See Fitzpatrick 2003, p. 453.

precisely in legalistic, 'self-help' terms. In other words, in response to a perceived infringement of sovereignty (a fundamental breach of law, a failure to respect private property) a state will exercise its coercive interpretation, waging war as a way of establishing its legalistic claim to have had its abstract rights violated. This sets in motion counter-claims, also regulated by force.

In that sense, then, almost definitionally a modern war is simultaneously a fundamental violation of international law by each side in the perception of the other, *and* is the regulatory mechanism by which the content of that legal relationship is fleshed out: a clash of coercion, by which the *effective interpretation* of the disputed law is decided. This is the sense in which there is a 'close morphological link . . . a clear connection . . . between the parties to a lawsuit and the combatants in an armed conflict'.[101]

War is simultaneously a violation of international law *and international law in action*.

> [I]nternational law appears as a means of struggle at the heart of an unstable order which is at one and the same time the locus and that which is at stake . . . Far from being opposed to one another in principle . . . international associative law and the right to subordination reveal themselves as complementary and both bearers of violence.[102]

We have not got very far in delimiting legal relations. Given that Pashukanis sees the norms of international law 'finding their force' in a situation of international peace, 'objectivity and compromise',[103] we can say that the most clearly 'law-like' behaviour is that where agreed legal norms regulate peaceable behaviour without controversy. Opposing this, we can see 'pure politics' in those very rare situations where similarly agreed legal norms are callously ignored in a political crisis. This leaves a vast mid-range of behaviours and relationships. Can we distinguish some of that behaviour as 'not-legal'?

In his discussion of the Kantian legacy of bourgeois jurisprudence, Pashukanis makes the paradox clear. Law is bounded by 'pure politics' on one side and

---

[101] Pashukanis 1978, p. 118.

[102] Robelin 1994, p. 159. '[L]e droit international apparaît comme un moyen de lutte au sein de l'ordre instable qui en est à la fois le lieu et l'enjeu . . . Loin de s'opposer dans leur principe . . . le droit international associatif et la droît de subordination s'avèrant complimentaires et prteurs tous deux des formes de violence'.

[103] Pashukanis 1980b, p. 179.

'pure morality' on the other, but in trying to systematise law's position vis-à-vis either one of these limits, it slips inexorably into the other.

> [I]f the independence of law from morality is being asserted, law merges with the state as a result of the strong emphasis on the aspect of external coercion. . . . [I]f law is being contrasted with the state, that is to say with effective dominance, then the aspect of duty in the sense of *Ought* . . . comes into play without fail and we are confronted . . . by a united front of law and morality.[104]

If law is distinguished from 'political' behaviour, in other words, then it is not clear what makes it legal as distinct from moral. But on the other hand, '[i]f legal obligation has nothing in common with "inner" moral duty, then there is no way of differentiating between subjection to law and subjection to authority as such'.[105] This is precisely the question of what is and is not law, how we are to distinguish between legal and non-legal activity. And mainstream theory cannot help us. 'Bourgeois legal philosophy exhausts itself in this fundamental contradiction, this endless struggle with its own premises'.[106]

There is in fact no way out. 'Legal obligation can find no independent validity and wavers between two extremes: subjection to external coercion, and "free" moral duty.'[107] The problem *is* actually intractable. In the commodity-form theory, law is simultaneously a form inhering between two free, abstract individuals *and* a necessary subjection to coercion. For this reason, there *is no* neat solution. It is not the legal theory which is paradoxical, but the relations that it represents.

> As always, the contradictions in the system here too reflects the contradictions in real life, that is in the social environment which produced the form of morality and law as they exist. The contradiction between the individual and the social, between the private and the universal, which bourgeois philosophy is unable to do away with, despite all its efforts, is the very basis of life in bourgeois society as a society of commodity producers. This contradiction is embodied in the actual interrelations of people who cannot regard their private endeavours as social aspirations except in the absurd and mystified form of the value of commodities.[108]

---

104 Pashukanis 1978, p. 164.
105 Pashukanis 1978, p. 163.
106 Pashukanis 1978, pp. 163–4.
107 Pashukanis 1978, p. 165.
108 Ibid.

The fact is that legal relations cannot be separated off either from moral or from 'political' relations with any systematicity. *This does not represent the failure of the theory but the peculiar nature of modernity*. Just as the wealth of society under capitalism appears as an 'immense collection of commodities',[109] so 'society presents itself as an endless chain of legal relationships'.[110] Just as commodification extends beyond its immediate boundary and appears to invest intangibles with exchange-values, so the legal form will burst its banks, as I show in Chapter Three, and take on new forms *on the basis of its essential form*, attempting to regulate all spheres of social life.

This is why it is not *just* hypocrisy that 'every state violating international law also tries to depict the matter as if there had been no violation whatsoever'.[111] The saturation of social relations by the legal form is such that it behoves social agents to 'legalise' any and all activities. Insofar as those relations will therefore be carried out, to some extent at least, on the basis of sovereign equality between the parties, they *do* have a legal character.

Law is not a discrete category. At the extremes of 'moral' or 'political' behaviour, other dynamics may be clearly dominant, but the great mass of relations lie somewhere between those poles, and are governed at least in part by legal logic. The fact that a 'political' logic will also be discernible does not mean the behaviour is not in part law-driven. There is, after all, no such thing as a 'purely' legal act. At the very moment of legal action a subject implies 'political' action in the form of direct coercive violence.

Therefore the 'impurity' of legal actions, and the impossibility of discerning any sharp boundaries to their sphere, any hermetic realm of law, far from undermining the commodity-form theory, vindicates it. The theological debates in mainstream jurisprudence about a pure theory of law are a product of lack of rigour, an attempt to carve out a separate legal realm. More than anything else, the theoretical insights of that odd couple, Pashukanis and McDougal, prove that that is impossible.

6. The violence of the legal form

I have tried to provide a systematic, if general, theory of the mapping of content into the legal form. Of course, to understand the dynamics by which

[109] Marx 1976, p. 125.
[110] Pashukanis 1980a, p. 62.
[111] Pashukanis 1980b, p. 179.

specific international laws are codified we must investigate the power relations between states at those particular moments.

We should not fall into the trap of thinking that the coercion immanent in law must be explicit or physical, nor that the direct and formal participants in the process of law are the only players in the power-game that it implies. The networks of obligation and informal imperialism are more intricate than that.

Despite the importance of the UN in international law, it is in no real way a superordinate authority, and therefore there is no monopoly of legitimate coercion and hence interpretation internationally. The only bodies able to provide the necessary coercion for international law are the subjects of that law themselves, the states. Given the extraordinary disparities of power between those states, and given that the real content of the legal regulation will be the struggle between them, it is no wonder that *materially effective* international law, as opposed to the high phrases and noble interpretations of the idealists, has favoured the stronger states and their clients.

International law is a relationship and a process: it is not a fixed set of rules but a *way of deciding the rules*. And the coercion of at least one of the players, or its threat, is necessary as the medium by which particular contents will actualise the broader content of competitive struggle within the legal form.

The accusation that Pashukanis has no theory of politics is quite wide of the mark. In his theory, the constitutive interpenetration of the 'political' and the 'legal' is paramount. The political – the violent, the coercive – lies at the heart of the legal, and nowhere is that more evident than in international law.

So far I have argued this at a theoretical level. It is even more clear when the history of international law is examined.

Chapter Five

States, Markets and the Sea: Issues in the History of International Law

1. The invisibility of history

Serious history is hard to come by in international law. Just as the relative proliferation of jurisprudence of domestic law has had little impact on the 'wasteland' of international legal theory, '[l]egal history is known to be one of the most cultivated and most fertile fields of legal science, but, strangely, this observation does not apply to the science of international law'.[1]

This situation has recently begun to improve:[2] the birth in 1999 of the *Journal of the History of International Law* is perhaps the most obvious and important sign of this. It is, however, early days, and the literature on the topic is still remarkably small.[3]

[1] Nussbaum 1947, p. 293.

[2] Even, according to Koskenniemi 2002a, 'dramatically' (p. 9). Butkevych can still argue, however, that the history of international law 'is far from being properly studied, is undeveloped as a branch of knowledge and harbours problems of both theoretical and methodological nature' (Butkevych 2003, p. 189).

[3] This is particularly the case for histories of international law in general, as the most recent and extensive bibliography of the subject (though one that does not claim to be comprehensive) makes clear (Macalister-Smith and Schwietzke 1999, p. 136). There are other shorter bibliographies in Nussbaum 1947 (pp. 293–8) and Grewe 2000 (pp. 733–4). Several of the items listed are of limited value to the modern international legal historian except as curios, by Nussbaum's own admission (p. 297). Of the items Nussbaum and Grewe list, the most useful today are Butler and Maccoby 1928 and Walker 1899 (neither of which are mentioned by Macalister-Smith and Schwietzke, and both of which, the Walker particularly, Nussbaum dismisses too readily), Nys 1894 and the 1984 articles by Preiser, Verosta, Scupin, Grewe and Kimminich

This lack of history conditions and is conditioned by the field's similar lack of theory (also, not coincidentally, a condition in the early stages of improvement). The eclipse of theory during the nineteenth century and after has acted to naturalise international law and seal it off from jurisprudential and/or historical analysis.[4]

Of course despite the triumph of doctrine, writers are aware that international law has a past: many of the enormous number of modern textbooks offer brief and sometimes useful overviews of the history of international law since antiquity, usually in their introductory chapters.[5] However, with their brusque attitude to theory, these works tend to raise more questions than they answer.

See for example Shearer on the birth of international law.

> [B]y the fifteenth and sixteenth centuries jurists had begun to take into account the evolution of a community of independent sovereign states and to think and write about different problems of the law of nations, realising

---

in the *Encyclopedia of Public International Law*. None of the bibliographies mention Hosack 1882, which though hardly scientifically rigorous, deserves to be listed in a comprehensive survey. For invaluable work focusing on the role of international law in colonialism and imperialism since the 15th century, see Fisch 1984, summarised in English in Fisch 2000. For the early writers, from 1480 to 1645, focusing on Vitoria, Suárez, Gentili and Grotius see Kennedy 1986b. There is of course an enormous secondary literature on Grotius: for the most important recent analysis see Tuck 1999, pp. 78–108. For an overview of international law and legal debates in the nineteenth century, see Kennedy 1996. For the history of international law between 1870 and 1960 see the indispensable Koskenniemi 2002a. For an overview of current directions in international legal history research see Hueck 2001.

[4] This is vividly illustrated in a remark by Manning, made towards the end of the 1800s. Discussing the conduct of the Romans and ancient Greeks vis-à-vis foreign governments, he claims that such relations are not international law because 'these usages . . . were not adopted from any sense of right deduced from that source' – ie., from the law of nations itself (Manning 1875, p. 10. He is right that this is not 'international law', but for the wrong reasons). In other words, to qualify as international law, behaviour has to self-consciously derive from international law. This ahistorical and recursive definition closes off the international legal form from investigation, defining it by reference to itself. This formulation precludes any serious historical analysis of international law, and could only have come to seem sufficient at a time when most international behaviour was precisely so self-referentially conceived, when international law had become universalised and naturalised.

[5] See for example, Shearer 1994, pp. 7–14; Schwarzenberger 1967, pp. 18–25; Shaw 2003, pp. 13–31. Malanczuk 1997, pp. 9–34 is one of the better of the modern introductions. Interestingly, in some cases the older, though still modern 'technical' rather than theoretical works, retain more of the spirit of theoretical enquiry in their histories than more recent textbooks. Lawrence 1910, pp. 17–53 and Manning 1875, pp. 8–65 are exemplary.

> the necessity for some body of rules to regulate certain aspects of the relations between such states.[6]

This formulation embeds incorrect and untheorised assumptions (international law as a body of rules) alongside a simple *statement* of the very historical processes that need *explanation* (the evolution of sovereign states as international legal agents) if history is to make sense of the development of international law.

The best chronological overview is Grewe's monumental work,[7] and it is to that that readers wanting an overview of the historical development of international law since the fifteenth century should look. The book is politically and theoretically controversial, and it has to be read in the light of Martti Koskenniemi's devastating critique:[8] in particular he rightly excoriates Grewe's abstract theory of power (as a 'somewhat mystical source of political authority')[9] and ahistorical history ('the monotonous rhythm of *the eternal return of the same*').[10]

Nonetheless, Grewe's very focus on the relation of international law to power that underpins much of Koskennemi's attack can be seen, from another optic, as invaluable. From a radical materialist perspective, one can dismiss the realist 'apology of brute force' and 'colossal moral insensitivity'[11] while learning from (and attempting to ground in nuanced historical context) Grewe's unsentimental sense of the political realities underlying international law, rather than seeing that law's history as the self-unfolding of ideas (let alone a teleology of freedom). Even so stern a critic as Koskenniemi acknowledges this possibility.[12]

---

6 Shearer 1994, p. 9.

7 Grewe 2000.

8 The claim that Grewe is not 'polemical or partisan' (Neff 2001, p. 252) seems naïve. Grewe draws heavily, among others, on Carl Schmitt, and his work seems to some critics at the very least too concerned with power-politics over questions of doctrine and 'internal dialogue' (Landauer 2003, p. 201); at worst, tainted by Schmitt's Nazism. Koskenniemi searingly points out Grewe's silence over the question of the Holocaust (Koskenniemi 2002b, pp. 747–748), and his refusal ever to apportion historical blame that leads to 'perverse exculpation of the German atrocities' (p. 747), casting a 'dark shadow upon the whole book' (p. 748).

9 Koskenniemi 2002b, p. 747.

10 Koskenniemi 2002b, p. 750. Emphasis in original.

11 Koskenniemi 2002b, pp. 748–750.

12 'Brief sections deal with intellectual developments and academic doctrines, interpreted predominantly as ideological justification of the policies of the epoch's dominant power. I have no problem with treating legal doctrine in this way . . . [it is]

Here, rather than give a chronological account or an overview of all the key writers and debates in international law historically, I attempt to so draw on Grewe (and others) selectively to examine certain key themes in the history of international law, to point out some inadequacies in existing theories, and to focus on strands of continuity and change in the epochs of international law. My approach is informed by, and tests, the commodity-form theory of (international) law outlined above, and historical materialism more generally. I argue that it is only through examining the changing nature of exchange and market relations across communities and eventually nation-states that the changing nature of international law can be made sense of.

2. Origins and prehistory: an eternity of international law?

Dating the origin of international law is controversial. The question is whether it is fundamentally a modern institution, constituting a break with the past, or whether it predates modernity.

The 'prevailing view' is that international law 'emerged in Europe in the period after the Peace of Westphalia (1648)'[13] The iconic date of IR and international law are unsurprisingly shared, 1648 being seen as the death of a premodern feudal order and its replacement with 'the modern system of international law and international relations, which takes as its starting point the principle of territorial sovereignty'.[14]

This obscures the complexities of history on both sides of 1648, and it is not only theoretical iconoclasts who know the supposed 'conventional view' to be gravely simplistic.[15] By that date the feudal *respublica Christiana*, for

---

certainly more credible than the old-fashioned international law orothdoxy that treats the early writers as humanist heroes, anachronistically representing what modern lawyers have the custom of admiring in themselves.' (Koskenniemi 2002b, p. 749). Similarly when for example Koskenniemi acknowledges that Grewe's argument that the official British opposition to the slave trade was derived from its economic and political interest 'is probably not altogether wrong' (p. 749) (and is, incidentally, an analysis shared by the Marxist Left (see Morton 1989, pp. 414–15), what disturbs him – quite rightly – is not the argument but the abstract realism and aristocratic moralism that underpins it. One can still, of course, learn from the former.

[13] Malanczuk 1997, p. 9. Bederman describes the view that international law is a product of the 'modern . . . mind' as 'an article of faith' (Bederman 2001, p. 1). See Brownlie 1984.

[14] Werner 1999, p. 319. This essay suffers from obscurantism as much as from the schematicism highlighted here.

[15] From a realist perspective, for example, Stephen Krasner cheerfully debunks the

example, had already been systematically undermined in international law as well as international relations for more than a century.[16] Conversely, the Treaty of Westphalia leaves in place enough continuities with the past that it 'does not close the final chapter of the multilayered system of authority in Europe'. '[T]he confinement of the transcendental institutions and the erosion of their authority . . . did not start, and certainly did not end either, with the Peace.'[17]

But the view that in the absence of the supposed radical break of 1648, international law can in fact be detected in antiquity, runs the risk of being even more schematic. Korff, for example, is adamant that though

> [f]or a long time writers on international law took it for granted that the subject of their studies was a relatively recent product of modern civilization . . . this theory had to be considerably altered and finally discarded. . . . [T]he ancient world knew very well the meaning of international relations and was making use of an elaborate system of institutions, well developed and firmly established . . . [T]here can be no more doubt on the question.[18]

The theory of ancient international law is a legalist variant of the ahistoricism of realist IR writers. Martin Wight famously described international politics as 'the realm of recurrence and repetition'.[19] The claim is that whatever the socio-historical circumstances, essentially the same dynamics of power politics will out in the international sphere, always 'the same old melodrama'.[20]

---

notion that 'Westphalia produced the modern sovereign state' in the pages of *Foreign Policy*, no less (Krasner 2001b).

[16] '[T]he dynamics at work in Europe's religious and political spheres meant that, at the break of the Thirty Years War, the respective universal authorities of the Pope and the Emperor had already been severely depleted by the joint actions of the Reformation and the centralization of government both within and without the Holy Roman Empire'. (Beaulac 2000, p. 176.)

[17] Beaulac 2000, pp. 150–1, p. 169. See also Osiander 1994, p. 44: 'the peacemakers far from regarded themselves as innovators. There was consensus among them that the settlement should bring a return to the *status quo ante bellum*, the main problem then being to define the *terminus ante quem*. The Emperor pressed for a date around 1630, but this would have introduced change with regard to the pre-war state. His opponents carried the day, essentially turning the clock back to 1618 in temporal and to 1624 in religious matters.'

[18] Korff 1924, p. 246. Korff's explanation for the supposedly flawed mainstream view is that 'our teachers of the nineteenth century . . . were not acquainted with the history of the ancient civilizations'. This is absurd, as a brief look at the citations found in Grotius, Bodin, Pufendorf and others quickly makes clear.

[19] Wight 1966, p. 26.

[20] Ibid.

Korff puts the case without Wight's subtlety, indeed with gung-ho historical philistinism, linking the political and legal to posit a theory of eternal international sameness.

> The fact that the fundamental principles of international intercourse always were and are even in our day identical all over the world proves their inward potential strength and vitality. But at the same time this also justifies the theory that international law is a necessary consequence of any civilization. . . . The binding force of . . . international obligations has remained exactly the same since the times of Rameses or Murdoc, Pericles and Cicero, to those of Napoleon, George V of England or the Tsars of Russia. The mere fact of neighborly cohabitation creates moral and legal obligations, which in the course of time crystallize into a system of international law.[21]

Of course there were agreements and treaties between political bodies in antiquity – Korff cites the famous 1280 BC treaty between Ramses II and Hattusilis III of the Hittites, among others.[22] And those treaties do contain elements which seem intelligible to the modern international lawyer: there are clauses guaranteeing borders, agreeing on the extradition of refugees, agreeing to operate a defensive alliance against third parties, and so on.[23] But to borrow Justin Rosenberg's critique of realism, what is missing in Korff's story is

> an account of those conditions of social power within a system which result . . . from the reproduction of the core institutions which reflect its historical character, which position the individuals in terms of access to resources and which define the terrain of interaction. . . . [I]t involves the . . . 'state of nature' fallacy . . . to assume that there ever were social systems in which power [or, we can add, law] could be understood without recognizing this dimension.[24]

What is missing, in other words, is history itself. What passes for it has been bled of social content. The idea that the written agreements between rulers of pre-feudal antique political entities and the modern edifice of international law are straightforwardly two specimens of the same species is absurd.

---

[21] Korff 1924, p. 248.
[22] Korff 1924, p. 249.
[23] The 1280 BC treaty is translated and reproduced, alongside many others from antiquity, in Grewe 1995, pp. 18–23.
[24] Rosenberg 1994, p. 28.

There are of course far more sophisticated attempts than Korff's.[25] In his thoughtful defence of the notion that international law existed in antiquity, David Bederman has engaged explicitly with these questions, mindful of the 'ruinous reasoning that compels some writers to suggest that modern doctrines of international law can trace their lineage directly back to ancient times'.[26] Despite attempting to answer charges of ahistoricism with specific evidence of ancient international legal categories, he accepts that 'no measure of care . . . can inoculate [him] . . . from the criticism that this project suffers from a false essentialism of equating modern (if not current) concepts to events transpiring two to three millennia ago'.[27] Such essentialism can perhaps be seen in his acknowledgement that he believes 'that there is an essential unity in the nature of State behaviour in ancient times', 'at very different times in antiquity'[28] – and, surely, to allow the comparative method, in modernity.

Militating against the visions of international law in antiquity is the simple fact that '[t]ill there were nations, in the sense of independent political communities possessed of sovereign power, there could be no true International Law'.[29] When there were no sovereign nation-states, there could be no law whose subjects are those nation-states. The term 'international law' cannot rigorously be applied to pre-medieval society. Any such use should be read as contained by invisible scare-quotes.

> If one believes that one can research these premodern arrangements and agreements in various regions in the same way as one researches the present international law, then one would seriously misunderstand these arrangements or agreements by projecting the prevalent notion of international law onto the past.[30]

Bederman himself admits that '"international law" may not consistently convey the sense of international relations in antiquity'.[31]

---

[25] See for example Preiser 1984b, who at least introduces some notion of periodicity.
[26] Bederman 2001, p. 6.
[27] Bederman 2001, p. 14.
[28] Bederman 2001, pp. 2–3.
[29] Lawrence 1910, p. 23.
[30] Onuma 2000, p. 59.
[31] Bederman 2001, p. 14. One response to this complex question of nomenclature is to acknowledge then ignore it, as Macalister-Smith and Schwietzke cheerfully do in their bibliographical outline: 'the term "international law" is used in this survey regardless of any question whether that law existed at an earlier time, in today's sense,

This cannot, however, be the end of the argument. Having insisted on the historical *rupture* represented by international law, it is also important to understand what elements there are of continuity and development. In other words, why '[s]uch rudiments of it [international law] as existed in the Middle Ages'[32] were there, and precisely what the relationship is between premodern and modern regulation between political entities. Can it really be true, as Manning claims, that '[t]hese usages were sometimes *coincident* with the law of nations, but . . . as far as they may be available at the present day, have little value beyond what curiosity may attach to them'?[33] Are they merely curios, the similarities pure coincidence?

In his essay on international law, Pashukanis seems to accept the existence of antique international law, and to deny its historical particularity.

> As a separate force which set itself off from society, the state only finally emerged in the modern bourgeois capitalist period. But it by no means follows from this that the contemporary forms of international legal intercourse, and the individual institutions of international law, only arose in the most recent times. On the contrary, they trace their history to the most ancient periods of class and even pre-class society. To the extent that exchange was not initially made between individuals, but among tribes and communities, it may be affirmed that the institutions of international law are the most ancient of legal institutions in general. Collisions between tribes, territorial disputes, disputes over borders – and agreements as one of the elements in these disputes – are found in the very earliest stages of human history. The tribal pre-state life of the Iroquois, and of the ancient Germans, saw the conclusion of alliances between tribes. The development of class society and the appearance of state authority make contracts and agreements among authorities possible. The treaty between Pharoah Rameses II and the King of the Hittites is one of the oldest surviving documents of this type.[34]

---

or what it may have been called then, and regardless of what the contents of the concept may have been at any given time in history.' (Macalister-Smith and Schwietzke 1999, p. 137.)

[32] Lawrence 1910, p. 23.

[33] Manning 1875, p. 10. Emphasis mine. Manning, somewhat confusingly, describes them instead as 'examples of the customary law of nations at a remote period' (p. 10), which makes sense only if he posits a radical distinction between 'remote' customary international law and (modern) international law. This leaves untheorised what, if anything, is shared – ie., what the legal form is.

[34] Pashukanis 1980b, p. 175. Pages 327–8 below.

However, this passage must be read as part of his broader argument in which both continuity *and rupture* are stressed. Shortly earlier, for example, Pashukanis stresses that '[t]he spread and development of international law occurred on the basis of the spread and development of the capitalist mode of production',[35] and makes an even stronger claim, that 'international law owes its existence to the fact that the bourgeoisie exercises its domination over the proletariat and over the colonial countries'.[36] This is obviously a historically specific argument. So how are we to reconcile these two apparently contradictory claims about the historicity of international law?

In fact, the object of Pashukanis's historical analysis is *not*, straightforwardly, international law: '[t]urning now', he says, 'to consider the *legal form* of international law'.[37] He is not talking about premodern international *law*, but 'the contemporary *forms* of international legal intercourse, and the *individual institutions* of international law'. He carefully *avoids* claiming to be talking about international law *tout court*.

What can be traced across the historical rupture to modernity is not international law but some of its institutions – particular ways of regulating certain arrangements – on the basis, more fundamentally, of its *forms* – based, of course, on the legal form itself.

Pashukanis is arguing that it is the maintenance of the same form in radically different social contexts which explains i) the *roots* of international law in premodern systems, and ii) the distinct nature of international law as a modern, universalised social form ('the state only fully becomes the subject of international law as the bourgeois state').[38] The *legal form* – the form whereby the bearers of abstract rights and commodities confront each – has existed in various historical conjunctures, but it was only with the rise of sovereign states that *international law* can be considered to have been born, and it is with the triumph of capitalism and its commodification of all social relations that the legal form universalised and became modern international law.

Crucially, its social content changed, even as the form maintained. That is why the continuity of the legal form between international law and what one might term proto-international law does not mean that there was not a radical break with the spread of the sovereign state form, market relations and

---

[35] Pashukanis 1980b, pp. 171–2. Page 324 below.
[36] Pashukanis 1980b, p. 172. Page 325 below.
[37] Pashukanis 1980b, p. 173. Emphasis mine. Page 325 below.
[38] Pashukanis 1980b, p. 172. Page 327 below.

ultimately capitalism. The sharing of the legal form is evidence of commodity exchange across cultures, but the social context in which that exchange occurs, and therefore the specific social meanings that the legal form will embody, are historically specific.

Take for example the changing nature of relations mediated by treaties. As Onuma points out,

> in the treaty between Rameses II of Egypt and Hatsilsi III of the Hittites . . . the subjects making promises were Rameses and Hatsilsi, not the state or empire of Egypt and the Hittites. This practice of 'treaty' making between politico-military or politico-religious leaders under their names, not under the names of 'states,' could also be found in Africa, America, Asia and Europe, and lasted well into the modern period, i.e., until the 19th century.[39]

These early agreements cannot be considered 'international' law – the subjects are neither sovereign states, nor nations. Nor, though, are they simply relations between individuals. These are clearly relations mediated by the legal form, between political entities – inter-polity, 'intercommunity law or intersocietal law'[40] – and as such they are related to, though radically different from, modern international law.

Compare a much later, though still dynastic, approach to treaties.

> The victory of the bourgeois perspective over the feudal-patrimonial perspective was expressed, among other things, in the denial of the binding force of dynastic treaties for the state. Thus in 1790 the National Assembly of France rejected the obligations which flowed from the family treaty of the house of Bourbon (1761), on the grounds that Louis XV had acted as a representative of the dynasty and not as a representative of France.[41]

The legal form – the process of the clash of abstract sovereign rights – is shared in the different treaties, across millennia. The social content, however, differs radically. It is not that the treaties of the Bourbons cannot be considered international law – unlike Ramses II, the absolutist monarchs embodied a burgeoning early-modern state, so that their 'personal' or 'familial' relations are nonetheless 'international' relations.[42] However, the move to a

---

[39] Onuma 2000, p. 59 footnote 167.
[40] Onuma 2000, p. 58.
[41] Pashukanis 1980b, p. 174. Page 327 below.
[42] Even those who opposed the modern, bourgeois use of international law by the

self-consciously *national* rather than dynastic subject of international law represents a massive political shift, the ascendancy of the bourgeois nation-state.

The continuity of the legal form must not disguise the epochal shifts of social relations in changing international subjectivity and the political content of international law. One of the most important moments in this process is precisely the nineteenth-century bourgeois triumph, of which the National Assembly's ruling was an early expression. It is this that has made 'the real historical content of international law . . . the struggle between capitalist states'.[43]

An earlier epochal moment is 'the period of the formation of absolute monarchies', 'the formation of a system of independent states which have . . . a sufficiently strong central power to enable each of them to act as a single whole'.[44] It was then, when the European system became one of sovereign states, new juridical agents, and thereby related according to the legal form that had inhered between previously existing polities, that we can begin to talk about a genuinely 'international' law.[45]

The argument that international law was present in feudalism or antiquity must be rejected. But the international legal form was not born from a void. Its homology with earlier relations is important. International law is historically specific, but can only be understood by reference to its roots.

Grewe wrestles to negotiate this dialectic of continuation and change. He claims that 'an international legal order' *did* exist in three cases in antiquity, having as its minimum necessary (though not sufficient) conditions 'a plurality of relatively independent (although not necessarily equal ranking) bodies politic which are linked to each other in political, economic and cultural relationships and which are not subject to a superimposed authority'.[46]

French National Assembly conceived of their own project as one of international law: 'German monarcho-reactionary professors . . . find that the National Assembly violated international law in this action' (Pashukanis 1980b, p. 174. Page 327 below).

[43] Pashukanis 1980b, p. 172. Page 325 below.

[44] Pashukanis 1980b, p. 173. Page 326 below.

[45] Onuma 2000 is adamant that the only correct formulation would be 'European international law' (p. 58). Although this is a useful corrective to the implied ahistorical universalism in talking about 'international law' in (say) the seventeenth century I think it runs the risk of obscuring the important and specific role of the relations between Europe and the non-European world in the birth of international law, as well as distracting attention from what it was precisely that allowed international law to become a universal system (processes Onuma does a good job of drawing attention to).

[46] Grewe 2000, p. 7. The three historical cases he cites are i) the Middle East between 1450 and 1200 BC (the period of the famous 1280 BC treaty described above); ii) the

He does *not* claim the existence of premodern international law – only of an 'international legal order'. His use of the term 'international' is unfortunate, as it obscures the specificity of 'nationhood' as a modern phenomenon tied to the rise of capitalism and the state-form.[47] Nonetheless, Grewe commendably counterposes international law and 'international legal order',[48] in an attempt to argue for the premodern existence of the legal *form* in relations between polities. He is careful to stress the incommensurability of this inter-polity law and international law.

> Above all, the assumption of an uninterrupted continuity of the international legal order must be limited by an acknowledgment of the impossibility of proving a context for the principles and the practice of a law of nations [again, an unfortunate phrase] reaching back beyond the immediately preceding epoch. . . . The hypothesis of continuity is thus reduced to involve only some conceptions and ideas underlying the principles and practice of international law. . . . Wengler's account of the historical development of the international legal order remains . . . accurate, based as it is on the starting point that today's legal order, which is factually valid for the whole world and which is designated 'international law', does not reach back further . . . than the last phase of the occidental Middle Ages.[49]

Grewe's perspicacity is obvious, but so are the limitations of his theoretical horizons. Without a conception of the legal form, his attempts to explain what is shared between different systems of inter-polity law – 'some conceptions and ideas' – is vague and ungrounded. The commodity-form theory of law allows us to understand the legal form that unites premodern legal systems and modern international law itself, without glossing over the historical rupture that the move to that law represented.

---

relations between Greek city-states, Persian Empire and Carthage between 600 and 338 BC; and iii) the Roman-Hellenistic world between the 4th Century BC and the development of the Roman Empire, around 168 BC (Grewe 2000, p. 10). A similar attempt to negotiate continuity and difference is in Steiger 2001, in his distinction between the 'law between political powers' and the 'law of nations', the former including 'the normative rules between political powers in the classical antiquity, the late antiquity and the Middle Ages'. Despite sharing some legal concepts, he acknowledges that these structures differ 'fundamentally from the present international law', and necessitate different conceptual apparatus for study (p. 181).

[47] See Anderson 1983 for one of the most influential statements of this thesis.

[48] '[T]his book . . . in its presentation of the historical development of international law does not extend to the international legal orders of Antiquity' (Grewe 2000, p. 10).

[49] Grewe 2000, p. 9.

There is an important variant of the theory of the transhistorical nature of international law which must also be addressed: the claim that such a law existed not, or not only, in the premodern West, but in non-Western societies.

2.1. *Pre-colonial theory: the non-Western birth of international law?*

These recent arguments are motivated to redress a problem in the literature – Eurocentrism. Traditionally, international law has been seen straightforwardly as a product of European civilisation. At its most stark, the claim is that 'international law as it now stands is a product of the European mind and has practically been "received" . . . lock, stock and barrel by American and Asian states.'[50]

In response, a variety of writers have marshalled evidence for the influence of non-Western norms, 'and claimed that Asian or African nations had played an important role in the development of international law'.[51] Some have performed an invaluable service in nuancing the historical record. However, it is important to disentangle the various arguments made under this sort of revisionist rubric.

One problem with the anti-Eurocentric argument is that it contains two distinct but often elided positions. In Onuma's words, the arguments are that non-Western regions 'had, or contributed to the development of, international law'.[52] These are, of course, different claims, of which the second – that non-Western polities contributed to the development of international law – is much more nuanced than the first.

The cruder version states that in the non-Western world in diverse periods, international law existed.[53] This claim is as ahistorical as the theories of 'antique international law' described above, and the same criticism – that it fails to analyse the specific forms of premodern regulations – can be made of it. Writers in this tradition

> tended to take the concept of international law for granted, and were interested in demonstrating how earlier studies had ignored the existence of this

[50] Verzijl, 1968, p. 442. See Anand 1983, pp. 1–9 for a list of other examples of Eurocentrism in the literature.

[51] Onuma 2000, p. 57.

[52] Onuma 2000, p. 61.

[53] See for example Anand, who claims that '[w]e shall try to see . . . the origin and development of the law of the sea not from the seventeenth century in Europe, as is usually done, but from the thus far neglected period of Asian maritime history' (Anand 1983, p. 6). This criticism should not detract from a fascinating and invaluable book.

particular notion of international law in Asia or in Africa. Their claim was basically that 'We too had international law.'[54]

As Onuma points out, these writers 'basically projected the notion of international law prevalent in the twentieth century onto their own past'.[55] It may be true that

> whenever human beings organize groups or societies such as clans, tribes, ethnic groups, religious groups, nations and the like, and are engaged in commercial or cultural intercourse, or armed conflicts among such groups, it is always necessary to make agreements. . . .[56]

But we cannot understand these relations 'without scrutinizing . . . the form, substance and nature of their norms regulating relations among independent groups'.[57] Labelling them 'international law' does not do this.

The claim that such law existed in ancient India, or Africa, is sometimes adduced without argument, simply by reference to the existence of interacting polities.[58] All these examples may tell us is of the existence of a legal form in relations between polities – and even then, that would have to be proved case by case.

> One might be able to demonstrate that there were certain normative relations between independent groups in certain regions of Africa at certain periods. . . . It is true that the rule of *pacta sunt servanda* in the naïve and general sense is valid regardless of the time and region. However, the substance of such a suprahistorical and universal rule would be so vague and equivocal, lacking the strictly binding character of law, that specific legal consequences could hardly be deduced from it.[59]

While specific (legal) relations between abstract subjects in a regular exchange process tend towards systematisation (though not necessarily to the peace-

---

[54] Onuma 2000, p. 61. See for example many of the writers in Anand 1972; Elias 1972. For an early version of this kind of argument, see Viswanatha 1925.

[55] Onuma 2000, p. 61.

[56] Onuma 2000, p. 58.

[57] Onuma 2000, p. 61.

[58] See for example the introduction to Elias's influential work (Elias 1972).

[59] Onuma 2000, pp. 39–40, footnote 98. Onuma is here talking about relations between African rulers and merchants on one hand and Europeans on the other, but his point about the 'vagueness' of *pacta sunt servanda* between the parties is equally true for relations between African polities. Onuma is wrong to imply that the basis of the law is in a 'strong' *pacta sunt servanda* as some kind of *Grundnorm*. This is a Kelsenist position, open to all the criticisms of Kelsen.

ful resolution of conflicting claims), the relations may be so contingent, unstable or random that a legal form does not inhere between the subjects, even if it applies for the duration of specific exchanges. The simple fact of relations between polities is not enough even to claim the legal form.

Obviously, there is no contradiction between the critique of Eurocentrist theory and a belief in the European basis of international law – Sinha, for example, writing from 'within a broad research agenda of anti-colonial international law scholarship',[60] accepts international law's 'parochial origin and growth in Europe', claiming that 'it has become universal and it governs states of all civilisations, European and non-European'.[61] As Bull and Watson put it, '[b]ecause it was in fact Europe and not America, Asia, or Africa that first dominated and, in so doing, unified the world, it is not our perspective but the historical record itself that can be called Eurocentric'.[62]

However, to put it thus risks underestimating the importance of the interaction between the European and non-European worlds in the creation of international law. Alexandrowicz's work is seminal here, with its thesis that international law was born in part because of the influence of non-Western traditions. Contrary to the conventional interpretation that a previously Christian-European international law has universalised and globalised, he claims that international law, which had been universal from the sixteenth to the eighteenth centuries, in the nineteenth century, '[p]aradoxical as it may seem, . . . then started contracting into a regional (purely European) legal system, abandoning its centuries-old tradition of universality based on the natural law doctrine'.[63]

> The . . . question may arise to what extent did treaty and diplomatic relations with the participation of a number of East Indian Sovereigns exercise an impact on the formulation of principles of the law of nations [in the sixteenth through eighteenth centuries]. The European powers, in their contacts with East Indian Sovereigns, often discovered a similarity of ideas with them as far as principles of inter-State relations were concerned. Failing similarity, they tried to impose on them their own ideas and whenever they were not able or ready to do so, they accepted certain legal concepts from Eastern tradition.[64]

---

60 Gathii 1998, p. 184.
61 Sinha 1996, p. 15.
62 Bull and Watson 1984, p. 2.
63 Alexandrowicz 1967, p. 2.
64 Alexandrowicz 1967, pp. 1–2.

His investigation stops with the nineteenth century because it was only then, he claims, that 'the contribution of Asian countries to the further development of international law was insignificant'.[65] In earlier interactions

> a confrontation of two worlds took place on a footing of equality and the ensuing commercial and political transactions, far from being in a legal vacuum, were governed by the law of nations as adjusted to local inter-State custom.[66]

There is no question that Western legal scholars knew of, and were influenced by, regulated behaviour, even the legal form, between non-Western polities. Grotius famously pointed out in his *Mare Liberum* that '[t]hese islands of which we speak, now have and always have had their own kings, their own government, their own laws, and their own legal systems'. The Portuguese 'do not go there as sovereigns but as foreigners. Indeed they only reside there by suffrance'.[67]

However, even Alexandrowicz's line is ultimately a derivation of the too-simple position that 'we [here Asia] too had international law'. He envisages the 'legal concepts' of the East, conceived as broadly similar to those of the West, merging to create universalist international law. The model is arithmetic: Western international law plus Eastern international law equals universalist international law. In this formulation it is a given that the principles in the East *were* international legal principles, which could be added to Western international law. Just as the West had international law, then, so had the East.

This leaves Alexandrowicz open to the criticisms made of Anand and others above. More fundamentally, his explanation of the development of international society is too simplistic. In this arithmetic model, historical change occurs through the addition of separate sets of ideas one to the other. There is no sense of social totality. A theoretical alternative has to be formulated which understands the kind of historical rupture represented by international law.

A new order was created, in which the inchoate legal forms between polities began to be conceptualised as a universal *international law*. It is a *world-historic result* of the early colonial experience of transatlantic and eastern trade.

---

[65] Alexandrowicz 1967, p. 2.
[66] Alexandrowicz 1967, p. 224.
[67] Grotius 2000, p. 14.

International law is not one Western system, nor one Western plus one Eastern system – it is the dialectical result of the very process of conflictual, expanding inter-polity interaction in an age of early state forms and mercantile colonialism. That is the way in which East and West, New World and Old World are inextricable in the formation of international law. Some practices and principles may appear to be maintained from an earlier age, but of course a continued practice in a changed social context is no longer the same practice.

International law embodies the violence of colonialism and the abstraction of commodity exchange. It is not that the contribution of non-Western polities to international law has been *obscured* by colonialism, nor that (Western) international law's spread across the world is the *result* of colonialism:[68] it is that international law *is* colonialism.

3. Colonialism and international law: the birth of a new order

A fundamental moment in inter-polity law, or proto-international law, occurred with the discovery of the 'New World', and the rapacious mercantile colonialism which followed it. It was of course not the mere existence of the New World which affected international legal thinking, in some nebulous idealist flurry. This is not a claim about the effect of 'encountering the other': it was specifically the appropriatory relationship between Europe and the Americas that developed international law.

This has long been openly acknowledged. The British Foreign Secretary put it matter-of-factly in 1884, quoting a Cambridge professor of international law.

> [I]t is obvious that the discovery of America . . . naturally gave rise to a vast number of disputes which the scanty International Code of the Middle Ages was quite unable to settle. 'That Code . . . possessed no means of unravelling complications with regard to the character of the acts necessary in order to obtain dominion over newly discovered territory . . . .'[69]

What this misses is the *break* with the 'International Code of the Middle Ages' and the first stirrings of true international law that the shock of the Americas necessitated.

---

[68] See Lachs 1987: 'international law flowered in the colonial era when Europe was at its most articulate and demanding' (p. 37).

[69] Carmichael 1884, pp. 161–2.

The pre-1492 inter-polity order had been characterised by the gradual collapse of the Papacy and the Holy Roman Empire as great powers, ongoing for around 200 and 250 years respectively. However, in the anarchic politics of late feudalism, the faded remnants of these institutions insisted on their own importance.[70] In the forms of the inter-polity legal community, for example, the Papacy continued to claim enormous power.

'The international legal community was identical to the Christian community, united in the Roman Church.'[71] Though generally the widespread adoption of notions from Roman law was predicated on the idea of equality in exchange, the Papacy stressed particular aspects of that law in inter-polity law to construct a stratified order of law,[72] with *ius divinum* – holy law – at its apex, above *ius gentium*.

In its original form *ius gentium* 'had nothing to do with the modern law of nations':[73] it was the law applicable between Roman citizens and non-citizens. Even in the usage of the later Middle Ages, that earlier sense lingered. However, as the polities of feudal Europe interacted in the absence of an Imperium (notwithstanding claims by the rump of the Carolingian Empire, which were only finally abandoned by Francis II as late as 1806) the meaning of *ius gentium* changed. Grewe's claim that '*ius gentium* included the fundamental structural principles of the law of nations' is correct,[74] so long as 'nations' is read as 'polities'. *Ius gentium* was not identical to the inter-polity legal order, but it was an important part of its structure.

Given the influence of *ius gentium*, and given that the *ius divinum* was held to be above it, this 'implied the existence of a supreme law-making power in the *Vicarius Dei*'[75] – the vicar of Christ, the Pope. Indeed, 'the papacy fre-

[70] 'It seems that there exists a particular dialectic necessity behind the tendency of declining powers and decaying institutions to exaggerate their ideological claims for superior dominion which equates with the degree to which their actual downfall had occurred. The Late Middle Ages provided a striking example of this experience. The intensity of claims for universal dominion on the part of the Empire and Papacy increased in proportion to the degree to which they had declined in power.' Grewe 2000, p. 46.

[71] Grewe 2000, p. 51.

[72] Grewe 2000, pp. 83–7.

[73] Nussbaum 1947, p. 19.

[74] Grewe 2000, p. 88. It is misleading of Grewe to state elsewhere that 'the character of . . . [*ius gentium*] was essentially that of the "law of nations" in our modern understanding of the term' (p. 88).

[75] Grewe 2000, p. 88.

quently claimed a legislative power binding upon all Christian nations',[76] while the Emperor was, formally at least, *primus inter pares*.[77]

In fact, though, 'the papacy was unable to acquire the position of a generally recognised and effective organ of law-making within the medieval international legal order', and that 'was even more valid for the Emperor'.[78] The point, however, is that the legal categories themselves were subordinate to overarching spatio-political entities. The continued overarching agency of the empire and the papacy – weak as it may have been – was a corollary of the relatively atomised, shifting polities of vassal feudalism, entities that 'were not "states" in the modern sense of the word'.[79]

These categories – legal and political – were changing by the end of the fifteenth century. The 'discovery' of the Americas sounded a death-knell to what remained of the medieval spatio-political integument, though it took a long time for these categories completely to decay.

Columbus's journey itself was an attempt to find a westward route to 'Cathay' and the Spice Islands for the purposes of mercantile enrichment. The growing strength of a merchant class was one of the underlying conditions – necessary but by no means sufficient – for the burgeoning change in the social system, of which the emergence of the early-modern state form was one symptom. It was in this context that Columbus's 'discovery' – unlike the visit to the Americas of the Vikings five centuries before him – had such a profound effect on the world's political economy, and on its legal categories.

By means of the Treaty of Tordesillas, on 2 July 1494, Spain and Portugal, with Pope Julius II's sanction, divided the world between them with a demarcation line 370 miles west of the Cape Verde Islands – east of that was deemed Portuguese, west Spanish. The world was divided by a *raya*, or global line. These lines were of fundamental importance in the changing nature of early international law.

The Treaty of Tordesillas is the most famous of the global lines of division drawn in the immediate aftermath of the discovery of America, and was a modification of Pope Alexander VI's *inter caetera divinae* of 4 May 1493, in which the *raya* was drawn 100 miles west of the same islands. In fact, five edicts were issued in quick succession by the Pope after special envoys from

[76] Grewe 2000, p. 88.
[77] Grewe 2000, p. 89.
[78] Ibid.
[79] Grewe 2000, p. 61.

Spain arrived in the Vatican to give notice of Columbus's journey and the discoveries. These edicts, with their varying placing of the *raya*, reflected the wrangling between Spain and Portugal, jockeying for position with the Pope for the largest possible share of the world.[80]

Although such demarcation lines between Spain and Portugal already existed, these new lines were a fundamentally important break with tradition. The earlier lines 'were not yet global. Even the Portuguese line of 1443 . . . [and the] *Inter caetera* of March 13, 1456 . . . are also not global in this sense. They reach "*usque ad Indos*," but India is still thought to be located in the east'.[81] These post-1492 *raya*, however, were 'the first global lines of division and distribution', predicated on 'the first scientific concept of the true form of our planet'.[82]

Of course the attempt to divide the globe between Spain and Portugal failed. The *raya* was unsustainable. But the kind of division of the world it represented remained crucially important, and survived into later lines of division of very different kinds. The fact of the New World fundamentally altered the socio-spatial landscape on which premodern, 'proto-international' law was predicated.

> [I]n 1492, when a 'new world' really did emerge, the structure of all traditional concepts of the *center* and *age* of the earth also had to change. European princes and nations now saw a vast, formerly unknown, non-European space arise beside them.
>
> Most essential and decisive for the following centuries, however, was the fact that the emerging new world did not appear as a new enemy but rather as *free space* – an area open to European occupation and expansion. For 300 years, this was a tremendous affirmation of Europe both as the center of the earth and as an old continent. But it also destroyed previously held concrete concepts of the center and age of the earth because it initiated an internal European struggle for this new world that in turn led to a new spatial order of the earth with new divisions. Obviously, when an old world sees a new one arise beside it, it is dialectically challenged and is no longer old in the same sense.[83]

---

[80] Grewe 2000, pp. 235–7.
[81] Schmitt 1996, p. 32 footnote 3.
[82] Schmitt 1996, p. 32.
[83] Schmitt 1996, p. 30.

The *raya*, even as mechanisms for 'crude seizures of land' represented '*global linear thinking*'[84] – a new, scientific conception underpinning an international law in flux, for which for the first time a *global* subjectivity was understood to exist.

The writings of Vitoria are crucial to understanding this moment, as Anghie has made clear, as has Carl Schmitt in an important, though elliptical, 1950 essay.[85] Vitoria is poised on a fulcrum, looking backward with scholastic method, while confronting a new and fundamental problem – 'the justification of European land appropriations as a whole'.[86]

Medieval inter-polity law was predicated on the idea of the world as ordered by the existence a *respublica Christiana*, in which the various polities were defined either as enemies or members of that *respublica*. The attempt of Vitoria and others to fit the 'New World' into that model could not succeed. Vitoria 'no longer recognized the spatial order of the medieval *respublica Christiana*'.[87] The status of the native Americans was *not given* in the medieval schema, and was thus subject to disputation, undermining the supposedly totalising traditional explanation of the world. In the writings of the time, the attempt by the European powers to apply existing concepts to this new global order – thereby undermining those concepts, and paving the way for new ones – can be seen.

The *raya* of 1494 itself was an essentially premodern, feudal division, between

> two princes, both recognizing the same spiritual authority and the same international law. . . . [T]he *raya* presupposed that Christian peoples and princes had the right to be granted a missionary mandate by the pope, on the basis of which they could pursue their missionary activities.[88]

However, in the context of the 'New World', the feudal notions on which that division is based are undermined by the increasingly obvious inadequacy of their model of the world. A premodern line of division was drawn onto a newly (post-feudal) scientific conception of the world, for the purpose of the exploitative distribution of a global order between two burgeoning

[84] Schmitt 1996, p. 31. Emphasis in original.
[85] Anghie 1996. Schmitt 1996.
[86] Schmitt 1996, p. 43.
[87] Schmitt 1996, p. 50.
[88] Schmitt 1996, p. 34.

mercantilist states. It is no surprise that Vitoria's apparently traditional concepts contain contradictory impulses.

Vitoria is not the modern thinker nor the liberal he is sometimes painted.[89] His spatial conceptualisation of early colonialism represents the last, brilliant applications of premodern categories to new problems, in such a manner and context that they pave the way for later, early modern theories.

Writing in a scholastic tradition – indeed, displaying 'perfection of . . . scholastic method', Vitoria 'obtained within a scholastic-theological debate',[90] and did not distinguish theology and law. There is no sense in his work of international law as 'a secular discipline of a technical legal character'.[91] But in his *De indis y de iure belli relectiones*, the application of pre-existing philosophical methods in these new circumstances led to new kinds of theory. This is at the heart of Vitoria's paradoxical proto-modernity.

Though he comes down firmly in favour of the Spanish *conquista*, in Vitoria's hands the scholastic method 'is one of extraordinary impartiality, objectivity and neutrality'.[92] By its rigorous application, he rejects 'unconditionally'

> all legal titles of the pope and the emperor deriving from claims to world domination . . . as inappropriate and illegitimate. . . . [I]t is repeatedly emphasized that native Americans, though they may be barbarians, are not animals and are no less human than the European land appropriators. . . . [T]his amounted to a rejection of a particular type of argument put forward at that time . . . [that] presented the natives as savages and barbarians . . . in order to place them outside the law and to make their land free for appropriation.[93]

Drawing on Augustine arguments, Vitoria 'emphasizes that non-Christian Indians may not be deprived of their rights for the benefit of Christian Europeans', because he 'treats Christians and non-Christians as equals in legal terms, at least from the standpoint of international law'.[94] The massive strains such ideas placed on the *respublica Christiana* model of inter-polity law led Vitoria to address the problem of jurisdiction over the 'Indians' by mov-

---

89 Nussbaum 1947, p. 63.
90 Schmitt 1996, p. 44.
91 Nussbaum 1947, p. 60. See also Schmitt 1996, p. 56, quoting an unnamed 'especially critical 19th century Hegelian': 'Vitoria was in no sense one of "the forerunners of modern lawyers dealing with constitutional questions"'.
92 Schmitt 1996, p. 44.
93 Schmitt 1996, pp. 44–5.
94 Schmitt 1996, p. 47.

ing away from 'the universal system of divine law administered by the Pope' towards a 'universal natural law system of *jus gentium*, whose rules may be ascertained by reason'.[95]

Of course, reason here is applied to religious categories, but the move from a divine toward a secular law is discernible, even though it is precisely Vitoria's application of a Christian-scholastic method, in changing circumstances, which pushes him in that direction. 'The lack of any historical concept at such a crucial time had to lead to a suspension and displacement of the predominant Eurocentric view of the world and of history in the *respublica Christiana* of the Middle Ages.'[96]

The move towards a concept of natural law – still religious, but no longer vested in the Pope – raised the question of the new basis of legal authority. For Vitoria, the answer lies in his inchoate theory of sovereignty. '[N]atural law administered by sovereigns rather than divine law articulated by the Pope becomes the source of international law governing Spanish-India relations'.[97] Vitoria finds the source of such sovereignty in the theory of 'just war'. A sovereign, for Vitoria, has the right to wage such a war. However, Vitoria's theory of just war remains embedded within the conceptualisations of the *respublica Christiana*, according to which only Christian powers – sovereigns – can wage just wars. The native Americans have no such right, and therefore no effective sovereignty.

> War, the right to wage it and by victory to acquire title over territory and people, resides only with the Spanish who are Europe's Christian emissaries in the Americas. Indians, as pagans, exist in Vitoria's legal framework as subjects against whom war may be waged and without a right to wage a just war themselves.[98]

The beginnings of an international law of independent sovereign powers is thus predicated on a colonial disempowering of non-Western subjects. The 'darker history of sovereignty', as Anghie claims, is that the 'doctrine acquired its character through the colonial encounter'.[99]

However, for a modern international law, the notion of a war defined by its 'just cause' is unsustainable.

---

[95] Liu 1999, p. 173.
[96] Schmitt 1996, p. 50.
[97] Anghie 1996, p. 325.
[98] Harris 2000.
[99] Anghie 1996, p. 335.

> Based on relations between states, post-medieval European international law from the 16th to the 20th century sought to repress the *iusta causa*. The formal reference point for the determination of a just war was no longer the authority of the Church in international law but rather the *equal sovereignty of states*. Instead of *iusta causa*, the order of international law between states was based on *iustus hostis*. Any war between states, between equal sovereigns, was legitimate.[100]

Vitoria's theory of sovereignty is therefore premodern, rather than protomodern.[101] However, clearly the move to a system where legal authority is based on the legitimate waging of war was a move towards modern international law. Again Vitoria's thinking is contradictory. It can be argued that the colonial *content* of sovereignty in Vitoria – the premodern right to wage 'just war' – is less fundamental than his focus on the *fact* of sovereignty as the basis of international legal agency, combined with a remarkable sense of reciprocity, which is a residue of his scholasticism and its 'extraordinary impartiality, objectivity and neutrality'.

Of course the undermining of non-European agency was of central importance in the colonialism of early international law. But the basis by which sovereign agency was denied to non-Western powers had to change over centuries, as Vitoria's premodern 'just war'-based justification became increasingly anachronistic. It was, for example, replaced by the concept of 'civilization' from the eighteenth century, reaching its strongest point during the nineteenth.[102] Thus the *content* of the colonialism in international law was mutable according to historical circumstances. However, without overarching authority, the contradiction between equality of juristic right and disparity of political power is not only intrinsic to international law, it is very fact by which international law is made binding *as law*. It could be described as the form, rather than content, of colonialism in international law, and it is visible in inchoate form in Vitoria's discourses.

---

[100] Schmitt 1996, p. 63. Emphasis in original.

[101] On the question of just cause, 'Vitoria's thinking belongs to the international law of the Christian Middle Ages rather than to the modern international law between European states' (Schmitt 1996, p. 63).

[102] Schmitt 1996, p. 50. Grewe 2000, pp. 445–58. It is worth pointing out that precursors of such 'civilisation' theories are clearly evident in writings as early as Gentili's, whose justifications for Spanish colonial intervention was that they made war 'on the Indians, who practised abominable lewdness even with beasts, and who ate human flesh, slaying men for that purpose' (quoted in Gowan 2001, p. 151). The theory of civilisation is examined in detail in the following chapter.

Despite denying the 'Indians' sovereignty, for example, Vitoria grants them 'dominion' over their own property, and crucially insists that 'all the Spaniards' rights vis-à-vis the barbarians are also valid in reverse – they are reversible as *iura contraria*, as rights of barbarians vis-à-vis Spaniards – unconditionally reciprocal and invertible'.[103] Because the natives have meaningful ownership over their lands, the mere 'discovery' of the Americas does not give the Spanish ownership 'any more than if it had been they [the natives] who had discovered us'.[104]

That eventually, however, was impossible. It was obvious to Vitoria as to everyone else that the Spaniards were 'much more powerful' than the natives.[105]

> Vitoria's right to settlement and commerce is only *formally reciprocal*, while it is *materially unilateral* or at least extremely one-sided. There was little chance in Vitoria's day that American Indians would paddle in their canoes to Europe in order to claim their natural right of settlement.[106]

The disparity of material culture was such that it was the very 'objectivity' of law that gave it in service to the strong – the coloniser. That contradictory colonialism-in-equality is at the heart of international law, even where weaker polities *are* granted sovereign agency (as the 'Indians', here, are not).

For Vitoria, the underlying reason for this equality and reciprocity was commercial equality. It is the fact that the natives have ownership over their property that renders them capable of trade, and grants them reciprocal legal rights. The freedom to trade is at the heart of his definition of social agency – he cites the natives' 'system of exchange' as evidence that they are fully human and competent[107] – as well as his legal order. In his view, the ultimate justification for the *conquista*, a war of the Spanish against the 'Indians', would be '[i]f barbarians opposed the right of free passage and free missions, of *liberum commercium* and free propaganda'.[108] At the heart of this bundle of concepts was the freedom of trade.

Initially, the Spanish crown had been more interested in its struggle with France for the control of Italy than in Columbus's cack-handed adventures.

---

103 Schmitt 1996, p. 49.
104 Victoria [sic] 1964 (no pagination).
105 Victoria 1964.
106 Fisch 2000, p. 8. Emphasis in original.
107 Victoria 1964.
108 Schmitt 1996, p. 51.

'Its attitude only changed when other adventurers discovered massive wealth.'[109] The discovery of Aztec gold in 1517 excited the attention of the increasingly powerful Spanish merchant class. Vitoria was addressing the issues raised by this sudden mercantile interest. It is therefore no surprise that he argues that

> [i]f the Indian natives wish to prevent the Spaniards from enjoying any of their . . . rights under the law of nations, for instance, trade or other above-named matter . . . they do them a wrong. Therefore if it be necessary, in order to preserve their right, that they should go to war, they may lawfully do so.[110]

Once again, the fact that this is an argument in favour of colonialist exploitation is obscured by juridical equality, and reciprocal rights and duties. 'Neither may the native princes hinder their subjects from carrying on trade with the Spanish; nor, on the other hand, may the princes of Spain prevent commerce with the natives'.[111] The absurdity of the idea that Spain might 'prevent commerce' when its entire colonial strategy revolved around the brutal extraction of goods and bullion from America is, juridically speaking, irrelevant.

The colonial encounter is central to the development of international law. But this centrality is not reducible to the colonialism of *content*, the fact that certain legal categories were invested with Western bias, though the fleshing out of such historical specificities is important. Colonialism is in the very *form*, the structure of international law itself, predicated on global trade between inherently unequal polities, with unequal coercive violence implied in the very commodity form. This unequal coercion is what forces particular content into the legal form.

This is what I have called colonialism-in-equality. It was present at the end of the fifteenth century, when the fact of the New World forced a crisis in medieval juristic concepts. It is still present – indeed central to international law – as Jörg Fisch acidly points out, observing that 'Grenada has exactly the same right to intervene in the United States as the United States has to intervene in Grenada'.[112] As I will argue in the next chapter, the legal contents of colonialism vary widely: the form persists.

---

109 Harman 1999, p. 165. See pp. 161–5 for Columbus's disastrous expeditions.
110 Victoria 1964.
111 Ibid.
112 Fisch 2000, p. 12.

3.1. *Amity lines: colonialism beyond law's boundaries*

The *respublica Christiana* was crumbling. The 17th century, with the strengthening of the sovereign state exemplified in absolutism and mercantilism, saw a systematisation of the international legal order, exemplified in the works of Grotius in theory and the Westphalia peace in practice (which, for all the necessary correctives about envisaging it as too-absolute a change, was an important step).[113] There was a break with the past.

The era between 1492 and 1648 – what Grewe calls 'the Spanish Age'[114] – was a time of contradiction. The crisis of the Middle Ages had not yet been resolved by the rise of a internally coherent alternative system. If, very broadly, the post-Grotian international law of 'mature absolutism'[115] was a 'modern' system based on bounded sovereign states, the international law of 'the Spanish Age' was an unstable law, which in retrospect – and mindful of the dangers of teleology – can be understand as a law in transition.

The instability of law mirrored the instability of politics, which had been greatly exacerbated by Europeans' arrival in the New World.

> As a result of the overseas discoveries, the State system in its *statu nascendi* at the turn from the fifteenth to the sixteenth centuries was immediately threatened by a loss of stability. It risked being dissolved in the immense distances of the overseas regions, and having its basic assumptions overturned as a result of the revolutionary effect that colonial expansion had on the distribution of power in Europe.[116]

The initial attempts to deal with this insecurity, the *raya*, could not last. The jostling for position of the various burgeoning European states in an international community in which Papal and Imperial authority were no longer key – the competitive process misleadingly termed 'balance of power' – made such high-handed attempts at division based on Papal power unsustainable.

---

[113] Beaulac, one of the most careful debunkers of the 'Westphalian orthodoxy' (Beaulac 2000) cannot quite square the circle of his impressive critical history, in which Westphalia is 'nothing more than another step' on the historical journal ending ultimately in sovereign equality (p. 169), with the fact that the 'mythical character of the Westphalian model' expresses 'the resolving nature of Westphalia as an *idea-force*' (pp. 176–7. Emphasis in original). The continuities he is right to point out – he even sees Westphalia *shoring up* the moribund Empire – do not mean that it did not occur at a moment of transition, in a complex of continuity, denial and change.

[114] Grewe 2000, pp. 135–275.

[115] Grewe 2000, p. 137.

[116] Grewe 2000, p. 152.

> According to the structural rules of the new balance of power system, no privileged position of individual powers could be maintained unless it rested on a predominance of political power; by its very nature this system granted all nations an equal chance of free political expression on a global scale. It was contrary to the true character of the balance of power system to recognise the authority of the Pope for settling disputes over colonial territories. Corresponding attempts by the Spanish to master problems of this kind by returning to the universalistic ideas of law and order which had evolved during the Late Middle Ages, were doomed to fail sooner or later because of this inherent contradiction.[117]

It was in this context that the struggle of England, France and Holland against Spain and Portugal led to the *inversion* of the global lines of division: the *raya* were replaced, it is generally held, with the lines of amity. First agreed in the Peace of Cateau-Cambrésis in 1559 – not formalised in the treaty, but orally agreed between the participants – these were lines separating 'the European sphere of peace and the law of nations from an overseas sphere in which there was neither peace nor law'.[118] Francis Drake is famously supposed to have described this formula as 'No peace beyond the line'. Though the details (and even the existence) of the lines are not without controversy, similar agreements seem to have been made between France and Spain in Vervins in 1598, and between England and Spain in London in 1604 (though the wrangling around this treaty was evidence of the beginnings of the end of the amity system).[119]

---

[117] Grewe 2000, pp. 153–4.

[118] Grewe 2000, p. 154.

[119] Grewe 2000, pp. 155, 158. This story of the amity lines has been more or less agreed on by many writers over many years and from widely diverging perspectives (See for example Burn 1951, p. 17; Johnson 1991, p. 42; Beer 1922, pp. 7–8; Quinn 2000, pp. 55–6; Crouse 1940, p. 2; Green and Dickason 1989, pp. 35–6; Davenport 1917, p. 3). In his careful historical work, however, Fisch denies that such lines ever existed (Fisch 1984, Chapters 2 and 3). 'The sentence "No peace beyond the line" is, from the point of view of international law, a legend.' (Fisch 1986, p. 11.) '[T]hese lines were an invention of the French and the English in the 17th century . . . as an instrument against Spanish claims. They pretended that the European peace treaties were not valid overseas so as to be legally entitled to attack the Spanish possessions especially in America at any time. The Spaniards constantly and consistently rejected these claims – and they were right. There is not one single European peace treaty in which you can find a clause instituting something like an amity line.' (Fisch, personal communication.) This is an invaluable corrective to those who have seen the lines 'enshrined' in the treaty of Cateau-Cambrésis (Williams 1984, p. 73. See also Lloyd 1996, p. 4). Fisch's searching work demands a rethink of the lines. However, while such divisions

This was, in dramatically literal fashion, an attempt to delineate a *European* law of nations, alongside a zone where might made right – where 'force could be used freely and ruthlessly'.[120] The amity lines are central to the claim, contra Alexandrowicz, that 'the international legal order of the Spanish Age . . . remained essentially an international legal order of occidental "Christendom"'.[121] The argument is that if non-Christian non-occidental polities were bracketed off as *beyond law*, then surely the legal order ends at the borders of the law. But this, of course, is too simplistic. The 'agonal' zone beyond law was fundamentally functional – indeed, invaluable and necessary – to the 'lawful' zone of Europe in an unstable time. It was 'a tremendous *exoneration* of the internal European problematic'.[122] International law and the international system, in other words, was predicated on its own opposite, the anarchic zone 'beyond the line'.

> [T]he designation of a conflict zone at once freed the area on this side of the line – a sphere of peace and order ruled by European public law – from the immediate threat of those events beyond the line, which would not have been the case had there been no such zone. The designation of a conflict zone outside Europe contributed also to the bracketing of European wars.[123]

The system was temporary. The lines were a reflection of the struggle between the European powers to establish overseas commercial/colonial presence. They represented the failure of the Spanish attempt to define whole areas of the world as exclusively Spanish, in the *raya*:[124] this political content was

---

may not have been formalised in treaties, Fisch's claim that '[n]o such agreement was ever made' (Fisch 1986, p. 10) seems to be contradicted by the letter of the Spanish plenipotentiaries to King Philip, dated 13 March 1559 (in Davenport 1917, pp. 220–221). Such lines may not have been 'enshrined', but even informal or semi-formal agreements might indicate the division of the world on the basis described – though with less crude vigour and more countervailing tendencies than the usual story might imply. It can also be argued that even if Fisch is right that the Spanish never agreed these terms, that they were invented by the French and English, insofar as the argument developed here is regarding the *global conception* embodied in such lines, the very fact of their being so posited early in the seventeenth century, disputed or not, is evidence that the model they embedded was functional to the new global thinking of (at least some) European powers (and not only the English and French – the Dutch also used such linearly divided conceptions in the early- to mid-seventeenth century (Grewe 2000, pp. 157, 159)).

[120] Schmitt 1996, p. 37.

[121] Grewe 2000, p. 152.

[122] Schmitt 1996, p. 37. Emphasis in original.

[123] Schmitt 1996, p. 40.

[124] Some of these, such as the Treaty of Tordesillas, were in fact in their original

transformed in the amity lines, though on the basis of a continuing scientific division of the world and global thinking at the service of colonialism. But as the dominant maritime power, Spain quickly adopted and supported the amity lines. Where they operated, overseas colonial possessions were not recognised, but were up for grabs: beyond the line, might made right, and that might was pre-eminently Spanish.

That changed, however, with the seventeenth century. Although agreements containing amity lines continued up as far as 1634,[125] the strain was showing as early as 1604, when the English negotiators 'refused to recognise this principle [of no peace beyond the line] in the Anglo-Spanish peace'.[126] This was an attempt by England to be recognised as a colonial power with as much right to formally recognised possessions as the Spanish. A fudge was agreed, under which 'everything remained as undecided as it had been before'.[127]

The growing power of the English and especially the Dutch East India Companies meant that the lines, representing Spanish refusal to acknowledge the *political-juristic* equality of other powers in terms of their right to recognised colonial possessions and status, were growing more and more unsustainable. Not surprisingly, given the indeterminacy of (international) law, both sides in these disputes were able to marshal support from within international law canon.[128] What shifted the Spanish was not the brilliance of any legal argument, but the changing geo-political situation.

The 1630 Anglo-Spanish Peace of Madrid was something of a halfway house. It fudged once again the issue of the freedom or otherwise of English overseas trade, but

---

formulations more advantageous to Portugal. However, Spain became the major overseas power in this epoch, with the decline of Portugese maritime power and trading monopolies in the East. Thus the collapse of the *raya* and their reformulation into the lines of amity was the result of attempts of other European powers to undermine specifically Spanish maritime power. The supposed 'beneficiary' of Tordesillas, Portugal, was less of a factor. For the decline of Portugal in the later sixteenth and seventeenth centuries see for example Furber 1976, pp. 31, 33; Rothermund 1981, pp. 22–4.

[125] The famous declaration made by Cardinal Richelieu on 1 July 1634, 'according to which French seafarers were forbidden to attack Spanish and Portuguese ships on this side of the Tropic of Cancer, but were given liberty to do so beyond this line if the Spanish and Portuguese refused the free access to their Indian and American lands and seas' (Schmitt 1996, p. 36).

[126] Grewe 2000, p. 158.

[127] Grewe 2000, p. 159.

[128] See for example the debate between England and Spain in 1604, outlined in Grewe 2000, pp. 158–9.

> [f]or the first time . . . this treaty provided expressly that henceforth there would be peace beyond the line, that prizes captured there would be restored and that compensation was due even when capture took place beyond the line. For the first time a European treaty bearing on the overseas territories started from the express assumption that peace should also govern beyond the line, and that the provisions of the treaty should be applied even there.[129]

The final death knell of the amity lines sounded, with neat symbolic timing, in the iconic year of 1648 itself, when for the first time, Spain recognised another colonial power: Holland, the most powerful of the new maritime-mercantile forces – a 'commercial thalassocracy'.[130] Spain bowed to the inevitable with the Treaty of Münster and 'formally conceded to the Netherlands the right of "navigation and traffic in the East and West Indies"',[131] as well as recognising all Dutch colonial possessions. 'The Spanish colonial monopoly was broken and the demarcation line had become irrelevant.'[132]

The amity lines have been controversial in international law. They represent a peculiar episode. 'The association between international law and universality is so ingrained that pointing to this connection appears tautological.'[133] The paradox of the amity lines is that such a universal system was predicated on its own partial abnegation.

It has become a cliché of critical theories to claim that something-or-other is defined by its own negation: in this case, this is no dialectical sleight of hand. For the burgeoning state system of Europe, the 'New World' was an opportunity, because of its massive resources, and a threat, because Europe risked 'having its basic assumptions overturned as a result of the revolutionary effect that colonial expansion had on the distribution of power in Europe'.[134]

The lines of amity were functional for a brief but vital time, in the period before 'mature Absolutism', of the 'early modern state, the subject and creator of the international legal order'.[135] During this time, the limits of state territory 'were not yet sharply and unambiguously drawn'.

---

129 Grewe 2000, p. 159.
130 Furber 1976, p. 50.
131 Grewe 2000, p. 160.
132 Ibid.
133 Anghie 1999, p. 1.
134 Grewe 2000, p. 152.
135 Grewe 2000, p. 171.

> This was also true in respect of the limits of power and competence in relationships between States, and in respect of the unity and extent of internal State authority. The process of concentration of public power in the person of the absolute monarch or . . . the general process of the accumulation of State-like powers and competence, did not reach a stage where the structure of the modern State was basically completed until the end of the Spanish Age.[136]

During this period of unstable state-forms, characterised by the coexistence of modernising and premodern tendencies, the legal order that the 'New World' had unleashed was rigidly circumscribed – and thus protected. This was *not* a precursor of the later international law for which the only legal agents were the European nation-states. *Pace* Alexandrowicz, the international legal order of the nineteenth century was not an order of European public law: it was rather, in one sense, a return to Vitoria, an order in which only the European powers were conceived as *agents* of international law, but where that law itself *was* perceived as universal. In other words, those nineteenth-century colonies, like the Americas in Vitoria's work, existed within the remit of international law, but possessed no agency.[137] During the period of the amity lines, in contrast, *there was no law* beyond the line.

In the particular circumstances of the early state system, this was, to put it crudely, a necessary safety-valve for the development of that system, and of the very law suspended beyond the line.

4. The development of sovereignty: from politics to abstraction

The bearer of abstract rights is the subject of the legal form. Sovereignty is the legitimating principle by which that subject in modern international law – the state – faces others. The historical development of sovereignty is clearly central to the forms of international law.

Sovereignty is not a given, and its modern form must be unpicked. The concept of 'sovereign equality', for example, is so fundamental – often definitional – to modern international law that it seems counterintuitive to

---

[136] Grewe 2000, pp. 171–2.
[137] See Anghie 1999.

separate the two words.[138] However, there is no necessity that states which recognise each other's sovereignty will also relate to each other as equals on a legal plane. What is primarily conceded in the recognition of another's sovereignty is the principle that internally, each power has the right to decide its own policies. It is a theory of independence, not equality.

> [I]n the international context the theory of sovereignty has never implied more than the claim to independence . . . it has only denied that there exists above the community a supreme power of the kind which, within the community, it has been its purpose to sustain.[139]

The first systematic theory of sovereignty was that of Bodin in the sixteenth century. It revolves around the absolute right of the sovereign to rule internally, but Bodin is clear and explicit that sovereignty does not imply equality between sovereigns.

> [I]n the case of the sovereign prince who puts himself under the protection of another, does he lose his sovereign authority thereby and become a subject? It would seem that if he recognizes a greater than himself, he is no longer sovereign. Nevertheless I hold that he does remain an sovereign, and in no sense becomes a subject. . . . [I]t is said that in treaties of alliance between sovereign princes, those that put themselves under the protection of one greater than themselves do not become his subjects. Even when, in treaties of an unequal alliance, it is expressly stated that one of the parties will defend the authority of the other, this does not make the latter the subject of the former. Our protégés and clients are as free as we are ourselves, even though they may not be our equals in wealth, in power, or in honour.[140]

What distinguishes Bodin's treatment of inequality between sovereigns from mainstream jurists' acknowledgement of 'obvious factual differences in reality'[141] is that Bodin's theory of sovereignty does not counterpose that reality

---

[138] Malanczuk 1997, p. 3, for example: 'International law . . . is primarily concerned with the legal regulation of states which are organized as territorial entities, are limited in number and consider themselves, in spite of the obvious factual differences in reality, in formal terms as "sovereign" and "equal"'. See also the Charter of the United Nations, of which Article 2 (1) reads '[t]he Organization is based on the principle of the sovereign equality of all its Members.'

[139] Hinsley 1986, p. 158.

[140] Bodin 1955, Book I, Chapters VI and VII. No pagination.

[141] Malanczuk 1997, p. 3.

and the legal system. In Bodin's discussion of 'unequal treaties' the inequality of sovereigns is formally, legalistically conceptualised. For modern international law, such inequality is a problem of the separate realm of 'politics', abstracted from law:

> publicists found in the concept of legal equality a political principle of equality. . . . [W]hatever their real inequalities, in the nominal [legal] world of indivisible corporate persons with a unified will, all states were politically equal.[142]

Sovereignty has obviously changed. Is it true, as Louis Halle claims, that in the sphere of international relations, '[n]o change has been more radical than that brought about by the recent rise of the concept that all nations are equal'?[143] What are the processes by which sovereignty has become sovereign equality?[144]

In Vitoria we see the first stirrings of sovereignty theory, though it is inconsistent and partial. Vitoria does link sovereignty with the early state – defined as 'a perfect community'[145] – but he cannot coherently define that supposed bearer of sovereignty. '[T]he essence of the difficulty', he admits, 'is in saying what a perfect community is'.[146] Vitoria's answer – 'that a thing is called perfect when it is completed whole' – is tautologous.[147] 'Neither does it help to define the sovereign as the ultimate authority within the community, for even this proposition is subject to complex qualifications; the complicated hierarchies of the time defy Vitoria.'[148] Ultimately, Vitoria takes refuge in empiricism, simply listing examples of what he deems sovereign kingdoms.

There were specific social reasons that an 'objective' theory of sovereign state-hood eluded Vitoria. In the sixteenth century,

> the power of the state has not been consolidated in any significant way. Authority is too dispersed and hierarchies, while established theoretically, are too confusing and uncertain for Vitoria to use them convincingly as a means of structuring sovereignty doctrine. . . . The task of identifying sovereign authority and defining the powers wielded by such an authority, in

[142] Klein 1974, pp. 8–9.
[143] Halle 1974, p. xi.
[144] '[T]he concept of sovereignty underpins a principle of sovereign equality that has attained almost an ontological position in the structure of the international legal system.' (Kingsbury 1998, p. 600.)
[145] Victoria 1964.
[146] Ibid.
[147] Anghie 1996, p. 329.
[148] Ibid.

> the complex political systems of Renaissance Europe proved extraordinarily difficult, and the techniques and conceptual distinctions used by Vitoria for this purpose were problematic and ambiguous.[149]

Vitoria's reliance on just-war theory to define sovereignty, along with Christian presuppositions as to which authorities can wage such wars, is subjective and medieval. Until the age of mature absolutism, sovereignty theory could not look to the states as self-evident legal agents.

The 'unequal sovereignty' theories of Bodin are historically specific to an age when feudal hierarchies and permeable territorial borders still existed in the early-modern state forms. He is acutely aware of that remaining feudal hierarchy, and of the problems it poses for his theory. The tensions between feudal and early modern conceptions are clear in his writing.

> We have already said that an absolute sovereign is one who, under God, holds by the sword alone. If he holds of another he is not sovereign. But this raises a difficulty. If those who hold anything at all of another in faith and homage are not sovereigns, there are hardly any sovereign princes in the world. On the other hand if we concede that those who do so hold in faith and homage are sovereigns, we are in effect saying the vassal and his lord, the servant and his master, are equals in honour, power, and authority.[150]

Bodin's imperfect solution is to pose absolute sovereignty as a cut-off point in a hierarchy of power. He appears to contradict himself: in his chapter on 'Tributary Princes' 'France alone emerges from this survey with an unqualified claim to be a sovereign state with no limitation whatsoever'.[151] Later, however, like Vitoria he resorts to empiricism and describes the monarchs of 'France, Spain, England, Scotland, Ethiopia, Turkey, Persia and Moscovy' as 'sovereign absolutely'.[152] The implied model is that at a certain point, a critical mass of feudal political power becomes absolute sovereignty. In this way, Bodin is able (somewhat unstably) to perceive sovereignty as discrete – a modern conception – and yet as part of a feudal hierarchy. His insistence that sovereignty does not equal equality is conditioned by the transitional history in which he was writing.

---

149 Anghie 1996, pp. 329–30.
150 Bodin 1955, Chapter IX.
151 M.J. Tooley's editorial insert in Bodin, 1955.
152 Bodin 1992, p. 114.

The modernising nature of Bodin's theory of absolute and discrete sovereignty compared to Vitoria's are manifest, for example, in his de facto secularism. Vitoria's just-war conception of sovereignty means that for him 'the Saracens [and native Americans et al] can never be truly sovereign'.[153] Bodin, by contrast, whose theory derives from *objective development of political power*, accepts without question the sovereign nature of Ethiopia, Turkey and Persia.

However, it would be a mistake to perceive Bodin as a writer struggling to free theory from the shackles of feudalism. Just as the structures of the early modern state were born *out of* the very feudal forms they changed, so Bodin's 'superficial modernity' is 'firmly rooted within the framework of Renaissance knowledge'.[154] Bodin is addressing problems *of feudalism*, 'responding to underlying changes in the political situation':[155] 'he feels that the aggregation of social classes which feudalism has developed can only attain the unity and order of the true state life through a power dominating and regulating all alike'.[156]

We can go further – Bodin's theory of absolute sovereignty was designed precisely as an attack on anti-feudal arguments, like those of the radical Huguenot theorists of the 1570s, the *monarchomachi*, who argued for the right of the populace to rebel against kings who exceeded their authority.[157] This political conservatism, however, did not stop Bodin's theory having radical implications vis-à-vis the feudal order.[158]

Modernism in theory, as in social life, was born from the categories that preceded it – the very attempt to perpetuate which leads to their transformation. It is only later that the feudal

> epistemic edifice underlying Bodin's reasoning is thoroughly demolished in the early seventeenth century, while the logical core of the theory of sov-

[153] Anghie 1996, p. 330.
[154] Bartelson 1995, p. 141.
[155] Hinsley 1986, p. 179.
[156] Dunning 1896, p. 91.
[157] Wood and Wood 1997, p. 74: Mattern 1928, p. 7.
[158] Beaulac 2003a suffers from an idealism which sees the very word 'sovereignty' playing 'a leading part in creating and transforming reality' (p. 2) rather than being an expression of the underlying political-economic changes, but stresses that sovereignty, for Bodin, was a concept designed to legitimate kingship, and that 'the reality associated with the word was eventually transposed from the internal to the international plane' (p. 26). (Beaulac stresses the importance of Vattel as the agent of this 'transposition' (Beaulac 2003b).)

> ereignty is retained, articulated and refined . . . until it becomes the centrepiece of the new cognitive and political order.[159]

With the consolidation of the state of the seventeenth century the debate over sovereignty changed. In this century of the English revolution, the arguments around the nature of sovereignty were largely focused *internally*, on the question of who had the right to sovereign power. The debates, for example, were between advocates of absolute royal sovereignty, such as Thomas Hobbes and Sir Robert Filmer, and advocates of various forms of 'popular sovereignty'.[160] The question of state equality – a question of the interaction of the governments *externally* – was not the focus.

Implicitly, however, in the early part of this period there was still no intrinsic link made between sovereignty and equality. Grotius, for example, 'never applied the theory of natural equality to the society of separate states, except in certain particular instances and for a limited purpose'.[161] His arguments in *Mare Liberum*, for example, are for free and equal access to the sea, but this 'was not intended to establish a like equality in respect to all rights'.[162] In *De Jure Belli ac Pacis*, for example, Grotius in distinguishing various types of treaties, describes unequal treaties thus.

> From equal treaties, the nature of unequal treaties may easily be understood. And where two powers contract, this inequality may be on the side either of the superior, or of the inferior power. A superior power may be said to make an unequal treaty, when it promises assistance without stipulating for any return, or gives greater advantages than it engages to receive. And on the part of the inferior power this inequality subsists when . . . her privileges are unduly depressed; so that engagements of this kind may be called injunctions or commands rather than treaties. And these may, or may not, be attended with a diminution of their sovereign power.[163]

Treaties which institutionalise the inequality of their parties, then, do not necessarily impair the sovereignty of either party: equality and sovereignty were not mutually constitutive.

---

159 Bartelson 1995, p. 143.
160 See Wood and Wood 1997, pp. 72–7.
161 Dickinson 1920, p. 34.
162 Dickinson 1920, p. 53.
163 Grotius 2001, p. 136.

Pashukanis is therefore wrong to claim that in Grotius's system 'sovereign states . . . are counterposed to one another in exactly the same way as are individual property owners with equal rights'.[164] However, the strengthening of the states and the state system led to a strengthening of the international legal order in which those states were conceived of as abstract juridical subjects – and this *was* an equalising tendency.[165]

For early theorists such as Vitoria, property could still be conceptualised as feudal property – a non-absolute, permeable form. The 'absolute and complete *dominium*' of Roman property had been replaced by feudal property, 'a complex of dependent and derivative rights'.[166] It was on the basis of this feudal property that Vitoria could perceive the native Americans as having effective *ownership* over their lands, without sovereignty. After all, 'medieval property . . . was converted into a dependency of medieval polity':[167] legal ownership said nothing about effective political control. Ownership and sovereignty were separate.

The sovereignty of a state *is* its subjectivity in an international legal order – that was clear even for Vitoria. At the core of a true legal order are juridical agents conceived as equal owners of alienable property. With the period of mature absolutism, the 'demolition of feudal hierarchy' '[t]he political and the proprietary organizations have again become separate and co-ordinate'.[168] As permeable – what Anderson calls 'conditional'[169] – feudal property ebbed away and the state took absolute (and absolutist) possession of itself and its colonies, and such absolute property came to underpin the social system.

---

[164] Pashukanis 1980, p. 176.

[165] For Osiander, this tendency toward equality is 'the unavoidable corollary of autonomy' in the Westphalian system (Osiander 1994, p. 87). In seeing equality in this manner, rather than as a slow, hedged-around juridical tendency as the result of *conflictual* (commodified) relations, Osiander depicts the 'balance of power' as 'a consensus principle' (p. 132) rather than, as would emerge from the analysis here, at best an always-already-failing 'hidden hand'-type attempt to smooth over the very conflictual reality of which emergent abstract equality was an expression. Despite obvious points of convergence in terms of a sense of dynamic, Osiander's stress on 'the role of consensus in the international politics of Europe in the last three centuries and a half' (p. 12) (in some ways a development of the work of Bull and Watson on the expansion of international society (Bull and Watson 1984)) stands in contrast to the analysis here, for which conflictual economic and coercive political-economic tendencies are key.

[166] Noyes 1943, p. 78.

[167] Ibid.

[168] Ibid.

[169] Anderson 1974, p. 425.

This is the point at which, for Grotius (and in international law in general) 'relations between states . . . [are] relations between the owners of private property'.[170] The tendency was for sovereignty and property to become inextricable. This is the moment at which sovereignty shakes off the last of its feudal residues.

In the older feudal conception, the rights concomitant on ownership were circumscribed by an overarching sovereign political power. At this later time, paradoxically, the very *disaggregation* of political power from property, as property became absolute, *aggregated* property and equality with sovereignty in international law. As subjects of a legal order, the agents of international law were definitionally property owners: at the same time, their independence and international legal subjectivity was already established as their sovereignty. Sovereignty and equality of proprietorial status linked.

In the seventeeth-century work of Pufendorf, the last legacy of feudal property is still visible. Pufendorf 'took his theory of sovereignty from Grotius',[171] but he explicitly recognises the equality of states. As the theory of sovereignty he takes from Grotius does not preclude inequality, Pufendorf cannot derive the equality he asserts from state sovereignty.[172] The fact that he recognises state equality in a world of radically politically unequal states is testimony to the pressures towards juridical abstraction in the period of mature absolutism, during the consolidation of the international legal order. However, with sovereignty still retaining something of its feudal particularism, Pufendorf instead locates equality using the last throes of radical natural-law methodology.

Borrowing from Hobbes, he sees states as existing in a state of nature. Unlike Hobbes, however, he sees 'the law of nature' placing states 'in a natural equality'.[173] 'It is an equality for which actual inequalities and differences are of no importance. . . . States are equal by their very nature; it is a fundamental equality that is inherent in their existence and is therefore absolute and unlimited.'[174]

---

[170] Pashukanis 1980b, p. 176.

[171] Dickinson 1920, p. 79. For an alternative account of Pufendorf, stressing his differences with Grotius, see Tuck 1999, pp. 140–65.

[172] Kooijmans's claim that for Pufendorf, 'equality . . . derives its meaning from the sovereignty of the state' is therefore wrong (Kooijmans 1964, p. 79), though much else in his analysis of Pufendorf is pertinent and useful (Kooijmans 1964, pp. 75–80).

[173] Quoted in Dickinson 1920, p. 81.

[174] Kooijmans 1964, p. 79.

Though as Dickinson puts it, this is 'the first time the principle of state equality was expressly derived from the application of familiar theories of natural law',[175] it is perhaps more apt to think of Pufendorf as at the *end* of a lineage of theory, one which separated sovereignty and ownership. The consolidation of absolute property, and absolutist power in the sovereign states, meant the end of theories predicated on feudal 'political' sovereignty, rather than on abstract property ownership.[176]

This is clear in the very different theory of equality found in the early eighteenth-century positivists, such as Johann Jakob Moser (1701–85). For Moser, the disaggregation of sovereignty and property was impossible. Accordingly for him, the equality pertaining to property owners *was* derived from sovereignty.

> That state is called sovereign, which is independent, that means to whom no other state or lord has the right to command in secular matters. . . . Independence entails equal rights. With regard to the rights, ensuing from independence, all fully sovereign states are equal; semi-sovereign states, however, are not equal to them. . . . As the smallest free state has just as many rights in this respect as the greatest, all sovereign states, whether they are great or small, are perfectly equal.[177]

Equality for Moser did not inhere in some state of nature, but in the very *fact* of a community of sovereign independent states. 'Equality becomes a necessary fundamental principle and starting-point for inter-stately relations'.[178]

Positivism as a theory is a product of the age after the crisis of feudalism has been resolved, and the structures of the modern state are in place. Moser's

---

[175] Dickinson 1920, p. 82.

[176] This is not to suggest that Pufendorf was operating in a straightforwardly feudal model. Clearly he was not. He was acutely conscious of parameters of '*regularity* and *irregularity*' (Schröder 1999, p. 967) in the discussion of sovereignty. The notion of an 'irregular' political form pathological to a 'regular' one is evidence of a generalising, abstracting tendency. The variety of political forms of 'actually-existing' sovereignty 'deeply concerned' Pufendorf (Schröder 1999, p. 967), particularly the 'mis-shapen Monster' (Pufendorf quoted in Schröder 1999, p. 966), what remained of the Holy Roman Empire. The impulse to systematisation of sovereignty bespeaks a modernising cast of mind, but his acute fascination with its particularities, excellently brought out in Schröder 1999, is evidence of Pufendorf's continual focus on sovereignty as politically specific – a premodern conception. It is symbolically perfect, and no coincidence, that it was the decaying rump of the great premodern Empire which gave Pufendorf the focus for a conception of sovereignty still stained by feudal particularism.

[177] Moser quoted in Kooijmans 1964, p. 90. See Moser 1959.

[178] Kooijmans 1964, p. 90.

'observational' method means that the abstract equality he claims had to have been well-established in fact for him to assert it. In his approach, 'principles could properly be established by examples'.[179]

This is in contrast to Pufendorf and other naturalists: schematically speaking, Pashukanis is right that natural-law theory, against which positivism rebelled, 'was the revolutionary banner under which the bourgeoisie conducted its revolutionary battle with feudal society'.[180] The theory had taken the ahistoricism, rigour and objectivity of medieval scholasticism and *secularised* and *radicalised* it by positing a natural law that would inhere, as Grotius famously claimed, whether or not God existed.[181] Thus for example, where the universalisation of the principle of abstract equality was a revolutionary measure occasioned by the spread of absolute property, natural-law theory was able to assert this principle *even where premodern forms of unequal sovereignty survived*. Pufendorf's assertion that equality inheres in the very state of nature may not stand up to scientific scrutiny, but it served a radical – a revolutionary – purpose in the face of the long-drawn-out survival of the Holy Roman Empire, which denied the equality of sovereignty.

The 'historico-pragmatic'[182] methodology of positivism, by contrast, proceeds by systematising 'actual international customs and treaties and the study of international practice'.[183] As Nussbaum argues vis-à-vis Moser, though, the

> purely factual or 'observational' approach . . . was bound to fail . . . [because] law cannot be perceived as a traveler perceives the shifting scenery. Observation can be no more than the first step in building up a legal discipline.[184]

Of course, there *is* theory in Moser and positivism, but it is often implicit.

For example, Moser's claim that all states are equal must, for him, proceed from observation. However, obviously all states are *not* politically equal. But Moser is not talking about political equality. Like Pufendorf, he is referring

[179] Walker 1981, p. 339. See pp. 283–95 on Moser's preference for induction and his antipathy to theory, philosophy and 'rationality and system' as opposed to 'fact' (p. 283).

[180] Pashukanis 1980a, p. 97.

[181] Schmitt 1996, p. 57. '17th and 18th century philosophers and jurists from Grotius to Christian Wolff consistently developed this moral doctrine of late scholasticism into a still more general, more neutral and purely human *ius naturale et gentium*'.

[182] Pashukanis 1980b, p. 177. Page 330 below.

[183] Ibid.

[184] Nussbaum 1947, pp. 167–8.

to *abstract* equality. The paradox is that as a positivist, Moser believed himself to be observing actual state behaviour,[185] and yet his theory of equality *and therefore of sovereignty* can only be a theory of states' *abstract* rights. This is evidence of the consolidation of the abstract edifice of international law.

What Moser is 'merely observing' in his theory of equal sovereignty, is the aftermath of the triumph of abstract juridical categorisation in the international sphere. His claim to be 'exclusively concerned . . . with the ways in which European rulers and states customarily "behave" in their negotiations'[186] is therefore highly ideological. Political facts are rendered less, not more visible, in the very positivism which claims to focus on them.

I have stressed that the formal categories of an abstract and equal juridical relationship presume unequal forces of coercion. The ugly facts of political coercion are not pathological to law, but intrinsic to it. This means that law, and international law in particular, not only *is* a system predicated on coercive political violence *but is its own ideological obfuscation of that fact*. Law disguises its own brutal core.

Positivism is a product of the triumph of that structure, and operates as justification for that self-justifying system. It is at the very triumph of equality, when that radical concept so subversive to the feudal inter-polity order becomes normalised, naturalised and universalised, as half of a dyad with sovereignty, that the ongoing political depredations of the system become *invisible* to international law, and are impervious to its analysis.

> This brings us to modern international law. Right up to the present, the principle of the equality of states is connected with the notion of sovereignty. . . . [I]t led to consequences that were in sharp contrast with the requirements of actual practice.[187]

The legacy of positivism is very strong in modern international law. It remained the 'informing philosophy'[188] of nineteenth-century international law, and its 'pragmatic', anti-theoretical tendencies are marked in the managerialism that takes the place of international legal theory.

The early history of sovereignty is i) the history of the collapse and reappropriation of feudal categories; ii) their reconstitution according to the exigencies of consolidated states and the absolute property rights concomitant

185 Nussbaum 1947, p. 165.
186 Ibid.
187 Kooijmans 1964, p. 91.
188 Anghie 1999, p. 78.

on a burgeoning global market; and iii) the self-camouflaging of a politically unequal and coercive system by the juridical forms which express it.

4.1. *Absolute ownership and Roman law*

I have argued that a legal order is a reflection of commodity exchange. This is of course not equivalent to modern capitalism, which is characterised by the development of productive forces driven by the process of competitive accumulation. However, part of the process of capitalism is the commodification of all aspects of life.

An examination of the influences on international law, and the premodern precursors of that law – the inter-polity codes up to the fifteenth century – illustrates the intimate relation between commodity exchange and the legal form. Roman legal proprietary concepts were hugely important for Grotius and seventeenth-century international law, for example – '[w]herever possible writers on international law tried to bolster their teachings by citations from Roman sources'[189] – evidence of the centrality of the Roman concept of absolute property to that legal order.

> [T]he Roman legal system became essentially concerned with regulation of informal relationships of contract and exchange between private citizens. Its fundamental orientation lay in economic transactions. . . . The real thrust of Republican jurisprudence . . . was not public or criminal law, but civil law governing suits between disputing parties over property, that formed the peculiar province of its remarkable advance. . . . The economic growth of commodity exchange in Italy . . . [during the Roman imperial system] thus found its juridical reflection in the creation of an unexampled commercial law in the later republic. The great, decisive accomplishment of the new Roman law was thus . . . its invention of the concept of 'absolute property'. . . .[190]

Perry Anderson may overstate the case in claiming that the revival of Roman law by the end of the Middle Ages 'was fundamentally propitious to the growth of free capital in town and country':[191] after all, as Ellen Wood points

[189] Nussbaum 1947, p. 18. See also: 'up to the eighteenth century, the highly refined terminology of Roman legal learning was invariably adopted by writers on international law'.

[190] Anderson 1974, pp. 65–6.

[191] Anderson 1974, p. 25.

out, 'capitalism originated in the one European country [England] where Roman law was least influential'.[192] Its influence on proto-international law, though, was marked.

Of course, the specific *contents* of the forms of Roman law were often not suitable for inter-polity or international law, or indeed the domestic law of these early polities. But jurists removed 'the large portions of Roman civil law that were strictly related to the historical conditions of Antiquity'.[193] Not that the adoption of Roman law was straightforwardly a reflection of modernising tendencies: though '*economically*, it answered to vital interests of the commercial and manufacturing bourgeoisie', '*politically*, the revival of Roman law corresponded to the constitutional exigencies of the reorganized feudal States of the epoch'.[194] Anderson expresses this brilliantly.

> For the Roman legal system . . . comprised two distinct – and apparently contrary – sectors: civil law regulating economic transactions between citizens, and public law governing political relations between the State and its subjects. . . . The juridically unconditional character of private property consecrated by the one found its contradictory counterpart in the formally absolute nature of the imperial sovereignty exercised by the other. . . . It was the theoretical principles of this political *imperium* which exercised a profound influence and attraction on the new monarchies of the Renaissance. If the rebirth of notions of Quiritary ownership both translated and promoted the general growth of commodity exchange in the transitional economies of the epoch, the revival of authoritarian prerogatives of the Dominate expressed and consolidated the concentration of aristocratic class power in a centralized State apparatus that was the noble reaction to it. Ulpian's famous maxim . . . 'the ruler's will has force of law' – became a constitutional ideal of Renaissance monarchies all over the West.[195]

This is the very contradiction examined above in the discussion of Grotius and Pufendorf – the disjuncture between a sovereignty inhering in the political facts of absolutist rule and a society of equal property owners. For Roman law in its own age, the contradiction was resolved because the absolute sovereign, the Republic, and the absolute property owners, the citizens, operated

---

192 Wood 1991, p. 50.
193 Anderson 1974b, p. 24.
194 Anderson 1974b, pp. 26–7. Emphasis in original.
195 Anderson 1974b, p. 27.

at different juridical levels. For an international law, it is the very states in which sovereignty inheres that are treated as the owners of property – the Roman law contradiction becomes acute precisely in early international law.

The move to positivism illustrates the fact that the imperial 'political' theory of sovereignty could not hold, and was replaced by an abstract juridical one. The resolution of that conceptual contradiction represented the triumph of the 'economic' aspects of Roman law over its 'political' aspects, with the universalisation of a commodity-exchange system.

5. From maritime law to international law

The law of the sea has come to be one category within the wider edifice of international law. Particularly as the technical possibilities of exploitation of the marine environment grow, it has come to be considered a resource at the disposal of the sovereign states.[196]

This was not always the case. International maritime trade's central importance in the development of the early sovereign state posited the sea not as a resource, but an *arena*, for trade, a backdrop to the clash of equal ownership rights. The seventeenth-century debates over the freedom of the seas were about effective control over the very arena in which sovereign states met, interacted and defined each other.

Maritime law has been at the heart of international law since its earliest incarnation. Certain key issues in international law and relations cannot be made sense of without understanding the centrality of the sea in international law: the fundamental relationship between international law and international trade; the consolidation of the state in the seventeenth century; and the transition to modern capitalism.

5.1. *Early codes: the mercantile maritime roots of international law*

It was not only Roman law which governed relations in the market place. Since at least the twelfth century, much commodity exchange between merchants had been governed by institutions like the law merchant – 'an

[196] For illustration, see the debates in Oxman et al. 1983. Though they argue furiously as to the best strategy for America to take, the contributors to this volume share the historically new exploitative view of the sea.

international code so that traders from all parts were familiar with the rights and obligations it enforced'.[197]

From the start law merchant was inextricably associated with international trade and maritime law, and is a fundamentally important influence on the development of international law. Few legal systems better illustrate Pashukanis's point about law being an expression of commodity exchange.

> Actual law, where created, reflected precisely this commercial need. . . . 'Out of his own needs and his own views the merchant of the Middle Ages created the Law Merchant.' The law did little more than echo the existing sentiments of the merchant community.[198]

The relation between related early maritime law and inter-polity, proto-international law is obvious. Evolving 'to meet changing, growing requirements of international commerce',[199] this was a 'maritime law [which] tended to become a law common to all nations and peoples'.[200]

Though not strictly part of the codified law merchant, the famous early maritime codes such as the *Rôles d'Oléron* of the twelfth century or the *Consolato del Mare* of the fourteenth century share many of its important features. Most fundamentally, they 'were a reflection of merchant desires',[201] caused by '[t]he very great expansion of medieval commerce . . . [o]riginating in the practice of merchants and seamen'.[202]

These mercantile codes dealt with rights and duties pertaining to shipbuilding and selling, but in their rules of prize law – designed to protect neutral property – they also covered maritime warfare. For merchants trading internationally, in other words, the distinction between private 'economic' and public 'political' law was meaningless. Questions of property *were* questions of political power – thus for example the *Consolato* decrees that 'neutral goods on enemy ships and neutral ships carrying enemy goods should not be subject to capture by a belligerent'.[203]

---

197 Morton 1989, p. 74.

198 Trakman 1983, p. 9. As Anderson says in a revealing footnote, '[t]he comparative advance of [non-Roman] legal rules governing commenda-type operations and maritime trade in the Middle Ages is not surprising' (Anderson 1974b, p. 26 footnote 17).

199 Sanborn 1930, p. 127.

200 Sanborn 1930, p. 40.

201 Trakman 1983, p. 9.

202 Walker 1899, p. 116.

203 Nussbaum 1947, p. 32.

This is a historical illustration of the argument above, that political coercion is embedded in the commodity form, and only obscured where an overarching sovereign becomes final arbiter of legal rules. Thus in the very earliest premodern forms of the inter-polity law that became international law, there is no separation of public and private law, and that most quintessentially public of legal orders – international law itself – *is* the 'private' law of commodity exchange.[204]

Grotius is clear on this, arguing that because states are juridically like property-owning individuals, 'the same reasoning applies' to 'private estates and . . . private law' and 'the territory of peoples and public law'.[205] It is not that the 'original' inter-polity law was that of 'peaceful' commodity exchange, and that questions of public law were overlaid on those foundations: it is that in its purest form, without an overarching arbiter, *there is no distinction* between private and public. *Questions of exchange are questions of coercion.*

These early maritime codes lacked a vital, defining universality of international law. This was a reflection of the fact that trade was still, despite the expansion of medieval commerce, not the economic motor of the society. 'Commercial capital, in the first instance, is simply the mediating movement between extremes it does not dominate and preconditions it does not create.'[206] The law only held where and when commodity exchange was likely to occur. The theoretical upheavals in law in the works of Vitoria, Grotius, Pufendorf and others are the result of a revolutionary change in the socio-economic order: the transition from feudalism.

> There can be no doubt . . . that the great revolutions that took place in trade in the sixteenth and seventeenth centuries, along with the geographical discoveries of that epoch, and which rapidly advanced the development of commercial capital, were a major moment in promoting the transition from the feudal to the capitalist mode of production. The sudden expansion of the world market, the multiplication of commodities in circulation, the competition among the European nations for the seizure of Asiatic products and American treasures, the colonial system, all made a fundamental contribution towards shattering the feudal barriers to production.[207]

---

[204] For an argument that the distinction between public and private international law does not reflect a fundamental organic separation, but is the result of the consolidation of the bourgeois state, see Cutler 1997.

[205] Grotius 2000, p. 29.

[206] Marx 1981, p. 447.

[207] Marx 1981, p. 450.

The argument is *not* that the growth of mercantile capitalism led directly to this change: 'this development, taken by itself, is insufficient to explain the transition from one mode of production to the other'.[208] Contrary to the arguments of Sweezy, Wallerstein and others writing in what Mooers calls 'the market-relations model',[209] mercantile capitalism per se was not a 'creative force': it is necessary, but not sufficient, for a transition to productive capitalism.[210]

There is a substantial debate, particularly within Marxism, over precisely what was the nature of the transition from feudalism to capitalism, and when it occurred.[211] Below, I will make a case that the seventeenth century's political forms were transitional to capitalism. It should be borne in mind, though, that whether or not Europe in the seventeenth century and even eighteenth century *is* deemed so transitional, it is undeniable that this mercantilist era saw the massive expansion of international trade, central to the structure of the most powerful European states. It is during this period that the categories concomitant on that trade – the legal forms – begin to universalise. This was the birth of true international law. As trade became global, and definitional to sovereign states, the international order could not but become an international legal order.

Whether or not one agrees with the transition thesis, and sees this as part of the birth of international capitalism, has huge ramifications for the analysis of the specific political content in the legal forms, but will *not* make a fundamental difference to the analysis of the universalisation of those forms and the legal order itself. This is because, as Chris Arthur and others have pointed out, while productive capitalism *as a mode of production* differs fundamentally

---

[208] Marx 1981, p. 444.

[209] Mooers 1991, p. 5.

[210] Sweezy 1978 (p. 42, for long-distance trade as a 'creative force'); Wallerstein 1983, especially pp. 30–1 and pp. 40–3.

[211] One of the best overviews of this debate is Mooers 1991, pp. 5–43. The starting point for the early arguments is Hilton (ed.) 1978. Against the Sweezy-Wallerstein position are arguments that the growth of capitalism came from within the feudal mode of production – a famous example is Dobb 1963. Drawing on Dobb and nuancing his arguments is Brenner (1977, 1985a and 1985b), who has become the most well-known and influential of the school known as 'political Marxism', which stresses the role of class struggle rather than the development of forces of production in the transition to capitalism. Wood (1991, 1999) is another eloquent example of this school. A critique of this current is Harman 1998, which makes several persuasive criticisms about political Marxism's failure to conceptualise changes in productive forces, but suffers from a tendency to schematise its opponent's arguments. A more sympathetic and open-minded critique of Wood is Barker 1997.

from mercantile capitalism, *at the level of the value-form* 'nothing changes when the form of simple circulation becomes the bearer of a capital circuit'.[212] In other words, the commodity-form analysis of the birth of the modern international legal order holds whether or not one agrees with Marx – as I do – that this epoch of mercantile capitalism 'had an overwhelming influence on . . . the rise of the capitalist mode'.[213]

I do not want to minimise the importance of the debate on transition: merely to point out that the spread of a world market is the fundamental moment of the international legal form, whether that market is deemed transitional to capitalism or not. Given the utterly central importance of mercantilism and the seventeenth-century market to international law, however, it is important not only to acknowledge the fact of that market but to make sense of its historical nature. We cannot understand why and how it is so central without that understanding.

5.2. *Lineages of the mercantilist state*

A key aspect of the transition debate in historical materialism is the nature of the absolutist state. Even among those who agree that the epoch was of 'a society in transition, with both feudal and capitalist forms of exploitation existing side by side',[214] the question of the state form itself is controversial.

Neither Marx nor Engels ever offered a systematic theory of absolutism: the closest was Engels's claim that it 'was . . . balancing the nobles and the burghers against one another'.[215] This model of a state balancing between two opposing social forces – the 'equilibrist-transitional paradigm'[216] – is unsatisfactory. It is highly unconvincing that a state could 'balance' between opposing forces for as long as three hundred years.[217] This theory underplays the specificity of absolutism, and fails to account for the form's own internal dynamics.

An examination of these dynamics is beyond the remit of this essay. For the best known – and magisterial – attempt to grant specificity to the

[212] Chris Arthur, personal communication.
[213] Marx 1981, p. 451.
[214] Harman 1998, p. 97.
[215] Engels 1902, p. 209.
[216] Teschke 2003, p. 157.
[217] Harman 1998, a modern restatement of the theory, describes French absolutism as starting 'in the late 15th and early 16th centuries' and being maintained until the 18th (presumably until 1789) (Harman 1998, pp. 97, 100).

absolutist form while acknowledging that it is a form for a society in transition, Perry Anderson's work is key. Though he stresses the 'feudal' nature of absolutism, the transition is key in his understanding of the peculiarities of the state form. 'The rule of the absolutist state was that of the feudal nobility in the epoch of transition to capitalism'.[218]

There was, of course, no single model of absolutism. In fact, there were several European polities such as England, Switzerland and Poland, where

> for reasons having to do with specific resolutions of preceding class conflicts on the basis of different social property-relations – absolutism never took hold. Even those polities conventionally taken to be absolutist – Spain, Austria, Russia, Prussia, Sweden or Denmark – had very different chronologies, dynamics, and characteristics. . . .[219]

However, for the historian of international law, the focus on these states' internal dynamics to point out their differences leaves relatively unexplored their *external* dynamics, in which certain shared characteristics between absolutist and non-absolutist states are visible. From this perspective, though care must be exercised, it is possible to make generalisations about the various state forms ranging from the 'high' absolutism of the French model even to the English non-absolutist model.

> [A]longside these specific characteristics of the absolutist State, certain general characteristics of State development were established during this Age which also marked the British type of aristocratic parliamentary State. These involved the development of a closed national mercantile trading and commercial system; the link between the modern State and modern capitalism became particularly close and intense during this Age. States developed into sovereign, closed and ever more self-sufficient economic entities. . . . The spirit of economic competition joined the political and military rivalries between States. The wars of this age were all essentially trade wars, beginning with the English-Dutch dispute over the Navigation Act and leading to the continental blockade of the Napoleonic Era.[220]

There were of course unique political forms in each country. But one risks obscuring as much as illuminating in focusing so carefully on the specifics

[218] Anderson 1974b, p. 42.
[219] Teschke 2003, p. 153.
[220] Grewe 2000, p. 319.

of a state form internally that the shared changes in European states in general goes unnoticed.[221]

Even more than the epoch of the absolutist state this is the epoch of the *mercantilist* state – it is in the very fabric of the most powerful sovereign states of this age that they are international, maritime and mercantilist. Mercantilism (and its laws) was crucial for the consolidation of the sovereign state – absolutist or otherwise – and a transition to a capitalist world economy.

It has been pointed out that some of the bundles of ideas associated with various 'mercantilist' writers 'reflected medieval patterns of thought, others anticipated liberal theories of a later age'.[222] Mercantilism 'seldom possessed a unified system of policy, or even a harmonious set of doctrines',[223] and supposedly therefore 'did not constitute a coherent system'.[224]

However, it is wrong to claim that therefore 'there was no such thing as a mercantilist *system* of economic regulation'.[225] One does not have to posit a 'consistent long-term policy divorced from the reality of temporal economic conditions'[226] to accept that there was a certain underlying programme to mercantilism – whatever its codifiers thought of it, and however they disagreed.

The guiding doctrine of mercantilism as economic philosophy is usually held to be the favourable balance of trade. As one of its early advocates put it,

> [t]he ordinary means therefore to encrease our wealth and treasure is by Forraign Trade, wherein we must ever observe this rule; to sell more to strangers yearly than wee consume of theirs in value. . . . That part of our stock which is not returned to us in wares must necessarily be brought home in treasure.[227]

---

[221] As Teschke does in his detailed examination of the internal and self-contained structure of French absolutism (Teschke 2003, pp. 167–81). This is a deeply impressive close analysis, but it risks missing wood for trees.

[222] Rothermar 1981, p. 1.

[223] Thomas 1926, p. 3.

[224] Rothermar 1981, p. 1.

[225] Supple 1959, p. 229.

[226] Supple 1959, p. 225. It is indicative of Supple's idealism and an implicit individualist theory of history that he cannot conceive of an economic system unless it has 'an overall and integrated content based upon conscious thought' (p. 225). If this were true it would probably deny *any* systematicity to *any* economic policy.

[227] Mun quoted in Buck 1942, p. 13. See also <www.socserv2.socsci.mcmaster.ca/~econ/ugcm/3113/mun/treasure.txt>.

However, it is in fact arguable that the relentless equation of this theory – or indeed of any other specific economic measures – with mercantilism is misleading.

> Nor is it fair to the Mercantilist to identify his policy with the theory (once held as a dogma) of the Balance of Trade. The Mercantile System was by no means the outcome of the failure to distinguish between Wealth and Money. Various fallacies entered at various times into the kaleidoscopic shiftings of mercantile policy, but they were not of its essence. Individual mercantilists emphasised the need for bullion regulations, tariff barriers, navigation laws and the like; but these were only various tendencies that came into prominence at various stages of mercantile policy.[228]

The 'shifting combination of tendencies' varied with political context: what they were all geared towards, however, was 'the increase of national power'.[229] 'The core of mercantilism is the strengthening of the State in material resources; it is the economic side of nationalism'.[230]

This underlying conception was intrinsically international.

> [It] presupposed the existence of political units which were also conceived of as economic units, i.e. states. . . . The programme also depended on the existence of not only bilateral but multilateral trade among such units and on the availability of political instruments . . . which enabled the government to influence these relations.[231]

International and maritime law was a vital part of the mercantilist state-building process. I will examine three key legal strategies deployed to this end: the Navigation Acts; the structure of the East India Companies; and the debates over the freedom of the seas.

5.2.1. *The Navigation Acts*

> Originally devised in the seventeenth century as a weapon directed against England's maritime rivals, the large number of statutes affecting shipping

---

[228] Thomas 1926, p. 3.
[229] Ibid.
[230] Ibid. The theory of mercantilism as at core about state-building was seminally expressed by Schmoller in 1884 (reprinted Schmoller 1967). The most influential modern reformulation of Schmollerian ideas is Heckscher's monumental 1932 work (reprinted Heckscher 1994). For a harsh critique of Heckscher see Coleman 1969.
[231] Rothermar 1981, p. 2.

> which together constituted the Navigation Laws formed the keystone of an imposing edifice of restriction.[232]

These acts were classic maritime protectionism, and the cornerstone of England's mercantilist policy. The most famous and important of these acts was that of 1651, by which Cromwell 'forbade, with some exceptions, participation by foreign ships in certain English and colonial trades'.[233] Specifically,

> all traffic with the English colonies had to pass over England. Imports from overseas, as well as all traffic with European ports, were restricted exclusively to English ships, while ships flying foreign flags would only be admitted to English ports if they carried goods which originated in the flag State. All intermediate trade under foreign flags was prohibited.[234]

As well as a general strategy of economic protection, designed to maintain a colonial trade monopoly and bolster English maritime industry, this was a specific attack on the Dutch. 'With these acts Cromwell and Parliament signaled their intention to challenge the Dutch for maritime supremacy and to assert their own sovereignty in the Atlantic.'[235] The sting was the prohibition of the intermediate re-export trade, which was of vital importance to the Dutch.[236] The Anglo-Dutch war which followed was a massive boost to the English mercantilist strategy, as an enormous number of Dutch ships[237] were taken and added to the English merchant fleet, accelerating a fleet-expansion programme which was already ongoing.[238]

The Navigation Acts were only a specifically English – and specifically juridical – version of a general European tendency towards the consolidation of the sovereign state through protected overseas trade. The famous French variant of mercantilism Colbertism, named after the statesman Jean Baptiste Colbert, contained similar provisions. In Colbert's own words,

---

232 Palmer 1990, p. 40.

233 Davis 1962, p. 12.

234 Grewe 2000, p. 296.

235 Linebaugh and Rediker 2000, p. 145.

236 Grewe 2000, p. 297. Rothermar points to the central importance of re-exports to Dutch maritime trade as a reason for the lack of Dutch mercantilist literature: 'the full programme was of immediate relevance only to such states which had both a considerable home market and a substantial share in foreign trade' (Rothermar 1981, p. 4).

237 The lowest estimate is 1,000 ships (Davis 1962, p. 12).

238 Davis 1962, pp. 10–11.

> We must establish a system of protective tariffs . . . we must make possible for France the overseas transportation of its own products, develop the colonies and link them together with France through our trade policy; we must eliminate all mediators between France and India and must develop the fleet in order to protect the merchant marine.[239]

The use of maritime law gave the English version of mercantilism a particular precision and formality. The Navigation Laws were a juristic codification of, and aid to, the tendency towards the state trading monopolies central to mercantilism. Law was thus central to the construction of English mercantilism.

5.2.2. *The East India Companies*

The trade with India in the seventeenth century was built on monopoly companies: the Dutch, English and French East India Companies, and many smaller companies such as the Danish, the Scottish 'Darien' Company, the Ostend Company and others, all competing.[240]

There were various reasons that the companies had been set up as monopolies.

> By the 1590s, the Portuguese experience had shown that overseas trade east of the Cape of Good Hope needed to be organized as a national monopoly for four main reasons. The first . . . was the need of military protection in dangerous seas. The Portuguese had amply demonstrated that the advantages to a European nation of the use of such 'passes' [*cartazes*, which controlled access to trade] depended on their issuance by a single authority rather than by individual traders. Thirdly, it was generally understood that individual Europeans, acting solely on their own authority, could not negotiate effectively with Asian princes, great or small. Finally, if the Portuguese example of setting up trading factories under their exclusive authority on Asian soil was to be followed, the effective operation of such 'enclaves' depended upon their being under one authority.[241]

This is not to suggest, of course, that there was no controversy about the monopoly nature of the trade: there was, most famously the anonymous *Considerations upon the East India Trade*.[242] But in addition to the four prag-

---

[239] Colbert's 1643 letter to Mazarin, quoted in Grewe 2000, p. 296.
[240] See Furber 1976, pp. 185–229 for a discussion of the various companies.
[241] Furber 1976, p. 185.
[242] For a discussion of this and other anti-monopolist arguments, see Thomas 1926, pp. 16–20.

matic arguments outlined above, and underlying the mercantilist nature of the East India Companies, the close relation between a state-authorised monopoly and the state itself, especially in an era when the later separation between economics and politics had not yet ossified, meant that the boundaries between the company and the state were permeable, and the monopoly trade could be used to underpin political (state) control. *The monopoly nature of these companies was the means by which their parent state retained control over its colonial possessions in an era of increasingly bounded sovereignty*. As Grewe puts it:

> The monopoly of trade was inseparably linked with a characteristic, very specific and important feature of colonial history, namely the large privileged trading companies. These companies were, at least in the history of English and Dutch expansion, the principal engines of colonial enterprise and organisers of the overseas settlements. In other States' colonisations they were also the organisational and legal forms by which colonial territories were politically and economically attached to the parent country.[243]

The particular legal structure of these agents of maritime trade was thus a vital component in the consolidation of Western colonialism. A crucial legal aspect was the fact that these companies possessed a degree of sovereignty in international law (the exact degree was controversial).[244]

Grewe brilliantly dissects the meaning of the companies' uncertain status in the context of a system of sovereign states which were mercantile *and colonialist*. Put simply, in the fifteenth and sixteenth centuries the lines of amity divided the world to legitimate 'primitive accumulation' of colonial plunder: in the new global order such lines could no longer be drawn, but nor were the colonial powers politically powerful enough to ensure hegemony through the hidden coercion in the legal form (which is necessitated in an epoch of worldwide juridical state equality, as I argue below). Politicians were well aware that the legal status of their colonial possessions was problematic.[245] The East India Companies were the perfect agents to police this 'transitional' colonialism, because of their indistinct legal status.

> [T]he specific, semi-State, semi-private intermediate position that the trading companies asserted . . . made it possible to avoid a complete transfer to

[243] Grewe 2000, p. 298.
[244] Grewe 2000, p. 302.
[245] Grewe 2000, p. 298.

> the overseas colonial sphere of the European concept of State, with all of its far-reaching legal consequences and associated concepts of sovereignty, nation-State, State territory and State borders.
>
> The intermediate position of the trading companies was the main reason that the legal ambiguity 'beyond the line' was not transformed directly into a situation where the strict rules of a law of nations applied, which was in conformity with the limited geographic extension and narrow political circumstances of Europe.
>
> Since it was not the States themselves which were confronting each other, but rather corporations, which were regarded as or at least pretended to be more or less self-reliant, a separate, flexible system of colonial law of nations developed.[246]

The status of the East India Companies, even more than the Navigation Acts, was part of a system of colonialist/mercantilist state consolidation, structured through maritime law.

> Mercantile companies were state-created institutions that used violence in the pursuit of economic gain and political power for both the state and non-state actors. With these institutions state rulers were able to exploit non-state coercive capabilities in conquering or colonizing large areas of the globe. With them, todays' theoretical and practical distinctions – between the economic and political and between state and non-state actors – were meaningless.[247]

5.2.3. *The freedom of the seas: a dissident interpretation*

The Navigation Acts and East India Companies illustrate how the particular *contents* of seventeenth-century maritime law could consolidate the sovereign colonial state. Here I address the more fundamental point of how the very

---

246 Grewe 2000, p. 298. An almost exactly similar analysis was developed by Lindley almost seventy five years before Grewe: 'Formed in most cases, at all events from the point of view of the shareholders, for the purpose of earning dividends, these corporations have proved to be the instruments by which enormous areas have been brought under the dominion of the States under whose auspices they were created, and in this way they have been utilized by all the important colonizing Powers. The special field of their operations has been territory which the State creating them was not at the time prepared to administer directly, but which offered good prospects from the point of view of trade or industrial exploitation' (Lindley 1926, p. 91).

247 Thomson 1994, p. 41. In its focus on the role of non-state violence in the burgeoning international system, this book is invaluable for stressing that the boundaries between the economic and political are 'neither self-evident nor eternal' (p. 5).

postulates underpinning maritime and international law in this period were marshalled to the mercantilist state-strengthening programme.

The seventeenth-century 'battle of the books' between Grotius and Selden is the high point of the debate over the freedom of the seas.[248] Grotius was first to lay out his theory. In 1603, a Dutch Admiral Heemskerck, sailing in the service of a company merged with the East India Company,[249] caught a Portuguese vessel the *Catharina*, worth the enormous sum of 3.4 million florins.[250] This was duly declared prize, and distributed among the shareholders of the Dutch East India Company. However, '[a]mong the shareholders of the "Company" were Mennonites and other Anabaptists who, on religious grounds, rejected the use of force in principle'.[251]

This was of great concern to the Dutch authorities, and not because of questions of abstract theology. It was the fact that the fervour of those objections was so strong that the dissident shareholders looked set to undermine the Dutch government's monopolistic colonial trade.

> [S]ome . . . threatened to form a new company which, abstaining from anything of the nature of warlike operations, should devote its energies solely to pure commerce. But the Government, which had conferred the monopoly of the Indian trade upon the Dutch Company, would naturally not permit a competing company to come into existence.[252]

In an attempt to quell this 'strong sectarian feeling against prize',[253] the Company employed Grotius to write an opinion justifying its seizure. It was the twelfth chapter of this treatise, *De Jure Praedae*, that was published in 1608 as *Mare Liberum*, in which he argued for the freedom of the seas, that 'navigation is free to all persons whatsover'.[254]

The conventional, and so far as it goes quite correct, interpretation of *Mare Liberum* is that it was written as an attack on the Portuguese[255] claims to a monopoly on Indian trade based on the papal bestowals of the late fifteenth

---

[248] Grewe 2000, p. 266. For a still-invaluable overview of the debate, including the works of many lesser authors than Grotius and Selden, see Fulton 1911, pp. 338–77.
[249] Dumbauld 1969, p. 26.
[250] Zemanek 1999, p. 49 footnote 2.
[251] Zemanek 1999, p. 50. See also Tuck 1999, pp. 79–81.
[252] Knight 1925, p. 82.
[253] Ibid.
[254] Grotius 2000, p. 12.
[255] And by extension the Portuguese-Spanish, the one having come under the dominion of the other in 1580.

and sixteenth Centuries. The assertion of free seas was thus a blow against the residues of premodern imperial global division, and for the system of sovereign mercantile powers. Maritime legal arguments here were deployed in favour of the burgeoning global commercial system.

However, an important fact about Grotius's theory is ignored in most of the literature. Grotius's support for equal trading access *was not* equivalent to a position for some abstract *laissez-faire* free trade, but was inextricably an argument for the right to wield coercive political power – violence – under certain circumstances. *His very argument for 'free seas' is justification for an act of violent maritime plunder.*

> [T]he Dutch were justified in making war upon the Portuguese, and hence in capturing their property as prize, because the Portuguese claimed a monopoly of trade with the Indies and interfered with the right of the Dutch to trade there.[256]

In other words, for Grotius the 'political' and the 'economic' are not separated in the international sphere. The international legal argument for free and equal access to trade was simultaneously an argument for the strengthening of the violent mercantile state. Richard Tuck has superbly brought out the radicalism of Grotius's position: the Dutch in the Indies 'were waging an offensive war, in order to open up trade routes and make a lot of money'. In legitimating this use of force, that 'seemed to be violating some of the most fundamental principles of international relations', Grotius was forced to 'a fundamental revision of those principles, and in the process . . . he fundamentally revised Western political thought itself'.[257]

There is an even more startling realisation about the arguments for free seas. It is usually claimed that Selden's arguments against Grotius in *Mare Clausum* (1635) represent a backward-looking jurisprudence. Selden claims that states do *not* have an automatic right of free and equal maritime access, but that sovereignty can extend over the waters.[258] This seems hard to reconcile with a modern attitude to freedom of commerce, central to the commodity form and thus the legal form. This argument for the 'progressive'

---

[256] Dumbauld 1969, pp. 27–8. In Ellen Wood's words, Grotius's work 'is striking for its ideological opportunism, transparently constructed to defend the very particular practices of the Dutch in their quest for commercial domination in the early seventeenth century' (Wood 2003, p. 68).

[257] Tuck 1999, pp. 80–81.

[258] For an invaluable exposition of Selden's argument see Christianson 1996, pp. 246–81.

Grotius, whose thesis 'revailed with governments and courts',[259] against 'reactionary' Selden, whose '*Mare Clausum* became an anachronism which was no longer necessary,'[260] is often repeated.

Closer examination shows that matters are not so simple. The apparent stark contrast between Grotius's and Selden's positions disguises a deeper convergence – and not only the banality that the contrasting positions are both taken for reasons of political exigency.[261]

Selden's argument revolves not around arbitrary divisions of the world at the behest of some putative overarching sovereign, but at a basic, pragmatic level of *effective authority*. He *agrees* with Grotius that the Portuguese and Spanish have no right to claim sovereignty over the open oceans because 'the two Iberian nations did not have sufficient sea-power at their disposal, actually to rule over the oceans effectively'.[262] Selden is at pains to use this criterion of effectiveness. He points out, in countering Grotius's preposterous argument that the waves resist possession because of their permanent movement, that the same is true of rivers but that no one disputed that they were a sovereign possession. He stresses that there is nothing ineffable in the substance of water which evades possession – '[t]aking possession of the sea and controlling it only required a fleet'.[263]

The nature of Selden's claims for sovereignty over the seas is thus radically different from – indeed counterposed to – the Iberian claims of maritime dominion. In 1625, for example, Seraphin de Freitas published *De Iusto Imperii Lusitanorum imperio asiatico adversus Grotii Mare Liberum*, in the service of the Spanish king. It claimed that Spain had jurisdiction over *all* the world's oceans, effective sovereignty notwithstanding. Freitas talked piously of the 'heavy burden' Spain had taken upon itself, and used irredeemably medieval categories predicated on Papal authority and the 'just war' Christians could wage against heathens to justify 'the Portuguese policy of seeking to break the Islamic monopoly on trade and navigation in the Indian Ocean in order to win this monopoly for themselves'.[264] Even these anachronistic categories

[259] Nussbaum 1947, p. 108.
[260] Anand 1982, p. 229.
[261] Grotius wrote on behalf of the Dutch East India Company, and Selden by the 'express command' of King Charles I of England (Anand 1982, p. 105).
[262] Grewe 2000, p. 267.
[263] Grewe 2000, p. 268.
[264] Grewe 2000, p. 260.

were offered in the service of the Spanish mercantile state. But the idea that Freitas and Selden have more in common than Selden and Grotius is absurd.

Claims such as Teschke's that Selden had 'adopted the Spanish position',[265] fundamentally miss the point. When Selden claims large parts of the seas around the British Isles, it is not based on the whim of a universal authority like the Pope, or of nature, but because, he says, it is under actual British control. This was highly questionable – the British were stretching the grounds of credibility. But that does not undermine the fundamentals of Selden's jurisprudence. The problem is not with his categories, but in the fact that British claims about them were untrue.

Even in dispute, Selden and Grotius share a conception of the inextricably political and coercive nature of the sovereign, trading, mercantile state. It is this that makes them both early modernists. In fact, contrary to the generally held position, Selden's jurisprudence is both more rigorous and more modern. Grotius fell back on scholastic methodologies by positing an abstract order: the seas should be free because that is natural law. Selden, in contrast, grounds his theory – and his attack on Iberian claims – in the actual practice of states. He 'thus took the *most radical* of positions against the Spanish'.[266]

Attempts to identify the 'progressiveness' or otherwise of these theories in their content are doomed to failure, and are predicated on the erroneous conception of international law as a body of static rules. There is no contradiction in seeing both Selden and Grotius as operating within a shared early modernist paradigm. Social content cannot be sought solely in the rule itself, but rather in the predicates that a particular norm may well share *with its own opposite*.

Stark evidence for this can be found in the fact that a few years after he wrote *Mare Liberum*, Grotius, still operating very much on behalf of the Dutch mercantile state, argued an exactly contradictory position to his earlier one. This turnaround came in 1613, when he accompanied a Dutch mission to England on an attempt to resolve a dispute over the ejection of English merchants from Spice Island ports claimed by the Dutch.[267]

At this point (before Selden's *Mare Clausum*) the English were arguing that they had 'a just right to a free Trade into the East Indies and every part

[265] Teschke 2003, p. 201.
[266] Grewe 2000, p. 267. Emphasis mine.
[267] For a detailed overview of Grotius's arguments during the dispute, see De Pauw 1965, pp. 46–61.

thereof . . . by the Law of Nations'.[268] They even quoted verbatim from *Mare Liberum* against its author.[269] Grotius was too serious a thinker to revert, Freitas-like, to a feudal defence of maritime monopoly. Instead, he countered that the Dutch had acquired monopolies in the East 'by contracts or treaties'.[270]

The English delegation reported the Dutch position thus:

> [T]hey say it was not well said of us to affirm that the Contracts they had made were against the Law of Nations, for that there was nothing more lawful or usual than for men to contract for the sale of their commodities, as well for the present as for the future; and he that had the power to sell had the power to promise.[271]

The power to sell imbued the power to promise, and Grotius claimed that the trading partners of the Dutch had promised – had *contracted* – to trade only with them. With a masterstroke, Grotius constructs the arguments for monopoly and closed ports, *against* free seas, *on the basis of contract theory* that underpins law. In terms of modernist rigour, this is a great improvement on his earlier natural-law conception of free seas, and it is this later conception of contractual monopoly that makes its way into his better known work, *De Jure Belli ac Pacis*.[272] Also in that later work, there is a wholesale acceptance of arguments later found in Selden for effective occupation granting sovereignty over coastal waters.

> It seems clear . . . that sovereignty over a part of the sea is acquired in the same way as sovereignty elsewhere, that is . . . through the instrumentality of persons and of territory. It is gained through the instrumentality of person if, for example, a fleet, which is an army afloat, is stationed at some point of the sea; by means of territory, in so far as those who sail over the part of the sea along the coast may be constrained from the land no less than if they should be upon the land itself.[273]

---

268 Quoted in Zemanek 1999, p. 56.
269 Anand 1982, p. 96.
270 Anand 1982, p. 97.
271 Quoted in Zemanek 1999, p. 57.
272 'I recall that the question has been raised, whether it is permissible for a people to make an agreement with another people to sell to it alone products of a certain kind. . . . I think that this is allowable. . . . Such an arrangement to purchase . . . is not at variance with the law of nature' (Grotius quoted in Zemanek 1999, p. 59).
273 Grotius quoted in Ngantcha 1990, p. 14.

'Not much remains of the doctrine of the eternal freedom of trade which he had announced in the most absolute terms possible in his youth'.[274]

Contrary to the claims of Nussbaum and others, there is nothing inexorable about the freedom of the seas as a concomitant of modernity and capitalism. Indeed one writer on the modern law of the sea is confident enough to open his book with the breezy claim that '[t]here are today no more doubts that the cherished Grotian concept of the freedom of the seas does not apply to all the areas of the globe that belong to the sea in the geographical sense'.[275] Teschke's claim that modern capitalism leads to 'the "de-bordering" of the sea . . . the shift from . . . John Seldon . . . to Adam Smith'[276] is thus far too simplistic.

Grotius and Selden share a legal theory predicated on the sovereign mercantile state as a political-economic agent,[277] and on the sea as the arena in which that agency is exercised. It is this relationship to maritime and international law, not the substance of a particular legal position, that distinguishes the modern maritime polity from the feudal.

5.3. *Excursus: mercantilism and the transition to capitalism*

I have said that the commodity-form theory of international law remains intact whether or not it is held that the absolutist state, or sixteenth-century political forms more generally, are forms of society in transition to capitalism. I will, though, conclude this chapter with a defence of one such 'transitional form' theory. It is necessary to address this question because the nature of the transition has ramifications for the nature of capitalism, and the conflictual relations embedded in the legal form.

This section is a brief reply to Benno Teschke's searching and impressive critique of transition theory. Teschke is one of the few writers in IR – and one of fewer Marxists – who has investigated the structures and forms of mercantilism with anything approaching the attention they deserve.

Though he accepts that mercantilism 'promoted for the first time a public economic policy on a "national" scale' and represented 'a step in the direc-

---

[274] De Pauw 1965, p. 70.
[275] Ngantcha 1990, p. 6.
[276] Teschke 2003, p. 204.
[277] 'Political-economic' here designating not two conjoined concepts but a unitary one.

tion of a bounded economic territory',[278] he stresses that it only did so in terms of 'external closure', not 'internal uniformity',[279] indeed that it 'entrenched a politically differentiated internal sphere of production' and cannot therefore be considered a transitional form towards the capitalist state.

> When capitalism burst on the international scene in the nineteenth century, most parts of the world had already been territorially demarcated by mercantilism. Bounded, though not fixed or static, territoriality preceded the rise of capitalism.[280]

This is an expression of Teschke's more general, and controversial, argument, which is that mercantilism is not only *not* part of a transition to modern capitalism, but that it operated as a *block* to it.

> Early modern mercantilism not only failed to establish a new logic of international economic relations . . . it did not even generate any unintended consequences which would have pushed this system in the direction of modern capitalism and thus modern international relations.[281]

Moreover, '[t]he construction of an open homogeneous home market, an economically unified space based on the complete mobility, i.e., commodification, of all factors of production, was impossible to achieve under mercantilism'.[282]

There are two levels of criticism one can level at Teschke: empirical and methodological. Empirically, one does not have to be a Sweezyite to acknowledge the tendencies toward the growth of productive forces and the early self-expansion of capital that can occur on the basis of mercantile trade. There is nothing automatic in these trends, and they depend on a number of variables, crucially the configuration of the domestic economy. I have argued, following Marx, that mercantile capitalism is a necessary but not sufficient condition for the development of modern industrial capitalism.

Foreign trade does not by any means always stimulate the productive forces – the opposite can be the case, as exemplified in early Spanish mercantilism, or sixteenth-century Poland.[283] But that given the right domestic circumstances foreign trade *can* stimulate production for exchange is undeniable.

---

278 Teschke 2003, p. 198.
279 Teschke 2003, p. 209.
280 Ibid.
281 Teschke 2003, p. 205.
282 Teschke 2003, p. 210.
283 In Spain, the American gold brought into the country led to the export of raw materials, cheap imports and the underdevelopment of domestic production (see

> Domestic demand alone, owing to its low elasticity, could not have launched proto-industrialization. It had to be assisted and supplemented by the expansion of foreign demand which, though perhaps not functioning as the 'engine of growth', certainly played the role of 'handmaiden of growth'. Under contemporary conditions, the 'appropriation of foreign purchasing power' . . . presented the only possibility of overcoming the limitation of domestic markets and of increasing the demand for industrial products . . . Indeed, precisely this combination between relatively well developing domestic demand and the expanding foreign demand accounted for England's lead over the other European countries [in the seventeenth and early eighteenth centuries].[284]

In Britain, for example, 'Asian trade in its later phase when it was dominated by textiles not only stimulated re-export but competed with internal production and forced the producers to aim at greater efficiency'.[285]

This empirical response, however, does not get at the heart of Teschke's theory. After all, he freely admits that 'the stimulus of market exchange could orient production in the direction of production for exchange, that is production of exchange value',[286] and that '[t]rade-driven military demand promoted the development of new industries – armaments, shipbuilding, metallurgy, textiles etc'.[287] But Teschke sees mercantilism as unable to transform the specific pre-capitalist social relations of exploitation: indeed he claims that it 'tended merely to intensify' their extra-economic appropriation of surplus.[288] The promotion of production was 'always in the "antediluvian" form of state-granted monopolies'.[289]

Teschke continually counterposes the mercantilist form with an abstract, ideal-typical form that he holds as definitional to capitalism, that mercantilism cannot possibly match.[290] It is in this methodology that the fundamental

---

Perrotta 1993). In Poland, the export of agricultural products 'created a very difficult situation for the industrial production' (Malowist 1959, p. 187 and throughout).

284 Kriedte 1981, p. 33.

285 Rothermar 1981, p. 61.

286 Teschke 2003, p. 205.

287 Teschke 2003, p. 208.

288 Teschke 2003, p. 205.

289 Teschke 2003, p. 208.

290 This is not to say that Teschke does not analyse the specificity of the non-capitalist forms under discussion. Far from it. His treatment of mercantilism is perhaps the slightest of these, but this is no criticism given that the detailed and minute exposition of what he sees as the specific social dynamics of absolutism, of medieval polities, of post-feudal-crisis lordship, are very impressive achievements. However, when

flaw in his approach lies – his hypostatisation, his methodological focus on an abstract form of capitalism. He has a static understanding of a bundle of concepts associated with modern capitalism – free markets in land, labour and capital, the separation of politics and economics – which he sees as the *sine qua non* of capitalism. These concepts are indeed central to capitalism – however, in a dynamic conception they must be understood as *tendencies*. Otherwise, one is forced to pathologise 'actually-existing' capitalism, in all its imperfect complexity.

Discussing the monopoly companies, for example, Teschke derides the idea that these could be in any way transitional to modern capitalism, because of their public/private form.

> Such a structural nexus between the economic and the political constitutes, of course, the opposite of modern capitalism, which was expressed in the sphere of maritime trade in the shift to 'open door' principles, allowing the free flow of goods in open markets. Here, competition is regulated only by the price mechanism and not through domestic monopolies and war. Under-pricing rather than out-gunning characterises capitalist trade.[291]

Teschke's approach is one of radical 'political Marxism', an approach for which 'class struggle is the exclusive source of social transformation'.[292] It is an irony of this school that one of the strongest critiques it has levelled at alternative paradigms can be turned against it.

Ellen Wood, for example, herself associated with 'political Marxism', has pointed out that '[s]ince historians first began explaining the emergence of capitalism, there has scarcely existed an explanation that did not begin by assuming the very thing that needed to be explained'.[293] Yet it is precisely this tendency to assume the contours of capitalism which undermines Teschke's account. For Teschke, the *differentia specifica* of capitalism is its separation of

---

it comes to his polemical point that the supposedly transitional forms of absolutism and mercantilism are not, in fact, transitional at all, his methodology is to counter-pose these forms to an *abstract* capitalism.

291 Teschke 2003, p. 204. In the original draft of this passage, in the PhD of which this book is a revision, Teschke acknowledges the importance of international law to these changes of social form, saying that modern capitalism 'in the sphere of maritime trade is precisely expressed in international law in the shift to "open door" principles' (Teshke 2001, p. 273).

292 Callinicos 1999, p. 10. For a critique, see Callinicos 1990b.

293 Wood 1999, p. 3.

politics and economics: political penetration into the economic sphere is thus fundamentally incompatible with the capitalist mode of production.

Of course, actually-existing capitalism is replete with examples of the political intruding into the economic, such as the post-war welfare state systems and nationalised industries, and the development of capitalism in the post-war developing world.

> By the mid-1970s the state in Bangladesh was holding 85 percent of the assets of what it termed 'modern industrial enterprise'; in Turkey the state was responsible for 40 percent of value added in industry in 1964; in Algeria the state moved from being the employer of 15 percent of the workers in industry, construction and trade in 1965 to 51 percent in 1972; and in Brazil the state became responsible for more than 60 percent of all investment by the mid 1970s.[294]

In those countries, in other words, large, sometimes dominant sectors of capitalist industry were run by a state whose 'monopolistic position – founded finally in its ability to use force, to collect taxes – permits . . . [it] to organise the pricing of its products', rather than submit to the 'pure' price mechanism. 'And commonly we find nation-states, relying ultimately on their monopoly of force, altering the domestic price-structure, and altering the flows of surplus-value.'[295]

This is a description of modern capitalism. An extremely similar formulation in Teschke, however, is evidence of the *non*-capitalist nature of the mercantile state, because for it

> [w]ealth was obtained only in the sphere of circulation . . . a principle that worked only because price differentials were artificially, i.e., politically and militarily, maintained through monopolies, preventing economic competition.[296]

Teschke's theory must lead him to see the penetration of state into capitalism as pathological to capitalism itself, which seems extraordinary, given the scale of this penetration, and its centrality to the very existence of particular national capitals. And not only minor economies: much the same kind of state penetration has been visible in the world's major capitalist economies, in the shape of massive – systemically sustaining – arms spending, which

[294] Binns 1984, p. 52.
[295] Barker 1978, p. 29.
[296] Teschke 2003, p. 200.

also, and very directly, allows the monopoly power of the state to bypass the 'free market' price mechanism.

> The single most important sectoral investment trend in the economy [in the 1980s] . . . is the rush to mine the motherlode at the Defence Department. Predictably, the new arms race has been the most important impetus in the recovery of key industrial sectors, supplying half the increased demand in aerospace and a fifth in primary and fabricated metals. . . . For the old 'Fordist' industrial core of the American economy . . . the Pentagon has been the chief instrument of restructuring.[297]

The arms economy has been central to the penetration of the 'political' state into the 'economic' sphere in modern capitalism, with the concomitant bypassing of the price-mechanism that is, for Teschke, a defining feature of capitalism.

> The significance of military expenditure is that it means that a substantial portion of every national economy is regulated not by local, let alone world markets, but by direct . . . relations between the state concerned, and either local defence contractors or other states.[298]

The only refuge left for Teschke's formalism is to claim that the separation of politics and economics remains central, that despite its scale the interpenetration remains parasitic on a form of self-expanding value predicated on free-market competition, and that in contrast, the state-monopoly profits derived from the sphere of circulation are the *basis* of the mercantilist system. This is quite true, but it does not end the argument.

The point is precisely that *in this historical conjuncture*, in the hands of a newly consolidated colonial state, the very maintenance of that 'mercantile' capitalism was part of the necessary conditions for, and spur to, the passage to modern capitalism. Teschke's paradigm blinds him to the way the very abstract categories of capitalism he hypostasises were born out of pre-existing categories.

For example, Teschke rightly mentions the centrality of free wage-labour for capitalism.[299] Wage-labour does not universalise under mercantilism, and Teschke therefore denies that mercantilism is a transitional form. He does not engage at all with that tradition of historical materialism mentioned above

---

297 Davis 1986, pp. 242–3.
298 Callinicos 1987, p. 100.
299 See for example Teschke 2003, p. 206.

which, while not questioning the tendency to free wage-labour in capitalism, considers unfree forms an 'anomalous necessity' at certain times. Because of that, crucially, he does not see how a lack of universal wage-labour in the specific context of mercantilism is precisely a component in the early *creation* of capitalism *predicated* on wage-labour.

This is brilliantly illustrated by Linebaugh and Rediker, in a provocative section worth quoting at length.

> If Cromwell inaugurated the maritime state and Charles II realized its promise, finally displacing the Dutch as the hegemonic Atlantic power, it was because of advisers such as Sir William Petty (1623–1687), the father of political economy. . . . Petty . . . had begun his working life as a cabin boy at sea. He was part of England's conquering army in Ireland. . . . Such experiences gave him a clear understanding of the primary importance of land, labor, and transatlantic connections. Labor, he believed, was the 'father . . . of wealth, as lands are the mother.' Labor had to be mobile – and labor policies transatlantic – because lands were far-flung. . . . [Though he focused partly on slavery] Petty's main point . . . was that ships and sailors were the real basis of English wealth and power. 'Husbandmen, Seamen, Soldiers, Artizans, and merchants, are the very Pillars of any Common-Wealth,' he wrote, but the seaman was perhaps most important of all. . . . 'The Labour of Seamen, and Freight of Ships, is always of the nature of an Exported Commodity, the overplus whereof above what is Imported, brings home money, etc.' Sailors thus produced surplus value above the costs of production, including their own subsistence. . . . Petty thus originated the labor theory of value by refusing to think of workers in moral terms. . . . His method of thinking was essential to the genesis and the long-term planning of the maritime state. . . .[300]

Thus it was that the early stirrings of the labour theory of value, inextricably bound up with a conception of wage-labour as central to profit, of labour-power as a surplus-producing commodity, was born precisely because of the peculiarities of the wage-labour of sailors on mercantile adventures in the service of a maritime state. Teschke cannot draw the obvious conclusion that these are forms of a society *in transition*.

---

[300] Linebaugh and Rediker 2000, pp. 146–7.

Instead, his rigid separation of economics and politics underlies his claim that the order of 'multiple bounded territories' – separate sovereign states – 'formed the historical legacy in which the subsequent new logic of modern capitalism and free trade had to operate'.[301] For Teschke, the logic of the state and the logic of capitalism are entirely contingent.

Given the scale and massive importance of state-capital penetration to capitalism and to the form of the modern state, it would seem sensible, rather than opposing a concrete state to an abstract capitalism, as Teschke does, to accept that the capitalist system itself contains the 'statist' dynamic. 'Just as it is essential to insist on the "political" dimension of seemingly economic relations, so too we need to explore the "economic" face of apparently political phenomena like states.'[302]

Teschke cannot follow Barker's sensible advice, because he has taken capitalism at its own word. Rather than conceptualising the separation of politics and economics as a tendency, with an ideological component, he has understood it to be an absolute truth more important to the definition of capitalism than the actual composition of capitalism at any particular time. His is a curiously static and – paradoxically, given his immense historical erudition – ahistorical capitalism.[303]

Because of what he sees as the definitional separation of politics and economics, at the core of Teschke's refusal to see mercantilism as related to capitalism is the centrality of war to the mercantile system. Counterposing the 'under-pricing' he sees as central to capitalism from the 'out-gunning' of mercantilism, he points out the 'extra-economic' competition in mercantialism, for which, '[c]ommerce, strategy and security formed one undifferentiated whole'.[304]

In contrast, I have insisted, despite the tendency for the separation of economics and politics in capitalism, on the fundamental embeddedness of the

---

[301] This formulation is in the first draft of his book: Teschke 2001, p. 281.

[302] Barker 1997, p. 59.

[303] It is a similar – and similarly paradoxical – abstraction which underlines Colin Barker's sympathetic critique of Ellen Wood as being 'not "Trotskyist"' (Barker 1997, p. 53). This is not the sectarianism it might sound like – Barker is drawing attention specifically to Trotsky's theory of 'combined and uneven development' (See Trotsky 1969, pp. 144–57; 1997, pp. 25–37). In considering capitalism to have always intrinsically been an international mode of production (rather than one inhering in a particular country), and always to take specific shapes depending on the historical-geographical context in which it is born, this tenet of 'Trotskyism' is strongly antipathetic to abstracted theories of capitalism.

[304] Teschke 2003, p. 203.

political in the economic form. Against Teschke's theory of war as inimical to capitalism, there is a tradition of Marxist writing in which the political coercion in the economic form *is precisely expressed in war*.[305]

These theories, most famously those of Lenin[306] and Bukharin,[307] were formulated to explain the growth of monopoly capitalism in the early years of the twentieth century, and the First World War. Teschke's theory, presumably, could only address those shifts with the assertion that the monopoly must be an atavistic, pre-capitalist form. Not so Bukharin, in whose brilliant work the concentration of capital and the growth of the monopoly form marks the explicit penetration of state and capital.

War, for Teschke, must be contingent to capitalism, fundamentally unrelated to capitalist pressures of competitive accumulation. For Bukharin, in contrast, '[c]apitalist society is unthinkable without armaments, as it is unthinkable without wars.'[308] Because as the process of early twentieth-century monopolisation continued, Bukharin claimed (if perhaps too schematically), ever larger firms buy each other up, until they have become trusts, which tend towards state-capitalist trusts.

> To say . . . that wars are *caused* by the ammunition industry, would be a cheap assertion. The ammunition industry is by no means a branch of

[305] In drawing on this theory, the picture of international development I have outlined differs from that of many of those labelled 'historical sociologists'. Taking Charles Tilly as an example, his well-known assertion that '[w]ar made the state and the state made war' (Tilly 1975, p. 42) clearly has much in common with the dynamic I have suggested, for which war and imperialist coercion is central to the development of the mercantile state. However, he carefully distinguishes the 'logics of capital and coercion' (Tilly 1992, pp. 16–20). Though he acknowledges that the two can and often do interpenetrate – in addition to the 'capital-intensive' and 'coercion-intensive' modes, in which each of those dynamics prevails in the formation of a state, he stresses the existence of a 'capitalized-coercion mode' (Tilly 1992) – that interpenetration is understood as on the foundation of *separate logics* (see also Giddens 1985, p. 326). Schematically, 'Tilly's framework made coercion . . . into a predominantly territorial (feudal, monarchical) phenomenon, while capital (cities, merchants) tended to become inherently pacifistic' (Glete 2001, p. 49. Glete's own analysis, drawing on organisational theory, plausibly stresses the important changes and bureaucratisation that development of permanent military organisations brought but imports anachronistic notions such as 'innovative entrepreneurship'). The notion of 'reciprocating logics' creating a 'motor' of modernity is perhaps somewhat closer, but still epistemically counterposed (Reyna 1999, p. 58). By contrast, the depiction of mercantialism I have given and the 'Bukharinite' Marxism I draw on below sees capital-logic to *be* a coercive logic, and the international political coercive logic at this historical conjuncture to be an expression of capital.

[306] Lenin 1939.

[307] Bukharin 1987.

[308] Bukharin 1987, p. 127.

production existing for itself, it is not an artificially created evil which in turn calls forth the 'battle of nations'. It ought to be obvious ... that armaments are an indispensable attribute of state power, an attribute that has a very definite function in the struggle among state capitalist trusts. ... [J]ust as it is true that not low prices cause competition but, on the contrary, competition causes low prices, it is equally true that not the existence of arms is the prime cause and the moving force in wars ... but, on the contrary, the inevitableness of economic conflicts conditions the existence of arms.[309]

Bukharin's analysis is predicated on an understanding of the permeability of the membrane that separates politics and economics in capitalism.

If the old feudal 'policy of blood and iron' was able to serve here, externally, as a model, this was possibly only because the moving springs of modern economic life drive capital along the road of aggressive politics and the militarisation of social life.[310]

Bukharin sees military competition in monopoly capitalism as an expression of the same competitive dynamic associated with capitalist economics. It is no coincidence that it is at the international, inter-state-capital level that Bukharin sees this continuity between the forms of competition being made manifest – because it is without a superordinate authority that the coercive regulation implied in the commodity form must be at the hands of the economic agents themselves. The early twentieth-century war-capitalism that Bukharin analyses is a historically specific form of a more general tendency inherent in the coercive market form. In Colin Barker's words:

The constitution of a system of private property requires, as a necessary correlate, the constitution of a system of 'defence' or coercive power. ... The analysis of the very 'base' of capitalist society, of its kernel of social productive relations, requires not simply an 'economic' theory but equally a theory of jurisprudence, a theory of politics, *and a theory of war*.[311]

This gives the lie to Teschke's claims that the war-based exchange of mercantilism is antipathetic to capitalism. Bukharin and Barker have taken us back to Pashukanis. This was the very crux of Chapter Four above, of the politics embedded in the commodity, and the legal, forms. This is rendered

---

309 Bukharin 1987, p. 127.
310 Bukharin 1987, p. 128.
311 Barker 1997, p. 53. Emphasis mine.

incomprehensible by the assumptions of Teschke's analysis. The binding force of international law – the coercion at the heart of the commodity/juridical – must remain a mystery to him.

5.4. *Categories and dialectics*

I have argued that Teschke is wrong to claim that mercantilism cannot be transitional to capitalism, and that the categories with which he makes that judgement fundamentally hamper his understanding of the international system, the relation between states and capital, and international law, which were so central in the transition to capitalism itself. With the alternative dialectical theory derived from Pashukanis, not only can we make better sense of those, but it becomes clear that it is the lack of superordinate stability which is one of the strongest countervailing factors to capitalism's tendency to institutionalise the separation of economics and politics. That is why the coercion in the legal (commodity) form is more evident in international than domestic law, because it is without the generally stabilising force of an overarching authority.

In other words, the rigid separation of categories not only obscures the transitional nature of mercantilism, but makes international law itself incomprehensible. The analysis of mercantilism as central to the transition to capitalism is not simply an addendum to the commodity-form analysis of international law: it is constructed on exactly that theory's dialectical formulations about the nature of commodity exchange.

There will be times when the international system is more acutely unstable than usual. In those times, the specifically capitalist forms of exchange will become manifest in political, coercive, violent forms – unstable capitalism in particular politicises exchange, and makes it war. It is that which underpins Bukharin's theory: he was depicting the capitalist system at what might have been its barbaric death.

That is what makes it so plausible that the epoch of mercantilism *can* be understood as transitional to capitalism. Again, there are unstable capitalist forms, politicising exchange and making it war. Unstable this time – and enthusiastically deploying international law as part of the system's self-stabilising strategies – not because of capitalism's imminent death, but in the first traumatic stirrings of its birth.

Chapter Six

Imperialism, Sovereignty and International Law

1. The nature of the relation

I have stressed the coercion implicit in the legal relationship. This raises the question of the relationship between international law and the systematic coercion of imperialism. This theme is neglected in the literature. 'A very major deficiency in the doctrinal analysis of international law is that no systematic undertaking is usually offered of the influence of colonialism in the development of the basic conceptual framework of the subject.'[1] Though some writers have started to fill this colonialism-shaped gap,[2] the deficiency remains, and is complicated by a lack of conceptual clarity about what precisely is being examined.

To analyse the relations between law and imperialism it is not sufficient to focus on the international law *of* formal imperialism. Imperialism, in this model, becomes a *problem for* international law, a phenomenon on which international law, conceived as rules, must pass judgement. While there is invaluable work pursued on these lines,[3] as a conceptualisation it is

[1] Carty 1996, p. 5.

[2] Grovogui 1996, Anghie 1999 and Koskenniemi 2000 and 2002 Chapter 1 are exemplary. Fitzpatrick engages illuminatingly with the issue in Fitzpatrick 2001, pp. 146–82. See also Riles 1995 – though it suffers from a tendency to recycle postmodernist platitudes, the piece takes colonialism seriously as a constituent of international law and international law seriously as a constituent of social reality.

[3] One of the most important such works is Lindley 1926. For a much less sophisticated example written in a spirit of crass colonial managerialism (and illuminating

inadequate. International law is a constituent part of the dynamic of modernity: if, as I argue, imperialism must also be so considered, the question is not one of the international law of imperialism, but of the imperialism of international law.

Of course imperialism and international law are not reducible to each other: but they are mutually constituting. The specific interconnections of imperialism and international law vary with historical context, and analysis must start by interrogating that specificity. Only through doing so will common threads become clear, and a general theory of imperialism and international law can emerge.

1.1. *Specificity versus breadth*

Imperialism is a contentious category: even establishing a working definition of it is not simple.

> Imperialism can be defined very broadly or very narrowly – as the domination, throughout history, of small countries by stronger states, or as the policy pursued by the Great Powers in the last third of the nineteenth century of formally subordinating most of the rest of the world to their rule.[4]

The classical Marxist definition of imperialism, of which the most powerful centre of gravity is Lenin's extraordinarily influential 1916 pamphlet,[5] 'is more specific than the broad definition, more general than the narrow one. Imperialism is neither a universal feature of human society nor a particular policy but "a special stage in the development of capitalism"'.[6]

Lenin, famously, related imperialism directly to the epoch of monopoly capitalism.[7] Not surprisingly for a work which was more an examination of

---

for that), see Lawrence 1913. For a more recent version see the brief Reisman 1976. For an ill-timed legal defence of a form of direct colonialism (questionably distinguished from imperialism) see Marshall Brown 1945. For an overview of the conjuncture between missionary activity, international law and imperialism see Cole 1940. One very interesting article is Rodriguez 1921, which pragmatically – almost cheerfully – accepts the existence of an American empire (confessing that the expression 'may be perhaps a trifle shocking' (p. 530)) and concerns itself with mechanisms of representation within it.

[4] Callinicos 1994, p. 14.

[5] Lenin 1939.

[6] Callinicos 1994, p. 14.

[7] He saw five 'basic features' as central. '1) The concentration of production and capital developed to such a high stage that it created monopolies which play a decisive role in economic life. 2) The merging of bank capital with industrial capital, and

the specifics of the First World War than a general theory of capitalist imperialism,[8] his categorising of certain 'basic features' as the essence of imperialism has been questioned. Finance capital, for example, the emergence of which he saw as central, was developed much more extensively in some less successful imperialist powers, such as Germany, than in, say, Britain. More crucially, he claimed that the export of capital was key to imperialism, a claim that cannot hold water – some imperialist powers, like the US and Japan, in fact *imported* capital up to 1914.[9]

However, in two aspects in particular, Lenin's theory remains trenchant. One is his focus on monopoly capitalism, after 1870, to explain the sudden rise of 'new imperialism', or what Callinicos calls 'classical imperialism'. The scale of this transformation of the globe can hardly be exaggerated. In 1860 the European colonial possessions constituted 148 million inhabitants and 2.7 million miles: by 1914 the still-ongoing process of expansion had brought 568 million people and 29 million miles into the European orbit.[10] Lenin's relating of this extraordinary transformation of global politics to a similarly momentous shift in the structure of capitalism – from free trade to monopoly concerns – remains key to understanding the change.

More fundamentally, for Lenin imperialism is not simply a *policy* of the stronger powers. The territorial division of the world by these powers is, in fact, just an aspect (though one of the most visible and important) of a dynamic in capitalism itself. Investigating 'classical' or 'new' imperialism, then, is a way in to understanding the shape of modern capitalism: the formal colonial policies are a mode of articulation of this fundamental structure.

---

the creation, on the basis of this "finance capital", of a financial oligarchy. 3) The export of capital, which has become extremely important, as distinguished from the export of commodities. 4) The formation of international capitalist monopolies which share the world among themselves. 5) The territorial division of the whole world among the greatest capitalist powers is completed.' Lenin 1939, p. 89.

[8] 'Lenin's theory of imperialism . . . is less a theory of its necessary economic generation and limitations than the theory of the concrete class forces which, unleashed by imperialism, are at work within it: *the theory of the concrete world situation created by imperialism*. . . . [W]hat primarily interests him is this concrete world situation and the class alignments created by it . . . above all, how, because of its different momentum in different countries, the development of monopoly capitalism itself invalidates the temporary peaceful distribution of "spheres of interest" and other compromises, and drives it to conflicts which can only be resolved by force – in other words, by war.' Lukács 1970, pp. 43–4.

[9] Callinicos 1994, p. 14.

[10] See Barratt Brown 1974, for more figures illustrating the massive expansion of colonial holdings.

These core insights of Lenin's theory are extended and systematised in Bukharin's nuanced understanding of the relation between the state and the market in capitalism. The interpenetration of the monopoly concerns, finance capital and the state

> has led to the conversion of each developed 'national system' of capitalism into a state-capitalist trust. . . . [T]he process of development of the productive forces drives these 'national' systems into the most acute conflicts in their competitive struggle for the world market.[11]

Heated debates over the nature of imperialism continue.[12] It is often argued that 'the concept of imperialism can be utterly economistic, if it is derived directly from Lenin and Bukharin'.[13] Doubtless it can be, but I will try to show that this is not inevitable.

Callinicos has summarised this theory and its implications, which underpins my own analysis of classical imperialism, admirably.

> 1. Imperialism is the stage in capitalist development where i) the concentration and centralisation of the integration of private monopoly capital and the state; and ii) the internationalisation of the productive forces tends to compel capitals to compete for markets, investments and raw materials at the global level.
>
> 2. Among the main consequences of these two tendencies are the following: i) competition between capitals takes on the form of military rivalries among nation-states; ii) the relations among nation states are unequal; the uneven and combined development of capitalism allows a small number of advanced capitalist states (the imperialist countries), by virtue of their productive resources and military strength, to dominate the rest of the world; iii) uneven and combined development under imperialism further intensifies military competition and gives rise to wars, including both wars among the imperialist powers themselves and those arising from the struggles of oppressed nations against imperialist domination.[14]

---

[11] Bukharin 1982, pp. 16–17.

[12] For the best introductions to the debates in historical materialism, see Brewer 1980, and Owen and Sutcliffe 1972. For the major classical positions within Marxism, see Lenin 1939; Luxemburg 1951; Bukharin 1987. This is only a sample from a vast literature.

[13] Panitch in Gowan, Panitch and Shaw 2001, p. 17.

[14] Callinicos 1994, pp. 16–17.

There is an obvious distinction between capitalist domination and such pre-capitalist exploitation as the rapacious Iberian adventures in the Americas. Early global commercial/mercantile adventuring was part of an epochal shift, but it was not 'capitalist', based as it was on direct extraction. 'To avoid confusion between pre-capitalist colonialism and capitalist world domination . . . the term "imperialism" is often used for the latter'.[15] I have argued, however, that there is both rupture and continuity between early mercantile colonialism and the modern international system.

The question is, what are the relations between the general phenomenon of the domination 'of small countries by stronger states' – if not trans-historically then at least under capitalism, or even since the early mercantile colonialism of Spain – and the specifics of particular imperialisms? Halliday makes this point well, in response to those who stress the economic causes of new imperialism.

> One can, however, approach the issue of economic causes in another way, by turning on its head the . . . argument of how specific, or distinctive, the period of 1870–1945 really was. . . . [T]he opposite may, in retrospect, be closer to the mark. For set in the broader scale of European domination over a five century epoch, from 1492 onwards, the establishment of colonial rule from 1870 onwards, while distinctive in genesis and form, was but one chapter in a longer process by which European political and economic power subjugated the world. . . . Globalization is in this sense a continuation of colonialism, and of what preceded it, mercantilism and free trade. It is this drive not only to expand, but also to force the rest of the world to conform to it, which characterizes modern capitalism, and within which the colonial period played a significant, but partial, role. The location of the post-1870 period in this broader period should, therefore serve to strengthen, not weaken, the argument which sets this phenomenon in an economic perspective.[16]

This is precisely right. The challenge is to unite generalisation with specificity. In what follows, imperialism is the political-military rivalry between

---

[15] Alavi 1991, p. 94.

[16] Halliday 1998, p. 9. An earlier, unpublished version of this paper concludes this section with this point about the variety of forms of political domination taken over the various economic epochs: 'That different forms, and paces, of domination succeeded each other, with phases of intense expansion followed by ones of stagnation and retreat, serves to indicate that at different phases of development of the strongest economies the latter had different needs.'

capitalist states that manifests the changing integration of capital and monopoly capital with those states. Formal imperialism is only one, in some ways an anomalous, phase of this. And just as mercantilism is distinct from but directly related to capitalism, so earlier colonialism is distinct from but related to general and to 'new' imperialism.

The following broad outline of imperialism identifies various phases, characterised by particular international legal dynamics. I focus largely on British imperialism, as it exemplifies these various trends well.

2. The crisis of mercantile colonialism

Mercantilism was a system born of the seventeenth century. With useful iconic timing, one of its most potent symbols and powerful agents, the East India Company, was set up in 1600; the most important Navigation Acts, the high points of mercantilist policy, date from 1651; Colbert's famous letter to Mazarin (outlining the French variant of mercantilism) dates from 1643.

Of course, the mercantilist monopolies, by definition, excluded some who wished to trade. There was increasing criticism of these monopolies from the second half of the seventeenth century.[17] Such criticisms reached critical mass in the eighteenth century, and demands for the alternative of 'free trade' grew in coherence and volume.[18] 1776 can serve as a symbolic year for the end of mercantilism as a dominant system: it was the year both of the American Declaration of Independence, a 'revolt against the mercantilist colonial policy of England';[19] and of the publication by Adam Smith of *The Wealth of Nations*, a free-trade manifesto as well as a masterly work of political economy.

As industry slowly consolidated and trade networks flourished, the necessity for mercantilism, as an economic-political strategy for state-building, waned with its own success. '[A]t the end of the seventeenth century state regulation of economic life was breaking down'.[20] This is reflected in the

[17] Hutchison 1988.

[18] Though its early expressions were less than perfectly rigorous or coherent, and drew on previous writings, the cry of *'laissez-faire'* was first explicitly raised by the physiocrats in the middle of the eighteenth century (Huberman 1936, p. 143). For arguments that the physiocrats' theories were easily adaptable to burgeoning capitalism see Barber 1967, pp. 20–1; Roll 1973, pp. 128–37.

[19] Huberman 1936, p. 137.

[20] Roll 1973, p. 92.

patchy and incoherent application of supposedly mercantilist policies, and in the controversies around mercantilism that did not begin but reached their apogee with Adam Smith.

It was most particularly the colonial policies of mercantilism that early capitalism strained against. The theory was that

> the value of colonies depended on their ability to act as exclusive markets for the manufactures of the mother country, to supply in exchange raw materials and other produce which would otherwise have to be bought from foreign countries, and to form a reservoir of cheap labour.[21]

In fact, though, '[f]rom the point of view of foreign commerce alone the mercantilists were . . . led increasingly to demand a greater freedom of trade'.[22] The somewhat anomalous longevity of the monopoly rights of the East India Company, which lasted to 1813, disguises the fact that mercantilism was undermined by its own successes relatively early on.

> Free trade suffered many set-backs, but over the eighteenth century as a whole it was undoubtedly progressing. . . . By the end of the seventeenth century the regulated company was ceasing to be the dominant form of organization in international trade.[23]

The continuing use of proxies such as the monopoly trading companies to maintain dominance – colonialism – has led to the formalist claim that it is 'doubtful whether it is proper to speak of eighteenth century English imperialism'.[24] This is to ignore the lessons of the previous chapter about the interpenetration of state and capital in these companies: it was after all through increased military expenditure, the Royal Navy and the East India Company that London continued to dominate the world market through colonial conquest in these years.[25]

---

[21] Roll 1973, p. 84.
[22] Ibid.
[23] Roll 1973, p. 93.
[24] Schumpeter 1955, p. 18.
[25] Brewer 1990. Evidence for the interpenetration of the monopoly companies, the states, war and commerce is provided by the Seven Years' War (1756–1763) that sucked in Prussia, France, Austria, Russia and Britain. This was the culmination of a war between Britain and France for the control of Indian and North American colonies, that started in 1746 with conflict between a French army of natives and the private troops of the East India Company (in North America the fighting began in earnest in 1755) (Morton 1989, pp. 262–3). The war ended with Britain 'protecting and enlarging its lucrative colonial empire and opening vast new territories in North America and the Caribbean' (Linebaugh and Rediker 2000, p. 212. See also Morton 1989, p. 266).

The conquests of this time, and the network of colonialism, did not necessitate a set of complex international legal structures. Slavery, for example, was 'at the heart of the entire system',[26] central not only to the American southern plantation economies but to the northern economies which exported products to the slave plantations of the Caribbean and southern mainland, but despite 'the pervasiveness, the ubiquity, of that central element' the slave trade itself was effected without either formal rule or even the para-state entities of the monopoly companies taking control.

This is not to say that the slave trade was *invisible* in international law. The 1713 Treaty of Utrecht that ended the War of the Spanish Succession, for example, included at British insistence a clause giving them a monopoly of supplying slaves to the Spanish American colonies.[27] However, the trade was conducted without direct rule, and was restricted to relatively small areas of the African coast (though its effects went much further),[28] so no international legal structures were necessary specifically to shape the relations between Britain and African polities.

In India, where direct rule *was* exerted, the quasi-sovereign, non-state nature of the East India Company removed the need for formal juridical control by the home state. In the Americas, 'the eighteenth century . . . Atlantic empire, commercial in its essence, [was] a sprawl of semi-self-governing communities, weakly and fitfully controlled from the metropolitan center'. The 'emerging administrative structures of the empire . . . [were] piecemeal and superficial'.[29]

Generally, European states did not want to take on the burdens of formal colonial rule. There was, then, no explicit international law *of colonies* during this period. Of course this does mean that imperialism was not affecting inter-

---

[26] Bailyn 2000, p. 654.

[27] Morton 1989, p. 252. For the full details of the clause see Umozurike pp. 7–8. Note the continuing importance of monopoly companies – the rights were given over to the South Sea Company.

[28] See for example Manning 1990. In Umozurike's words: 'Africa was the loser all the way through. The trade resulted in misery, death, destruction and impoverishment. . . . The trade depopulated large areas of the continent. . . . The slave trade negated political, economic, cultural and social development; it stultified the growth of civilization and destroyed what civilization there was. . . . The debilitating effect, the instability, the sense of inferiority, guilt and subservience caused to the Africans by the slave trade were only such as to make them easy preys for the next European design – colonialism' (Umozurike 1979, pp. 4–5).

[29] Bailyn 2000, p. 649, p. 654.

national legal structures. The very silence of international law regarding the colonies was structurally important, to international law itself and to European imperialism.

Control of the colonies was one of the principle means by which the European states vied with each other.[30] It was precisely the importance of the colonies in an age of European state-consolidation – mercantilism – which explains why international law denied the colonies legal existence, let alone agency. This was international law as European international law – 'the international legal order could with good reason be called the "droit public de l'Europe"'[31] – predicated on the systematic legal ignoring of the colonial world.

However, the growing inadequacy of mercantilist structures during the eighteenth century resulted in tensions between the processes of early European capitalism and colonialism on the one hand, and juridical structures on the other. The mercantilist 'minimalism' of international law would no longer do. Changes in the international legal structure were precipitated by crises of British colonial power in India and North America, the results of a changing capitalism and of inter-imperialist war, as well as of the growing revolutionary current of the late eighteenth century, against which the ossifying structures of mercantile colonialism could not stand.

The colonised around the world were not quiescent – there were rebellions throughout the eighteenth century. Slave revolts shook the Caribbean colonies, and reverberated throughout North America.[32] The Declaration of Independence of 1776 was informed by these events in a contradictory way, positively by the fact of political struggles and the spread of revolutionary ideas, and negatively by fear of slave uprisings. The American revolutionaries 'were moved by the militancy of slaves in the 1770s to attack slavery as they expanded the arguments for human freedom':[33] on the other hand, the Declaration of Independence, while bidding 'a final adieu to Britain' blamed King George

---

[30] 'The overseas world as a means for correcting European power relations and proportions and as a premium for the possession of European hegemony: this was the idea at the centre of French policy and the motive for French colonial expansion. 'During this period, the newly discovered continents were only an object of European political maneuvering.' Grewe 2000, p. 295.

[31] Grewe 2000, p. 295.

[32] For a list of rebellions see Linebaugh and Rediker 2000, pp. 223–7.

[33] Linebaugh and Rediker 2000, p. 227. For an overview of the contradictory relationship between slave revolts and the American Revolutionary ideals, see pp. 211–47.

III for inciting slave rebellions, saying he had 'excited domestic insurrections amongst us'.[34]

The Indian and North American cases illustrate two possible directions in the evolution of an international capitalist structure and legal order under strain. In India Britain retained its power: in North America the colony was able to assert its independence – quite deliberately using a discourse of sovereignty *in* and *of* international law to define itself as an agent in the international legal universe.[35] Where British imperialism succeeded just as much as where it failed, the international legal order had to accommodate the changing nature of international capitalism.

The monopoly nature of the Indian trade could not survive in the face of the rapidly expanding capitalist market – hence the end of the East India Company's monopoly in 1813. But the seeds of that change can be seen in the 1773 Regulating Act, which by ceding political control to the British state acknowledged that the monopoly companies had outlived their usefulness as agents of colonialism. Their sidestepping of juridical forms was no longer appropriate. India was simply too profitable to be left in the control of a company which was structured to treat it as a treasure-chest.[36] By taking it over *politically* in 1773, the British state helped insitutionalise the separation of politics and economics associated with mature capitalism.

> [The British government took] partial control over the administration of the conquered provinces. Ostensibly aimed at checking the oppression of the Company's rule the real effect of the Act was to systematise the exploitation of India, which was now too profitable to be allowed to continue in private hands. It marks the beginning of the transition from the first stage of British penetration, in which India was a source of certain valuable commodities which could not be produced at home, to the second stage in which

[34] Zinn 1995, p. 72.

[35] 'By declaring that "these United Colonies are . . . Free and Independent States [and] . . . have the full power to levy war, conclude peace, contract alliances, establish commerce, and do all other acts and things which Independent States may of right do," [Declaration of Independence §35] the Declaration announced America's intention to be included within the family of nations. The Declaration was, essentially and legally, an assertion of sovereignty constituted by the law of nations as much as a political instrument to separate from England. . . . American intellectuals, grounded in the philosophies of the day, viewed the law of nations as *constituting* sovereignty.' (Sylvester 1999, pp. 9–10. Emphasis in original.)

[36] Which is why the British state had taken a direct share of the spoils since 1767. See Morton 1989, p. 262.

> it became an important market for British manufactured goods, especially cotton textiles.[37]

As capitalism matured and mercantilism crumbled, international law began to be forced to *accommodate* the colonies, to recognise them as existing within the international legal universe. This was the effect of establishing formal British political control over India. Even though the relation was one of straightforward direct control of the colony, this was a fundamental shift from the structured silence that had characterised international law till then.

Where colonialism succeeded, international law had to recognise the colony's subservient existence. The alternative was more dramatic: when it became clear that the American insurgents would not be contained by Britain, it became inevitable that they be recognised as an independent state. That was the result of failed colonialism.

2.1. *The imperialism of recognition*

Vattel, the pre-eminent theorist of the law of nations of the period, argued that '[f]or a nation to have the right to act immediately in this large society, it is sufficient that it is truly sovereign and independent, that is, that it governs itself by its own authority and by its laws'.[38] Thus he derived the requirement of effectiveness from his theory of sovereignty. At the same time, he restricted the right of revolt to resistance against an 'intolerable tyrant'.[39] Of course, there are no objective criteria for judging which tyrant is intolerable, whether a nation is truly sovereign, whether it governs itself, and so on. Conflicting theories of recognition were developed during the eighteenth century, with regard to these questions, according to which writers could support or condemn the recognition of the United States.[40]

---

[37] Morton 1989, pp. 262–263. The Pitts India Act of 1784 set up a board of control in Britain to control the company's military, civil and revenue affairs, leaving it only its monopoly of trade. The Industrial Revolution was not merely something which happened *to* colonialism, but was in part a result *of* it. The massive demands of the large-scale colonial wars – for standardised arms, tools and uniforms for the professional armies – were powerful spurs to technological and industrial innovation. Mercantile colonialism undermined itself, necessitating a new kind of colonialism. See Morton 1989, pp. 274–275.

[38] Vattel's *The Law of Nations*, Book 1, §4, quoted in Grewe 2000, p. 345.

[39] Grewe 2000, p. 345.

[40] Grewe 2000, p. 346.

The doctrine of effectiveness found in Vattel and writers such as von Martens was gaining ground, with a positivism which treated facts of state control as primary, rather than notions of traditional authority. This principle became 'a fundamental and guiding precedent',[41] and is still in place in modern international law: 'effective control is generally accepted as the necessary condition for recognition'.[42]

It is no surprise that France, still antagonistic to Britain, was the first state to recognise the political independence of the US, concluding a treaty of commerce and a defensive alliance in 1778. This recognition was justified explicitly on the grounds 'that the United States was factually independent'.[43] In the writings of those who opposed the principle of effectiveness and therefore this act of recognition, two different criticisms are bundled together. One, straightforwardly backward-looking, is the notion that legitimacy resides in the traditional dynastic powers.[44] But the other, more hard-headed, is that recognition is a political act.

This was, and remains, quite correct. The imputation of effectivity is still subjective: the decision to recognise is political. Thus for example Johann von Steck criticised the French recognition of the US, because 'recognition of a new State seceding from its parent country had to be regarded as "premature" and as "unfriendly intervention" unless the parent country had renounced its sovereignty'.[45]

Of course to claim, based on this political understanding of recognition, that such recognition is *illegitimate,* is to stick to the implausible theory of international law as a body of rules. If it is instead understood as a process, then such politically informed manipulation and creation of legal facts is precisely *the constitutive fabric of international law itself.* Recognition, in this case, might be criticised as imperialist, immoral, stupid, or many other things, but it is nonsensical to criticise it as illegal.

The French recognition of the US was not simply an objective recognition of facts, but was a political reaction to a changing situation, and an interventionist act, designed to undermine British power.[46] The overthrowing of

---

[41] Grewe 2000, p. 348.
[42] Peterson 1982, p. 329.
[43] Grewe 2000, p. 347.
[44] Grewe 2000, p. 346.
[45] Quoted in Grewe 2000, p. 346.
[46] For a full discussion of the debates between Britain and France on this point, see Grewe 2000, pp. 346–8.

colonialism and the reconstitution of an ex-colony as an agent in the order of international law and politics was therefore informed by a dynamic of *ongoing inter-imperialist rivalry*. This is crucial – *the defeat of formal imperialism does not mean the end of an imperialist order, and even the very legal fabric of post-colonialism can be constitutive of such an order, in a new form.*

The Monroe Doctrine of 1823 is interesting in this regard. Although not framed as a piece of international law – it 'must be regarded as having a descriptive and rhetorical rather than a legal character'[47] – the document is extremely important to the international, and international legal, order. It frames a conception of American imperialism, by which the US proclaimed its 'proprietary interest' in Latin America, and its refusal to countenance European interference.[48]

In the words of an American policy-maker:

> In its advocacy of the Monroe Doctrine the United States considers its own interest. The integrity of other American nations is an incident, not an end. While this may seem based on selfishness alone, the author of the Doctrine had no higher or more generous motive in its declaration.[49]

The irony is that this clear statement of imperial interest was '[i]ssued in 1823 when the countries of Latin America were winning independence from Spanish control',[50] inspired by the French Revolution of 1789 and the Haitian Revolution in 1803. '[T]he US recognized the most important of the new states almost immediately'.[51] The Monroe Doctrine, in other words, was part of the US's policy of recognition. *It was in the recognition of formally independent postcolonial states that the US's newly modulated imperialism articulated itself.*

The same instincts can be seen in Britain, which was almost as quick to recognise the new states (over which it had a great deal of economic control). The 'flexible' foreign secretary Canning[52] straddled the dialectic of formal freedom and factual control in the new imperialism admirably only a year after the Monroe Doctrine: 'Spanish America is free, and if we do not mismanage our affairs sadly she is *English*.'[53]

---

[47] Fenwick 1939, p. 257. At the time it was written, the declaration was 'prophetic' rather than descriptive (Hobsbawm 1962, p. 131).

[48] Chomsky 1987, p. 59.

[49] Robert Lansing, Woodrow Wilson's Secretary of State, quoted in Chomsky 1987, p. 59.

[50] Zinn 1995, p. 290.

[51] Hobsbawm 1962, p. 138.

[52] Hobsbawm 1962, p. 131.

[53] Quoted in Rosenberg 1994, p. 170. Of course, British ambitions were dashed. 'In

The strategic imperialism of recognition is one of the most visible ways in which international law and imperialism intersect in post-mercantilist capitalism. With this strategy, modern imperialism starts. In contrast, the formal carving up of the world in the late nineteenth century was in some ways an *interruption*. By contrast to such 'classical' imperialism, for this modern free-trade imperialism that commenced in the eighteenth century, formal sovereign independence not only does not preclude domination, but can, through recognition, *be the very institution by which domination is exercised.*

That this is an imperialism of modern capitalism can be seen in the fact that it 'was based on the presumed separation of economics and politics': in the Monroe Doctrine 'European states could carry on as much trade as possible in the Western Hemisphere, but must not do anything political'.[54] With his hard-headed understanding of the penetration of power-politics into an international legal order, Schmitt was clear about the centrality of recognition.

> He looked for the key to the coexistence of independent *Grossräume* in the practice of recognition, because the structural transformation of the spatial order of international law has been reflected in the conceptual transformation of recognition throughout centuries past and particularly in the last [ie. nineteenth] century.[55]

As capitalism and imperialism matured, the specific interventionary tactics of recognition did also, their contents evolving while the process continued.

> According to the Tobar Doctrine, based on a 1907 agreement, only those governments should be recognized which are 'legal' in the sense of a 'democratic' constitution. In practice, what was meant concretely by 'legal' and 'democratic' was decided by the US, which defined, interpreted and sanctioned these terms. In Schmitt's estimation, such a doctrine had a clearly interventionist character. It meant that the US could effectively control every constitutional and governmental change in every country in the Western Hemisphere.[56]

---

point of fact, the British did mismanage their affairs very sadly' (Hitchens 1990, p. 154). For the innovative international legal arguments around Britain's recognition of these states see Talmon 1998, pp. 49–59.

[54] Ulmen 1987, p. 58.

[55] Ulmen 1987, p. 65.

[56] Ulmen 1987, p. 67.

The intervention of recognition illustrates the complicity of imperialism and positivism. This theory of international law which claimed to abstract away from all but the 'objective truth' about states was constructed of subjective categories such as 'effective sovereignty' which *could not but be* evaluated, recognised and thereby actualised by powerful states within the international community. The seeming objectivity is predicated on power.[57]

Not that imperialism always uses recognition.

> There was no rush to recognize the many liberal governments established in 1848, though Britain, France, and the United States clearly sympathized with them. . . . Intervention was avoided . . . if the prospect of counterintervention was too great.[58]

But it is undeniable that '[g]overnments can affect a new regime's chances for survival with their recognition policy',[59] and that recognition of a state's formal independence can therefore be part of imperialism. 'Recognition was granted by states, not in accordance with any international principle, but according to the powerful and unpredictable expedience of competition for colonies.'[60]

This was true in 1778. It was true in 1828, when Russia and the US recognised Dom Miguel's government in Portugal; it was true in the refusal of the western powers to recognize the Bolshevik government in 1918; it was true in the recognition of Franco's regime in 1936 by Italy and Germany; and it continues to be true today. The use of recognition as 'a political weapon' is acknowledged even in some mainstream textbooks.[61]

There is no monolithic imperialist agenda according to which recognition will or will not be granted. Definitionally, the international order of imperialism is one of inter-imperialist rivalry, of bitter squabbling and disagreement

---

[57] Anghie gets something of the flavour of this. '[R]ecognition doctrine was not merely, or even primarily, concerned with ascertaining or establishing the legal status of the entity under scrutiny, rather, it was about affirming the power of the European states to claim sovereignty, to reinforce their authority to make such determination and, consequently, to make sovereignty a possession that they could then proceed to dispense, deny, create, or grant partially.' Anghie 1999, p. 66. However, Anghie overstates his case. Recognition *was* very importantly about the bolstering or creation of the legal status of an entity, even if for the purposes of the powerful state. If it were simply that the *act* of recognition 'reinforced the authority' of the recogniser, there would be no advantage ever to not-recognising.

[58] Peterson 1982, p. 329.

[59] Ibid.

[60] Anghie 1999, p. 46.

[61] Douglas 1961, p. 10. See also Aristodemou 1994, p. 534.

and *realpolitik*, of mistakes and failures as well as successes. The controversies of recognition reflect that.[62] Nonetheless, '[a]lmost all the Great Powers succumbed to the temptation to use the institution of recognition to pressure other countries.'[63]

The strategy has been expressed coldly by the functionaries of those powers.

> A 1927 Memorandum of the U.S. State Department stated: 'We do control the destinies of Central America and we do so for the simple reason that the national interest absolutely dictates such a course. . . . Until now Central America has always understood that governments which we recognize and support stay in power, while those we do not recognize and support fall.'[64]

3. Ad-hoc legality in the nineteenth century

In the early years of the nineteenth century, the anti-monopolism of industrial capitalism was the dominant force in British international affairs,[65] as evidenced by the aggressive 'free-market' imperialism of Britain towards Latin America, which became 'an almost total economic dependency of Britain',[66] and the ending of the East India Company's monopoly in 1812, which transformed the economic nature of Britain's relationship with Asia.

> [A]s the industrialist vested interest prevailed in Britain, the East India mercantile interests (not to mention the Indian ones) were pressed back. India was systematically deindustrialized and became in turn a market for Lancashire cottons. This was not merely a gratifying extension of Lancashire's markets. It was a major landmark in world history. For since the dawn of time Europe had always imported more from the East than she had sold there. . . .[67]

---

[62] This can be seen, for example, in the debates over recognition of states in the morass of Yugoslavia's dissolution, and the ignoring, under German pressure, of the counsel of the Badinter commission – set up to advise on this issue – vis-à-vis the recognition of Croatia and Bosnia-Herzegovina (Samary 1995, p. 121).

[63] Lukashak 1991, p. 152.

[64] Lukashak 1991, p. 157 footnote 33.

[65] Though mercantilism was not swept away overnight: it was only in 1858, for example, that the East India Company finally dissolved.

[66] Hobsbawm 1962, p. 53. By 1820 it took more than a quarter as much of British cotton cloths as Europe: by 1840 it took nearly half as much again as Europe.

[67] Hobsbawm 1962, pp. 53–4.

Legally speaking, the increasing separation of economics and politics and the fact that the British domination inhered in its economic power meant that mechanisms of direct rule were still generally unnecessary. Where states established themselves, as in Latin America, recognising them – and thereby accelerating the spread of the sovereign state form – was the imperialist strategy. Where polities did not take that form, as in Africa, no such recognition was necessary.

> The years 1815–1870 constituted the heyday of British predominance overseas. But in Britain, too, successive prime ministers from Castlereagh onwards opposed the formalization of British rule. As Macauley pointed out in 1833: 'To trade with civilized men is infinitely more profitable than to govern savages'. Britain's 'empire of free trade' was maintained by unchallenged naval supremacy and the absence of serious industrial or diplomatic competition from potential European rivals. Britain's advocacy of free trade was firmly grounded in self-interest. Colonization was understood to be contrary to free trade and colonies were regarded as an economic burden.[68]

Legal regulation existed between the controlling and controlled polities during this time, and it slowly extended its reach. But it was far from systematic: that was what defined it.

3.1. *Positivism and its sources*

With the spread of positivism and the withering of residual notions of natural law, international legal categories were held to inhere in the practice of states. This makes the decision of what constitutes relevant practice enormously important, as does the question of who has the power to decide this relevance.

Positivism's very institutionalisation of a distinct study of international law, for which the 1836 publication of Henry Wheaton's *Elements of International Law* is a key moment, was itself part of this process. As international law became a science,[69] subjective judgements (of those with the power to enforce them) took the form of objective categories: international law naturalised imperialist decisions.

---

[68] Koskenniemi 2000, pp. 5–6.
[69] Anghie 1999, pp. 18–22.

Perhaps more importantly, international law emerged not only as a science but as a *profession*,[70] which prescribed its own relevant terrain. If international lawyers agreed that a polity was not a sovereign state, this was not only an act of ideological closure, it was also a juridical *decree*: without being accorded the rights of sovereignty, a polity was *not sovereign*.

For positivism, the question of the sources of international law was central: the idealism of natural-law theory was unacceptable, yet international law had to come from somewhere. In the positivist answer lay the tools necessary for the ad-hoc imperialism of the nineteenth century.

> The teleological basis . . . [of natural law] was unacceptable to positivists, for whom treaties and custom had replaced natural law as the exclusive and primary source of international law. Treaties were an expression of sovereign will. Furthermore, positivists argued, the practice of states was also a manifestation of sovereign will and could suggest consent – either expressly or implicitly – to a set of customary laws. Thus, for positivists, treaties and the developing body of custom were the best guides to the proper rules of international behaviour.[71]

The subjective and ad-hoc nature of custom is obvious. Far from being self-explanatory, what is 'customary' is debatable and debated,[72] and will of course be marshalled to political projects.

As to treaties, imperialist politics inhere not only in the contents of treaties but in their form, because it is through recognition of international legal sovereignty that the agency to engage in treaties inheres. Thus an imperialist power had to consider with which polities, and how, it would conclude treaties, because to do so seemed to imply the recognition of sovereignty in the treaty-partner. Although, as in Latin America, the recognition of sovereignty could sometimes be of advantage to a particular imperialism, it was not always so. How to engage in international intercourse without spreading the bacillus of sovereignty was a problem for positivism, and one that was overcome with one of the most important framing concepts of nineteenth- and early twentieth-century international law. That concept, steeped in mutually constituting vagueness, imperialism and legalism, was 'civilisation'.

---

[70] Koskenniemi 2000, pp. 18–19; 2002 Chapter 1.

[71] Anghie 1999, p. 13.

[72] Custom 'is drawn from the opinions of "writers" . . . who usually differ decisively with each other on every occasion' (Pashukanis 1980, p. 182).

3.2. *'Civilisation': a counterintuitive materialist analysis*

The standard of 'civilisation' began to emerge in the middle of the 1800s as a criterion without which a state could not engage in international legal relations.[73] In 1846, the third edition of Wheaton's textbook amended its original definition of international law as one between 'civilized, Christian nations' to one 'among civilized nations'.[74] In 1856, the Ottoman Empire was admitted into 'civilised' European society.

The standard emerged in response to a difficulty facing positivist jurisprudence. There were certain polities with which the European powers were dealing which had more or less absolute control over a more or less clearly defined territory. In other words, they 'easily met both the Austinian definition of sovereignty and the requirement of control over territory'.[75] What was more, treaties had been struck with many of them.

Using the framework of the extremely important 1843 Foreign Jurisdiction Act, for example, Britain concluded a treaty with Turkey in 1844, followed by many others in the next quarter century.[76] These treaties raised theoretical difficulties.

> [A]lthough positivists asserted that non-European societies were officially excluded from the realm of international law, numerous treaties had been entered into between these supposedly non-existent societies and European states and trading companies. . . . Furthermore, these treaties, and the state practices that followed, suggested that both the European and non-European parties understood themselves to be entering into legal relations. . . . The nineteenth-century European states . . . relied very heavily on treaties with non-European societies in expanding their colonial empires, and in so doing, demonstrated a lamentable disregard for the systematically established and elaborated positivist assertion that non-European peoples were outside the scope of law.[77]

How, then, if at all, was international legal personality to be denied these polities?

---

[73] The indispensable work on this is Gong 1984.
[74] Gong 1984, p. 54.
[75] Anghie 1999, p. 27.
[76] Johnston 1973, p. 37.
[77] Anghie 1999, pp. 38–9.

> The broad response was that Asian states, for example, could be formally 'sovereign'; but unless they satisfied the criteria of membership in civilized international society, they lacked the comprehensive range of powers enjoyed by the European sovereigns who constituted international society.[78]

'Civilization', therefore, was a standard that established a taxonomy of polities, whereby powers could be deemed 'savage', 'barbarous', 'civilised' or 'semi-civilised'.[79] This did not by any means finally answer the question of what legal capacity flowed from the treaties concluded – positivist theorists tied themselves in knots trying to deal with the conundrum.[80] But it did formalise the frankly ad-hoc responses to the question: 'So anomalous are those not-full sovereign states', one writer judiciously opined, 'that no hard and fast general rule can be laid down with regard to their position within the Family of Nations'.[81]

These treaties *predate* the development of the theory of civilisation, and are not systematic. The Framing Act of 1843 institutionalised this ad-hoc approach: when the collapse of the monopoly companies necessitated a framework for state intervention abroad, Britain instituted the new law 'designed to set out basic principles for the exercise of foreign jurisdiction in foreign countries'.

> The new act of 1843 replaced the former specific acts for individual countries with a framework for a complete system of exterritorial jurisdiction. It provided that such jurisdiction as Her Majesty acquired in a foreign country was to be held and exercised 'in the same and as ample a manner as if Her Majesty had acquired that jurisdiction by the cession or conquest of territory.' . . . This procedure obviously pleased administrators in Whitehall. The act did not purport to create or grant jurisdiction; it merely provided for its exercise. The actual jurisdiction and its extent had to be established otherwise, generally by treaty. . . . But it might also be obtained by 'grant, usage, sufferance and other lawful means. . . . The 1843 act was general and enabling – authorizing and legitimizing the use of *whatever jurisdiction might be obtained* in foreign countries. . . . Generally *legislators avoided creating a general system* allowing the establishment or operation of wide, jurisdictional powers.[82]

---

78 Anghie 1999, p. 28.
79 Gong 1984, p. 28 and elsewhere.
80 Gong 1984, pp. 60–3.
81 Oppenheim quoted in Gong 1984, p. 57.
82 Johnston 1973, pp. 36–7. Emphasis mine.

The act existed at the intersection of domestic and international law. In defining the boundaries of British jurisdiction in an overseas territory, it was a medium by which the international spread of British law was a kind of vanguard for international law itself, because the extent of the British jurisdiction was decided by treaty with another power. Those treaties were flexible – characterised by 'vagueness'[83] – and driven by economic motives. 'The need for such exterritorial privileges arose primarily in the case of merchants in a foreign country'.[84] Generally this was about the penetration of large companies and concerns.

The flexibility of such treaties was to the immense advantage of the more powerful state, and was often imposed at gunpoint.

> [I]t was principally by using force or threatening to use force that European states compelled non-European states to enter into 'treaties' that basically entitled the European powers to whatever they pleased. . . . Under the positivist system, it was legal to use coercion to compel parties to enter into treaties that were then legally binding.[85]

These were profoundly unequal treaties – 'unequal not only because they were the product of unequal power, but because they embodied unequal obligations'.[86] Were the parties formally equal, such treaties would have been impossible.

> '[U]nequal treaties' can be defined as those treaties which fulfil at least two of the following three related conditions: (1) they impose unequal obligations in practice; (2) they are imposed through the use or threat of force; and (3) they are perceived to be 'unjust treaties', often because they impair the sovereignty of one of the treaty parties.[87]

A classic example is the 1842 Treaty of Nanking, concluded at the end of the first of Britain's Opium Wars with China. It was vital to Britain that it dictate terms, not only as the trade 'was absolutely vital to British imperial interests',[88] but because the war 'had also the more general object of breaking

[83] Johnston 1973, p. 38.
[84] Johnston 1973, p. 34; cf., 'Rights to trade were an important part of such treaties', Anghie 1999, p. 41.
[85] Anghie 1999, pp. 40–1.
[86] Anghie 1999, p. 41.
[87] Gong 1984, p. 67.
[88] Newsinger 2001, p. 58.

down the barriers which prevented the export of British goods to China'.[89] At the end of the war, Britain threatened to bombard Nanking, and forced the Chinese to accept utterly punitive and degrading terms, against their will.[90]

These unequal treaties – ad hoc and flexible both in their one-sided and often vague content *and* in their blithely coercive application – were central to the creation of nineteenth-century imperialist international law. The treaties were instigated for the interests of the powerful states, coerced onto the 'partners', and the standard of civilisation was a flexible instrument to rationalise and contain this unequal realpolitik in the fabric of law.

Gong is surely right that 'the standard of "civilization" influenced all three components in "unequal treaties"'. However, he is wrong to put the category of 'civilisation' first, and claim that '[t]he power and proclivity of the Europeans to impose their standard of "civilization" on the non-European countries . . . made "unequal treaties" almost inevitable', that '[u]nequal legal obligations rose *because* qualities of legal capacity arising out of differences in civilization are manifested in . . . the positive law of nations"'.[91] This is idealist, and leaves unexplained how and why the category arose in the first place. The reverse, in fact, is more exact – it was the imposition of unequal treaties for imperialist reasons that threw up and nourished the legitimating concept of civilization.

It is important to reiterate that it was the *real* fabric of actually-existing international law that was constituted by these treaties. By contrast, Anghie, for example, claims that coercion created 'ostensibly' legal instruments;[92] that 'non-European peoples were governed not by general principles of international law, but by the regimes created by these unequal treaties';[93] that 'the parties most knowledgeable about treaty making had no illusions about the legal status of these treaties';[94] that '[j]urists had some perception of . . . [their] fraudulence'. This is to posit some abstract, ideal-type international law against which reality is deemed lacking.

Let us be clear – these unequal treaties were not ostensibly but *really* legal, they *created* the general principles of international law: they are not fraudu-

[89] Morton 1989, p. 397.
[90] See Gong 1984, p. 67; for a fuller exposition Anghie 1999, p. 41.
[91] Gong 1984, p. 68. Emphases mine.
[92] Anghie 1999, p. 40.
[93] Anghie 1999, p. 41.
[94] Anghie 1999, p. 42.

lent, but the truth of nineteenth-century international law. That is the law we inherited.

There is a final, counterintuitive point to be made about 'civilisation'. The polities with which these imperialist unequal treaties were concluded – Siam, Morocco, China, Japan, Zanzibar, Madagascar, Muscat, and others[95] – were territorially bounded and internally sovereign. In other words, it was not with regard to 'uncivilised' powers that the standard was framed, *but to those powers that would be deemed 'semi-civilized'*.[96] These states were 'grudgingly granted . . . partial legal personality'.[97] They were 'in a kind of limbo: "they are some parts within the circle of the Family of Nations, they remain for the other parts outside"'.[98]

It was the treaties with these powers that were central to the development of civilisation theory in positivism. 'Civilisation' emerged as a category to deal with the problem of these developed, internally sovereign polities. It is therefore not true that '[a]ll non-European societies, regardless of whether they were regarded as completely primitive or relatively advanced, were outside the sphere of law'.[99] It was precisely the *partial* inclusion of these states into the sphere of law that was generative of the continuum of civilisation.

In other words, Anghie is precisely wrong when he claims that despite the 'different classifications for the non-Europeans' and the 'distinctions . . . made . . . between the societies of Asia, Africa, and the Pacific', '[b]asically . . . these classifications were irrelevant in terms of the broad issue of the central distinction between the civilized and the uncivilized'.[100] That is *not* the central distinction. It would be a postmodern commonplace to claim that civilisation (or anything else) is defined by its 'other', in this case the 'uncivilised'.[101] However, in this instance the crucial antithesis of 'civilised'

---

[95] Johnston 1973, p. 37.

[96] See Johnston 1973, p. 59. Although the act 'provided a basis for the regularization of jurisdiction in the Gold Coast', 'it referred to problems elsewhere, especially in the Levant'.

[97] Gong 1984, p. 56.

[98] Gong 1984, p. 57, quoting Oppenheim.

[99] Anghie 1999, p. 31.

[100] Anghie 1999, pp. 30–1.

[101] 'More generally, the nineteenth century offers us an example of a much broader theme: the importance of the existence of the "other" for the progress and development of the discipline itself.' (Anghie 1999, p. 79.) On reading this, on the penultimate page of a powerful, genuinely original article which has thus-far avoided this modern-day banality, the heart sinks. In Terry Eagleton's words, 'otherness is not the most fertile of intellectual furrows' (Eagleton 2001, p. 19).

was '*semi*-civilised' – those states which were neither beyond the purview of law, nor sovereign, but 'quasi-sovereign'.[102]

This helps explain why, though the standard of civilization begins to appear in the middle of the century, 'the culmination of the process by which the standard of "civilization" emerged [was] not at the middle, but at the end of the nineteenth century'[103] – *after* the use of unequal treaties with 'semi-civilised' powers was well established. Semi-civilised is not, as it might appear, a mediating fudge between two opposites, but *the generative problematic for the taxonomy of 'civilisation'*. Because 'civilisation' is not a discursive strategy for 'othering', but a result of the paradoxes of actually-existing sovereignty.

3.3. *Into Africa*

British 'influence' in Africa waxed slowly throughout the nineteenth century. Where the early- and mid-century was characterised by ad-hoc international law and legislation, as the century progressed and capitalist penetration extended, the law formalised, and hardened.[104]

The British interest was especially strong around West Africa, and centred on the slave trade by sea – first its support, then its suppression. This meant that British troops, merchants and administrators were based around the fringes of the African coast. During the seventeenth century, '[w]hile slaves were the only important export from West Africa, no attempts were made to penetrate the interior'.[105] When Britain banned the trade in 1807, and extended the ban to all its colonies in 1833, it was in part a response to the decreasing profitability of slavery,[106] and it heralded a slow change in British interest.

Still, at first, the British were focused on their 'footholds' on the African coasts[107] – now as bases for the campaign against the slavers. But partly as a result of these activities the sheer exploitability of Africa became obvious to

---

[102] The term, ironically, is from Anghie 1999, p. 43, whose enthusiasm for overstating the generative power of stark 'alterity' does not stop him developing a nuanced analysis of specifics which evades that framework. Interestingly, Grovogui uses precisely the same terminology to describe the status of the East India Company and similar bodies (Grovogui 1996, pp. 68–9).

[103] Gong 1984, p. 32.

[104] This chronology is illustrated in Johnston 1973. The first of his chapters on British 'influence' mid-century is called 'Ad Hoc Arrangements for West Africa': the first on the passage to the 1880s 'The Law Hardens'.

[105] Morton 1989, p. 414.

[106] Morton 1989, p. 415: Umozurike 1979, p. 5: Williams 1966, p. 208.

[107] Hobsbawm 1962, p. 135.

Britain and other European powers.[108] This lay behind the mid-century spate of 'explorers' mapping Africa. None of these explorers 'were or could be unaware of the economic dimension of their travels'.[109] At first the European expansion into Africa progressed piecemeal and gradually: it was not until the 1870s that the value of African resources became clear and the pace of penetration sped up markedly.[110]

In Britain it was agreed that 'a world lying open to British trade and safeguarded by the British navy . . . was more cheaply exploited without the administrative costs of occupation'.[111] This was why the burgeoning British imperialism in Africa worked within the ad-hoc strictures of the 1843 Act. However, in Africa, the polities were very different to the 'quasi-sovereigns' that had been unequal partners in other legislation.

> The similarity in formal appearance of the individual orders for countries in the Orient and North Africa was pinned on the fact that in each of those countries a somewhat recognizable and well-established government could be discerned. . . . The Foreign Jurisdiction Act of 1843 provided a workable basis to arrange relations between the two kinds of society. But when the act was used in West Africa problems of adaptation arose. The area was a disparate collection of political units, ranging from kingdoms to petty chieftaincies and local tribes. Some of the societies were large in size and population, with well-organized political and military machines. Other groups were small and weak, at the mercy of stronger neighbors. The latter group were more frequently spread along the West African coast and it was

[108] 'For more than a generation the British navy was actively employed on the African coast, hunting down slavers of the smaller nationalities, and it was in the course of these activities that the foundation of British power in West Africa was laid. It was soon discovered that this area could produce palm oil, cocoa and other valuable foodstuffs and raw materials and an extensive trade grew up' (Morton 1989, p. 415).

[109] Hobsbawm 1975, p. 67. He continues: 'To explore meant not only to know, but to develop, to bring the unknown and therefore by definition backward and barbarous into the light of civilisation and progress; to clothe the immorality of savage nakedness with shirts and trousers, which a beneficent providence manufactured in Bolton and Roubaix, to bring the goods of Birmingham which inevitably dragged civilisation in their wake.'

[110] 'British exports to sub-Saharan Africa had risen from about 1.5 million pounds in the late 1840s to about 5 millions in 1871', but then 'they doubled in the 1870s to reach about 10 millions in the early 1880s' (Hobsbawm 1975, p. 68).

[111] Hobsbawm 1962, p. 135.

with these littoral groups that British traders and adventurers made first contact.[112]

Throughout the middle of the nineteenth century, legal relations between the imperialists and the African polities were usefully vague. Before 1843, the British had extended a network of nebulously conceived 'influence', often achieved through alliance with some local power or other. This was not unsuccessful: an 1842 select committee commended the Gold Coast administrator George Maclean's establishment of 'a very wholesome influence over a coast not much less than 150 miles in extent, and to a considerable distance inland'. They did note, however, that the jurisdiction was 'irregular', and – given the slowly increasing trade and traffic – considered it 'desirable that this jurisdiction be better defined and understood'.[113]

After that point, 'the Foreign Jurisdiction Act of 1843 provided a basis for the regularization of jurisdiction in the Gold Coast'.[114] However, the supposed 'regularisation' of British jurisdiction under the act was itself 'arranged in vague terms', and 'did little to clarify or define the extent and nature of British jurisdiction'.[115]

For the most part, general enabling laws like that of 1843 were the medium by which British jurisdiction spread. It was also possible for specific legislation, such as the 1871 West Africa Settlements Act, to be used. But what characterised the legal intervention until the end of the 1870s was an 'easy spread of jurisdiction',[116] characterised by a 'loose, fluid approach'[117] due to the 'uncivilised' nature of the African polities.

All this was changing, though, by the 1880s, as a new form of imperialism took shape.

4. The Berlin Conference and the 'scramble for Africa'

Towards the end of the nineteenth century, British overseas predominance had eroded and the European powers were increasingly coming into competition with each other over African territories. This was a time of increas-

[112] Johnston 1973, p. 57.
[113] Quoted in Johnston 1973, pp. 58–59.
[114] Johnston 1973, p. 59.
[115] Johnston 1973, p. 60.
[116] Johnston 1973, p. 123.
[117] Johnston 1973, p. 117.

ing concentration and monopolisation of capital in the West, and it was these monopolies that were especially active in the carving up of Africa: 'By the time the scramble was over, more than 75 per cent of British territory south of the Sahara was acquired by chartered companies'.[118] These monopolies were very different from the mercantilist ones, which had been the agents of a burgeoning, not-yet fully powerful state. These, by contrast, were phenomena of developed industrial capitalism.

> The . . . transition . . . to monopoly capitalism had . . . profoundly affected colonial interactions. Where once free mercantilist competition dominated inter-European relations, new explorers, merchants, and settlers now sought exclusive territorial control of trade and mineral prospects. This nascent demand for territory drew the opposition of both Africans and rival colonialists. As a result, the demand by new monopolistic societies for national protection and assistance grew ever louder.[119]

Grovogui's peculiar term 'free mercantilist competition' captures something of the nature of commercial expansion into Africa in the second half of the nineteenth century. Although the nineteenth century was associated with free trade, '[e]xpansion . . . had always been conducted by mercantile associations . . . led by ambitious capitalists such as George Goldie, William Mackinnon and Cecil Rhodes'.[120] The previous mercantile companies had been able to act as semi-sovereign states, but by this time formal state authority was clearly defined and fully developed. Where in the sixteenth and seventeenth centuries the state had turned to the companies to exercise political authority, now the companies turned to the state.

Material responsibility for the colony should always be left to the company.

> The problem was that the companies either resorted to protectionist practices (in breach of their charters), proved unable to administer territories granted to them, or failed to forestall expansion by other powers. Governmental interference was required to protect traders and settlers or to prevent anarchy and, eventually, to take over formal rule. In West Africa, for example, Sir George Goldie's United (National) African Company had started out in the Niger region in 1879 where France and Germany were

[118] Koskenniemi 2000, p. 9. For more on the role of the companies, see especially Flint 1988.

[119] Grovogui 1996, p. 82.

[120] Koskenniemi 2000, p. 9.

> also seeking possessions. In 1883, Sir Percy Anderson, the head of the Foreign Office's African bureau wrote: 'Action seems to be forced on us.... Protectorates are unwelcome burdens, but in this case it is ... a question between British protectorates, which would be unwelcome, and French protectorates, which would be fatal'.[121]

The European powers bickered dangerously over Africa, and '[i]n order to avoid a catastrophe',[122] Wilhelm I of Germany, with the support of France, called the Berlin Conference, to take place in 1884 and 1885. In this forum, the imperialists divided up Africa – 'haggling and bargaining'[123] – agreeing a framework for their interaction.[124]

The conference (at which '[t]he political discourse was not that of power politics but of international law'[125]), in agreeing the reaches of the various empires, sped up the international legal formalisation of imperialism. 'The hardening of legal theory during the 1880s was associated with new developments in the law governing protection and foreign jurisdiction that arose as a result of the discussions of the Berlin Conference of 1884–1885.'[126]

The extent of this formalisation should not be overstated. It is wrong to suggest, as Grovogui does, that the 1885 Act 'signaled the absolute rule of positive law' in Africa. In fact, for some time ad-hoc methods could still operate under the terms of the treaty. It was not, for instance, true that the notorious Article 35 of the Act, under which the powers recognised 'the obligation to ensure the establishment of authority in the regions occupied by them' meant the acquisition of trading rights in an area was now 'followed by the establishment of a "zone of influence," accompanied by the proclamation of a protectorate'.[127] Protectorates *had*, by this time, become 'the main form of European influence in Africa',[128] but this was not the result of the act.

> [N]o criteria for 'authority' were laid down. Chartering a company would suffice.... The rule was also limited in space and time: it was to apply only

[121] Koskenniemi 2000, p. 10.
[122] Umozurike 1979, p. 24.
[123] Johnston 1973, p. 167.
[124] See Koskenniemi 2002, pp. 121–7. For a detailed discussion see Johnston 1973, pp. 167–225. For an excellent collection on the conference, see Förster et al. 1988.
[125] Wesseling 1997, p. 89.
[126] Johnston 1973, p. 167.
[127] Grovogui 1996, p. 86.
[128] Koskenniemi 2000, p. 15.

> to *new* acquisitions and only to acquisitions on the coasts – at a time when there was practically no coast any longer to occupy.[129]

Protectorates were spreading not because of the Act but because of the failure of the monopoly companies. Far from the Act institutionalising formal power, 'at a British proposal, protectorates were excluded from Article 35',[130] so did not have to 'establish authority'. In effect, this meant that a protectorate 'avoided the financial and administrative burdens for keeping the peace'.[131] 'Often this legal instrument was chosen in order to safe-guard all the advantages of economic exploitation for the protector without burdening it with full international responsibility for the territory under its rule.'[132] If, then, the 1885 act meant the spread of protectorates, it was not in recognition of the necessity to formalise rule but, for the British at least, *in a continuing attempt to avoid it.*

Having said which, the Conference was an important moment in the formalisation of the international legal structure of imperialism. Merely by institutionalising a particular state's responsibility for a particular territory, the already-ongoing process of legal formalisation – the 'hardening of the law' – was aided. In fact, the British conception of the protectorate as different from formal legal control was considered 'extremely doubtful'.[133] Neither the French nor the Germans insisted on the tendentious British view,[134] and the most active of the increasing number of professional international lawyers opposed it.[135]

The British were swimming against the tide. The failure of the companies to ensure stability meant that increasing political and formal legal regulation was inevitable. The transformation of 'protectorates' into full colonies is evidence of that.

> Madagascar became a French protectorate in 1885 and a French colony in 1896. Korea became a Japanese protectorate in 1905 and a Japanese colony in 1910. Numerous British protectorates such as the Gambia, the Gold Coast, Nigeria and Kenya later became Crown colonies.[136]

---

129 Umozurike 1979, p. 25.
130 Koskenniemi 2000, p. 15.
131 Ibid.
132 Grewe 2000, p. 473.
133 Ibid. See also Koskenniemi 2000, p. 15.
134 Grewe 2000, p. 473.
135 Koskenniemi 2000, p. 23.
136 Grewe 2000, p. 473.

In effect, though for the British not in design, the protectorate became a *stage* in the progressive international legalisation of relations between colony and empire.

However, the British were not alone in still trying to avoid the costs of formal administration. After the Act many chartered companies were set up – by all the major powers – to take control of exploitation and, resentfully, administration, of African and other regions: among them were the Royal Niger Company in 1886; the British East Africa Company in 1888; the British South Africa Company in 1889; the German East Africa Company in 1885; the German New Guinea Company in 1886; and the Portuguese Mozambique Company in 1891.

But these companies were only a slightly more convincing attempt than the British 'protectorate' scheme to exercise authority without administration. They did not last long.[137] These companies 'lacked . . . the right to make war and peace . . . and the trade monopoly' which had given their predecessors their 'great political and international legal importance' and 'economic power'. Their very structure allowed for – and therefore because of their own inefficiency demanded – the legitimating authority of their home states.[138]

To this extent the Berlin Conference was a failure. Its various evasions could not withstand the pressure to formalise and legalise colonial control. 'Even Bismarck was no longer able to consider . . . using the trading companies to interrupt the global inter-relationship between Europe and the overseas colonies and to isolate the two spheres . . . one against the other'.[139] The tendency from the mid-1880s onwards was for the progressive codification of colonial rule, whereby the colonies became part of the political unity of the home state. This was the beginning of the age of the large, formal empire.

There was one other strategy pursued at the Berlin Conference – the setting up of the now-notorious 'Congo Free State'. This was a nominally inde-

---

[137] Grewe 2000, p. 468. For example, the grandly named Imperial British East Africa Company was chartered towards the end of 1888, and its agents withdrawn from Uganda in 1891, necessitating the establishment of a protectorate. See also Koskenniemi 2000, p. 11.

[138] Grewe 2000, p. 468. He continues: 'The new companies were all subject to strict public control. The Charter of the British North Borneo Company stipulated that . . . the designation of the director charged with leadership functions in Borneo required the consent of the Colonial Minister. . . . [A]ll disputes between [the company] . . . and the indigenous princes had to be submitted to him for resolution.'

[139] Grewe 2000, p. 470.

pendent state at the mouths and basin of the Congo, separate from Belgium, but under the sovereignty of the Belgian king Leopold II. It was born out of the International Commission of the Congo (ICC), a body put in place to minimise inter-imperialist confrontation in the area,[140] and the International Association of the Congo, a business, which provided 'the embryo of its [the state's] government'.[141]

The degeneration of the Congo Free State into an exploitative regime of the most savage and murderous brutality is well documented.[142] What is interesting from the point of view of international law and imperialism is the fact that, like the other measures of the 1885 Act, it was a strategy 'of avoiding formal sovereignty [over the territory] but reaping the benefits'.[143] This led it to take the most extraordinary hybrid forms. When still the ICC, it was a neutral state for which '[n]othing was exact', combining 'the double nature of a state and an international colony': it was 'an institution endowed by legal fiction with the attributes of an autonomous state'.[144]

However, for Grovogui to describe this as a 'fiction' is misleading. The Congo Free State was little more than Leopold's private estate, but it *was* designated a state, whatever the motivations of such designation and however fragile the resulting entity, and it *was* 'recognised by the United States and the European powers as an independent and sovereign member of the international legal community'.[145] Grewe picks up immediately on the most crucial point: 'this enterprise . . . *demonstrated the transfer of the European conception of the State to the African colonial sphere*'.[146]

Here, this was specifically as a means to colonial power. The status of the new polity allowed Leopold's depredations: in Koskenniemi's apposite and chilling phrase, this was 'sovereignty as terror'.[147] Though the social *content*

---

[140] The ICC achieved the agreement of the imperialist powers in the 'Congo Free State' by providing for free trade and navigation in the region. See Grovogui 1996, p. 84; Koskenniemi 2000, pp. 12–13.

[141] Grovogui 1996, p. 85.

[142] See Hochschild 1999. Also Stengers 1969; Pakenham 1992, p. 600.

[143] Koskenniemi 2000, p. 13.

[144] Grovogui 1996, p. 85. (The 'double nature' description is Grovogui quoting Riccardo Pierantoni.)

[145] Grewe 2000, p. 471.

[146] Ibid. Emphasis mine.

[147] Koskenniemi 2002a, p. 155. See pp. 159–66 for the debate among international lawyers, and their 'blind spot . . . towards the atrocities that went on at the same time in "normal" or "legitimate" French or German colonies in Africa' (p. 165).

of the ICC/Congo Free State was highly peculiar (in an attempt to avoid colonial responsibility), it was given the *form* of the juridically sovereign, independent state.

The tendency towards juridical formalisation visible in the recurring colonial lineage of chartered company authority, to protectorate, to colony, reaches the ultimate expression of sovereign state. This is not to say that it was inevitable that the colonies would ultimately be recognised as sovereign, but it is to admit that there were tendencies in that direction even before factoring in the agitation from the colonised.

The pressures towards juridical recognition of the colonies were strong. With the spread and universalisation of commodification under capitalism, law – including international law – had a similar universalising dynamic, with a tendency towards the realisation of the juridical sovereignty of polities.

4.1. *Mandates, colonies and sovereignty: tendencies and countertendencies*

The history of Africa between the Berlin Act up until the Second World War seems to contradict the idea of a dynamic of juridical sovereignty: the tendency during this period was to bring more and more of the African continent under direct and formal colonial rule. 'With the exception of Egypt (since 1922), Ethiopia (for part of the period) and Liberia, the whole of Africa came under colonial subjugation.'[148] The colonies were by now regarded 'as part and parcel of the colonizing states', whose 'sovereign powers' extended over them.

For the ex-German colonies won in World War One, however, the new system of mandates was devised by the victorious powers.[149] The various colonial possessions were divided into A, B and C Mandates, supposedly according to their 'standard of development'.[150] Of course these categories could not be objective.

---

148 Umozurike 1979, p. 51.

149 See Umozurike 1979, pp. 56–61 for an overview of the system.

150 Umozurike 1979, p. 57. Ottoman Arabs were considered 'most' developed and were 'A Mandates'; '[m]ost African and some Pacific island territories were placed under category B or parallel legal arrangements. South West Africa and another group of German dependencies in the Pacific were ranked as C mandates, reserved for the "least evolved"' (Grovogui 1996, p. 127).

> The three categories of mandate, it appears, were designed to reflect different political realities in the territories rather than different stages of development among the colonized. These circumstances were: the strength of the nationalists; the degree of political and economic involvement of European capital; and the existence of a political and religious elite predisposed to embrace values that intersected with Europeans' desires for the territories.[151]

In addition to the politics of assignation of mandate-type, there was the question of which power or powers received overlordship over which mandate. The allocation was at the behest of the Permanent Mandate Commission, an international body of the League of Nations,[152] and was determined by jostlings between the imperialist powers.

> [P]olitical, economic and strategic interests were central to the design of the mandate system and the ensuing allocation of territories. In this regard, one cannot help but notice that phosphate was the reason that Nauru, an eight-square-mile island in the South Pacific inhabited by two thousand people, was assigned to three mandatory powers.[153]

The mandate system and the solidification of the victorious colonialists' holds over 'their own' possessions makes clear that the dynamic towards the juridically independent sovereign state was partial and contradictory. However, even these developments are not so one-sided as they might appear.

The bringing of the colonies under the acknowledged sovereign control of the home power was after all the failure of nineteenth-century colonialism, which had striven to avoid formal administrative control. The move to full, formal colonialism, was thus symptomatic of the general *extension* of the framework of sovereignty. The full development of this trend would only be seen in the self-determination of polities with the sovereign form, but even this was an acknowledgement that these territories must fall under *some*

---

[151] Grovogui 1996, p. 128.

[152] It also theoretically acted as a kind of ombudsman, which locals could petition with protests about the running of a territory, but this did not stop the appalling depredations being carried out under the mandate system's aegis. Initially this right to petition was extended only to citizens of the mandate powers themselves. Though it was later granted to native populations, the right was hedged with many caveats and was administered with politically determined interpretation by the Commission. For examples of some of the iniquities of the mandate regimes see Umozurike 1979, pp. 59–60.

[153] Grovogui 1996, p. 127.

sovereignty – even that of a colonial power. The imperialist powers were able to turn this to their own ends for some decades, but they were capitulating to a dynamic towards the universal juridical regulation of international relations.

There was increasingly vocal opposition to formal colonialism from Africans, exemplified in the four Pan-African Congresses held between 1900 and 1927. Though not a powerful force, these meetings petitioned the League, and made it impossible to ignore the fact that grass-roots opposition to the imperialist powers was growing.[154] Meanwhile, at the heart of the still-new juridical strategy of formal colonialism was an instability, whereby sovereignty was used on the one hand to define a territory that had been previously defined by its exclusion from the universe of sovereignty, and on the other to deny its independence. The attempt was to decouple sovereignty from sovereign independence. Where once sovereignty was a problem to be avoided, or at best a strategy the deployment of which should be carefully considered, now it was thrust upon the powers, and they were left to rationalise it.[155]

The same dynamic towards sovereignty was also embedded in the other form of institutional imperialism, the mandate system. At one level this was yet another successful attempt by the imperialists to avoid the costs of formal rule. However, Article 22 of the League of Nations covenant, which enshrined the system, provided that for those 'peoples not yet able to stand by themselves under the strenuous conditions of the modern world', 'the tutelage . . . should be entrusted to advanced nations who by reason of their resources, their experience or their geographical position can best undertake this responsibility, and who are willing to accept it'.

The construction here was that the African territories needed teaching in the ways of civilisation and sovereignty. But of course, this was an admission that they could learn. The natives, it is claimed, have not *yet* learnt to stand by themselves.[156] These categories through which the mandates were

---

[154] Umozurike 1979, pp. 53–6.

[155] It is perhaps a reflection of imperialist anxiety resulting from this that the discourse of imperialism in these years became markedly more crude than the measured *realpolitik* of Bismarck or the British Foreign Office of the late nineteenth century (on Bismarck see Grewe 2000, pp. 469–70: on the FO see Koskenniemi 2000, p. 10). 'We hold these countries', opined Frederick Lugard, Britain's representative to the Mandate Commission, in 1923, 'because it is the genius of our race to colonize, to trade, and to govern' (quoted in Umozurike 1979, p. 53).

[156] These constructions were justified by 'liberal' companion platitudes to the muscular colonial ideology of Lugard (see above), and which were no more sophisticated.

conceived undermined them, by *containing their own end*. The ramifications were enormous for international law, as Grewe makes clear.

> All of these criteria deviated considerably from the traditional ideology of colonial imperialism with its sharp distinctions between 'civilised' nations, 'barbarous' and 'semi-barbarous' communities, and 'savages', which reserved full legal personality to the first group only. Some of the peoples placed under mandate were 'provisionally recognised' in their 'existence as independent nations'. *They were thus offered the prospect of full recognition of their independence under international law.*[157]

This was more than a hypothetical possibility. 'Iraq was released from its mandate in 1932, and negotiations on the emancipation of Syria and Lebanon were initiated'.[158]

Of course this was not the end of the problem: in most cases the powers would hardly hand over independent sovereignty without resistance, and would argue that the claims of the colonised that they were ready for self-determination were premature. 'The question now arises as to who is competent to decide when a ward is fledged for political autonomy.'[159]

The mandate system did not lead to a smooth transition to independent sovereignty. But the notion of trusteeship did contain a sense of its own finite nature. Tutelage as a principle implies the question that gives Azikiwe the title of a section in his 1931 essay: 'After Tutelage What?'[160] However much the imperialists might try to deny it, the obvious answer was sovereignty, in its fully developed form of sovereign independence.

'Critics' of colonialism 'insisted . . . that the European powers act as "colonialists with a conscience" . . . as trustees for the natives' (Grovogui 1996, p. 112).

[157] Grewe 2000, p. 582. Emphasis mine.

[158] Ibid.

[159] Azikiwe 1931, p. 298.

[160] Azikiwe 1931, p. 297. Now a period piece, Azikiwe's article is fascinating in that it embeds many of the contradictions of 'liberal' thought of the time. This black scholar critical of imperialism does not dispute that 'the Permanent Mandates Commission is doing remarkably fine work for humanity' (p. 292). Problems in the mandate system are seen as pathological to that system, rather than engendered by it (p. 293). However, the piece illustrates how even one who accepted much of the ideological baggage of inter-war 'liberal' 'humanitarian' imperialism – arguably especially such a one – was driven by the logic of those structures ultimately to do away with them: '[T]he dual mandate principle entails more than trusteeship, it entails social progress and social progress entails a liberality of attitude and equal opportunities so that these adolescents will reap the benefit of a realistic and not a fictitious mandates principle' (p. 294).

5. The empire of sovereignty

It seems counterintuitive, given that late-nineteenth- and early-twentieth-century formal colonialism is usually deemed exemplary of capitalist imperialism, to consider it a relatively short-lived transitional form of the phenomenon. However, the history of imperialism in Africa is the history of a resentful, reluctant failure to withstand the trend towards independent sovereignty.

Of course the history of decolonisation and sovereignty was not an inexorable teleology. Italy's 1935 invasion and annexation of Abyssinia, for example, were about the snuffing out of a sovereign state, in which the major imperialist powers were complicit.[161] And where it did occur, decolonisation was often hard won by the mass action by those at the sharp end of imperialism, in the colonies themselves.[162] But despite countertendencies, the juridical form of independent sovereignty was one which imperialism itself tended to universalise.

Capitalism's tendency is to generalise, and as Pashukanis has made clear, capitalism is *juridical* capitalism. This imperialism of sovereignty is the imperialism of international law, which is the imperialism of juridical relations.

It is this model that informs Justin Rosenberg's seminal Marxist genealogy of anarchy and the modern capitalist state form, which he sees ending in 'the empire of civil society'.[163] He is clear that sovereignty is 'a form of political rule peculiar to capitalism',[164] predicated on 'the separation of political functions between public and private spheres'.[165]

Rosenberg exaggerates this separation. In his model, the 'separation of political functions between public and private spheres . . . [is] the *form* of both class power and state power under capitalism',[166] which means the slightest elision of the boundaries of state and market is deemed subversive of the very capitalist character of the state.[167] This is an ideal-type analysis of capitalism. There is no room for Rosenberg to examine the actual constitutive

[161] Umozurike 1979, pp. 66–77.
[162] For a brief overview see Hobsbawm 1994, pp. 199–222.
[163] Rosenberg 1994, pp. 123–58.
[164] Rosenberg 1994, p. 123.
[165] Rosenberg 1994, p. 129.
[166] Ibid. Emphasis in original.
[167] He claims, for example, that 'by extending its direct ownership through nationalization . . . the *sovereign* character of [the capitalist state's] . . . rule diminishes' (Rosenberg 1994, pp. 127–8).

interpenetration of 'public' and 'private' in the history of actually-existing capitalism, explained in the work of Bukharin and others as the result of countertendencies to the separation of spheres within capitalism itself.

Despite this criticism, however, Rosenberg's work remains a brilliant and vital starting point for the genealogy of sovereignty: although the separation of public and private is not *definitional* to capitalism, it is most certainly a strong tendency. And sovereignty as a relation – both between state and citizen, and between states – is a corollary of this tendency.

Rosenberg insists that 'we should define sovereignty primarily not . . . as a kind of residual legal paramountcy',[168] and so far as it goes, this is quite true – to *define* sovereignty juridically would tell us nothing about the social relations it expresses. The juridical nature of sovereignty, though, is not a mere gloss on those relations, but *is* them. There is nothing 'residual' about the legal paramountcy of sovereignty – it is the same phenomenon Rosenberg examines, viewed with another optic.

The dynamic in the nineteenth century by which sovereignty – always intrinsically juridical – 'extends and expands its reach and scope',[169] illustrates that what Rosenberg calls capitalism's 'empire of civil society' is also the empire of sovereignty, which is the empire of international law.[170]

Along with the 'hardening' of law in the nineteenth century went the expansion of its geographic scope. In 1850, for example, the British colonial secretary commented favourably on the results of the 1843 Foreign Jurisdiction Act.

> [A] jurisdiction has been acquired by H.M. in the Territories adjacent to the Forts on the Gold Coast, and . . . by this means the neighbouring Chiefs and Tribes have been induced to have recourse to a great extent to British Tribunals for the repression of crime, and to relinquish their own barbarous usages.[171]

---

168 Rosenberg 1994, p. 129. There is an implication in Rosenberg that the juridical status is in some way *derived from* the fundamental relations of sovereignty, which is related to the simplistic view that law is a 'superstructural' add-on. He acknowledges, though, that without the 'legal paramountcy' of sovereignty, 'there would be no sovereign states' (p. 129).

169 Anghie 1999, p. 80.

170 At its most abstract, the notion of the dynamic logic of sovereignty and international law can be seen in Allott's idea of 'cumulative' stages of self-determination between 800 AD and the present day, stages that are 'incremental rather than metamorphic' (Allott 1993, p. 181). This article is marred by an opaque style and idealist method, but it contains a fascinating genealogy of self-determination.

171 Quoted in Johnston 1973, p. 61.

In the mid-nineteenth century, juridical control of areas was considered of such importance that the extension of law was deliberately ordered by the British Colonial Office.

> The Colonial Office . . . issued an Order in Council [in 1850] . . . for the regulation of British jurisdiction over British subjects residing in countries adjacent to the colony but under the dominion of native princes. The order provided that the first step for British authorities was to obtain grants of jurisdiction by treaty from 'competent chiefs'. . . . The order stated distinctly that the Foreign Jurisdiction Act alone was not sufficient to afford the crown any jurisdiction.[172]

Here was the transition to a new period. It was no longer enough for British influence that jurisdiction be *asserted* – it had to *formally encompass* other territories. In the interaction of capitalist and non-capitalist polities, the commodity-form of law began to formalise relations as the market economy encroached on pre-existing modes of production, distribution and exchange. The imperialism of law was not accomplished by fiat but by actual jurisdictional extension.

The agency of the colonised was channelled into juridical relations, especially, at first, in their interactions with the imperial power. Obviously, this 'juridicalisation' raised the question of the legal status of the polity with which the European sovereign state was dealing, and the universalisation of international law in Africa began.

In a direct way, the European powers were the agents of this spread, as the precepts of international law were those that underpinned their political-economic agenda.

> [B]y looking at nineteenth-century international law one could . . . speak of a process through which civilization was . . . internationalized. . . . Especially from the middle of the nineteenth century, the Europeans introduced new standards in international relations. States had to provide the framework for all legitimate human activities, from safe trading to a just legal system, based on enlightened Western concepts of law. This was defined as civilization. Where there was no civilized state, territories were open to occupation by any civilized state [which would, of course, bring with it its laws].[173]

---

[172] Johnston 1973, p. 63.

[173] Geyer and Paulmann 2001, pp. 9–10. See also Fisch 2001.

International law was not universalised without the acquiescence and active agency of non-European powers. The gradual extension of juridical relations which culminated in the generalisation of sovereignty and international law reached polities eager to become equal partners in the new international system.

The process is visible, progressing much faster than in Africa and from a more formal basis, in China. In 1864 the third edition of Henry Wheaton's *Elements of International Law* was translated into classical Chinese, and the translation made 'mandatory reading for all top Chinese/Manchu officials and provincial governors'.[174] The structures of international law were increasingly unavoidable for polities pulled into the world capitalist market, as the bureaucrats of the Chinese state realised. Although for many decades 'China applied international law in only a limited fashion',[175] its gradual adoption was not at the gunpoint, but was because of its genuine use to the Chinese state in a new international environment.[176]

Similar pressures lay behind the acceptance of international law by Siam and Japan.[177] Japan in particular, where Wheaton and other textbooks had been available in translation since the 1860s,[178] was quick to use international legal methods not merely to adapt to international capitalism but to conduct its own imperialism. 'Engaging in the terms of international law did not cause Japan to become the imperialist nation it did. Fluently using the terms of this science, however, legitimated its imperialist claims.'[179]

---

[174] Liu 1999a, p. 169. See also Liu 1999b; Gong 1984 pp. 152–7. For a list of other works of Western international law translated and influential in China in the following two decades, see Lee 2002, p. 47.

[175] Gong 1984, p. 154.

[176] For an example of China's successful application of international law, see Gong 1984, p. 154. 'China achieved a first success using international law in 1864 while Prussia and Denmark were at war in Europe. The Prussian minister to China had seized three Danish merchant ships as war prizes. After Prince Kung used international law to argue China's neutrality, the Prussian minister returned the ships with compensation. This incident seemed to prove the utility of a knowledge of international law.'

[177] Gong 1984, pp. 224–5, pp. 180–7. For an overview of the East Asian reception of international law, see Lee 2002.

[178] Gong 1984, p. 182. In Japan as in China, bureaucrats were forced to study international law from Wheaton and others (Anand 2003, p. 19).

[179] Dudden 1999, p. 186, and throughout for an excellent investigation of Japan's encounter with international law, based on a model in which '[t]he vocabulary of international law could not be separated . . . from the material conditions of industrializing capitalism' (p. 168).

It used the specific structures of nineteenth-century pre-universal international law – '[r]ecognizing an advantage in employing international law in Korea, Japan modelled the "unequal treaty" it imposed on Korea after the "unequal treaties" the West had imposed on Japan'.[180] But it also very quickly used the logic of *universal* international law predicated on sovereign equality for its own imperialist ends, employing the politics of recognition.

> Japan challenged the traditional system of international relations in Northeast Asia by denying China's historic suzerain role over Korea in Article I of the treaty which stated, 'Corea being an independent State enjoys the same Sovereign rights as does Japan'.[181]

This universalising – imperialist – logic of international law was put with admirable simplicity by the nineteenth-century jurist W.E. Hall in his textbook, for whom '[s]tates outside European civilization must formally enter the circle of law-governed countries'.[182] In this sense, though the process of decolonisation that commenced after the Second World War represents 'a radical change in international law in relation to colonialism'[183] in its *content*, it is a continuation of the universalising trend in the *form*.

Even in content, the rupture is not absolute: the UN charter proclaimed the 'equal rights and self-determination of peoples', but it did not insist on immediate self-government of colonies. Instead, it retained a variant of the mandate system but made more explicit the dynamic of universalism. Thus 'non-self-governing territories' were to be ruled by their colonial masters with the aim 'to develop self-government'. Mandates were replaced with 'trusteeships', the rule of which was to be carried out with the objective of the 'progressive development towards self-government or independence'.[184] Even

---

[180] Gong 1984, p. 183.

[181] Gong 1984, p. 184.

[182] Hall 1884, p. 40. He goes on: 'They must do something with the acquiescence of the latter, or of some of them, which amounts to an acceptance of law in its entirety beyond all possible misconstruction.'

[183] Umozurike 1979, p. 79.

[184] For a critical overview of the trusteeship system, see Grovogui 1996, pp. 151–3. Grovogui in fact claims that '[h]indsight now shows that colonial relations worsened under the trusteeship system. The move away from the formalism of the mandate enabled colonial powers to divest themselves of most of the requirements of the mandate, including the legally defined duties of the trustee. According to natives who petitioned the Trusteeship Council during its early existence, the trustee powers intensified their exploitation of the territories after they were no longer restrained by intrusive prescriptions' (p. 153). Grovogui's claims are very plausible, and illustrate

Churchill, the 'diehard' imperialist,[185] accepted the ideology of 'the progressive evolution of self-governing institutions in the regions and peoples which owe allegiance to the British Crown'.[186]

The trend towards self-determination gathered momentum. In the face of the opposition of the colonised, 'by the late 1950s it had become clear to the surviving old empires that formal colonialism had to be liquidated'.[187] Formal colonialism broke first in Asia. 'By 1950 Asian decolonization was complete, except in Indochina.'[188] From there, the wave of opposition moved to north Africa and the Middle East, 'a series of popular movements, revolutionary coups and insurrections'[189] from Morocco to Egypt, Syria and Iraq. Finally, in the 1960s, the wave began to sweep over sub-Saharan Africa, heralded by the 'Declaration on the Granting of Independence to Colonial Countries and Peoples', adopted by the UN General Assembly in 1960. The collapse of the trustee system occurred 'after a surprisingly short period of time. For the most part, it hardly lasted a decade'.[190]

'After the cataclysm of World War II the nation-state tide reached full flood. By the mid-1970s even the Portuguese Empire had become a thing of the past'[191] – not, it must be stressed, without violent responses from colonial powers.[192] The UN General Assembly, which 'began as a sort of Euro-American club . . . has become a predominantly African and Asian organisation'.[193]

---

how the colonial powers could attempt to gain maximum advantage from almost any structure of colonialism, and that such 'advantage' was *still* seen in terms of the avoidance of formal overlordship. However, even if the trusteeship system was a step backwards for local people in terms of the lived conditions, it did represent a step along the line towards universalisation of international law, in its open treatment of trust-status as a stage along the way to full independence.

[185] Hobsbawm 1994, p. 211.

[186] Hansard, quoted in Umozurike 1979, p. 81. Ironically, Churchill said this during an attempt to exclude colonial subjects from the Atlantic Charter in 1941: even the defence of the most old-fashioned kind of formal imperialism had to be framed within a problematic of 'progressive evolution' towards independence.

[187] Hobsbawm 1994, p. 221.

[188] Hobsbawm 1994, p. 220.

[189] Ibid.

[190] Grewe 2000, p. 649. Though the exceptions are startling – for example, Namibia remained under the colonial control of South Africa until 1989, and the Federated States of Micronesia was only released from US administration in 1991.

[191] Anderson 1983, p. 113. For a comprehensive and chronological list of the expansion of the UN from 51 members in 1945 to 185 by 1997, see Marín-Bosch 1998, pp. 7–8.

[192] On the fourteen years of Portugese colonial war, for example, see among others Hargreaves 1996, p. 233; Springhall 2001, p. 179.

[193] Marín-Bosch 1998, p. 12.

As Benedict Anderson argues, '[t]he "last wave" of nationalisms, most of them in the colonial territories of Asia and Africa, was in its origins a response to the new-style global imperialism made possible by the achievements of industrial capitalism'.[194] That capitalism is a system of juridical abstraction, which explains the particular shape nationalism took:[195] anti-colonial movements became the culmination of the long-term tendency toward universalised juridical sovereignty, and the international law of which sovereign states are the subjects and agents.

International law has been profoundly changed by this historical shift, exemplified in the proclamations of the UN. 'Instead of a special colonial international law, there was now only a multitude of independent and formally equal member-States'.[196] Though the colonial powers – or more exactly certain sections of the ruling class in each colonial power – resisted the changes,[197] 'the vast majority of UN members sought to set in motion an irreversible process of decolonization'.[198] The United Nations, the 'raison d'être' of which appears to be '[t]he codification of International Law'[199] 'has . . . striven for universality'.[200]

This is not to suggest that empire of sovereignty was the result of the intrinsic content of the UN Charter.[201] Instead, the provisions of the UN Charter have come to be read in such a way, because though they were not intrinsically anti-colonial,[202] as the legal arguments by the colonial powers against decolonisation make clear, they embodied and were pushed forward by the mutually constituting dynamics of sovereignty and self-determination. Koskenniemi captures this seeming ineluctability.

> Nor were the Charter provisions on trusteeship and non-self-governing territories designed to attain the massive redistribution of sovereignty that decolonization meant in practice. That the relevant provisions were flexible

---

[194] Anderson 1983, p. 139.

[195] 'The need of a constantly expanding market for its products chases the bourgeoisie over the whole face of the globe. It must nestle everywhere, settle everywhere, establish connections everwhere.' (Marx and Engels 1987, pp. 19–20.) So with the juridical relations that this market implies.

[196] Grewe 2000, p. 649.

[197] See the discussion of Portugal and France in Marín-Bosch 1998, pp. 50–2.

[198] Marín-Bosch 1998, p. 52.

[199] Marín-Bosch 1998, p. 151.

[200] Marín-Bosch 1998, p. 9.

[201] Umozurike makes that mistake, claiming that '[t]he provisions of the charter of the U.N. are anti-colonialist' (Umozurike 1979, p. 94).

[202] See Koskenniemi 1995, p. 337.

> enough (despite colonial powers' constant legal objections to the interpretation of Chapter XI of the Charter so as to internationalize what was supposed to be a national trusteeship) to provide a basis for a programme of pushing into independence a much larger number of territories than were originally listed within the trusteeship system (11 territories) reformed these parts of the Charter into a veritable *de facto* peaceful change mechanism.[203]

'Equality', it appears, 'is infectious'.[204] Once sovereignty is granted to some politically weak polities, 'the tendency is irresistible to qualify still other members of the society as well'.[205] We can of course more exactly express this: the post-War drive to self-determination is not merely a change in the structure or content of international law, but the *culmination of the universalising and abstracting tendencies in international – legal – capitalism.*

In this sense it is therefore not enough to claim with Anghie that 'international law is now more open and cosmopolitan', or that it 'promoted the process of decolonization by formulating doctrines of self-determination where once it formulated doctrines of annexation and *terra nullius*':[206] while this is

---

[203] Koskenniemi 1995, p. 337.

[204] Jackson 1987, p. 538. Jackson distinguishes between juridical sovereignty and 'empirical statehood', and sees the modern international legal system of juridical equality as based on 'the contemporary moral-legal framework of the accommodative juridical regime' (p. 536), in contrast to the 'traditional empirical foundation of the competitive states-system' of 'positive sovereignty: the national will and capacity to become and remain independent'. 'International law in this sphere', he claims, 'is an acknowledgement of real statehood that is a consequence of successful state-building' (Jackson 1987 p. 536). He sees the focus on the 'juridical' rather than the 'real' aspects of sovereign statehood as underlying many of the problems of the third world – essentially, this is a problem of an 'accommodative' system. For a devastating critique of Jackson's liberal construction which completely writes out the complicity of the colonial powers in the very problems of underdevelopment that he terms 'quasi-statehood', see Grovogui 1996, pp. 182–4 and pp. 202–3. Here, I will only point out that Jackson's distinction between 'empirical statehood' or 'positive sovereignty' on one hand and 'juridical sovereignty' on the other is predicated on precisely the separation of politics and law that I have argued is impossible. While of course he is right that the various states of the world have vastly different capabilities, it is not a *pathology* or *mistake* that has led them to be treated as juridically equal – such a coexistence of real inequality and juridical equality is precisely the condition of capitalist modernity. He describes the situation as a 'new dualism' (Jackson 1987, p. 536) which it emphatically is not. To that extent, his putatively 'liberal' solutions, revolving around the move away from juridical equality towards 'a greater variety of international statuses including more intrusive forms of international trusteeship' (Jackson 1991, p. 202) are profoundly conservative, and conservatively utopian, harking nostalgically back to the mandate era.

[205] Miller 1985, p. 49.

[206] Anghie 1999, p. 75.

true his emphasis is exclusively on the *differences* between pre- and post-War international law. The continuities are also important, as they trace the dynamic of international legal development. Embedded even in colonialist international law doctrines was the germ-seed of self-determination and sovereignty.

Though for many years formal colonialism was expressed in international legal terms, the recent conversion of international law to decolonisation represents the *self-actualisation* of international law – the universalisation of the abstract juridical equality of its subjects. With the end of formal empire comes the apogee of the empire of sovereignty, and of international law.

5.1. *The international law of freedom?*

With the universalising of the legal form, modern international law is usually deemed antipathetic to imperialism. 'There is', the argument runs, 'in existence today a peremptory norm of general international law, a rule, that is to say, of *jus cogens*, which provides for the right of self-determination and thus prohibits colonial domination.'[207]

This position does not have to equate to a naïve belief that with the new international legal epoch, imperialist domination comes to an end. Umozurike, for example, warns of 'neo-colonialism', and is perfectly hard-headed about its coexistence with universal international law and self-determination.[208] However, he still sharply counterposes such 'neo-colonialism' from international law itself.

International law, he says

> must now provide the legal framework within which the New International Economic Order [of more equitable distribution] can be achieved. Though the main actions to redress neo-colonialism must be internal, international law is an additional medium.[209]

---

[207] Udechuku 1978, p. 15. For an almost identical formulation, see Umozurike 1979, p. 85: '[i]n present international law, colonialism is illegal for it runs against the *jus cogens* rules of self-determination and respect for fundamental human rights.'

[208] Umozurike 1979, pp. 126–38. See also Chimni 1993, p. 235: '[i]mperialism, it bears repeating, is just not another word for "colonialism" but refers to a particular stage in the global development of capitalism. . . . For those who associate imperialism with colonialism, the former phenomenon was extinguished with decolonisation or continues only in so far as decolonisation is not complete. Such a view veils the fact that colonialism not only existed before what is termed "the monopoly stage of capitalism" but is survived today by neo-colonialism'.

[209] Umozurike 1979, p. 138. See also pp. 128–9.

Here, 'neo-colonialism' – the continued existence of imperialism – is held to be a *political* phenomenon that can be remedied, in part, by recourse to international law, which *by its nature* is held to oppose it. This construction is supported neither by the facts of post-war history, nor by the analysis of international law and the legal form.

This is not to say that the ending of the era of formal colonialism was not a historically progressive moment: as Koskenniemi puts it, '[f]ormal sovereignty is useful . . . as an absolute barrier by a weak community against a more powerful one'.[210] Though the term 'absolute' is unclear and problematic, it is true that at a formal level the parcelling off of a sovereign state by the extension of international law gives a newly independent state a range of juridical, political and economic options which a dependent territory does not have.

> [T]he formation of a constitutionally independent state undoubtedly can act as the focus of crystallisation of an autonomous capitalist class: even a venal regime heavily dependent on external support is likely to promote some economic development in order to widen its social base . . . and activities designed to consolidate the territorial power of the new state – for example school and road building – will also create the conditions for capital accumulation. . . . The exclusive control of colonial and semi-colonial economies by individual metropolitan powers was now replaced by a more fluid state of affairs in which multinational corporations form a variety of Western states invested in the same country, giving the local state room for manoeuvre between them and the tax revenues to promote the expansion of native capital.[211]

This is why though '[s]overeignty is a dry, legal question for those nations who have acquired statehood . . . [it is] a passionate crusade for those who do not have it.'[212] Just as all the manifold oppressions and exploitations resulting from subjugation to the wage-form do not mean that such subjugation does not embed more emancipatory potential than slavery or serfdom, so despite all the serious problems that Grovogui and others have shown resulted from the adoption of the dominant sovereign state model by postcolonial

---

210 Koskenniemi 2000, p. 16.
211 Callinicos 1994, pp. 47–9.
212 Farley 1986, p. 9.

societies,[213] it did advance the potentiality for emancipatory politics. The insistence of the decolonization movements on self-determination drew on international legal principles articulated by the UN, and whatever critiques are made of the realities of post-colonialism, the importance of this wave should not be underestimated.

However, imperialism outlasts the transition to universalised juridical sovereignty, and not because postcolonial sovereignty is incomplete[214] or because 'the sovereignty acquired by the non-European state . . . was only tenuously connected with its own identity'.[215] Such imperialism is not something international law can successfully oppose, whatever its apparently anticolonial content[216] – it is embedded *in the very structures of which international law is an expression and a moment*. The movements for self-determination may have articulated the content of the legal norm of self-determination to emancipatory political effect, but it was in the very juridical forms and structures of those norms that imperialism had purchase.

The imperialism of international law means more than just the global spread of an international legal order with capitalism – it means that the power dynamics of political imperialism are embedded within the very juridical equality of sovereignty.

In their enormously influential book *Empire*, Hardt and Negri develop some of these ideas.

> The position of the newly sovereign nation-state cannot be understood when it is viewed in terms of the rosy U.N. imaginary of a harmonious concert of equal and autonomous national subjects. The postcolonial nation-state functions as an essential and subordinated element in the global organiza-

---

[213] Grovogui 1996, pp. 195–200 for an outline. See Nesiah 2003 for an example of this model's application in the case of the Western Sahara. Here, as elsewhere, choice 'is limited to alternatives that are state-centred' ('self-determination as independent statehood, integration with an existing state, or free association with an existing state') (Nesiah 2003, p. 18). For a similar argument with regard to the same case, also stressing the 'favour[ing of] territoriality over other forms of identity', see Castellino 1999 (p. 531).

[214] Grovogui 1996, p. 196: 'The current postcolonial crises suggest that the results of the dominant African strategy have been mixed at best. *Its failure to fully restore African sovereignty* and self-determination has had significant political and theoretical implications' (emphasis mine).

[215] Anghie 1999, p. 70.

[216] 'When empire is used to mean colonialism, then, it appears that, although things were different in the past, today *international law and institutions oppose empire*; they are against it, quite emphatically in fact.' Marks in Various 2003b, p. 902. Emphasis mine.

> tion of the capitalist market. . . . [N]ational liberation and national sovereignty are not just powerless against this global capitalist hierarchy but themselves contribute to its organization and functioning.[217]

Ultimately they take this insight in what I hold to be a quite wrong direction, claiming that '[t]he global capitalist hierarchy that subordinates the formally sovereign nation-states . . . is fundamentally different from the colonialist and imperialist circuits of international domination'.[218] I argue that the two are one.[219] However, Hardt and Negri's correction to the utopianism of some international lawyers is sharp. To borrow their provocative phrase about the triumph of national self-determination, if it is true that juridical sovereignty and the edifice of international law embed relations of imperialist domination, then it really is 'The Poisoned Gift of National Liberation'.[220]

6. New world order

There are important differences between imperialism during and after the Cold War. The move from a world that is, between 1945 and 1990, 'politically bipolar, but economically multipolar' to one that is 'politically as well as economically multipolar'[221] represents a vital shift in the structure of international relations, and the imperialism which informs it.[222] However, the shift away from 'Cold War imperialism' at the start of the 1990s did not fundamentally alter the nature of the problematic under investigation here – the articulation of imperialism in a world of juridically equal states.

The 1990–91 Gulf War is a crucial example.[223] A brief examination of this conflict and the debates around it can illustrate the realities of modern imperialism, of international law, and of the penetration of the two.

---

[217] Hardt and Negri 2000, p. 133.

[218] Hardt and Negri 2000, p. 135.

[219] For a critique that takes Hardt and Negri to task for positing an impersonal network of Empire, rather than of seeing the US as an overwhelmingly dominant capitalist power, see Callinicos 2002. For an alternative critique, that charges Callinicos with misreading Hardt and Negri on American power, see Green 2002.

[220] Hardt and Negri 2000, p. 132.

[221] Callinicos 1994, p. 27, p. 39.

[222] For an excellent overview of the differences between the two stages, see Callinicos 1994, pp. 27–55.

[223] For chronologies, see Blair 1992 and Travers 1993. For a discussion of the theoretical implications for IR, see Matthews 1993. For an overview of various positions and facts on the war, see Sifry and Cerf 1991. For critical positions see Bennis and

6.1. *Excursus: the Gulf War*

The war was an act of American imperialism, motivated by a desire to control the economic power of oil[224] as well as to establish authority in a suddenly no-longer bipolar world. 'As Bush and his advisers made plain in numerous speeches, the war drive in the Gulf was a means of reasserting American global political and military leadership.'[225] This, of course, as Fred Halliday has pointed out, is not necessarily an argument against the war. '[I]s everything imperialism does negative?' he asks, and concludes that 'if I have to make a choice between imperialism and fascism, I choose imperialism'.[226]

I will not rehearse the humanitarian catastrophe caused by the West's military response to Iraq's invasion of Kuwait in August 1990.[227] Nor will I reiterate the evidence that, contrary to Halliday's claim that '[t]he diplomatic option was tried and it failed', that '[p]eace *was* given a chance',[228] the decision to go to war was decided as early as 30 October 1990, and that numerous diplomatic alternatives to war were rebuffed by an intransigent US.[229] Instead I will focus on the point that Halliday concedes, that the war was 'conducted by an unsavoury set of powerful states'.[230]

Halliday's argument is that despite 'unsavoury' motives, the imperialism itself might constitute a progressive force. However, as Patrick Wilcken points out, '[t]he main problem with this type of approach is that, if these powerful states really are "unsavoury", what guarantee was there that the negoti-

Moushabeck 1991; Bresheeth and Yuval-Davis 1991; Chomsky 1992a, pp. 179–214, pp. 407–40. For the most systematic and nuanced defence of the war, see Halliday 1996, pp. 76–103.

224 Simons 1998, pp. 211–13.

225 Callinicos 1994, p. 44.

226 Halliday 1991, p. 16.

227 See Clark 1992a and 1992b. See also Middle East Watch 1991: however, though this report can be culled for information, it must be read alongside Norman Finkelstein's devastating critique, showing how its putatively open-handed reportage is replete with unstated ideological imbalance that 'perpetuated the Bush administration's central myth that Iraq was a powerful and dangerous adversary'. (Finkelstein 1996, p. 65. See pp. 57–65.)

228 Halliday 1996, p. 86. Emphasis in original.

229 For lists of these opportunities, see Chomsky 1992a, pp. 190–2, pp. 203–11. See also Falk 1994: 'It was very clear that the United States and its allies preferred to use force and war. . . . This feature very much constrained the search for a peaceful settlement. It is not necessarily sure that a peaceful settlement could have been achieved. . . . But there was certainly not a disposition on the part of the US and its major allies to resolve the conflict in that way.'

230 Fred Halliday quoted in *The Guardian* 11 February 1991.

ations, war and final settlement would be conducted satisfactorily?'[231] Halliday's point of view owes a great deal to Bill Warren's view of imperialism as the pioneer of capitalism.[232] The 'Warrenite' position 'rests on the fallacious assumption that the imperialist powers have a general interest in promoting "democratic change" in the Third World'.[233]

Halliday is quite right that questionable motives in themselves 'do not automatically discredit the war the Allies fought'.[234] However, these motivations are most interesting insofar as they illuminate the *underlying political-economic processes*: 'the logic of international relations is stronger than the logic of diplomacy'.[235] This opens into a radically different conception of imperialism from Halliday's and Warren's. The alternative perspective draws on Lenin and Bukharin's theory of imperialism as a *stage* of capitalism, alongside Trotsky's theory of 'combined and uneven development', a conception of the modern world as a *heterogeneous capitalist totality*. In this model, 'backward countries' develop in a 'planless, complex, combined character',[236] but are components of a 'world economy' that is

> not . . . a sum of national parts but . . . a mighty and independent reality . . . which in our epoch imperiously dominates the national markets. The productive forces of capitalist society have long ago outgrown the national boundaries.[237]

This means that 'Warren's measurements of capitalist progress in the Third World are not just platitudinous; they are also unilinear and one-dimensional – comparing not whole modes but the individual dimensions of each mode'.[238] In this 'combined and uneven' model, 'unsavoury' motives illuminate the depredations of actually-existing capitalism: there is no separate 'progressive' social dynamic that can operate, as it were, behind or despite the agents' motivations.

Imperialism is not a strategy of the advanced and powerful capitalist powers, and certainly not a means of transporting a capitalist mode of production, but is a *defining structural element of actually-existing capitalism* – which included Iraq as much as the allies. The active imperialist intervention of the

[231] Wilcken 1994, p. 34.
[232] Warren 1980.
[233] Callinicos 1994, p. 65.
[234] Halliday 1996, pp. 98–99.
[235] Trotsky 1969, p. 113.
[236] Trotsky 1997, p. 27.
[237] Trotsky 1969, p. 146.
[238] Sivanandan 1990, p. 166.

US, in this model, was not something that the US was *doing to* a non-capitalist society, but was a moment in the totalising, combined and uneven reality of *global capitalism*.

This is not to posit a conspiracy theory: the epoch of imperialism is one of inter-imperialist rivalry, and will be informed by all manner of failing, competing imperialist strategies. However, the structures of imperialism are consistent: the complaints of Halliday and countless others that in March 1991, the West did not 'finish Saddam off' fail to address this. 'Washington's failure to do so did not reflect some intellectual mistake, or lack of will power, but its calculation . . . that [its] . . . interests were better served by the survival of a weakened Ba'athist regime than by its replacement'.[239]

The point is not whether or not the US was correct in this assessment – the point is that leaving Saddam Hussein in power *was as much US imperialist strategy as the earlier bombing*. Similarly, the well-known fact that the US backed Hussein during the 1980s, during some of his worst excesses,[240] is more than simply evidence of US hypocrisy: that too was the US imperialist strategy, just as much as its later attacks. The shifts in policy reflect a consistency of imperialism.

Halliday's argument, that imperialism is a vanguard of capitalism and that 'unsavoury' motivations might be incidental to an underlying modernising dynamic, can be turned on its head. Discussing various actions, Richard Falk says:

> Such anti-genocidal interventions were in each instance *incidental* to the true rationale for recourse to war, which involved reactions to menacing aggressive policies that threatened core interests associated with the power, security and economic well-being of the intervening states.[241]

Falk argues, correctly, that emancipatory motivations *and therefore effects* are incidental even for interventions such as the 1979 invasion of Cambodia by Vietnam, which 'dislodging the Khmer Rouge, did, after more than a decade, help create a peace process for the country that included establishing democracy'. Armed with this analysis, though one might approve of the *incidental*

[239] Callinicos 1994, p. 65.
[240] See for example Wilcken 1994, p. 33.
[241] Falk 1997, pp. 119–20. Emphasis in original.

effects of an intervention – moves towards democracy, for example – it would make no sense to support the *intervention itself*.[242]

To support imperialism, no matter how honourable the motives, is to support the strategies that underpin imperialism as an epoch of global capitalism. It is no coincidence that the imperialist strategy has not brought about a material or political improvement in the region. This hope is predicated on the notion that a *moment* of imperialism – the military action – can be abstracted away from the whole structure and process of imperialism, and used for progressive ends. In fact however progressive such an action's stated aims, it is part of a historical process of domination and exploitation, for which brutal methods are more often than not effective. To try to pick pieces of imperialism to support and others to condemn is to fail to deal with it as a totality.

Such a conception underpins the argument that the international law of *formal* imperialism cannot be the most fundamental intersection of juridicalism and imperialism. If imperialism is totalising, it structures global capitalism, which is a legal system. The question then is how, in an era of formal equality of states, international law articulates imperialism.

6.2. *The limits of legalistic opposition*

Critics of post-war intervention by powerful states often pose their opposition in terms of the action's illegality. In this way, they subscribe to the counterposition between international law and imperialism.

Chomsky, for example, claims that for the US, '[d]iplomacy and international law have always been regarded as an annoying encumbrance'.[243] Geoff Simons claims that

> [t]he US manipulation of law and the international community over Iraq is part of a pattern. It is useful to remember some significant US violations of the UN Charter, UN resolutions and Conventions, treaty obligations and international law.[244]

Stressing that 'the list could easily be extended', he gives a list of what he claims are repeated US violations of international law between 1949 and 1995,

---

[242] Cf. Callinicos 2003, pp. 39–40, discussing the most recent attack on Iraq. '[I]ndeed American arms did overthrow Saddam Hussein's thoroughly evil regime. But all this does is remind us of the long-familiar moral fact that a wicked act – in this case, a war of aggression – can have some good consequences. This does not extinguish the evil consequences it has also brought. . . . Nor does it imply that we should support future wars of the same type'.

[243] Chomsky 1992a, p. 3.

[244] Simons 1998, p. 194.

including, among other examples, the Korean and Vietnam wars, the Cuban blockade, Grenadan and Panamanian invasions, and various less dramatic decisions such as refusals to refer disputes to the International Court of Justice.[245]

There are innumerable other examples of the legalistic opposition to imperialism, many of them constituting invaluable works of critical scholarship. The whole of Christopher Hitchens's magnificent polemic against Henry Kissinger, for example, is framed in these terms, as the evidence for the prosecution in a trial under 'common or customary international law'.[246] However, there is a fundamental problem with the legalist critique of imperialist interventions.

According to Chomsky, the US claims that the Gulf War was an act in defence of the rule of law – that the *ius ad bellum* governing 'permissible recourse to military force'[247] was on the side of the US – do not 'withstand even a moment's scrutiny'.[248] This is demonstrably untrue. In fact, for every Chomsky or Simons there is a Marc Weller,[249] a David Rivkin[250] or an Abram Chayes[251] for whom the attack *was* legal.[252] Some even saw the action as ushering in a new epoch of respect for international law.[253]

Chayes – hardly an unthinking apologist for the US[254] – went so far as to hold that under the authority of an Article 42 resolution of the UN Security Council,[255] which was eventually granted on 29 November 1990, with the

---

[245] Simons 1998, pp. 195–6.

[246] Hitchens 2001, p. ix. See pp. ix–xi, pp. 127–131, and throughout.

[247] Rivkin 1991, footnote 7 p. 59.

[248] Chomsky 1992b, p. 61. Seven years later he excoriates those who depict the 1999 bombing of Yugoslavia as perhaps legal in international law as 'the desperate efforts of ideologues to prove that circles are square' (Chomsky 1999, p. 150).

[249] Weller 1993.

[250] Rivkin 1991.

[251] Chayes 1991.

[252] Though there is disagreement among them on the precise parameters of that legality. Chayes represents the dissident wing of this position, in his view (as expressed by one of his opponents) that 'having brought the Security Council into play, the United States and its allies could not strike at Iraq without an explicit U.N. authorization' (Rivkin 1991, p. 55). For an overview of the debate over whether or not Security Council authorisation was required, see Rostow 1991, pp. 414–18.

[253] See for example Janis 1991.

[254] Chayes has at other times 'represented the Sandinista government in its effort to seek redress before the International Court of Justice for what it considered unlawful United States aggression' (Manas 1995, p. 247).

[255] Article 42: 'Should the Security Council consider that measures provided for in Article 41 [for measures short of military intervention in response to a threat to or breach of the peace] would be inadequate or have proved to be inadequate, it may

adoption by the Council of Resolution 678,[256] 'we could expect substantially universal agreement among international lawyers . . . that the use of force against Iraq would have been permissible'.[257] The only exceptions to this unanimity he foresaw was from 'Iraqi partisans'.[258] He would presumably include among these Ba'ath apparatchiks such critics of the war as Richard Falk.

In fact, Chayes's claim is no more realistic than Chomsky's. The Gulf War can plausibly be defended as either legal or illegal. There are pieces that treat it as a paradigmatic case of a legal war,[259] and there are others dedicated to proving its illegality.[260]

Saddam Hussein claimed various justifications for his invasion, 'arguing that Kuwait was *de jure* part of Iraq, that he had been invited in, and that Kuwait had harmed his interests'.[261] Halliday dismisses the first two as 'simply spurious': it is not entirely clear whether he means that the justifications were *untrue*, or *unacceptable as legal bases for argument*. The claims were, in fact, untrue – there is no meaningful sense in which Kuwait had been separated from Iraq by colonialism, inasmuch as '[i]f Kuwait was . . . an artificial and therefore illegitimate state, then so too was Iraq'.[262]

However, as a basis for law, that is not the point: the form of legal argument inheres not in the truth-value of the claims but in their categories. And this was, in Koskenniemi's terms, a classic 'ascending' argument, a legal argument derived from the 'apologetic' or 'realist' basis of sovereign state-hood. What made the Iraqi claim a *juridical* one structured by the process of international law is not its truth but its *form*, its derivation from the basic juridical units, 'ascending'/realist arguments based on sovereignty and 'descending'/cosmopolitan arguments based on overarching concepts such as 'justice, common interests, progress, nature of the world community'.[263]

---

take such action by air, sea, or land forces as may be necessary to maintain or restore international peace and security. Such action may include demonstrations, blockade, and other operations by air, sea, or land forces of Members of the United Nations.'

256 'Member States co-operating with the government of Kuwait, unless Iraq on or before 15 January 1991 fully implements the foregoing resolutions [including withdrawal from Kuwait and release of hostages], to use all necessary means to uphold and implement Security Council Resolution 660 and all subsequent relevant resolutions and to restore international peace and security in the area.'

257 Chayes 1991, p. 4.

258 Ibid.

259 Moore 1992.

260 Brugger 1991, among others.

261 Halliday 1996, p. 97.

262 Halliday 1996, p. 94.

263 Koskenniemi 1989, p. 40.

Though Halliday means it as a critique of the Iraqi claim, it is equally a *vindication* when he describes 'Iraq's historic title to Kuwait as . . . at best, debatable'.[264] That is exactly right – it is *possible to debate it* on the basis of Iraq's arguments. 'The body of law' is nothing but that debate. The fact that few people agree with the Iraqi position does not alter the *kind* of claim it is – a legal one.

Similarly, Iraq's second justification, that it had been invited in by the 'Democratic Government of Kuwait', was spurious, insofar as this body was effectively non-existent. However, Iraq formulated its claim with scrupulous legalism – intervention by invitation being generally deemed acceptable, certain conditions being met.[265] In fact, one international lawyer said that had the invitation happened as Iraq claimed, it would have been '[t]he paradigm case' of the consent necessary for legal justification.[266] This was then another legal argument for Iraq's invasion, articulated ascendingly, in terms of the 'defence' of Kuwaiti sovereignty, and descendingly, in terms of the 'justice' of defending a government that had supposedly overthrown the Al-Sabah regime in Kuwait.

The use of the third justification given, that Kuwait had harmed Iraqi interests by siphoning oil from the Iraqi part of the Rumaila oilfield and overproducing oil, costing Iraq $14 billion a year,[267] put Iraq, in Halliday's words, 'not so far out of line with international norms'.[268] Though it was certainly possible to argue that Saddam Hussein was operating according to a somewhat outdated view of legal regime,[269] this claim was also legalistically structured and structuring. An ascending formulation can easily be made that Kuwait was intruding on Iraqi sovereignty by its actions.

Obviously, the Iraqi legal case was opposed by most of the world. But the point is not that Iraq lost the legal argument but that it framed the argument legally. The dispute was one of the international legal order, predicated on juridical relations.

---

[264] Halliday 1996, p. 94. Similarly, Halliday's point that Iraq's justifications 'were contradictory' (p. 83) is true but not relevant to their status as legal argumentation.

[265] For various articulations of and disagreements over the conditions deemed necessary, see Hargrove 1991; Mullerson 1991; Wedgwood 1991; Doswald-Beck 1985.

[266] Hargrove 1991, p. 116.

[267] Simons 1998, p. 212.

[268] Halliday 1996, p. 97.

[269] Ibid.

The allied response was also framed by international law, in which Kuwaiti sovereignty was a key term. Against the first Iraqi point was mobilised an ascending defence of the Kuwaiti sovereign state as a legitimate entity in the international (legal) system. Against the second point it was insisted that the Al-Sabah regime was the recognised government, and that therefore the agency of sovereignty was withheld from the rump organisation that Saddam Hussein claimed spoke for Kuwait.

As to the third point, even if Iraq's claims about the Rumaila oilfield were accepted, it could quickly be claimed that Saddam's 'response to the economic harm caused was disproportionate'.[270] In an examination of *ius ad bellum* proportionality, the traditional mode of operation is to consider whether '[t]he probable good to be achieved by successful recourse to armed coercion . . . outweigh[s] the probable evil that the war will produce'.[271] This takes the shape of a moral question – '[p]roportionality is about the comparison of moral goods or values'[272] – which is therefore a descending response to Iraq's ascending claim.

Indeed, it was overwhelmingly descending arguments that framed the Allies' prosecution of the war. Bush's proclamation that '[i]f history teaches us anything, it is that we must resist aggression or it will destroy our freedoms' is paradigmatic:[273] against Iraq's recourse to the argument of sovereignty was arraigned the overarching normative argument of 'freedom'. In a more purely juridical formulation, Bush also claimed that 'America stands where it always has, against aggression, against those who would use force to replace the rule of law'.[274] Here the descending cosmopolitan concept mobilised against Iraq's ascending realist one is the ultimate abstraction of the legal process itself, the 'rule of law'.

The ascending/descending structure of international legal argument is reversible. There is nothing intrinsic to the fact that the opposition to Iraq for the most part took a descending form. 'To participate in international legal argument is essentially to be able to use concepts so that they can be fitted into both patterns'.[275] Legal support for the Allies' war must be explicable in

270 Ibid.
271 O'Brien 1981, p. 28.
272 Coates 1997, p. 176.
273 Quoted in Chomsky 1992a, p. 185.
274 Ibid.
275 Koskenniemi 1989, p. 452.

an ascending form, and of course it is, in terms of the defence/restoration of Kuwaiti sovereignty. One of the most eloquent expressions of this version is Peter Gowan's, who is rare in that he accepts the war was legal, but still stands in sharp opposition to it, and to the 'states'-rights' position that underpins it.

His articulation of the ascending legal defence is provocative.

> Condemnation of Iraqi aggression, variously expressed, was issued worldwide. . . . Within a Grotian, states' rights perspective [the basis of international law], annexation involved what we might call the killing of a sovereign state – the greatest injustice that could be committed within the terms of states' rights theory, and an act of state murder unprecedented in postwar history. . . . If states' rights are sacrosanct, this was a uniquely heinous crime.[276]

The international legal argument, for Gowan, is self-evident. 'There is no need to examine the factual details of the Gulf crisis in order to justify Desert Storm [the military action] within the terms of states' rights doctrine.'[277] This is an ascending defence of the legality of the war.

Law as a relation, rather than a body of rules, implies that 'law-ness' inheres in the form of argument, such as that between the allies and Iraq: this was a *legal* conflict, structured by and around *juridical concepts*. Obviously, then, we cannot prove that one or other side's position was legally 'correct': the whole point of the insight that international law is an indeterminate system is that it is fruitless to look for the resolution of legal argument in the arguments themselves.

As Koskenniemi puts it, the argumentative structure

> leads nowhere but into the *constant opposition, dissociation and association of points about concreteness and normativity* of the law. There is no end to this, however. The discursive structure is only a form of making arguments. It is not one for arriving at conclusions.[278]

The discursive structure is the articulation of juridical forms, a structured process of confrontation of international legal agents thrown up by the dynamics of capitalism.

---

[276] Gowan 1999, p. 147.
[277] Ibid.
[278] Koskenniemi 1989, p. 49. Emphasis in original.

The point is plain. Because international law is a process, not a set of norms, we cannot look to it to tell us whether or not the waging of the Gulf War, or as I will argue below the methods by which it was executed, were legal or illegal. For every claim there is a counter-claim, and 'legalist' opposition to the war is therefore ultimately toothless.

7. The universality of legalism

For every post-war imperialist intervention, this legal indeterminacy is obvious. However minor or massive the incident, the legal arguments are sustained and often bitter. Of course there is usually a majority on one side or the other: but the alternative position is always also structured in terms of legality.

Take 'Operation Just Cause', the US invasion of Panama at the end of 1989. Chomsky claims that the US's 'ritual gesture towards international law' was 'hardly intended seriously'.[279] And certainly the bulk of legal opinion was against the US, seeing the invasion as a violation of the UN Charter.[280] However, it is not the case that for the US, '[i]nternational law was presented as being irrelevant in the face of a conflict with such a person' as Noriega.[281]

In fact the legal case was carefully worked out, involving a descending claim about the necessity for humanitarian intervention; an ascending claim about sovereign rights of a state during war (based on Noriega's hyperbolic declaration that a war existed between the countries); a principle of 'intervention by invitation' only slightly less tenuous than that of the Iraqis in Kuwait;[282] and a claim of legitimate intervention as part of a campaign against drugs by the ingenious application of a 50–year-old Arbitration between the US and Canada designed to minimise cross-border air pollution.[283]

---

[279] Chomsky 1992a, p. 147.

[280] See for example Nanda 1990: Miller 1990.

[281] Johns and Johnson 1994, p. 68.

[282] By claiming the sanction of Endara, the opposition candidate who had claimed the presidency.

[283] See Ehrlich and O'Connell 1993, pp. 97–100. This claim was made with reference to the *United States vs Canada Trail Smelter* Arbitration of 1941, according to which '[n]o state has the right to use or permit the use of its territory in such a manner as to cause injury . . . to the territory of another or the properties or persons therein'. This arbitration has also been raised as possible justification for other acts of international intervention, for example the US-led attack on Afghanistan in 2001 (see Rowe 2002, p. 308 footnote 34).

The same unresolvably structured arguments – again with the weight of opinion against the US – have been batted back and forth in the case of the US invasion of Grenada in 1983.[284] The US's backing of the Nicaraguan Contras has been deemed illegal by the International Court of Justice in 1986, having previously been defended stridently by the US, all in legal terms.[285] The same indeterminate arguments hold whether or not a global superpower is directly involved: the Israeli commando raid on Beirut airport in 1968, for example, just as much as its 1982 invasion of Lebanon, has been seen as legal and as illegal.[286]

International law is everywhere. Legal argument permeates every international incident and the very fabric of the international system. And on its own, the dynamic of this argument resolves nothing.

7.1. *Politics and the end of the rule*

Of course, all this juristic reasoning might purely be a scrabbling for justification for ideological or propagandist purposes, 'to throw an ideological veil over the relations of will thus justified'.[287] Of course there is a strong ideological component involved in framing actions in international legal terms. But this cannot explain the sheer extent of juristic reasoning, the scale and penetration of the legal edifice internationally.

It is unconvincing to suggest that juridical relations are essentially contingent to the 'real' business of power politics, given that every moment of inter-

---

[284] The invasion of a small island with a (presumably nefarious) grip on the world nutmeg trade by the globe's most powerful state was named, with an irony-free hyperbole breathtaking in its crassness, Operation Urgent Fury. For an overview of the debate over the legality of the action see Davidson 1987, pp. 79–137. Davidson's own view, as he judiciously puts it, is that the justifications 'were unable to displace the presumption of illegality' (p. 124). The staunchest proponent of the invasion as legally justified, was, predictably, Moore. See Moore 1984. For an excellent bibliography and a critical evaluation of the legality of the law see Gosselin 1998. Mansell's claim that '[d]iplomatic attempts at legal justification were scarcely bothered with' are clearly overstated (Mansell 1997, p. 37).

[285] For the ICJ's condemnation, see Chomsky 1987, pp. 255–83. A defence, yet again, is offered by Moore – Moore 1986.

[286] For an analysis of the Beirut raid as illegal, see Falk 1969. Defending the legality of Israel's actions is Blum 1970. For a critical view of the legality of the 1982 Lebanon war, both in terms of *ius ad bellum* and *ius in bello*, see Finkelstein 1996, pp. 44–57. For a *ius in bello* critique, see Mallison and Mallison 1986, pp. 376–87. For a positive interpretation (of aggressive pro-Israeli partiality), see O'Brien 1991, pp. 133–47, pp. 173–215.

[287] Koskenniemi 2000b, p. 23.

national interaction and intervention is conceived in these terms. It makes more sense to see the world itself as structured by juridical forms.

There is another, paradoxical, problem with the claim that international law is merely an ideological gloss on power. International law is often singularly *ineffective* as an 'ideological veil over relations of will'. There is a large literature precisely bemoaning the 'failure' of international law to curb gross power relations, decrying 'the irrelevance of international law',[288] or its collapse into power politics.[289] Almost every legalist critique of intervention is some variant of this 'failure of international law' model. Not only does legal reasoning penetrate every aspect of international relations, but at the same time it seems to have too limited an effect on power politics. This is hard to square with the idea of international law as ideology to obscure the facts of power. How can something so ineffective be so universalising and tenacious?

It has become a cliché – though still something of a mystery – to claim that states generally *do* make sure that their behaviour is consistent with international law. This is what is generally conceived as 'the ineluctable relationship of law and politics'.[290] An often-quoted example is Franck's, that the US in the Persian Gulf enforced the rules of neutrality to its own perceived disadvantage, in allowing a shipment of Silkworm missiles to pass to Iran.[291]

While this is all very well, it is somewhat beside the point. After all, there are countless counter-examples when a state articulates a partisan, tendentious, minority interpretation of a law in an attempt to justify its acts. These apparent tendencies of 'law' to influence 'politics' and vice versa only appear contradictory – indeed only appear as tendencies at all – if one holds to the comforting fiction that international law is a body of rules, counterposed to politics.

International law permeates international society because it is a society of juridical forms. The 'rules' may be contingent: the legal forms of which they

[288] The phrase is from the title of Boyle 1980, a good example of the genre.

[289] See for example Briggs 1945, p. 678. 'In terms of power, the form given to the United Nations Organization is grounded realistically on a fact . . . the fact is the preponderant power of the British Empire, the Soviet Union, and the United States to maintain peace in the post-war world'.

[290] Hsiung 1997, p. 4. See also Kaplan and Katzenbach 1961; Deutsch and Hoffman 1971; Henkin 1979; Ringmar 1995. The flipside of this notion, also embedded in the 'ineluctable relationship', is that politics helps to 'structure' international law. Both these conceptions abstract and counterpose law and politics, then construct models for how these two abstractly distinguished systems 'interact'.

[291] Franck 1988, p. 707.

are expressions are not. The point is not, pace Franck, that the apparent 'rules' – at best momentary accretions of past decisions – *have an effect on* power politics: that may happen case to case, but it is not the fundamental articulation of international law and international relations. The point, rather, is that the 'power politics' of modernity *are the power politics of a juridically constructed system.*

The most realist, cynical, power-maximising state in the modern world-system is a realist, cynical and power-maximising juridical form. The *agents* of what realists might fondly suppose is 'pure power' are, in fact, defined by the abstract juridical structures of generalised commodity exchange. There is no separation of these juridical forms from 'pure politics' because there *is* no pure politics: there are instead the politics of sovereignty-in-anarchy, which are the politics of juridical units.

'[T]he questions as to whether and why states "obey" international law are no longer meaningful. It can now be seen that states neither obey nor disobey international law'.[292] It makes little sense to describe any particular action as 'legal' or 'illegal'.[293] Pace Franck, states do not act as they do because they want to 'obey' international law, nor even 'so as to demonstrate acceptance of the ideology of international law':[294] their 'political' actions articulate the juridical categories that define them.

Above the deep grammar of juridical forms, there is nothing to stop a legal argument continuing forever, simply switching from ascending to descending categories endlessly. Of course legal arguments do *not* go on forever. But their resolution is not a result of the internal logic of the concepts, but represents interpretation *backed by force.*

Such interpretation, of course, will be politically motivated, which is why the endless disputes over the contents of legal norms are windows into the strategic approaches of those involved. Some interpretations, though, carry more political weight than others. The traditional concern with legal obligation[295] – why obey the law? – must be replaced with an alternative concern

---

[292] Scott 1994, p. 325.

[293] With the possible exception of the very rare situation of unanimous interpretation. Even here, of course, the unanimity is contingent: the lack of argument does not inhere in the particular norm, and therefore though it might be true to describe a particular action as 'legal' or 'illegal' in this case, it would not be a stable category. It would only take a single dissenting opinion to undermine it.

[294] Scott 1994, p. 325.

[295] The classic starting point is Brierly 1958.

with *authoritative interpretation* – why obey the law as interpreted by a particular power?

The controversy over obligation revolves around whether it derives from some secularised overarching conception of justice or natural law, or on state consent. There are insurmountable problems with each these answers, which are clearly structured around the dyad that Koskenniemi outlines, and can therefore be countered endlessly.

There have been attempts to get round the impasse. Higgins, for example, sees 'reciprocity' as 'a central element' in obligation.

> If consensus, often tacit and sometimes unenthusiastic, is the basis of international law, then that consensus comes about because states perceive a reciprocal advantage in cautioning self-restraint. It rarely is in the national interest to violate international law, even though there might be short-term advantages in doing so. For law as a process of decision-making this is enough. The search for some other basis of obligation is unnecessary. . . .[296]

This is an international legal variant of the 'invisible hand' – international law as constituted by enlightened self-interest. However, Higgins rightly sees the interpretation of laws as central to the content of norms: it is precisely that interpretation which allows an endless spiral of disagreement. The claim that it is rarely advantageous 'to violate international law' therefore tells us almost nothing, as there is often no consensus on what would constitute a violation.

It is, in fact, meaningless to talk about 'obligation', as the understanding that international law is a set of juridical forms partly constitutive of modernity makes clear. A state is not *obligated* to behave as a sovereign juridical form – *that is what it is*. And at the level of particular norms, the fact of interpretation makes the question of 'obligation' equally unhelpful: a state is not 'obligated' by a decision it makes – that decision constitutes its actions.

Having interpreted international law and come to certain decisions, however – having arbitrarily reached the end of a rule – some states are able to make their position stick in the world, against the alternative interpretations of other states. They are able to actualise a particular interpretation of law in the world. Their interpretation does not become 'obligatory', but it *does* become the one that shapes the world, and it is vital to identify the basis of that ability.

---

[296] Higgins 1994, p. 16.

7.2. *Force and law*

Traditionally, force and international law are counterposed. The task of creating a just and peaceful world order is seen as one of 'substituting law for force'.[297] 'There are very few today', Higgins claims, 'who believe that international law cannot exist in the absence of effective sanctions'.[298]

This stands in stark contrast to Pashukanis's insight that a group 'capable of defending their conditions of existence in armed struggle' was 'the morphological precursor of the legal subject':[299] sanctions as relations of violence are intrinsic to the legal form. It is not merely utopian but fundamentally analytically wrong-headed to see the triumph of law as leading to a world without violence. The law is constituted by relations of violence.

Internationally, the states themselves, as juridical subjects, are the wielders of the violence that operates to enforce legal decisions. Violence may not always be used, but it is always implicit.[300] The subjectivity of the state is *as an agent of war and law*. '[I]nternational law comprehends as actors only continuing monopolies of force'.[301] The violence of the state is a constitutive element of its juridical existence.

Though this is denied by much international legal scholarship, it has been accepted by practitioners. Outlining the recognition doctrine of the US in the *Russian Reinsurance* case, Justice Lehman explained that a state would be recognised on 'the fall of one government establishment and the substitution of another governmental establishment which actually governs, *which is able to enforce its claims by military force*'.[302] The judge was unnerved enough by the apparently apologetic nature of this doctrine to explain that whatever the nature of the new regime's original claim to power, 'lawful or unlawful, its existence is a fact, and that fact cannot be destroyed by juridical concepts'.[303] In fact, of course, far from 'not being destroyed' by juridical concepts, the recognition of a state because of its capacity for violence is *constitutive* of them.

---

[297] Orth 1916, p. 341.

[298] Higgins 1994, p. 16.

[299] Pashukanis 1978, p. 134

[300] See, for example, the 'non-violent' coercion of the US to ensure that the votes on Resolution 678 went its way in the run-up to the Gulf War of 1990–91 (Simons 1998, pp. 197–8).

[301] Kennedy 1986a, p. 163.

[302] Quoted in Kennedy 1986a, p. 164. Emphasis in original.

[303] Ibid.

After World War II, the newly independent states relied, then, on their ability to use force for their juridical status in international law, and for the political power of which it is an expression. One result has been the rise of sub-imperialisms: 'Third World powers aspiring to . . . political and military domination on a regional scale'.[304] It is no surprise given this expansion of the variables and agents involved that international law has seen 'the growth of . . . new licensing techniques for the international use of armed force'.[305]

Violence is the constant backdrop, threat, and constituent of legal relations, so it is in the interests of states, particularly the powerful, to be able to use violence with few constraints. A *laissez-faire* attitude to the means of violence is, unsurprisingly, visible in legal debates over *ius in bello*, regarding the methods of war (traditionally counterposed to *ius ad bellum*, regarding the recourse to military force itself).[306]

Though some have argued, for example, that the conduct of the allies in the 1990–91 Gulf War constituted a series of crimes,[307] others have seen it as for the most part legally acceptable.[308] The notorious 'Turkey Shoot' of fleeing Iraqi forces on the Basra road is easily defensible from a legal point of view.[309]

Even the US strategy of *deliberately burying Iraqi troops alive* is not self-evidently illegal.[310] Hampson weighs up legal arguments for and against what she calls this 'innovative tactic',[311] and concludes only that one reading of the

---

[304] Callinicos 1994, p. 45. See in general pp. 45–54.

[305] Gottlieb 1968, p. 146.

[306] Rivkin 1991, p. 59 footnote 7, contains an admirably terse description of the difference between *ius ad bellum* and *ius in bello*. '*Jus in bello* governs the actual use of military force and contains a number of proscriptive and prescriptive themes, for example, proportionality, discrimination, impermissibility of direct attack on non-combatants, etc. In contrast, *jus ad bellum* provides normative principles for permissible recourse to military force. Both of these bodies of law are rooted in Judeo-Christian tradition . . . the Just War theory. Significantly, while the laws of war – *jus in bello* – have to be obeyed irrespective of the virtues of the underlying cause, the entire enterprise is illegitimate unless one's original resort to force – governed by *jus ad bellum* principles – was just.' See Halliday 1996, p. 97, on the tendency to elide the two in criticisms of the Gulf War.

[307] Most clearly Clark 1992a and 1992b.

[308] For example Greenwood 1993: Hampson 1993.

[309] As Halliday unsentimentally points out, '[t]he shootings . . . fell clearly within the legitimate use of force against combatants as defined in international law. Soldiers in retreat, but who have not surrendered, are not exempt from attack and never have been considered as such' (Halliday 1996, p. 101). See also Hampson 1993, p. 107.

[310] Using ploughs mounted on tanks, minefields were cleared, and the trenches that criss-crossed them filled with sand, killing the many soldiers within. The strategy is described and evidence for it cited in Hampson 1993, pp. 104–7 and Simons 1998, p. 9.

[311] Hampson 1993, p. 105.

law 'suggests' that the actions *might* be prohibited. In an equivocal conclusion, she closes with a wry pun: '[s]words would have been preferable to ploughshares'.[312] The most extraordinary forms of violence can thus be viewed as legal.[313]

There have been various forums designed to 'regulate' the conduct of war, perhaps most famously the 1899 Hague conference, of which it is said that it 'tried to order many areas of armed conflict', and was 'limited' but 'prophetic' in its humanitarian restriction of means of war.[314] In a brilliant dissident interpretation of the laws of war, however, af Jochnick and Normand have shown how the humanitarian motivations expressed at the conference were, with very few exceptions, subordinated to the elastic doctrine of 'military necessity'.[315] Even, for example, a much-vaunted ban on balloon-launched munitions was in fact 'understood . . . to operate only against non-dirigible balloons, which had proven useless for military purposes'.[316]

Because of the indeterminacy of law, it was always possible to criticise opponents for breaking the law with particular actions, and by doing so with a normative argument, that criticism could appear 'moral' and marshal support. 'Law served as a second front, where belligerents sought to mobilize public opinion behind the justice of their cause.'[317] As to the judgement of one's own state's activities, by contrast, the codified law was used a legitimising force.

> The deliberate vagueness of the Hague laws [as well, the writers later show, as those outlined in innumerable other international contexts including the Nuremberg Trials] provided ample room to maneuver on the battlefield, allowing belligerents to adopt any tactic deemed expedient, including the wholesale bombardment of civilian populations. The laws of war thus helped

---

312 Hampson 1993, p. 107. From the horrifying bathos of its opening sentence – 'The second issue that aroused concerns was the burying alive of Iraqi soldiers' (p. 105) to its considerations on the standards applied – 'The question then becomes whether death by suffocation . . . represents "unnecessary suffering"' (p. 106) – it is a quite extraordinary, and appalling, passage.

313 For a more thorough review of the legal justifications for violence – including against civilians – in the Gulf War, see af Jochnick and Normand 1994b.

314 Aldrich and Chinkin 2000, p. 90.

315 af Jochnick and Normand 1994a, pp. 72–5.

316 af Jochnick and Normand 1994a, p. 73.

317 af Jochnick and Normand 1994a, p. 77.

> to legitimate the very atrocities that they purportedly intended to deter, leading to the 'lawful' slaughter of civilians.[318]

Though the spread of juridical relations necessitated the 'juridicisation' of the conduct of war, laws could not hamper the exercise of violence essential to these relations.

This exercise of the violence intrinsic to international law is often, of course, manifest in intervention. This is despite international legal doctrine's supposed, and much-vaunted, opposition to such actions.

> [I]t is stated in remarkably absolute terms, that no state has any right whatsoever to intervene in any way whatsoever in the affairs of other states. Yet it remains a well-known fact that interventions are a persistent feature of international relations. How is the jurist to react to this phenomenon?[319]

Absolute state sovereignty and the constant intervention that undermines it mutually constitute each other, and the fabric of international law. That is the meaning of Koskenniemi's ascending/descending dyad, and of Pashukanis's insight that the coercive agent is the root-form of the legal subject. Understanding that the force, coercion, intervention of sovereign states is thus a structuring part of the contestation implied by law, brings us to the brink of understanding imperialism in a world of juridically equal states – a world of universal international law.

8. Serving two masters: the imperialism of international law

It is sometimes argued, against those with utopian hopes in this or that organisation of international regulation (usually the UN) that these bodies are hopelessly complicit in the fabric of imperialism: that the UN is, as the British Foreign Office called it in 1952, 'an instrument of Anglo-American foreign

---

318 Ibid.

319 Carty 1986, p. 87. See also the fascinating article by Necati Polat, Polat 1999. Polat argues 'that intervention and terrorism, two forms of international violence marginalized within the mainstream conceptualizations as mere deviances, may be more coherently viewed as *facets* of the system' (p. 67). Polat sees this as a consequence of the privileging of sovereignty as the conceptual basis of law, something he sees as contingent. I have argued that the privileging and universalisation of sovereignty was intrinsic to the legal form, and that therefore there is nothing contingent about the violence of law.

policy'.[320] The specific organisations of international society and international law are thus blamed for imperialism.

It is true that the history of the UN reveals a very high degree of complicity with the politics of power and imperialism.[321] So far as it goes, it is quite reasonable to take the view that 'the whole history of international bodies such as the United Nations shows that the hope of reform . . . is badly misplaced'.[322]

However, the history and politics of the UN, while perhaps highly conducive to imperialism, are not fundamentally constitutive of it. Modern capitalism is an imperialist system, and a juridical one. International law's constituent forms are constituent forms of global capitalism, and therefore of imperialism. This is why it is not merely propagandist that the US and other imperialist powers frame their actions in juridical terms.

Nevertheless, the mainstream view still sees imperialism as incidental or opposed to the equal sovereign state form that is the subject the law. Joseph Lockley, discussing the US policy of 'pan-Americanism', the crucial element of which was 'the independence and equality of the American nations',[323] expressed this starkly.

> The one [policy] is expressly intended to create and maintain a community of equal, cooperating nations; and the other is intended, presumably, to create and maintain an empire. The two policies, the two courses of action, lead in different directions. In which of these directions does the United States move? It cannot move in both at one and the same time. It cannot serve two masters.[324]

Of course, it has been evident that there was no contradiction between the spread of the sovereign state form and imperialism since at least the start of the nineteenth century when the US recognised the Latin American states. States categorically *can* serve the two masters of attempted regional or even

320 Quoted in Curtis 1998, p. 177.

321 Curtis 1998, pp. 173–92. See also Gowan 2003, which though it makes clear that the UN is not perfectly reliable as the US's 'chosen instrument of hegemony' (p. 27), also stresses that '[f]rom the start, Roosevelt was committed to wrapping the UN Wilsonian banners around an inner structure shaped as a breathtaking dictatorship by a handful of great powers.' (p. 9).

322 Blackie 1994, p. 70. See also Baxter 1999.

323 Lockley 1938, p. 234.

324 Ibid.

world dominance and of supporting the independent sovereign state form. The US has for decades been uniquely placed to succeed in both of these strategies.

One of the most interesting theories about the imperialism of law is that the spread of law itself constitutes an invaluable strategy for imperialism. In the expression of John Davies, Attorney-General in Ireland from 1606 to 1619, 'to give laws to a conquered people is the principal mark of a perfect conquest'.[325] It has been said that English law had the power of a Maxim gun in subjugating Africa to colonial rule.[326]

The mechanisms by which this imperialism of law is deemed to function are generally left unclear. Schmitt puts his finger on the core issue but, informed by an austere idealist philosophy, fails to identify the dynamics that it makes clear.

> A historically meaningful imperialism is not only or essentially military and maritime panoply, not only economic and financial prosperity; it is also this ability to determine in and of itself the content of political and legal concepts. This side of imperialism (I speak here not only of American imperialism) is . . . perhaps more dangerous than military oppression and economic exploitation. A people is first conquered when it acquiesces to a foreign vocabulary, a foreign conception of what is law, especially international law.[327]

Schmitt is right that this is not about American, or indeed any other specific imperialism, but about imperialism as a structuring process of the modern international system. However, in his model, he reduces this to what he somewhat nebulously terms a 'tyranny of values'.[328]

This is not what lies behind international law is a force for imperialism. The universalising dynamic in international law that saw the end of formal imperialism simultaneously embedded modern imperialism, *because of the particular structuring of the international system that it implies and extends.*

The fundamental subjects of international law are the sovereign states, which face each other as property owners, each with sole proprietary

---

[325] Quoted in Pawlisch 1985, p. 14. For an overview of this theory in the context of Ireland see the introduction 'Law as an instrument of colonization', Pawlisch 1985, pp. 3–14. See pp. 13–14 for a brief list of the imperialism of law in non-Irish cases. For more on Davies's view of law as a conquering force, see Carty 1996, pp. 32–5.

[326] Adewoye 1977, p. 14.

[327] Schmitt quoted in Ulmen 1987, p. 70.

[328] Ulmen 1987, p. 70.

ownership over their own territory, just as legal subjects in domestic law face each other as owners of commodities. There is no state to act as final arbiter of competing claims, and internationally the 'clear connection between . . . the parties to a lawsuit and the combatants in an armed conflict' *cannot attenuate*.[329] The means of violence remains in the hands of the very parties disagreeing over the interpretation of law. 'There is here, therefore, an antinomy, of right against right, both equally bearing the seal of the law of exchange. *Between equal rights, force decides*.'[330] And of course that force, the capacity for coercive violence that underpins the legal relation, is not distributed equally – this is 'the discrepancy between formal and material reciprocity'.[331]

This is why strong states are able to enforce their own interpretations of law. Intrinsically to the legal form, a contest of coercion occurs, or is implied, to back up the claim and counterclaim. And in the politically and militarily unequal modern world system, the distribution of power is such that the winner of that coercive contest is generally a foregone conclusion. *The international legal form assumes juridical equality and unequal violence.*

Thus, for example, the Gulf War derived from the juridical system of sovereignty and was assiduously legally argued on both sides, by formally equal subjects. Its outcome was expressed in legal terms and established legal facts on the ground. And that outcome *was never in doubt*, given the overwhelming military coercion the US could use to enforce its legal interpretation.

At this level of abstraction, this violence at the hands of the juridical subjects themselves is the violence of the market, of the commodity and of the legal form, but it is not *class*-violence. The necessity of coercion inheres in the exchange of commodities, not on a particular mode of production and exploitation.

Here, the insights of Lenin and Bukharin on the structure of the imperialist state can inform Pashukanis's legal theory. In an epoch of mature capitalism, of the consolidation and monopolisation of capitals, and the penetration of capitalist concerns into the state, that state cannot be understood as autonomous from capital.

Bukharin's theory of the state allows us to be more precise about the inequalities of power between states. These disparities, and state policies, are

---

329 Pashukanis 1978, p. 118

330 Marx 1976, p. 344. Emphasis mine.

331 Fisch 2000, p. 12.

neither contingent nor evidence of some putatively 'autonomous' dynamic of geopolitics. *As imperialist states*, they are powered by capitalist economics, and operating according to capitalist concerns. Marx famously described capitalists as 'warring brothers', and the wars of the twentieth century illustrate that in spectacularly bloody form.

The very imperialism of each state is a function of its capitalist nature. When it comes to international law, then, the point is that the more powerful state, with the coercive capacity to enforce its own interpretation of legal rules, is a more powerful *capitalist* state. Its interpretations and its coercive efforts are deployed for capital, which is predicated on class exploitation. This makes concrete the specific relations of the *capitalist* market that underpin modern international juridical relations, and shows how these relations of juridical equality will be actualised according to what is ultimately a *class* logic, rather than a market logic.

This is emphatically not to say that the more powerful state in an international legal relation takes the role of 'capitalist' and its opponent that of 'proletariat', nor that in any crudely instrumentalist way capitalist states only come to blows over narrowly economic issues. It is only to say that the strategic logic of capitalist states, particularly the powerful imperialist states, is ultimately derived from the exploitative logic of capitalism.

The international legal form assumes juridical equality and unequal violence of sovereign states. In the context of modern international capitalism, that unequal violence *is imperialism itself*. The necessity of this unequal violence derives precisely *from* the juridical equality: one of the legal subjects makes law out of the legal relation by means of their coercive power – their imperialist domination. Specifically in its universalised form, predicated on juridical equality and self-determination, *international law assumes imperialism*.

At the most abstract level, without violence there could be no legal form. In the concrete conjuncture of modern international capitalism, this means that without imperialism there could be no international law.

Conclusion
Against the Rule of Law

1. Ideas, ideology and contestation

On Friday 7 March 2003, 16 scholars of international law signed a letter in The *Guardian*, arguing that 'there is no justification under international law for the use of military force against Iraq'.[1] The letter was an attempt to use the language and argumentative structures of international law for a progressive end, against (though perhaps not all the signatories would describe the Iraq adventure thus) the imperialist ambitions of the US and UK.

What makes this letter so interesting for the theory of international law, and for questions of that law's potential progressive application, is that several of the signatories are associated with critical currents in the field. This raises the question, if a scholar

---

[1] See <http://www.guardian.co.uk/letters/story/0,3604,909275,00.html>. The writers were Ulf Bernitz, Nicolas Espejo-Yaksic, Agnes Hurwitz, Vaughan Lowe, Ben Saul, Katja Zielger, James Crawford, Susan Marks, Roger O'Keefe, Christine Chinkin, Gerry Simpson, Deborah Cass, Matthew Craven, Philippe Sands, Ralph Wilde and Pierre-Marie Dupuy. It is interesting that in a clear and not unsuccessful effort to increase their perceived authority, the writers open their letter with a self-description not as 'theorists' or 'scholars' but as 'teachers'. For progressives, there was a potential problem precisely in this recourse to expertise, with its maintenance of the 'mystery' of international law. David Kennedy has provocatively raised this issue in another context: 'We could imagine an international law which sought to disenchant its speakers from their own expert authority rather than to offer them the promise that theirs was the last, best, humanitarian position available. This would not be the international law of the multilateral left, of civil society and of human rights, but I think it would be an international law more attuned to human possibility, expert responsibility and political contestation.' (Kennedy in Various 2003c, p. 917).

acknowledges the indeterminacy of international law, say, how can and why would she claim that a particular act is 'illegal'?

At the heart of this (and other) attempts to insist on a progressive interpretation of international law – even conscious of that law's embeddedness into structures of power and inequality – is the notion that law is a contested space, in which a committed lawyer can expound an alternative, even radical, discourse. This is a 'critical-theoretical' variant of the jurists' practice of arguing an interpretation in the hopes of influencing opinion. The difference is that for the critical theorist, the claim that a particular act is 'illegal' is more theoretically fraught, and is perhaps less a bald statement of interpretation than a political intervention: in this model, international law is, in the words of Susan Marks, one of the letter's signatories, 'a strategic tool, which can be used for both good ends and bad ones, to constrain violence and legitimate it'.[2]

Such an approach is of course attractive, offering as it seems to a way of squaring practice with radical international law theory. After all, that international law is contested is a statement of the indeterminacy thesis; and that progressive ideas wrought from international law might impact the social world seems a corollary of the insights of ideology critique regarding the ideological currents and power of international law. It could be argued, then, that it is precisely the radical critique and theory of international law that seem to grant space for progressive practice.

Fundamental problems, however, remain. At the simplest level, these writers cannot back up their interpretations with force. The Iraq War went ahead, with the British and American governments insisting it was legal: this was actualised international law, or more precisely, juridical politics. It is unclear what the legal critique has achieved.

One could argue that it has shifted the debate and delegitimated the action. For example, one writer (unencumbered by critical theory) cites the international legal case against Henry Kissinger for crimes against humanity, and admits that while 'Kissinger is unlikely to be prosecuted any time soon, yet he is beginning to feel the heat of domestic and international vilification'.[3] In other words, while the legal arguments have had some concrete impact – it is at least satisfying that 'Kissinger does not travel without asking a foreign

---

[2] Unpublished notes 14 June 2003. See also Craven, Marks, Simpson and Wilde 2004. I am deeply indebted to Susan Marks for discussing the *Guardian* letter and the issues and debates surrounding it with me.

[3] Gottschalk 2003, p. 301.

government whether they could guarantee his round trip'[4] – the most sustained progressive point of the legal case against Kissinger is less that it will *win* by successfully prosecuting him, than that it will have an impact in 'the court of public opinion'.[5]

One problem is that even if this is true, if the ideological triumph of 'progressive' international law occurs *outside* the arena of international law, then no logical reason is adduced that the desired change in discourse is due to the specific 'international-law-ness' of the argument. In other words, it is quite possible that such a legitimation or delegitimation of a particular action might as well or better have been carried out by a *non*-international-legal argument – based on principles of justice, for example. Even where the legal nature of such a position *does* seem to strengthen its power, *it does so by undermining the structures and even legitimacy of international law itself.* This is the Pyrrhic, extra-legal victory of progressive international law.

As this book goes to press, in a decision no one on the progressive Left can fail to celebrate, the International Court of Justice has ruled that the huge 'West Bank barrier', the metres-high wall of concrete, barbed wire and mesh that Israel is constructing around and in the Palestinian occupied territories, is illegal and 'tantamount to de facto annexation'.[6] This has been described as – and surely is – a 'moral victory' for the Palestinians,[7] perhaps even one which 'shifts the debate'.[8] However, as Israel has made clear that it will ignore the (non-binding) ruling (arguing that it is one-sided, 'political', and/or that the ICJ has no jurisdiction in the case),[9] and the US has denounced it as 'a damaging distraction',[10] the very 'victory' of progressive international law also underlines the limitations of that law – 'nothing more than ink on paper'[11] – as an arena for change. Palestinian groups such as Hamas 'ask what the point is in fighting legal battles when Israel and the US are so ready to reject court rulings they do not like'.[12]

[4] Rotter in Various 2003a, p. 894.
[5] Gottschalk 2003, p. 302.
[6] <http://news.bbc.co.uk/1/hi/world/middle_east/3111159.stm>
[7] <http://news.bbc.co.uk/1/hi/world/middle_east/3880881.stm>
[8] *Guardian*, 10 July 2004. 'Barrier ruling shift the debate'.
[9] See among others <http://news.bbc.co.uk/1/hi/world/middle_east/3884135.stm>.
[10] <http://news.bbc.co.uk/1/hi/world/middle_east/3882175.stm>
[11] From an editorial in Saudi-Arabia's *Al-Watan*, quoted at <http://news.bbc.co.uk/1/hi/world/middle_east/3882793.stm>.
[12] *Guardian*, 10 July 2004. 'Barrier ruling shifts the debate'. It is testimony to the power of international law as an ideological legitimation that even having made this

Tellingly, the most concrete semi-official Palestinian plans to build on this ruling involve agitating for international sanctions, popular pressure and boycotts of Israeli goods.[13] In fact, one Palestinian negotiator has made it clear that for reasons of *realpolitik*, the Palestinians are unlikely to push for the UN Security Council to support the ruling and thereby strengthen the *legal* nature of the decision, as '[i]t would highlight America's role as a friend of Israel and I'm not sure the Palestinians actually want to isolate the Americans'.

In other words, precisely mindful of the political reality that underpins the forging and exposition of international law, the Palestinians are prepared to *self-stall* the 'international-law-ness' of their very international legal victory and will attempt instead to use it to mobilise *extra*-legal public opinion. This is an understanding that it is popular pressure from below rather than international law that represents the best hope for the Palestinian cause, and that the most 'progressive' international legal decision is best deployed insofar as it *leaves* the realm of international law.

In what is arguably the most famous legal blow against imperialism, the ICJ's 1986 decision in *Nicaragua vs. US*[14] held that the US support for the Contra guerillas against the Sandinista regime and mining of Nicaragua's harbours was illegal intervention into Nicaragua's domestic affairs. However, the US refused to recognize the ICJ's jurisdiction,[15] vetoed a Security Council resolution that would have enforced the judgement, and no restitution was made. From the left, one might argue that this evidences that the US has the power to flout law with impunity; alternatively, that the US's interpretation was the one made actual and that this illustrates the imperial actuality of international law. *Either way*, out of an apparent legal triumph for progressives, the international legal system itself is undermined as a site for activism.

There is a danger that basing 'progressive' critique *on* international law might, to a jurist's potential horror, precisely legitimate those actions for which powerful states are able to garner overwhelming or authoritative legal support. At the time the above letter was written to the *Guardian* expressing doubts over the legality of the Iraq War, it was thought possible that the US

---

point, a Hamas spokesman immediately continued: 'We already know what international law says: that we have the right of armed resistance against the occupation.

[13] *Guardian*, 10 July 2004. 'Barrier ruling shift the debate'.

[14] Available at <http://www.lawofwar.org/nicaraugua_v_us.htm>.

[15] The US ambassador to the UN, Jeanne Kirkpatrick, innumerately described the ICJ as a 'semi-legal, semi-juridical, semi-political body which nations sometimes accept and sometimes don't' (Meyer 1997).

and UK might obtain a Security Council resolution in support of their war, and mindful of that possibility, the letter concludes 'even with that authorisation, serious questions would remain. A lawful war is not necessarily a just, prudent or humanitarian war'.[16] However, if 'serious questions' mean that the writers, or some of them, would still not support such an 'authorised' war, then their more fundamental criticisms are not on grounds of law but of justice, prudence or humanitarianism. And by focusing not on those but on law, as Susan Marks has said, the attack on the war was neither fundamental nor stable. 'A Security Council resolution authorising the war might have been passed. . . . Was it right to run the risk that our legal advocacy might ultimately turn against our political goals?'[17]

More fundamentally, the critical application of international law risks not only legitimising particular actions, but the very structure of international law that critical theory has so devastatingly undermined. As David Kennedy has persuasively argued, in an exchange with the letter's authors, in which he stated his view that such an initiative 'ultimately does more harm than good',

> the increment in lost legitimacy to the war [itself not, as I have argued, a foregone conclusion] would have to be weighed against the increased increment in false belief about what international law is and what it can do, and the negative effects of that belief over time. A hard balance – but we could compare the result to that from a different kind of opposition, one which tried to oppose the war *and* get people over their tendency to invest international law with a wisdom it does not possess.[18]

Kennedy's concerns seem borne out by the experience of Susan Marks, who discovered once the war had commenced and she turned her attention to indeterminacy and how international law had been used to legitimate the war, that 'no-one seemed to want to hear this. If we had been unsure before as to whether people had exaggerated faith in international law, now it seemed absolutely clear that they did. Were we reaping what we had sown?'[19]

---

16 *Guardian*, 7 March 2003. 'War would be illegal'.

17 Personal communication. The question could also be asked now that 'every hand in the Security Council – some eagerly, others more sullenly – has gone up to endorse the puppet authority installed by the conquerors, ratifying their conquest' (Gowan 2003, p. 28).

18 David Kennedy 10 March 2003. I am grateful to David Kennedy for sharing these unpublished communications with me.

19 Personal communication.

Kennedy's alternative proposal – 'a group of international lawyers saying "international law doesn't know what it's doing here, folks . . ."'[20] – seems both less theoretically misleading *and* less inclined to fail in its argument-shifting aims.

The use of international law in progressive discourse, then, may shift opinion along the way, but seems ultimately to be theoretically disingenuous or self-defeating.

There have been attempts to theorise the 'space' opened up by law, focusing on law's dialectic and the radical appropriation of its categories. Though 'the founding violence persists in law, so does the founding dream that things might be otherwise',[21] so 'finding a utopian dimension to inhere in law may be truly radical'.[22] One of the most intriguing, though opaque, of these attempts is by Peter Fitzpatrick.[23]

Fitzpatrick acknowledges that law's 'determinate content' will respond to 'the demands of predominant power', but holds that such law can still 'pose a ruptural challenge' to '*imperium*' by virtue of its 'constituent ethics' – 'an insistence on equality, freedom, and impartiality within law, and an insistence on a regardful community of law'.[24] That community and those ethics are not simply posited, but are, it is argued, the result of the fact that law inevitably presumes its own transgression, some of those transgressions fundamentally challenging law's precepts, thereby implying a certain ethical landscape of law itself.

Though of considerably more theoretical precision than the various liberal lullabies about the nobility of the rule of law, this negatively derived 'community of law' cannot ultimately, I would argue, be mobilised against the imperial actuality of law, for two main reasons. One is that even the seemingly obviously fundamental violations are not so clear as Fitzpatrick seems to think. He holds for example that the US's notorious incarceration of 'enemy combatants' in Guantanamo Bay is a '[v]iolation which would negate or undermine the very hold of law and its processes' and thereby 'mark a divide between law and empire'.[25] In fact, of course, the US is adamant that '[b]oth

20 Personal communication.
21 Dean 2004, pp. 23–4.
22 Dean 2004, p. 23.
23 Fitzpatrick 2003.
24 Fitzpatrick 2003, p. 466.
25 Fitzpatrick 2003, p. 465.

international law and the US constitution sanction the detention':[26] the parameters of even supposedly fundamental transgressions are not self-evident but as indeterminate as the rest of law.

More importantly, the fact is that even where Fitzpatrick's 'ethics of the existent within law' *are* deemed to have been transgressed, even perhaps candidly by those with power, it is by no means beyond the dialectical virtuosity of those violators to claim that such breaches are necessary to protect the very values being breached (it is this sort of thinking that lay behind the famous, perhaps-apocryphal but all-too-credible pronouncement of an American officer in Vietnam that 'we had to destroy the village to save it'). Concretely, This underlines states' erosion of human rights in anti-terrorism legislation: to protect 'core values of democratic states ruled by law' those democratic states enact laws that undermine those core values.[27]

An example of a common international legal argument that takes such a shape is the discourse surrounding reprisals activity: 'Reprisals are illegitimate acts of warfare, not for the purpose of indicating abandonment of the laws of war, but, on the contrary, to force compliance to those laws.'[28] Such 'bad dialectics' flourish easily even at the level of the fundamental juridical units of international law:

> [T]he conventional rules associated with Westphalian sovereignty . . . can be violated through coercion. . . . The goal of those interventions . . . has been . . . to establish a stable polity that would, in the long run, conform with those very same rules.[29]

Given the flexibility of international law, it is questionable whether the appropriation of its categories – such as, say, a radical focus on the equality of states as a rebuke to concrete inequality – can be systematically progressive, let alone fundamentally emancipatory. If a space is opened, it is at the same time always-already closing – after all, the principle of equality is also part of the

[26] Paul Rosenzweig in Danzig and Rosenzweig 2004. Though on 28 June 2004 the US Supreme Court by a 6–3 decision insisted on the right of the detainees to query their treatment before an American court, a considerable blow to the Bush administration, it affirmed the government's right to detain 'enemy combatants' indefinitely and without charges or trail.

[27] See for example International Helsinki Federation for Human Rights 2003, p. 14 and throughout.

[28] Greenspan 1959, p. 408.

[29] Krasner 2001a, p. 334.

self-legitimation of the actually-existing international system. Some subversive appropriations are ignorable, and where not, they are reappropriable.

At a systemic level, for example, the demand of the developing countries for equitable global distribution, encapsulated in the New International Economic Order (NIEO) of the 1970s, was couched in international law's terms, such as those of 'self-determination'.[30] However, today's neoliberal international reality, as one textbook rather mildly puts it, 'does not at all seem to be the [NIEO's] radically restructured one'.[31] The claim that 'the less powerful' have been able 'to improve their positions in the international political order via the idea of international law' is deeply unconvincing, not only theoretically but empirically.[32] The demands for a new global political economy remain legitimate and urgent: the question is, though, just what the NIEO movement gained by couching its demands in terms of international law.[33]

Today, one category of international law seemingly ripe for 'appropriation' by the progressive Left is that of 'human rights'. Domestically, it is true that there have been cases where human-rights legislation has been used to hold governments to account. Norma Woods, for example, used the Human Rights Act to force the British prison service to take responsibility for the suicide of her son Colin Williamson while he was in custody.[34] The same language of human rights has also been used, however, by Madonna, in a case

---

[30] See for example Bedjaoui 1979, p. 184: 'The direct connection between Declaration 1514(XV) of 1960, which confirmed the intrinsic illegality of the "colonialist political order", and the Charter of Economic Rights and Duties of States of 1974, which tolled the bell for the "imperialist economic order", is undeniable. . . . The one is connected to the other by the umbilical cord represented by Declaration 2625(XXV) on the seven principles of international law, which ratifies the sovereign equality of States, the self-determination of peoples in every field, and international co-operation.'

[31] Weiss, Forsythe and Coate 2004, pp. 223–4 'To the contrary . . .' the authors continue frankly, 'the UN system has become increasingly free to function in the economic realm as it was designed to function – in the service of promoting a liberal capitalist order.'

[32] Scott 1994, p. 324.

[33] According to one of the new 'post-Seattle' generation of movements for social justice, the Network Institute for Global Democratization, the potential of the World Social Forum (a regular gathering of organisations and individuals 'opposed to neoliberalism and to domination of the world by capital and any form of imperialism' (paragraph 1 of the Charter of Principles of the WSF)) to bear 'a potential in serving as a basis for new initiatives and powers to democratize global decision making' comes explicitly in the aftermath of 'the *failure* of the New International Economic Order' (Nisula and Patomäki 2002, p. 4. Emphasis mine).

[34] <http://news.bbc.co.uk/1/hi/england/hampshire/dorset/3744347.stm>

at least partially settled in her favour, to complain that she might be visible to countryside walkers through the windows of her £9m house.[35]

This tragicomically absurd range of applicability implies at the very least that the discourse is becoming etiolated through overuse, and that any radical power it contains will have to be wrested from it. In the words of Bill Bowring, one eloquent proponent of this strategy, no matter that '[h]uman rights talk is often and increasingly the meaningless rhetoric of the powerful and the oppressor . . . it becomes real when articulating the present, not the endlessly deferred, claims of the oppressed.'[36]

There has been an enormous upsurge in publishing on human rights in international law. The claim that this literature reflects fundamental structural changes in the international system is discussed below. Here I focus on the notion of human rights as a contested ideological category, which can be used against those in power *even when* they themselves also invoke such rights – '[t]he question of human rights thus recovers the dimension eliminated in the process of instrumentalization in U.S. policy'.[37] The problem is that even if one agrees with Bowring that such a discourse might provide space for radical critique of power, that is not *all* it does, and in its less desirable forms it is considerably more than 'meaningless rhetoric'.

Such writing often articulates a vision of 'rights' that: i) derives from bourgeois 'negative rights which protect the individual from arbitrary state action and are associated with Western liberal democracies'[38] and thereby tacitly takes bourgeois capitalism for granted;[39] ii) updates the notion of the civilising mission of the West by producing what Orford calls a 'heroic narrative' in which the West 'is associated with attributes including freedom, creativity, authority, civilization, power, democracy, sovereignty and wealth',[40] and is the only agent capable of injecting them into a Third World cast as a passive object; and iii) by showing that the attempt to support 'human rights' involves international action, implies that human rights problems are intrinsically foreign, and that there are no abuses at home. 'Many American thus believe and perpetuate the quaint fiction that human rights problems exist

35 <http://news.bbc.co.uk/1/hi/england/wiltshire/3818659.stm>
36 Bowring n.d., no pagination.
37 Heuer and Schirmer 1998. No pagination.
38 Cheah 1997, p. 235.
39 This is expressed, in arid Althusserian form, in Lenoble 1986.
40 Orford 1999, p. 687.

only in places that must be reached by crossing large bodies of saltwater.'[41]

The point is not that the *substance* of particular conceptions of human rights cannot be marshalled to progressive discourse.[42] The point is that the attempt to appropriate *the international law of human rights* for that project is precisely *abstracting* of that substance, and thus abstracted is easily reappropriated by those in power. In addition, because 'the human rights regime . . . is composed of more than those legal rules and institutions that explicitly concern human rights',[43] such an 'appropriative' approach by implication legitimates not only specific other laws which may even 'facilitate or excuse' human rights abuses,[44] but the very edifice of international law and juridical forms that has been so swingeingly criticised (sometimes by those now attempting to appropriate the categories).

At best, it seems, in the ideological struggle for international law one can hope for occasional victories in a constant struggle over categories. These victories, however, will be predicated on legal forms that not only make the catagories ripe for counter-appropriation, but that can only be actualised in the coercive interpretations of the very states and other bodies whose interpretations and actions the radical lawyer is critiquing. However persuasive the subversive interpretation, in other words, it will be the interpretation of those with power that will inhere in the world. If a victory is claimed, then, it is likely to be 'in the court of public opinion', *outside* the law. By pulling beyond law, the very triumph of 'radical interpretation' that is deemed to vindicate a critical legal practice *upholds* the fundamental structural critique of international law.

2. The rule of law's new advocates

Traditionally, of course, in mainstream conservative and liberal traditions, it has been widely held that one of the best hopes for international peace is the rule of law (or as it is often rendered, the Rule of Law).[45] The iniquities and

---

[41] Donnelly 1992, pp. 264–5. In Simpson's felicitous phrase, this is the 'export theory of human rights' (Simpson 2001, pp. 347–8).

[42] Bowring is clear on this, in his call for a 'substantive account of human rights' (Bowring, n.d.).

[43] Kennedy 2002, p. 119.

[44] Ibid.

[45] See Walker 1988, p. 1.

instability of the international system are obvious, and the rule of law is often seen as the best defence against them. It can 'protect the weaker states against the superiority of the larger powers':[46] and in an era of nuclear weapons, 'the rule of law is our only alternative to mass destruction'.[47]

Such views are still expressed today.[48] Recently, however, defence of the rule of law has been deployed by a more critical modern project, known variously as 'cosmopolitan democracy',[49] 'global governance',[50] 'democratic governance',[51] but that I follow Peter Gowan in terming 'liberal cosmopolitanism'.[52] This is the most sophisticated recent reformulation of what one might call the international juridical project.

Though of course the various writers associated with this approach do not speak with one voice,[53] certain general arguments can be made about their radical liberal analyses and suggested reformulations of international society.

> [T]his discourse says that the Western liberal-democratic states are able to, and indeed are and must be understood above all as, spreading across the whole globe liberal-democratic values and régimes. We thus have the prospect of a globe which is entirely liberalised and democratised, and . . . this transformation of the globe will bring with it a new kind of world order – a cosmopolitan world order – going beyond the old Westphalian world order which was characterised by the absolute rights of states. . . . [T]his school of thought, which doesn't necessarily spell out all of its premises, is basically

[46] Friedmann 1968, p. 184.

[47] Douglas 1961, p. 32.

[48] For example, Koechler 1995. The authors of the *Guardian* letter themselves warn that a war without Security Council backing would 'seriously undermine the international rule of law'.

[49] The title of Archibugi and Held 1995.

[50] See the work of The Commission on Global Governance, at <http://www.medi-antics.com/maximedia/geneva/cgg1.htm>.

[51] See Global Governance Reform Project 2000.

[52] Gowan, Panitch and Shaw 2001, p. 4. The choice of terminology is important. In Gowan's words, '[t]hese people are not talking about a global democratic state. They are not, therefore, talking about cosmopolitan democracy. . . . What they are talking about is global governance. . . . That's why I say that these people are cosmopolitan *liberals*, not actually democrats, even though they may well say that they are democrats, and no doubt they are good democrats when it comes to domestic activities' (Gowan, Panitch and Shaw 2001, p. 5). Panitch points out that '[t]here are . . . cosmopolitan liberals who *are* liberal democrats' (p. 12), citing David Held, but this does not undermine Gowan's point, and neither does Shaw's attempt to distinguish himself from Held (pp. 21–2).

[53] See for example the various writers collected in Archibugi and Held 1995; Held, McGrew, Goldblatt and Perraton 1999; Shaw 2000; Kaldor 1999.

> saying that this is the way we're moving . . . and we should join this and get involved.[54]

In this approach, 'Rawls' philosophical conception of the Law of Peoples joins more empirical theories of political globalization'.[55] With its 'great stress on the importance of law and judicial systems',[56] the defence, extension and implied evolution of the rule of law itself is centrally important to the liberal-cosmopolitan project.

David Held, for example, considers that the rule of law must 'involve a central concern with distributional questions and matters of social justice'.[57]

> [A] basis might be established for the UN Charter system to generate political resources of its own, and to act as a politically independent decision-making centre. Thus, the UN could take a vital step towards shaking off the burden of the much-heard accusation that it operates 'double standards', functioning typically on behalf of the North and West . . . if the UN gained the means whereby it could begin to shake off this heritage, an important step could also be taken towards establishing and maintaining the 'rule of law' and its impartial administration in international affairs.[58]

A central criticism of this liberal-cosmopolitanism is its failure to see the continuities of political – imperial – power. As Callinicos puts it:

> [T]he mere fact of institutional proliferation [held to be key to the new structures of politics and power] tells us nothing about the actual relations of power that subsist among these networks of 'global governance'. To a large extent the institutions and regimes welcomed by Held, McGrew and their colleagues as the avatars of 'cosmopolitan democracy' have served further to institutionalize the American hegemony.[59]

Gowan makes a similar point with a detailed analysis of the specifics of American policy vis-à-vis Yugoslavia during the 1990s.[60] He concludes that

---

[54] Gowan in Gowan, Panitch and Shaw 2001, pp. 4–5. Gowan's contribution to this roundtable, pp. 4–10, is an excellent brief introduction to and critique of this school.

[55] Callinicos 2001, p. 76.

[56] Gowan in Gowan, Panitch and Shaw 2001, p. 6.

[57] Held 1995, p. 248.

[58] Held 1995, p. 269. For an excellent critique of Held accepting his own predicates, see Smith 2003.

[59] Callinicos 2001, p. 78. See more generally pp. 76–96.

[60] Gowan, Panitch and Shaw 2001, pp. 8–10.

'[t]he NATO war against Serbia on Kosovo was the consolidation of the US's political victory in Europe. Human rights and liberal-cosmopolitan rhetoric and the Hague Court were instruments of power-politics'.[61] In this critique, liberal-cosmopolitanism is 'the ideological form of a peculiar kind of imperial expansion'.[62] This indicates certain shifts in capitalism and imperialism. 'Excavating the material forces underlying this would require the decoding of economic globalisation.'[63]

For many of these writers, underpinning liberal-cosmopolitanism is a claim about the centrality – and desirability – of a putatively new legal and political regime of humanitarian intervention. The explosion of literature on this topic (some ideological aspects of which are discussed above), heralds, it is claimed, 'a particularly intense and almost revolutionary development of humanitarian law'.[64]

Much of the support for the new 'humanitarian intervention' is predicated on the idea that in the face of human-rights abuses, 'something must be done' and that non-intervention is 'inactive and negative', and is choosing to do nothing. Orford has brilliantly argued this to be an ideological and limiting conception, often predicated on the systematic forgetting of the relationship between economic imperialism and whatever crisis it is claimed military intervention must fix. The appearance of the militarized 'international community' as 'saviour and humanitarian',[65] in other words, is that 'community's' effacement of its own complicity in the crisis.[66]

> The international community had already intervened on a large scale in Yugoslavia [for example] before the security crisis erupted, through the

[61] Gowan, Panitch and Shaw 2001, pp. 9–10.

[62] Gowan, Panitch and Shaw 2001, p. 10.

[63] Ibid.

[64] Schindler 2003, p. 173. For critical takes on this literature see for example Cheah 1997: Koshy 1999. For an invaluable list of problems with the new 'human rights movement' see Kennedy 2002. Also Orford 1999 and 2003, though this perspicacious essay and invaluable book are marred by some postmodernist cliché, compared for example to her excellent earlier and closely related piece, Orford 1997. For a few examples of the view from within international law see Cassesse 1999a and 1999b: Glennon 1999: Zacklin 2000. For an attempt to 'develop' just-war theory to allow for such intervention within international law see Orend 1998.

[65] Orford 2003, p. 188.

[66] '[T]he narrative of intervention masks the involvement of international economic institutions and development agencies in shaping those societies that later erupt into humanitarian and security crises.' Orford 2003, p. 188.

> activities of international monetary institutions. Inactivity, in other words, is not the alternative to intervention.[67]

The disastrous effects of *this* kind of intervention, to pursue this example, should give very serious pause about advocating another carried out by precisely the same agents. The intervention we might want to make, instead, could be the 'acknowledging and seeking to prevent the destructive effects of international law and multilateralism as they operated in the former Yugoslavia and continue to operate in much of the world today.'[68]

Whether or not one agrees with Orford's political scepticism, the claims that such 'humanitarianism' is new, and is changing the international legal system, underpin the liberal-cosmopolitan defence of the rule of law, and must be evaluated.

2.1. *From war to policing?*

The Kosovo conflict of 1999 is deemed the 'decisive episode'[69] of the new regime of human-rights intervention. This type of action, it is claimed, represents '[t]he death of the restrictive old rules',[70] an 'evolution' which 'will have a transforming effect on international law'.[71] Tony Blair has claimed that '[w]e are witnessing the beginnings of a new doctrine of international community.'[72]

There is certainly a shift in the language of and justification for intervention. However, the novelty should not be exaggerated. Richard Falk argues that the basis for this intervention, the institutional recognition of human rights, is at least latent in already-existing international law.[73] Such 'humanitarian' actions are not entirely new.

> 'Humanitarian intervention' played an increasingly important role in the numerous cases of intervention which occurred during the nineteenth century. . . . Numerous 'humanitarian interventions' occurred. . . . The Treaty of London of 6 July 1827 justified the intervention of the European powers in

67 Orford 1997, p. 459.
68 Orford 1997, p. 485.
69 Callinicos 2001, p. 69.
70 Glennon 1999, p. 2.
71 Zacklin 2000, p. 22. See also Glennon 1999.
72 Quoted in Callinicos 2001, p. 70. For an analysis of one particular document as evidence of this putative epochal shift, see Halberstam 1993.
73 Falk 1995, pp. 171–174.

> favour of the rebellious Greeks . . . [in part] on the basis of the desire to 'stop the shedding of blood and mischiefs of all kinds which the prolongation of such a state of affairs could cause'.[74]

Rather than that humanitarian intervention is new, then, the liberal-cosmopolitan claim must be that in its recent articulation it has restructured international legal relations, fundamentally altering the forms of international law and the sovereignty of the state.[75] One of the most sustained formulations of this theory is by Kurt Mills, who sees sovereignty in its absolute form being 'chipped away' by human-rights concerns.[76]

> [T]he back of sovereignty has been broken. Its days as an absolute ordering principle are over. . . . The New Sovereignty increasingly includes greater respect for human rights and humanitarian principles. In addition, the sovereignty of the future will recognize a much wider array of loci of power and authority, such that rather than being able to point to a single sovereign centre, a much more ambiguous situation will emerge. . . .[77]

The resulting reconfiguration of sovereignty is strongly linked to a move towards international *criminalisation*. There has been a growth in the criminal prosecution of individuals, associated with the use of International War Crimes Trials,[78] and the barrier between the criminal prosecution of individuals for breaches of international law and the criminal prosecution of states themselves is permeable. These individuals are often tried for carrying out or ordering state policy, which implies a shared criminal culpability between individual and state.

Human rights are central to this elision, as it is human-rights abuses, simultaneously the acts of individuals and the policies of states, which are increasingly the focus of international legislative attention. As international problems are perceived as *criminal*, so the enforcement of supposed international norms becomes a matter of *policing*.

---

[74] Grewe 2000, pp. 489–90. Grewe lists eight other important nineteenth-century humanitarian interventions (pp. 487–96).

[75] Glennon 1999 embodies this perspective.

[76] Mills 1998, p. 41. 'Chipping away' is the least indignity sovereignty is deemed to have suffered. 'Others pictured sovereignty as perforated, defiled, cornered, eroded, extinct, anachronistic, bothersome, even interrogated.' (Bunck and Fowler 1995, p. 2: examples are given for each characterisation.)

[77] Mills 1998, pp. 194–5.

[78] Meron 1998.

Mary Kaldor puts the case well.

> The analysis of new wars suggests that what is needed is not peacekeeping but enforcement of cosmopolitan norms, i.e. enforcement of international humanitarian and human rights law. . . . Cosmopolitan law-enforcement is somewhere between soldiering and policing. . . . Policing has been the great lacuna of peacekeeping. . . . Given the unlikelihood of another old war, military forces will eventually have to be reoriented to combine military and policing tasks.[79]

This conception of 'new intervention' – though emphatically not the liberal-cosmopolitans' political conclusions – is key to the putatively new epoch of 'Empire' for Hardt and Negri.[80] Whatever one's criticisms of the book, it is to be saluted as one of the only works outside the international law corpus that has grasped the profundity of the change occurring, *if* the supposed shift towards 'police action' is in fact taking place.

> [A]lthough international courts do not have much power, public displays of their activities are still very important. Eventually a new judicial function must be formed. . . . Courts will have to be transformed gradually from an organ that simply decrees sentences against the vanquished to a judicial body . . . that dictate[s] and sanction[s] the interrelation among the moral order, the exercise of police action, and the mechanism legitimating imperial sovereignty.
>
> This kind of continual intervention . . . is really the logical form of the exercise of force that follows from a paradigm of legitimation based on a state of permanent exception and police action. Interventions are always exceptions even though they arise continually; they take the form of police actions because they are aimed at maintaining an internal order. . . .
>
> We have already seen that this juridical model cannot be constituted by the existing structures of international law. . . .[81]

---

[79] Kaldor 1999, pp. 124–5, and see p. 126 also. This important book builds on arguments from Kaldor 1997.

[80] Hardt and Negri 2000, p. 38.

[81] Hardt and Negri 2000, pp. 38–40. See also Fitzpatrick 2003, p. 464: '[T]his new condition of war . . . resembles more a perpetual police. . . . The mediations of law or of the juridical which could attend war and police action more conventionally perceived can here only be subsumed instrumentally within the "total" project, a project commensureate with the completeness of imperium itself. . . . [I]nternational law cannot extend to this condition of war'. Fitzpatrick's discussion of recent changes and his concept of *imperium* seem to dovetail with Hardt and Negri's notions, and it is

Apparently exemplifying this trend, Richard Haass, the Director of Policy Planning in the US State Department, went on record defending the US's right to attack Afghanistan in the wake of the atrocities of 11 September 2001. He argued that sovereignty is about 'responsibilities as well as rights'.[82] This is an extraordinary recomposition of sovereignty into an analogue of *citizenship*. In this innovative model, 'police action' is necessary when a state fails to fulfil its 'responsibilities'.

This posits, as Hardt and Negri imply, a juridical structure *above* the very states that would constitute it – 'from a harmonious order between states to a liberal-cosmopolitan order *above* states'.[83] This would represent a fundamental and radical shift in the structuring dynamic of international law, away from one derived from the equal sovereignty of its subjects. There have even been attempts from within international law to examine the structures that such a law, predicated on a hegemon, would take.[84]

Given the derivation of international law precisely from the *lack* of such an authority, this new 'hegemonic international law' (based on the notion that only the US as an overarching power 'will lay down international rules . . . determine what constitutes a crisis . . . distinguish between friend and foe and make the resulting decision on the use of force') in fact elides with 'hegemonic international law *nihilism*', in that the necessity of hegemon expresses the supposed failure of 'decentralised' international law.[85] There certainly is evidence for such disdain for international law among many of the 'neo-conservatives' of the Bush administration[86] – witness for example Richard Perle's blithe concession that the 2003 invasion of Iraq was illegal, and that international law had 'stood in the way of doing the right thing'.[87]

Two things must be pointed out against the implication of a sudden and fundamental shift. One is that such legal nihilism is not new. A *Wall Street*

---

something of a surprise that they are not referenced. In 1978, Carl Schmitt prefigured this thinking: 'The day *world politics* comes to the earth, it will be transformed into a *world police power*.' (Schmitt 1987, p. 80 (emphasis in original)).

82 Newsnight, BBC2, 14 September 2001.

83 Gowan in Gowan, Panitch and Shaw 2001, p. 5. Emphasis mine.

84 Vagts 2001; Alvarez 2003.

85 Rilling 2003, p. 3. Emphasis mine. According to Rilling the phrase 'hegemonic international law nihilism' comes from Norman Paech.

86 For a superb examination of the strategy of these neo-conservatives see Callinicos 2003.

87 'War critics astonished as US hawk admits invasion was illegal'. *Guardian*, 20 November 2003.

Journal editorial of the 1980s quoted a high-powered dinner-party conversation at which it was announced that 'we are only going to be able to talk sensibly about [the invasion of] Grenada if anyone who is an international lawyer agrees to keep his mouth shut'.[88] There has always been layer of technocrats within the American (and other) ruling class(es) who underestimate the extent to which their imperialism happily coexists with international law.[89] Anne-Marie Slaughter (by no means an illiberal reactionary) rushes to reassure: 'The United States needs international law acutely now because it offers a way to preserve our power and pursue our most important interests' – while, she adds quickly if not so convincingly, 'reassuring our friends and allies that they have no reason to fear us.'[90]

It is striking that the nihilists are not the 'mainstream'. Perle's announcement was in stark contrast to the official American position. In his speech of 17 March 2003, George Bush took the utterly traditional legal line that '[t]he United States of America has the sovereign authority to use force in assuring its own national security'.[91] Haass, after his own apparently 'Negri-an' reconstitution of sovereignty, immediately then continued: 'America was just intervened against. Are we supposed to treat Afghanistan's sovereignty – if indeed they are behind this – as absolute?'[92] This is straight back to the traditional model of international law, in which the structuring juridical concepts derive from sovereignty. If there *is*, then, an international legal dynamic in a new direction, it is clearly at an inchoate phase, is by no means inevitable or even dominant, and remains extremely hedged around by the more traditional structures of international law.

It makes sense therefore to see the articulation of humanitarianism as essentially ideological and propagandist.[93] There is considerable evidence that the

---

[88] See Mansell 1997, p. 37.

[89] A particularly anxious version is Casey and Rivkin 2000, who believe there is a 'new' international law and that it is a 'threat' to the US, due to its unacceptable restraints on the methods of statecraft: for example, its 'overly prescriptive and proscriptive' attitude to what they describe as 'so-called "collateral damage"'. Happily for Casey and Rivkin, their concerns about law's limits to power are misplaced. From the point of view of legal nihilism discussed here, it is interesting that their proposed solution is the 'restoring [of] the "law of nations"'. For Rubenfeld, international law 'may be used as a vehicle for anti-American resentments', and is 'a threat to democracy'. His article (Rubenfeld 2003) was printed in an issue of *The Wilson Quarterly* the cover of which demanded 'What Good Is International Law?'

[90] Slaughter 2003, p. 37.

[91] See <http://www.whitehouse.gov/news/releases/2003/03/20030317-7.html>.

[92] *Newsnight*, BBC2, 14 September 2001.

[93] Callinicos 2001, pp. 69–74, pp. 93–6.

doctrine obscures, or perhaps more charitably 'includes', less lofty concerns. In a public speech, for example, Bill Clinton gave a very different reading of the war over Kosovo from the 'humanitarian' one.

> [I]f we have learned anything after the Cold War, and our memories of World War II, it is that if our country is going to be prosperous and secure, we need a Europe that is safe, secure, free, united, a good partner with us for trading; they're wealthy enough to buy our products; and someone who will share the burdens of taking care of the problems of the world. . . . Now, that's what this Kosovo thing is all about.[94]

The point that Halliday makes about the Gulf War remains pertinent – hypocritical motives do not automatically invalidate actions. However, the evidence is that the drive to war did not derive from some new paradigm, but was geopolitical and economic, and was overlaid with the ideology of human rights, serving as a normative, descending justification for the breaching of whichever sovereignty the intervening powers chose.

The use of such justification is not new: in 1940, Schmitt made 'humanitarian' acts his exemplary case of intervention as a structuring dynamic of international law.[95] The most serious theoretical problem with the claim that 'new humanitarianism' is reconfiguring international relations lies in the idea that the sovereignty is now 'no longer' inviolable. This is predicated on the erroneous claim that the 'traditional' view of sovereignty was 'anti-interventionist'.[96]

In fact, of course, sovereignty has always been overridden by intervention. 'Great Powers', Callinicos says, 'have always asserted a right of intervention in the affairs of small countries':[97] international law *presumes* the capacity for the organised violence of intervention, *sovereignty assumes its own abnegation*, and it is the Great Powers which are particularly able to effect that.[98]

---

[94] Quoted in Callinicos 2001, pp. 72–3.
[95] Schmitt n.d.
[96] Glennon 1999, p. 2.
[97] Callinicos 2001, p. 93.
[98] It is thus quite wrong to claim that '[t]he traditional international law concept of sovereignty constitutes an important normative inhibition to military intervention'. Kingsbury seems to derive this from the fact that '[t]here have been extraordinarily few cases of recolonization of former colonies': however, though he is right that the 'death rate of sovereign states' has been low since 1945, sovereignty's assumption of intervention is not predicated on the *end* of sovereignty, but its constant penetration. (Kingsbury 1998, p. 618.)

The fact that intervention is written in to international law and relations is not news. A well-expressed understanding of it predates Koskenniemi's masterly analysis by more than half a century.

> The currently accepted international law is essentially a *status quo* law which grants to allegedly equal entities known as states certain substantive rights usually listed as the rights to existence, to independence, to equality, to jurisdiction, to property, and to intercourse. These are usually laid down in absolute terms, and it all makes a very orderly structure. At the same time that it supplies these substantive rights, the law sets up certain rules as to forms and procedures relating to treaties, diplomacy, and force, by which all these allegedly fundamental rights may be changed or destroyed. This dualism leads to some strange paradoxes: the right to existence, so elaborately and dogmatically set forth on the one hand, may be totally annihilated by the use of force provided for one the other hand, and the treaty of peace will be perfectly valid![99]

Sovereignty has never been immune from intervention, so the claim that in opening sovereignty up humanitarianism has fundamentally altered international law is manifestly false.

3. Against the rule of law

The liberal-cosmopolitan writers tend to combine analysis and prescription. 'Cosmopolitanism is normative and activist . . . it says: "Look, there is an inspiring dynamic opening up. If you join it you can bring it about."'[100] While their claims about the new international legal regimes may be wrong, the question remains, would a universalising rule of law be desirable? Whether or not we see 'an inspiring dynamic' unfolding, would we *want* to 'bring it about'?

Faced with the carnage of 11 September 2001 Fred Halliday has argued that '[t]he framework for addressing these issues, of conflict between states and of differences within them, is not cultural or civilisational at all, but universal, based on international law and the principles of the United Nations'.[101]

---

[99] Wild 1938, p. 482.
[100] Gowan in Gowan, Panitch and Shaw 2001, p. 6.
[101] Halliday in *The Observer*, 16 September 2001.

Given the widespread though mistaken belief that law is counterposed to power and war, the desire for a rule of law is not surprising. Its extension is held to be an emancipatory project, internationally and domestically. The rule of law, 'is necessary to achieve a well-ordered society in which the problems of knowledge, interest, and power are handled'.[102] According to one writer, in fact, it 'could . . . make possible the birth of a new civilization of unparalleled brilliance and enlightenment'.[103] Generally, these are the intentions that underpin the desire for an international rule of law, in its traditional or its modern cosmopolitan form.

But the rule of law is not a self-evident good. It is a concept that needs unpacking, and it has long had its critics,[104] most of whom focus on the fact that the rule of law is an abstract construction that is not only incapable of reflecting the complexities of reality, but actually serves to obscure them.

Many writers, of course, have defended the rule of law, some from the left. Perhaps most famously, E.P. Thompson, while stressing that historically law had been used by the ruling class as a repressive force for the defence of property rights,[105] also held that, 'the rule of law itself, the imposing of effective inhibitions upon power and the defence of the citizen from power's all-intrusive claims, seems to me to be an unqualified human good'.[106] Thompson's defence of law – according to which, the very ideological and legitimating function excoriated by the left also necessitated law's 'independence from gross manipulation' and 'inhibitions upon the actions of the rulers'[107] – was predicated on law's 'principles of equity and universality which, perforce,

---

[102] Barnett 1998, p. 325.

[103] Walker 1988, p. 406.

[104] For an overview of the debates see Craig 1995. Perhaps the most famous of the critics is Roberto Unger, in Unger 1976 pp. 176–81. See also the writers collected in Hutchinson and Monahan 1987. For a particularly splenetic attack on the Critical Legal Studies movements approach to the rule of law, see Walker 1988, pp. 256–87. Walker produces very much more heat than light, but is interesting as an example of the defensive outrage with which mainstream jurisprudence is capable of reacting to attacks on the fetishised object of its attention. Some of Walker's claims – for example, that there is a 'CLS-clerisy monopoly of legal coverage in the mass media' (p. 378) – are nothing short of absurd.

[105] This critique of law has been described as Thompson's 'basic aim' in his 1975 book *Whigs and Hunters* (Loughlin 1992, p. 215), though the book is now famous/notorious for a very different approach to the subject.

[106] Thompson 1975, p. 255. The arguments occasioned on the left by Thompson's approach are beyond the scope of this discussion. See among others Horwitz 1977; Merritt 1980; Fine 1984.

[107] Thompson 1975, pp. 263, 264.

had to be extended to all sorts and degrees of men'.[108] (The affinity to the above-described attempt to appropriate law's categories is clear.)

It is precisely this, law's *generalised abstraction*, however, that is at the basis of the most sophisticated radical critiques of law. Thompson's supposed 'corrective' reminder that 'there is a difference between arbitrary power and the rule of law',[109] is not only not a challenge to the CLS and form-analysis critique of abstract and abstracting law (which does not of course deny that formal equality is preferable to ruling-class will), but is constitutive of it.[110] '[T]he formal conception of the rule of law was always a mask for substantive inequalities in power'.[111]

This criticism, that the rule of law is abstracting, is quite correct (if itself rather abstract). The debate over the rule of law has tended to be about the operation of that rule domestically, but with the analysis here, that critique can be brought to bear on the desire for an international rule of law between states, and can be concretised to a considerable degree.

I have argued that it is vital to 'disentangle denial'. Seeing the state system as intrinsically constituted by the juridical forms that underpin international law, obviously I do not see such law as a weak or non-existent force. However, I am a 'denier' in the alternative sense that I see no prospect of a systematic progressive political project or emancipatory dynamic coming out of international law.

That law is made actual in the power-political wranglings of states, ultimately at the logic of capital, in the context of an imperialist system. The very social problems that liberal-cosmopolitan writers want to end are the results of the international system, which is the international legal system. The forms and relations of international law are the forms and relations of imperialism. Attempts to reform though law can only ever tinker with the surface level of institutions.

---

108 Thompson 1975, p. 264.

109 Thompson 1975, p. 266.

110 Merritt 1980 points this out (pp. 199–200). Cole rightly criticises Merritt for overstating Thompson's commitment to law *tout court* and for his borderline *ad hominem* attacks on Thompson, but quite misses the importance of Merritt's observation that (in Cole's words), '[t]he *real* structuralist critique . . . peers behind the screen of the law's formal equality' (Cole 2001. Emphasis in original).

111 Craig 1995, p. 45. See also Hutchinson and Monahan 1987, p. 114.

It would obviously be fatuous to deny that law could ever be put to reformist use. In his discussion of the Factory Acts, Marx himself certainly sees 'progress'. But the recourse to law can only ever be of limited progressive value, and not just, as Marx argues, because such 'progress' is always hedged by 'retrogression'.[112] There is another limiting factor specific to international law.

For Marx, the 'formulation, official recognition and proclamation by the state . . . [of the Factory Acts was] the result of a long class struggle'.[113] Crudely, the contending classes fought quite directly to fill the legal form with specific content, and at particular points the working class triumphed. That the ruling class could often turn these triumphs to its own advantage does not mean the battles were not worth having, or that the successes were not manifest in 'progressive law'. However, at an international level, the struggle over the legal form is far more mediated.

States, not classes or other social forces, are the fundamental contending agents of international law, and while their claims and counterclaims are informed by their own domestic class struggles, they do not 'represent' classes in any direct way. It is generally the opposing ruling classes of different states that clash with the legal form, each with their own class agenda. These internecine battles between the 'warring brothers' of the ruling class make up a great swathe of the international legal structure, and in them there is little purchase for a fundamentally progressive, subversive or radical legal position.

This is not to foreclose any possibility of 'progressive' international legal moments or decisions. On occasions, such as *Nicaragua vs. US*, a ruling may be given against the imperialist action of a powerful state. And there are some attempts to formulate a proactive progressive legal activism. Recently, for example, there has been an explosion of literature on the new international law of indigenous peoples: in the light of decisions such as Canada's *Delgamuukw vs. British Columbia* in 1997, which granted priority to aboriginal customary land use in the arbitration of land claims, many writers see such law as potentially useful to further self-determination among indigenous peoples.[114] The foregoing analysis does imply, though, that even if such self-

---

[112] Marx 1976, p. 395.

[113] Ibid.

[114] See Anaya 1996 and Keal 2003 which acknowledge the historic uses of international law in oppressing indigenous peoples but are still hopeful about its more progressive application now. For an overview of different structures of claim in such cases see Kingsbury 2001.

determination *is* effected and does not turn out to be a 'poisoned gift', such 'progressive' moments will be more tenuous, unstable and unlikely than their domestic counterparts, because unusual circumstances aside, given their fundamental juridical units, international legal decisions generally represent the triumph of (at least) one national ruling class, rather than an agent fighting for fundamental progressive change.

There is also a more profound sense in which radical change, or even the systematic amelioration of social and international problems, cannot come through law. As Pashukanis's form-analysis shows, the system that throws these problems up *is* the juridical system that underpins the law. Law is a relation between subjects abstracted of social context, facing each other in a relationship predicated on private property, dependent on coercion. Internationally, law's 'violence of abstraction' *is* the violence of war.

To fundamentally change the dynamics of the system it would be necessary not to reform the institutions but to *eradicate the forms of law* – which means the fundamental reformulation of the political-economic system of which they are expressions. The project to achieve this is the best hope for global emancipation, and it would mean the end of law.

4. The future of the theory

This book is, to echo Pashukanis, only a sketch, a general outline of public international law from a commodity-form perspective: much work could be done to develop the theory.

The various historical epochs of international (and pre-international interpolity) law still need in-depth examination. The tendencies and countertendencies linking the bourgeois state and the legal form might be illuminated by investigating the conjunctures of bourgeois international law and the non-liberal state – the international law of the Axis powers, say, or of Stalin's USSR. More generally there is great scope for the investigation of different phases of capitalism and the bodies and structures of international law that express and act on their historic political-economic particularities.

Within modern international law, the specifics contents of various legal norms could be interpreted (something which has perhaps been neglected here).[115] Having argued that international law is derived from a structure in

[115] As one contemporary example, one might examine Stephen Gill's work on the

which the 'public' and the 'private' spheres were not sharply differentiated, it could be invaluable to apply this theory to what *is* now conceived of as specifically 'economic' international law: the legal regimes of taxation, of business regulation and private international law.

Though this theory sees law as intimately bound up with capitalism and violence, it offers no blueprints for social regulation in a post-(international-) law society, which would be a post-capitalist society. For some, this is enough to discredit critiques of the rule of law.[116] We might choose to address this by arguing that the construction of alternative social relations would throw up regulatory forms capable of dealing with new social and international problems, and that during the process of transition it is inconceivable that the legal form would not inhere for some time. However, the fact is that the lack of a stated alternative to law in no way invalidates the commodity-form analysis. The legal form has been a black box at the heart of international law, which Pashukanis's theory unlocks. In turn, the specifics of international law itself make it an optic uniquely able to develop and correct the theory.

Of all the insights that the commodity-form approach offers, none is more important than the unapologetic response to those who call for the rule of law. The attempt to replace war and inequality with law is not merely utopian – it is precisely self-defeating. A world structured around international law cannot but be one of imperialist violence.

The chaotic and bloody world around us *is the rule of law.*

'new constitutionalism', by which through 'treaties . . . institutional arrangements . . . and laws' international neoliberalism is implied in law and international law (Gill 2000, 2003).

[116] See for example Barnet 1998, pp. 327–8. For a paranoid version of this critique, see Walker 1988, p. 378: 'CLS shows its weakness . . . when one asks what alternative to the rule of law it has to offer. CLS writers and their supporters play down this side of the argument, but it is plain enough that they envisage a dismantling of the constitutional checks on the exercise of government power, to be followed by a transfer of that power to themselves and their allies exclusively.' It is difficult to imagine the thought of a coup attempt by critical lawyers filling the functionaries of the state with horror.

Appendix: Pashukanis on International Law

The following essay (Pashukanis 1980b in the bibliography) is Pashukanis's entry 'International Law' from the three-volume *Encyclopaedia of State and Law* published between 1925 and 1927 by the Communist Academy. It is reproduced in Beirne and Sharlet 1980a, and is available online at: <http://www.uiuc.edu/ph/www/p-maggs/pashukanis.htm>. With sincere thanks to the translator Peter Maggs for making it available here. References are made in full in the footnotes, following Pashukanis's own slightly inconsistent formulations.

International law (*ius gentium, droit des gens, Völkerrecht*) is usually defined as the totality of norms regulating the relationships between states. Here is a typical definition: 'International law is the totality of norms defining the rights and duties of states in their mutual relations with one another'.[1] We find the same definition in the Germans Hareis, Holtsendorf, Bulmering, Liszt and Ulman; in the Belgian Rivie; in the Englishmen Westlake and Oppenheim; in the American Lawrence etc.

But absent from this formal, technical definition, of course, is any indication of the historical, ie. the class character of international law. It is extremely clear that bourgeois jurisprudence consciously or unconsciously strives to conceal this element of class. The historical examples adduced in any textbook of

[1] H. Bonfils, *Traite de droit international public* (1894), Paris, p. 1.

international law loudly proclaim that *modern international law is the legal form of the struggle of the capitalist states among themselves for domination over the rest of the world.* However, bourgeois jurists try, as much as possible, to silence this basic fact of intensified competitive struggle, and to affirm that the task of international law is 'to make possible for each state what none could do in isolation, by means of co-operation between many states'.[2]

Nor did the theorists of the Second International move far from these bourgeois jurists. Abandoning the class conception of the state, they were naturally compelled to discover in international law an instrument, standing outside and above classes, for the co-ordination of the interests of individual states and for the achievement of peace.

It was from this perspective that the well-known Bernstein,[3] and the equally-famous Renner,[4] approached international law. With great assiduity, both of these gentlemen stressed the 'peaceful functions of international law', but in so doing they forgot that the better part of its norms refer to naval and land warfare, ie. that it directly assumes a condition of open and armed struggle. But even the remaining part contains a significant share of norms and institutions which, although they refer to a condition of peace, in fact regulate the same struggle, albeit in another concealed form. Every struggle, including the struggle between imperialist states, must include an exchange as one of its components. And if exchanges are concluded then forms must also exist for their conclusion.

But the presence of these forms does not of course alter the real historical content hidden behind them. At a given stage of social development this content remains the struggle of capitalist states among themselves. Under the conditions of this struggle, every exchange is the continuation of one armed conflict and the prelude to the next. Here lies the basic trait of imperialism.

> Capitalists [wrote Lenin] divide the world, not out of any particular malice, but because the degree of concentration which has been reached forces them to adopt this method in order to receive profit. And they divide it 'in proportion to capital', 'in proportion to strength', because there cannot be any other method of division under commodity production and capitalism. But strength varies with the level of economic and political development.

[2] J. Louter, *Le droit international public positif* (1920), Oxford, p. 17.
[3] E. Bernstein, *Völkerrecht und Völkerpolitik* (1919).
[4] K. Renner, *Marxismus, Krieg und Internationale* (1918), Vienna.

> In order to know what is taking place, it is necessary to know what questions are decided by the changes in strength. The question of whether these changes are 'purely' economic or extra-economic (military, for example) is secondary. . . . To substitute the question of the content of the struggle and agreements (today peaceful, tomorrow warlike, the next day peaceful again), is to descend to sophistry.[5]

When Renner depicts the development of international law as the growth of institutions which ensure the general interest of all states, and when he tries to show that this development has been retarded by the larcenous and selfish policy of only one of the states, Great Britain, then he too descends to sophistry. He must, moreover, be in the service of Austro-German imperialism (Renner's book was published before the Central Powers were defeated by the *Entente*). Conversely, we can see that even those agreements between capitalist states which appear to be directed to the general interest are, in fact, for each of the participants a means for jealously protecting their particular interests, preventing the expansion of their rivals' influence, thwarting unilateral conquest, ie. in another form continuing the same struggle which will exist for as long as capitalist competition exists. One may instantiate any international organization, even the international commissions for the supervision of navigation on the erstwhile 'treaty rivers' (the Rhine, the Danube, and after Versailles, the Elbe and the Oder). Let us begin with the fact that the very composition of these commissions perfectly reflects specific relations of forces, and is usually the result of war. After the World War, therefore, Germany and Russia were ousted from the European Commission on the Danube. At the same time the Commission on the Rhine was transferred to Strasbourg and fell into French hands. Under the Treaty of Versailles, the very transformation of German rivers into treaty rivers, which were controlled by international commissions, was an act which divided the spoils among the victors. The International Administration of Tangiers, a port in Morocco where the interests of France, England and Spain intersect, is the same type of organization for joint exploitation and supervision. A final and typical example is the International Organization for the Extortion of Reparations from Germany: the reparation commission and all types of supervisory agencies envisioned

[5] V. I. Lenin, *Imperialism, the Highest Stage of Capitalism* (1917), *Collected Works*, vol. 22, p. 253.

by the expert's plan. As soon as some power feels strong enough to take the plunder into its exclusive possession, it starts to combat internationalization. Thus, at the 1883 London Conference, Tsarist Russia succeeded in placing the Kiliisky branch of the Danube outside the control of the European Commission provided for by the international treaty of 1889. The Commission for the Supervision of the Neutralization of the Suez Canal could not be constituted at all: it was eliminated by a separate agreement between England and France, whereby the first bought itself freedom of action in Egypt in exchange for the latter's taking of Morocco (English-French Convention of April 8th, 1904). The struggle among imperialist states for domination of the rest of the world is thus a basic factor in defining the nature and fate of the corresponding international organizations.

There remain the comparatively few and narrowly-specialized interstate agreements. These have a technical character and correspond to purposeful combines or so-called international administrative unions, for example the International Postal Union. These organizations do not serve primarily as an arena for the struggle between administrative groupings, but they occupy a secondary and subordinate position. The origin of most of these organizations was in the 1870s and 1880s, ie. in the period when capitalism had still not fully developed its monopoly and imperialist-traits. The intensified struggle for the division of the world has moved forward to such an extent since that time, that the actual ability of capitalist states to serve general economic and cultural needs has diminished rather than expanded. In this respect a very clear regression was marked by the World War in that it caused the downfall of a whole series of cultural (in particular) and, for example, scientific links.

The bourgeois jurists are not entirely mistaken, however, in considering international law as a function of some ideal cultural community which mutually connects individual states. But they do not see, or do not want to see, that this community reflects (conditionally and relatively, of course) the common interests of the commanding and ruling classes of different states which have identical class structures. The spread and development of international law occurred on the basis of the spread and development of the capitalist mode of production. However, in the feudal period the knights of every European country had their codes of military honour and, accordingly, their class law, which they applied in wars with one another; but they did not apply them in inter-class wars, for example in the suppression of burghers and the peasantry. The victory of the bourgeoisie, in all the European countries, had to lead to the establishment of new rules and new institutions of international law which protected the general and basic interests of the bourgeoisie, ie. bourgeois property. Here is the key to the modern law of war.

While in feudal Europe the class structure was reflected in the religious notion of a community of all Christians, the capitalist world created its concept of 'civilization' for the same purposes. The division of states into civilized and 'semi-civilized', integrated and 'semi-integrated' to the international community, explicitly reveals the second peculiarity of modern international law as the class law of the bourgeoisie. It appears to us as the totality of forms which the capitalist, bourgeois states apply in their relations with each other, while the remainder of the world is considered as a simple object of their completed transactions. Liszt, for example, teaches that 'the struggle with states and peoples who are outside the international community must not be judged according to the law of war, but according to the bases of the love for mankind and Christianity'. To assess the piquancy of this assertion recall that, at the time of the colonial wars, the representatives of these lofty principles, eg. the French in Madagascar and the Germans in Southwest Africa, liquidated the local population without regard for age and sex.

The real historical content of international law, therefore, is the struggle between capitalist states. International law owes its existence to the fact that the bourgeoisie exercises its domination over the proletariat and over the colonial countries. The latter are organized into a number of separate state-political trusts in competition with one another. With the emergence of Soviet states in the historical arena, international law assumes a different significance. It becomes the form of a temporary compromise between two antagonistic class systems. This compromise is effected for that period when one system (the bourgeois) is *already* unable to ensure its exclusive domination, and the other (proletarian and socialist) has not *yet* won it. It is in this sense that it seems possible, to us, to speak of international law in the transitional period. The significance of this transitional period consists in the fact that open struggle for destruction (intervention, blockade, non-recognition) is replaced by struggle within the limits of normal diplomatic relations and contractual exchange. International law becomes *inter-class* law, and its adaptation to this new function inevitably occurs in the form of a series of conflicts and crises. The concept of international law during the transitional period was first put forth, in Soviet literature, by E. Korovin.[6]

---

[6] E. Korovin, *International Law of the Transitional Period* (1924), Moscow.

Finally, international law assumes an entirely different meaning as the inter-state law of the Soviet states. It now ceases to be a form of temporary compromise behind which an intensified struggle for existence is hidden. Because of this the very opposition between international law and the state, so characteristic of the preceding period, disappears. The proletarian states, not having merged formally into one federation or union, must present in their mutual relationships an image of such a close economic, political and military unity, that the measure of 'modern' international law becomes inapplicable to them.

Turning now to consider the legal form of international law, we will first note that orthodox theory considers the subject of international legal relations to be the state as a whole, and only the state. 'Only states are subjects of international law, the bearers of international legal obligations and powers.'[7] The real historical premise for this viewpoint is the formation of a system of independent states which have, within their boundaries, a sufficiently strong central power to enable each of them to act as a single whole. 'The sovereignty of the state, ie. its independence from any authority standing above it – this is the basis of international law.'[8]

These premises were historically realized in Europe only at the end of the Middle Ages, in the period of the formation of absolute monarchies which consolidated their independence, with respect to Papal authority, and which severed internal resistance by the feudal lords. The economic basis of this was the development of mercantile capital. The emergence of standing armies, the prohibition of private wars, the instigation of state enterprises, customs and colonial policy – these are the real facts which lie at the heart of the theory of the state as the sole subject of the international legal community. The Catholic Church, which had claimed the position of supreme leader of all the Christian states, was delivered a decisive blow by the Reformation. The Treaty of Westphalia, which in 1648 proclaimed the basis of equality between the Catholic and the 'heretical' (Protestant) states, is considered the basic fact in the historical development of modern (ie. bourgeois) international law.

The revolutions of the seventeenth and eighteenth centuries made further strides along the same road. They completed the process of separating state rule from private rule, and transformed political power into a special force

---

[7] F. Liszt, *Das Völkerrecht* (1925), Berlin, sec. 5.

[8] Loening, *Die Gerichtsbarkeit über fremde Souverane* (1903), sec. 83.

and the state into a special subject. The legal relations of the state flowed independently, and they were not to be confused with those persons who at any given moment were the bearers of state authority. Having subordinated itself to the state machine, the bourgeoisie brought the principle of the public nature of authority to its clearest expression. It may be said that the state only fully becomes the subject of international law as the bourgeois state. The victory of the bourgeois perspective over the feudal-patrimonial perspective was expressed, among other things, in the denial of the binding force of dynastic treaties for the state. Thus, in 1790 the National Assembly of France rejected the obligations which flowed from the family treaty of the house of Bourbon (1761), on the grounds that Louis XV had acted as a representative of the dynasty and not as a representative of France.

It is typical that at the same time as French authors (Bonfils, for example) consider this rejection to be proper, German monarcho-reactionary professors (Heffken) find that the National Assembly violated international law in this action.

The Roman Papacy is a curious vestige of the Middle Ages. After the Church entered the constituency of Italy in 1870, the Pope continued extra territorially to enjoy the right to send and receive ambassadors, ie. he had certain essential attributes of sovereign authority. When bourgeois Jurists are forced to explain a phenomenon which contradicts their doctrine, they usually argue that the Papal throne occupies a quasi-international status and that it is not in the strict sense a subject of international law.

In fact, of course, the influence of the leader of the Catholic Church is no less in international affairs than that of the League of Nations. All authors classify the latter, as an exception, to be among the independent subjects of international law along with individual states.

As a separate force which set itself off from society, the state only finally emerged in the modern bourgeois capitalist period. But it by no means follows from this that the contemporary forms of international legal intercourse, and the individual institutions of international law, only arose in the most recent times. On the contrary, they trace their history to the most ancient periods of class and even pre-class society. To the extent that exchange was not initially made between individuals, but among tribes and communities, it may be affirmed that the institutions of international law are the most ancient of legal institutions in general. Collisions between tribes, territorial disputes, disputes over borders – and agreements as one of the elements in these disputes – are found in the very earliest stages of human history. The tribal pre-state life of the Iroquois, and of the ancient Germans, saw the conclusion of alliances between tribes. The development of class society and the appearance of state authority make contracts and agreements among authorities possible. The treaty between Pharaoh Ramses II and the King of the Hittites is one of the oldest surviving documents of this type. Other forms of relationships are equally universal: the inviolability of ambassadors; the custom of exchanging hostages; one might also point to the ransoming of prisoners, the neutrality of certain areas, and the right to asylum. All these practices were known and used by the peoples of the distant past. Ancient Rome observed various forms for the declaration of war *(ius fetiale)*, concluded treaties, received and sent ambassadors. The ambassadors of foreign countries enjoyed inviolability etc. A special college of herald-priests dealt with these rules in Rome, and the majority of legal rules were protected by the gods at that time. The sanction of religion did not, however, prevent the fact that they were sometimes violated in the grossest manner.

On the other hand, a series of rules were formed which related to international intercourse. These were necessary both for regulating conflicts among tribes and peoples, and also for ensuring commercial exchange between individuals who belonged to different clans and tribes. Later, these rules were extended to include state organizations. In this way so-called private international law developed.

For example, during the period when Athens was flourishing, there were no less than 45,000 foreign inhabitants. They enjoyed all civil rights and were protected by a representative elected from their midst (embryos of consular representation). The protection of foreigners thus applied to merchants who were temporary residents. We see the same phenomenon in ancient Rome where the special office of *praetor peregrinus* was instituted for the hearing of foreigners' judicial cases. Moreover, the so-called *actiones fictitiae* aided in overcoming those strict requirements of Roman procedure which gave the foreigner no possibility of defending his rights.

In the understanding of the Roman jurists, the law of nations (*ius gentium*) embraced equally that which is now termed public international law, and also that which is inaccurately termed private international law. Thus, for example, we read in the Digests:

> By this law of nations (*ius gentium*), wars are waged, nations are divided, kingdoms are founded, property is distributed, fields are enclosed, build-

> ings are erected, trade, purchases, sales, loans and obligations are established – with the exception of certain transactions that are conducted in civil law.[9]

From this list it seems that the essential characteristic of international law was deemed to be not merely that it regulated relations (borders, war, peace etc.) among states but, and in contrast to the *ius civile*, that it established the basis of a legal community devoid of local peculiarities and free from tribal and national colouration. These universal rules could be nothing other than a reflection of the general conditions of exchange transactions, ie. they were reduced to the bases of the equal rights of owners, the inviolability of ownership and the consequent compensations for damages and freedom of contract. The bond between the *ius gentium* – in the sense of laws inherent in all nations – and norms regulating the mutual relations of states, was consciously strengthened by the first theorist of international law, Hugo Grotius (1583–1684). His whole system depends on the fact that he considers relations between states to be relations between the owners of private property; he declares that the necessary conditions for the execution of exchange, ie. equivalent exchange between private owners, are the conditions for legal interaction between states. Sovereign states co-exist and are counterposed to one another in exactly the same way as are individual property owners with equal rights. Each state may 'freely' dispose of its own property, but it can gain access to another state's property only by means of a contract on the basis of compensation: *do ut des.*

The feudal-patrimonial structure greatly aided the theory of territorial rule in acquiring a clearly civilist hue. Suzerains or 'Landesherren' considered themselves as the owners of those holdings over which their authority extended; the holdings were thought of as their private right, a subject of alienation by the owner. Entering into relations with one another, they disposed of their holdings as owners dispose of their objects, and alienated them according to the system of private (Roman) law. From the very beginning, therefore, many of the institutions of international law had a private law foundation – including the theory of *modi aecuirendi dominii* in international relations. Other methods were also recognized: inheritance, dowry, gift, purchase and sale, exchange, occupation, prescription.

On the basis of natural-law doctrine, Grotius's ideas continued to be developed by subsequent theorists: Puffendorf (1632–1694), Tomasius

---

[9] 1, 5 *Digests*, 1, 1.

(1655–1728), Wolff (1679–1754), Vattel (1714–1767) and Burlamaki (1694–1748). These theorists laid the foundation for an abstract or philosphical theory of law. In contrast to this school, which had given preference to abstract concepts, there began the collection and systematization of actual international customs and treaties and the study of international practice. The forefather of this positive, historico-pragmatic school is considered to be Zouch (1590–1669), an Oxford professor and Admiralty judge; the Dutchman Binkerskuch (1673–1743), and Martens (1756–1821) were later representatives. The doctrine of natural law ceased to enjoy the recognition of most jurists in the second half of the nineteenth century. However, even in our day Grotius's formulae continue to exist in international law textbooks, under the guise of so-called 'basic or absolute rights' of the state. For example, Hareis in *Institutionen des Volkerrechts* (1888), lists four such 'basic rights': the right to self-preservation; the right to independence; the right to international exchange; and the right to respect.

We read exactly the same in Liszt:

> From this basic idea [international legal intercourse] directly follows a whole series of legal norms, by which are defined the mutual rights and obligations of states and do not require any special treaty recognition in order to have obligatory force.
>
> They comprise a firm [!] basis for all the unwritten legal rules of international law, and are its oldest, most important and holiest content.[10]

It is most obvious that we are dealing here with ideas drawn from the sphere of civil law relationships with a basis in equality between the parties.

To a certain degree the analogy may be extended. Bourgeois private law assumes that subjects are formally equal yet simultaneously permits real inequality in property, while bourgeois international law in principle recognizes that states have equal rights yet in reality they are unequal in their significance and their power. For instance, each state is formally free to select the means which it deems necessary to apply in the case of infringements of its right: 'however, when a major state lets it be known that it will meet injury with the threat of, or the direct use of force, a small state merely offers passive resistance or is compelled to concede.'[11] These dubious benefits of for-

[10] F. Liszt, *International Law* (1913), Russian translation from the 6th edition, edited by V. E. Grabar, p. 81.

[11] V. E. Grabar, *The Basis of Equality between States in Modern International Law* (1912), Publishing House of the Ministry of Foreign Affairs, 1.

mal equality are not enjoyed at all by those nations which have not developed capitalist civilization and which engage in international intercourse not as subjects, but as objects of the imperialist states' colonial policy.

In civil-law transactions, however, the relationships between the parties assume legal form not only because they derive from the logic of objects (from the logic of the exchange act, more accurately), but also because this form finds real support and defence in the apparatus of judicial and state authority. Legal existence is materialized in a special sphere, partitioned off from the intrusion of naked fact. In his language the lawyer expresses this by asserting that every subjective right depends upon an objective norm, and that private legal relationships arose because of the public legal order. Moreover, in international law the subjects of legal relationships are the states themselves as the bearers of sovereign authority. A series of logical contradictions follows from this. For the existence of international law it is necessary that states be sovereign (for sovereignty in any given case is equated with legal capacity). If there are no sovereign states then there are no subjects of the international law relationship, and there is no international law. But, on the other hand, if there are sovereign states, then does this mean that the norms of international law are not legal norms? For in the opposite case, they must possess an external power which constrains the state, ie. limits its sovereignty. Conclusion: for international law to exist it is necessary that states not be sovereign. Bourgeois jurisprudence has devoted a great amount of fruitless effort in solving this contradiction. For instance, Pruess – the author of the present German (Weimar) Constitution tended to the position of sacrificing the concept of sovereignty for the sake of international law. Conversely, writers such as Zorn and, most recently, Wendel, are more ready to abandon supra-state international law. However, these dogmatic arguments change nothing in reality. No matter how eloquently the existence of international law is proved, the fact of the absence of an organizational force, which could coerce a state with the same ease as a state coerces an individual person, remains a fact. The only real guarantee that the relationships between bourgeois states (and in the transitional period with states of another class type) will remain on the basis of equivalent exchange, ie. on a legal basis (on the basis of the mutual recognition of subjects), is the real balance of forces. Within the limits set by a given balance of forces, separate questions may be decided by compromises and by exchange, ie. on the basis of law. Even then there is the qualification that each government calls upon law when its interests demand it, and in every way will try to avoid fulfilling some norm if it is profitable for it.[12] In critical periods, when the balance of forces has fluctuated seriously, when 'vital interests' or even the very existence of a state are on the agenda, the fate of the norms of international law becomes extremely problematic.

This particularly relates to the imperialist period, with its unprecedented intensification of the competitive struggle which derives from the monopolisitic tendencies of finance capital, and from the fact that after the whole globe has already been divided then further expansion can only occur at the expense of robbing one's neighbour.

The best illustration of this is afforded by the last war, of 1914–1918, during which both sides continuously violated international law. With international law in such a lamentable condition, bourgeois jurists can be consoled only with the hope that, however deeply the balance was disturbed, it will nevertheless be reestablished: the most violent of wars must sometime be ended with peace, the political passions raised by it must gradually be reconciled, the governments will return to objectivity and compromise, and the norms of international law will once again find their force. However, in addition to this hope the fact is adduced, as an argument in favour of the positive nature of international law, that every state in violating international law also tries to depict the matter as if there had been no violation whatsoever. We find in Ulman, for example, this curious reference to state hypocrisy as proof of the positive nature of international law. Another group of jurists simply deny the very existence of international law. Among them is the founder of the English school of positivist jurisprudence, Austin. Defining 'law in the proper sense', as an order emanating from a definite authority and strengthened by a threat in the case of disobedience, he finds that international law is *contradictio in adjecto*. 'To the extent that it is law, it is not international; to the extent that it is truly international, it is not law.' Gumplowicz holds the same opinion: 'In a definite sense international law is not law inasmuch as state law also is not law.'[13] Lasson says: 'The norms of international law are but rules of state wisdom which the state follows having in mind its own welfare, and from which it can deviate as soon as its vital interests so demand.'[14]

---

[12] L. Oppenheim, *International Law*: A *Treatise* (1905), Longmans, Green & Co., vol. 1, p. 65.

[13] L. Gumplowicz, *Allgemeines Staatsrecht* (1907), sec. 415.

[14] G. Lasson, *Prinzip und Zukunft des Volkerrechts* (1871), p. 49.

But the perspective of Austin, Lasson, Gumplowicz and others is not shared by the majority of bourgeois jurists. The open denial of international law is politically unprofitable for the bourgeoisie since it exposes them to the masses and thus hinders preparations for new wars. It is much more profitable for the imperialists to act in the guise of pacifism and as the champions of international law.

Therefore, for example, the English writer Walker[15] censures the terminological cavils of Austin, who did not want to define international law as law in the proper sense, and who exclaims 'it is better to permit peace and passivity to reign without correct terminology, than to permit accuracy of language to exist with the spirit of lawlessness!'

Jurists who preach the cult of force in international relations are both useless to the bourgeoisie (it needs not preaching, but real force), and also dangerous because they conceal the irreconcilability of the contradictions of capitalist society, and because they compromise peace and tranquility needed even by a thief when he has had his fill and is digesting his spoils.

From the Marxist perspective this nihilist criticism of international law is in error since, while exposing fetishism in one area, it does so at the cost of consolidating it in others. The precarious, unstable and relative nature of international law is illustrated in comparison with the largely firm, steady and absolute nature of other types of law. In fact, we have here a difference in degree. For only in the imagination of jurists are all the legal relationships within a state dominated one hundred per cent by a single state 'will'. In fact, a major portion of civil law relationships are exercised under influence of pressures limited to the activities of subjects themselves. Furthermore, only by taking the viewpoint of legal fetishism is it possible to think that the legal form of a relationship changes or destroys its real and material essence. This essence, on the contrary, is always decisive. The formalization of our relationship with bourgeois states, by way of treaties, is part of our foreign policy, and is its continuation in a special form. A treaty obligation is nothing other than a special form of the concretization of economic and political relationships. But once the appropriate degree of concretization is reached, it may then be taken into consideration and, within certain limits, studied as a special subject. The reality of this object is no less than the reality of any constitution – both may be overturned by the intrusion of a revolutionary squall.

[15] T. A. Walker, A *History of the Law of Nations*, n.d., p. 19.

It is commonplace to distinguish a general and a special component in relation to the systematization of international law. The first contains the theory of the state as the subject of international law. Here lies the theory of sovereignty, the various forms of limiting sovereignty, the theory of international law and legal capacity etc. Starting from the traditional division of the state into three elements – authority, territory and population – most treatises include within this general component the regulation of territorial questions (borders, territorial waters, methods of territorial acquisition etc.), and population questions (citizenship, preference, etc.). The special component considers the organization and forms of international legal relationships – here lie diplomatic and consular representation, international courts and other international organizations, the theory of international treaties etc. Further conceptual areas are usually delineated as regulatory international legal agreements (transportation, commerce, navigation, post and telegraphy, the battle with epidemics, the protection of property etc.). Finally comes the part dedicated to the law of war. This is usually prefaced with a consideration of the peaceful means of settling conflicts (arbitration decisions). The law of war may be divided into the law of military war, the law of naval warfare and the theory of the rights and obligations of neutral states.

Sources of international law

To the extent that states have no external authority above them which could establish their norms of conduct, then in the technical legal sense the sources of international law are custom and treaty. In Liszt's opinion both of these sources may be reduced to one – this is the 'general legal ideology of states', which is expressed partly in the form of legal practice, and partly in the form of the direct and overt establishment of law by way of agreement. But since (a) it is not always easy to decide which ideology is general and which ideology is 'legal', and (b) the practice of the different states at any one time, and the practice of any one state at different times, are far from the same – in fact, therefore, the source of the norms of even customary international law is drawn from the opinions of 'writers', or scholars, who usually differ decisively with each other on every question. Common, therefore, are citations to the 'majority' or to the 'overwhelming' majority of authorities. If one further notes that each of these authorities consciously or unconsciously defends those positions which are or seem beneficial to his own state, then one can imagine how hopeless will be the application of customary international law to the decision of any serious dispute.

The norms of written international law, which are fixed in treaties and agreements, are of course distinguished by comparatively greater precision. But there are rather few such treaties which could establish general rules or, expressed in technical language, which could create objective international law. The most important of these are: the acts of the Congress of Vienna (1815); the Paris Declaration on the Law of Naval Warfare (1856); the Geneva Conventions (1856 and 1906); the General Acts of the Hague Peace Conference (1899 and 1907); the London Declaration on the Law of Naval Warfare (1909); the League of Nations Treaty (1919); and certain declarations of the Washington Conference (1921) etc. However, parts of these treaties were not concluded by all states – just by some of them – and therefore the norms created by these agreements may not, strictly speaking, assume the significance of norms of general international law. There are only particular international laws effective within the circle of states which signed them or which later adhered to them. There are, accordingly, few generally recognized written norms of international law.

Finally, the decisions of international tribunals, arbitration panels and other international organizations are usually adduced as sources of international law. Anglo-Saxon jurists add the judicial practice of national courts, especially so in prize cases and in internal legislation dealing with questions of international significance.

Bibliography

(Wherever possible I have used English translations of texts.)

Aceves, William J. 2001, 'Critical Jurisprudence and International Legal Scholarship: A Study of Equitable Distribution', *Columbia Journal of Transnational Law*, 39, 2: 299–393.

Adewoye, O. 1977, *The Judicial System in Southern Nigeria 1854–1954: Law and Justice in a Dependency*, London: Longman.

Akehurst, Michael 1987, *A Modern Introduction to International Law* (6th edition), London: Allen & Unwin.

Alavi, Hamza 1991, 'Colonial and Post-Colonial Societies' in Bottomore, Tom (editor), *A Dictionary of Marxist Thought*, Oxford: Blackwell.

Alcantara, Oscar L. 1996, 'Ideology, Historiography and International Legal Theory', *International Journal for the Semiotics of Law*, IX, 25: 39–79.

Aldrich, George H. and Christine M. Chinkin 2000, 'A Century of Achievement and Unfinished Work', *American Journal of International Law*, 94, 1: 90–98.

Alexandrowicz, C.H. 1967, *An Introduction to the History of the Law of Nations in the East Indies*, Oxford: Clarendon Press.

Allott, Philip 1993, 'Self-Determination – Absolute Right or Social Poetry?' in Tomuschat, Christian (editor), *Modern Law of Self-Determination*, Dordrecht: Martinus Nijhoff.

Alvarez, José E. 2003, 'Hegemonic International Law Revisited', *American Journal of International Law*, 97, 4: 873–887.

American Society of International Law 1954, *Proceedings*, 48.

Anand, R.P. (ed.) 1972, *Asian States and the Development of Universal International Law*, Delhi: Vikas Publication.

Anand, R.P. 1983, *Origin and Development of the Law of the Sea*, The Hague: Martinus Nijhoff.

Anand, R.P. 2003, 'Family of "Civilized" States and Japan: A Story of Humiliation, Assimiliation, Defiance and Confrontation', *Journal of the History of International Law*, 5: 1–75.

Anaya, S. James 1996, *Indigenous Peoples in International Law*, Oxford: Oxford University Press.

Anderson, Benedict 1983, *Imagined Communities*, London: Verso.

Anderson, Perry 1974a, *Passages from Antiquity to Feudalism*, London: Verso.

Anderson, Perry 1974b, *Lineages of the Absolutist State*, London: Verso.

Anderson, Stanley V. 1963, 'A Critique of Professor Myres S. McDougal's Doctrine of Interpretation by Major Purposes', *American Journal of International Law*, 57, 2: 378–383.

Anghie, Antony 1996, 'Francisco de Vitoria and the Colonial Origins of International Law', *Social and Legal Studies*, 5, 3: 321–336.

Anghie, Antony 1999, 'Finding the Peripheries: Sovereignty and Colonialism in Nineteenth-Century International Law', *Harvard International Law Journal*, 40, 1: 1–80.

Archibugi, Daniele and David Held 1995, *Cosmopolitan Democracy*, Cambridge: Polity.

Arend, Anthony Clark 1999, *Legal Rules and International Society*, New York: Oxford University Press USA.

Aristodemou, Mària 1994, 'Choice and Evasion in Judicial Recognition of Governments: Lessons from Somalia', *European Journal of International Law*, 5, 4: 532–555.

Arthur, Chris 1978, 'Introduction', in Pashukanis, Evgeny, *Law and Marxism: A General Theory*, London: InkLinks.

Arthur, Chris 1999, 'Systematic Dialectic', talk given to the Greenwich Postgraduate Seminar Series in Critical Political Economy.

Artous, Antoine 1999, *Marx, l'état et la politique*, Paris: Éditions Syllepse.

Austin, John 2000, *The Province of Jurisprudence Determined*, Amherst, NY: Prometheus Books.

Azikiwe, Ben N. 1931, 'Ethics of Colonial Imperialism', *Journal of Negro History*, 16, 3: 287–308.

Bailyn, Bernard 2000, 'The First British Empire: From Cambridge to Oxford', *William and Mary Quarterly*, LVII, 3: 647–655.

Bakan, Abigail B. 1987, 'Plantation Slavery and the Capitalist Mode of Production: An Analysis of the Development of the Jamaican Labour Force', *Studies in Political Economy*, 22: 73–99.

Balakrishnan, Gopal 2000, *The Enemy. An Intellectual Portrait of Carl Schmitt*, London: Verso.

Banaji, Jairus 1977, 'Modes of Production in a Materialist Conception of History', *Capital and Class*, 3: 1–44.

Banaji, Jairus 2003, 'The Fictions of Free Labour: Contract, Coercion and So-Called Unfree Labour', *Historical Materialism*, 11, 3: 69–95.

Barber, William J. 1967, *A History of Economic Thought*, London: Penguin.

Barker, Colin 1978, 'The State as Capital', *International Socialism*, 2, 1: 16–42.

Barker, Colin 1998, 'Industrialism, Capitalism, Value, Force and States: Some Theoretical Remarks', unpublished MS.

Barnett, Randy E. 1998, *The Structure of Liberty: Justice and the Rule of Law*, Oxford: Clarendon Press.

Barratt Brown, Michael 1974, *The Economics of Imperialism*, Harmandsworth: Penguin.

Barrow, Clyde W. 2000, 'The Marx Problem in Marxian State Theory', *Science and Society*, 64, 1: 87–118.

Bartelson, Jens 1995, *A Genealogy of Sovereignty*, Cambridge: Cambridge University Press.

Baxter, John 1999, 'Is the UN an Alternative to "Humanitarian Imperialism"?', *International Socialism*, 85: 57–72.

Beaulac, Stéphane 2000, 'The Westphalian Legal Orthodoxy – Myth or Reality?', *Journal of the History of International Law*, 2: 148–177.

Beaulac, Stéphane 2003a, 'The Social Power of Bodin's "Sovereignty" and International Law', *Melbourne Journal of International Law* 4, 1: 1–28.

Beaulac, Stéphane 2003b, 'Emer de Vattel and the Externalization of Sovereignty', *Journal of the History of International Law*, 5: 237–292.

Bederman, David J. 2001, *International Law in Antiquity*, Cambridge: Cambridge University Press.

Bedjaoui, Mohammed 1979, *Towards a New International Economic Order*, New York: Holmes & Meier.

Beer, George Louis 1922, *The Origins of the British Colonial System, 1578–1660*, New York: Macmillan.

Beirne, Piers and Robert Sharlet 1982, 'Pashukanis and Soviet Legality' in Beirne, Piers and Richard Quinney (eds.), *Marxism and Law*, New York: Wiley.

Beirne, Piers and Robert Sharlet 1990, 'Towards a General Theory of Law and Marxism: E.B. Pashukanis' in Beirne, Piers (ed.), *Revolution in Law*, London: M.E. Sharpe.

Bendersky, Joseph 1987, 'Carl Schmitt at Nuremburg', *Telos* 72: 91–96.

Bennis, Phyliss and Michel Moushabeck (editors) 1991, *Beyond the Storm: A Gulf Crisis Reader*, New York: Olive Branch Press.

Benson, Bruce L. 1991, *The Enterprise of Law: Justice Without the State*, San Francisco: Pacific Research Institute for Public Policy.

Binns, Peter 1980, 'Review Article: Law and Marxism', *Capital and Class*, 10: 100–113.

Binns, Pete 1984, 'Revolution and State Capitalism in the Third World', *International Socialism*, 2, 25: 37–68.

Binns, Peter and Mike Haynes 1980, 'New Theories of Eastern European Class Societies', *International Socialism*, 2, 7: 18–50.

Blackie, Duncan 1994, 'The United Nations and the politics of imperialism', *International Socialism*, 2, 63: 49–76.

Blair, Arthur H. 1992, *At War in the Gulf: A Chronology*, College Station, TX: Texas A&M University Press.

Blanke, Bernhard, Ulrich Jürgens and Hans Kastendiek 1978, 'On the Current Marxist Discussion on the Analysis of Form and Function of the Bourgeois State' in Holloway, John and Sol Picciotto (eds.), *State and Capital: A Marxist Debate*, London: Edward Arnold.

Blum, Yehuda 1970, 'The Beirut Raid and the International Double Standard', *American Journal of International Law*, 64, 1: 73–105.

Bodin, Jean 1955, *The Six Books of the Commonwealth*, Oxford: Basil Blackwell/ http://www.constitution.org/bodin/bodin_.htm.

Bodin, Jean 1992, *On Sovereignty: Four Chapters from* the Six Books of the Commonwealth, Cambridge: Cambridge University Press.

Boyle, Francis 1980, 'The Irrelevance of International Law: The Schism Between International Law and International Politics', *California Western International Law Journal*, 10: 193–219.

Bowett, Derek 1958, *Self-Defence in International Law*, Manchester: Manchester University Press.

Bowett, Derek 1972, 'Reprisals Involving Recourse to Armed Force', *American Journal of International Law*, 66, 1: 1–36.

Bowring, Bill n.d., 'Ideology Critique and International Law: Hegel, Marx, Habermas – and Susan Marks', unpublished manuscript.

von Braunmühl, Claudia 1978, 'On the Analysis of the Bourgeois Nation State within the World Market Context' in Holloway, John and Sol Picciotto (eds.), *State and Capital: A Marxist Debate*, London: Edward Arnold.

Brenner, Robert 1977, 'The Origins of Capitalist Development: A Critique of Neo-Smithian Marxism', *New Left Review*, 104: 25–92.

Brenner, Robert 1985a, 'Agrarian Class Structure and Economic Development in Pre-Industrial Europe' in Aston, T.H. and C.H.E. Philpin (eds.), *The Brenner Debate: Agrarian Class Structure and Economic Development in Pre-Industrial Europe*, Cambridge: Cambridge University Press.

Brenner, Robert 1985b, 'The Agrarian Roots of European Capitalism', in Aston, T.H. and C.H.E. Philpin (eds.), *The Brenner Debate: Agrarian Class Structure and Economic Development in Pre-Industrial Europe*, Cambridge: Cambridge University Press.

Bresheeth, Haim and Nira Yuval-Davis (eds.) 1991, *The Gulf War and the New World Order*, London: Zed Books.

Brewer, Anthony 1980, *Marxist Theories of Imperialism*, London: Routledge & Kegan Paul.

Brewer, John 1990, *The Sinews of Power*, Cambridge, MA: Harvard University Press.

Brierly, James L. 1958, *The Basis of Obligation in International Law*, Oxford: Clarendon Press.

Briggs, Herbert W. 1945, 'Power Politics and International Organization', *American Journal of International Law*, 39, 4: 664–679.

Brownlie, Ian 1963, *International Law and the Use of Force by States*, Oxford: Oxford University Press.

Brownlie, Ian 1984, 'The Expansion of International Society: The Consequences for the Law of Nations' in Bull, Hedley and Adam Watson (eds.), *The Expansion of International Society*, Oxford: Clarendon.

Brownlie, Ian 1990, *Principles of Public International Law* (4th edition), London: Oxford University Press.

Brugger, Bill 1991, 'Was the Gulf War "Just"?', *Australian Journal of International Affairs*, 45, 2: 161–169.

Buck, Philip W. 1942, *The Politics of Mercantilism*, New York: Henry Holt and Company.

Bukharin, N.I. 1982, *Selected Writings on the State and the Transition to Socialism*, New York: M.E. Sharpe.

Bukharin, Nikolai 1987, *Imperialism and World Economy*, London: Merlin.

Bull, Hedley 1975, 'New Directions in the Theory of International Relations', *International Studies*, 14: 277–86.

Bull, Hedley 1977, *The Anarchical Society*, London: Macmillan.

Bull, Hedley and Adam Watson (eds.) 1984, *The Expansion of International Society*, Oxford: Clarendon.

Bunck, Julie Marie and Michael Ross Fowler 1995, *Law, Power and the Sovereign State: The Evolution and Application of the Concept of Sovereignty*, University Park, PA: The Pennsylvania State University Press.

Burn, W.L. 1951, *The British West Indies*, London: Hutchinson House.

Butkevych, Olga V. 2003, 'History of Ancient International Law: Challenges and Prospects', *Journal of the History of International Law*, 5: 189–236.

Butler, Geoffrey and Simon Maccoby 1928, *The Development of International Law*, London: Longmans, Green and Co.

Byers, Michael 1999, *Custom, Power and the Power of Rules*, Cambridge: Cambridge University Press.

Cain, Maureen 1983, 'Introduction: Towards an Understanding of the International State', *International Journal of the Sociology of Law*, 11: 1–10.

Callinicos, Alex 1987, 'Imperialism, Capitalism and the State Today', *International Socialism*, 2, 35: 71–115.

Callinicos, Alex 1988, *Making History*, New York: Cornell.

Callinicos, Alex 1989, *Against Postmodernism*, Cambridge: Polity.

Callinicos, Alex 1990a, *Trotskyism*, Buckingham: Open University Press.

Callinicos, Alex 1990b, 'The Limits of "Political Marxism"', *New Left Review*, 184: 110–115.

Callinicos, Alex 1994, 'Marxism and Imperialism Today', in Callinicos, Alex, et al. (eds.), *Marxism and the New Imperialism*, London: Bookmarks.

Callinicos, Alex 1996, *The Revolutionary Ideas of Karl Marx* (revised second edition), London: Bookmarks.

Callinicos, Alex 1999, 'Capitalism, Competition and Profits: A Critique of Robert Brenner's Theory of Crisis', *Historical Materialism* 4: 9–31.

Callinicos, Alex 2001, *Against the Third Way*, Cambridge: Polity Press.

Callinicos, Alex 2002, 'The Actuality of Imperialism', *Millennium*, 31, 2: 319–326.

Callinicos, Alex 2003, *The New Mandarins of American Power*, Cambridge: Polity Press.

Carmichael, C.H.E. 1884, 'Grotius and the Literary History of the Law of Nations', text of a speech issued as a pamphlet.

Carothers, Thomas 1984, 'Legal Argumentation in International Crises: The Downing of Korean Air Lines Flight 007', *Harvard Law Review*, 97: 1198–1213.

Carty, Anthony 1986, *The Decay of International Law?*, Manchester: Manchester University Press.

Carty, Anthony 1991, 'Critical International Law: Recent Trends in the Theory of International Law', *European Journal of International Law*, 2: 66–96.

Carty, Anthony 1996, *Was Ireland Conquered? International Law and the Irish Question*, London: Pluto Press.

Carty, Anthony 2001, 'Carl Schmitt's Critique of Liberal International Legal Order Between 1933 and 1945', *Leiden Journal of International Law*, 14, 1: 25–76.

Casey, Lee A. and David B. Rivkin 2000, 'The Rocky Shoals of International Law', *The National Interest*, Winter 2000: 35–45.

Cass, Deborah Z. 1996, 'Navigating the Newstream: Recent Critical Scholarship in International Law', *Nordic Journal of International Law*, 65: 341–383.

Cassesse, Antonio 1999a, '*Ex iniuria ius oritur*: Are we Moving Towards International Legitimation of Forcible Humanitarian Countermeasures in the World Community?', *European Journal of International Law*, 10, 1: 23–30.

Cassesse, Antonio 1999b, 'A Follow-Up: Forcible Humanitarian Countermeasures and *Opinio Necessitatis*', *European Journal of International Law*, 10, 4: 791–799.

Castellino, Joshua 1999, 'Territoriality and Identity in International Law: The Struggle for Self-Determination in the Western Sahara', *Millennium*, 28, 3: 523–551.

Charlesworth, Hilary 1992, 'Subversive Trends in the Jurisprudence of International Law', *American Society for International Law Proceedings*, 86: 125–130.

Chase, Anthony 1997, *Law and History. The Evolution of the American Legal System*, New York: The New Press.

Chayes, Abram 1991, 'The Use of Force in the Persian Gulf' in Damrosch, Lori Fisler and David J. Scheffer (eds.), *Law and Force in the New International Order*, Boulder, Co.: Westview Press.

Cheah, Pheng 1997, 'Posit(ion)ing Human Rights in the Current Global Conjuncture', *Public Culture*, 9: 233–266.

Chimni, B.S. 1993, *International Law and World Order*, New Delhi: Sage Publications.

Chimni, B.S. 1999, 'Marxism and International Law: A Contemporary Analysis', *Economic and Political Weekly*, 6 February 1999: 337–349.

Chimni, B.S. 2002, 'Toward a Radical Third World Approach to Contemporary International Law', *ICCLP Review* [publication of the International Center for Comparative Law and Politics] 5, 2: 14–26.

Chomsky, Noam 1987, *Turning The Tide* (2nd edition), Montreal: Black Rose Books.

Chomsky, Noam 1992a, *Deterring Democracy* (revised edition), London: Vintage.

Chomsky, Noam 1992b, *What Uncle Sam Really Wants*, Berkeley, CA: Odonian Press.

Chomsky, Noam 1999, *The New Military Humanism: Lessons from Kosovo*, London: Pluto Press.

Christianson, Paul 1996, *Discourse on History, Law, and Governance in the Public Career of John Selden, 1610–1635*, Toronto: University of Toronto Press.

Clark, Ramsey 1992a, *War Crimes: A Report on U.S. War Crimes Against Iraq*, Washington: Maisonnaeve Press.

Clark, Ramsey 1992b, *The Fire This Time: U.S. War Crimes in the Gulf*, New York: Thunder's Mouth Press.

Clarke, Simon (ed.) 1991, *The State Debate*, London: Macmillan.

Cliff, Tony 1996, *State Capitalism in Russia*, London: Bookmarks.

Coates, A.J. 1997, *The Ethics of War*, Manchester: Manchester University Press.

Colbert, Evelyn 1948, *Retaliation in International Law*, New York: King's Crown Press.

Cole, Daniel H. 2001, '"An Unqualified Human Good": E.P. Thompson and the Rule of Law', *Journal of Law and Society*, 28, 2: 177–203.

Cole, H.M. 1940, 'Origins of the French Protectorate Over Catholic Missions in China', *American Journal of International Law*, 34, 3: 473–491.

Coleman, D.C. 1969, 'Eli Heckscher and the Idea of Mercantilism' in Coleman, D.C. (ed.), *Revisions in Mercantilism*, London: Methuen and Co.

Cotterrell, Roger 1980, 'Book Review: *Pashukanis: Selected Writings on Marxism and Law*', *British Journal of Law and Society*, 7.

Cotterrell, Roger 1996, *Law's Community: Legal Theory in Sociological Perspective*, Oxford: Oxford University Press.

Craig, Paul P. 1995, 'Formal and Substantive Conceptions of the Rule of Law', *Diritto Publico*: 35–55.

Craven, Matthew, Susan Marks, Gerry Simpson and Ralph Wilde 2004, 'We Are Teachers of International Law', *Leiden Journal of International Law*, 17, 2.

Crouse, Nellis M. 1940, *French Pioneers in the West Indies, 1624–1664*, New York: Columbia University Press.

Cruickshank, Albert and Vendulka Kubálková 1988, *Marxism and International Relations*, Oxford: Oxford University Press.

Curtis, Mark 1998, *The Great Deception: Anglo-American Power and World Order*, London: Pluto Press.

Cutler, Claire 1997, 'Artifice, Ideology and Paradox: the Public/Private Distinction in International Law', *Review of International Political Economy*, 4, 2: 261–285.

Cutler, Claire 1999, 'Globalization and the Rule of Law: Reconstituting Property, Capital and the State', paper delivered at the *Now More Than Ever: Historical Materialism and Globalisation* workshop at Warwick University, April 1999. <http://faculty.maxwell.syr.edu/merupert/Research/HM%20workshop/cutler.htm>.

Cutler, Claire 2001, 'Critical Reflections on the Westphalian Assumptions of International Law and Organization: a crisis of legitimacy', *Review of International Studies*, 27, 2: 133–150.

Danzig, David and Paul Rosenzweig 2004, 'Head to Head: Is the US Breaking the Law?', 10 March 2004, at <news.bbc.co.uk/1/hi/world/americas/3548399.stm>.

Davenport, Frances Gardiner 1917, *European Treaties Bearing on the History of the United States and Its Dependencies*, Washington, DC: Carnegie Institution of Washington.

Davidson, Scott 1987, *Grenada: A Study in Politics and the Limits of International Law*, Aldershot: Avebury.

Davis, Mike 1986, *Prisoners of the American Dream*, London: Verso.

Davis, Ralph 1962, *The Rise of the English Shipping Industry in the Seventeenth and Eighteenth Centuries*, Newton Abbot: David & Charles.

De Pauw, Frans 1965, *Grotius and the Law of the Sea*, Brussels: Université de Bruxelles Institut de Sociologie.

Dean, Jodi 2004, 'Zizek on Law', *Law and Critique*, 15: 1–24.

Derrida, Jacques 1976, *Of Grammatology*, Baltimore: The John Hopkins University Press.

Detter De Lupis, Ingrid 1987, *The Concept of International Law*, Stockholm: Norstedts Förlag.

Deutsch, Karl and Stanley Hoffman (eds.) 1971, *The Relevance of International Law*, Garden City, NY: Doubleday Anchor Books.

Dickinson, Edwin DeWitt 1920, *The Equality of States in International Law*, Cambridge, MA: Harvard University Press.

Dinstein, Yoram 1984, 'A Realistic Approach to International Law' in Grahl-Madsen, Atle and Jiri Toman (eds.), *The Spirit of Uppsala: Proceedings of the Joint UNITAR-Uppsala University Seminar on International Law and Organizatio for a New World Order (JUS 81), Uppsala 9–18 June 1981*, Berlin: Walter de Gruyter.

Dinstein, Yoram 1994, *War, Aggression and Self-Defence* (second edition), Cambridge: Grotius Publications.

Dobb, Maurice 1963, *Studies in the Development of Capitalism*, New York: International Publishers.

Doehring, Karl 2002, 'Book review: Carl Schmitt, *Le nomos de lat terre dans le droit des gens du Jus Publicum Europaeum*', *Journal of the History of International Law*, 4: 374–376.

Donnelly, Jack 1992, 'Human Rights in the New World Order', *World Policy Journal*, 9, 2: 249–277.

Douglas, William O. 1961, *The Rule of Law in World Affairs*, Santa Barbara, CA: Center for the Study of Democratic Institutions.

Doswald-Beck, Louise 1985, 'The Legal Validity of Military Intervention by Invitation of the Government', *British Yearbook of International Law*, 56: 189–252.

Dudden, Alexis 1999, 'Japan's Engagement with International Terms' in Liu, Lydia H. (ed.) *Tokens of Exchange: The Problem of Translation in Global Circulation*, Durham: Duke University Press.

Dumbauld, Edward 1969, *The Life and Legal Writings of Hugo Grotius*, Norman: University of Oklahoma Press.

Dunning, William A. 1896, 'Jean Bodin on Sovereignty', *Political Science Quarterly*, 11, 1: 82–104.

Eagleton, Terry 2001, 'A Spot of Firm Government', *London Review of Books*, 23, 16: 19–20.

Eckstein, George 1981, 'Hans Morgenthau: A Personal Memoir', *Social Research*, 48: 641–52.

Ehrlich, Thomas and Mary Ellen O'Connell 1993, *International Law and the Use of Force*, Boston: Little, Brown and Company.

Eldred, Michael 1984, *Critique of Competitive Freedom and the Bourgeois-Democratic State*, Copenhagen: Kurasje.

Elias, Taslim Olawale 1972, *Africa and the Development of International Law*, The Hague: Martinus Nijhoff.

Engels, Frederick 1902, *The Origin of the Family, Private Property and the State*, Chicago: C.H. Kerr and Company.

Engelskirchen, Howard 1992, 'Locating the Analysis of Legal Form: E.B. Pashukanis', *Rethinking Marxism*, 5, 1: 108–115.

Engelskirchen, Howard 1997, 'Consideration as the Commitment to Relinquish Autonomy', *Seton Hall Law Review*, 27, 2: 490–573.

Estreicher, Samuel and Paul B. Stephan 2003, 'Taking International Law Seriously', *Virginia Journal of International Law*, 44, 1: 1–4.

Falk, Richard 1968a, 'The Relevance of Political Context to the Nature and Functioning of International Law: An Intermediate View' in Deutsch, Karl W. and Stanley Hoffman (eds.), *The Relevance of International Law*, Cambridge, MA: Schenkman.

Falk, Richard 1968b, *Legal Order in a Violent World*, Princeton: Princeton University Press.

Falk, Richard 1969, 'The Beirut Raid and the International Law of Retaliation', *American Journal of International Law*, 63, 3: 415–43.

Falk, Richard 1970, *The Status of Law in International Society*, Princeton: Princeton University Press.

Falk, Richard 1975, *A Study of Future Worlds*, New York: The Free Press.

Falk, Richard 1980, 'The Shaping of World Order Studies: A Response', *The Review of Politics*, 42: 18–30.

Falk, Richard 1983, *The End of World Order: Essays on Normative International Relations*, New York: Holmes and Meier Publishers.

Falk, Richard 1985, 'The Grotian Quest' in Falk, Richard et al. (eds.) *International Law: A Contemporary Perspective*, Boulder: Westview Press.

Falk, Richard 1992, 'Democracy Died at the Gulf', *Viet Nam Generation Journal*, 4:1. <http://lists.village.virginia.edu/sixties/HTML_docs/TextsScholarly/Falk_Democracy_Died_01.html>.

Falk, Richard 1994, Speech at the 1994 Conference on Security Council Reform. <http://www.globalpolicy.org/security/conf94/falk.htm>.

Falk, Richard 1995, 'The World Order between Inter-State Law and the Law of Humanity: the Role of Civil Society Institutions' in Archibugi, Daniele and David Held (eds.), *Cosmopolitan Democracy: An Agenda for a New World Order*, Cambridge: Polity.

Falk, Richard 1997, 'The United Nations, the rule of law and humanitarian intervention', in Kaldor, Mary and Basker Vashee (eds.), *Restructuring the Global Military Sector. Volume 1: New Wars*, London: Pinter.

Farley, Lawrence T. 1986, *Plebiscites and Sovereignty: The Crisis of Political Illegitimacy*, Boulder: Westview Press.

Feinerman, James V. 1996, 'Chinese Participation in the International Legal Order: Rogue Elephant or Team Player?' in Lubman, Stanley (ed.), *China's Legal Reforms*, Oxford: Oxford University Press.

Feinman, Jay M. and Peter Gabel 1990, 'Contract Law as Ideology' in Kairys, David (ed.), *The Politics of Law: A Progressive Critique* (revised edition), New York: Pantheon Books.

Fenwick, Charles G. 1939, 'The Monroe Doctrine and the Declaration of Lima', *American Journal of International Law*, 33, 2: 257–268.

Fine, Bob 1979, 'Law and Class' in Fine, Bob et al. (eds.), *Capitalism and the Rule of Law*, London: Hutchinson.

Fine, Bob 1984, *Democracy and the Rule of Law*, London: Pluto Press.

Fine, Robert and Sol Picciotto 1992, 'On Marxist Critiques of Law' in Grigg-Spall, Ian and Paddy Ireland (eds.), *The Critical Lawyers' Handbook*, London: Pluto Press.

Finkelstein, Norman G. 1996, *The Rise and Fall of Palestine*, Minneapolis: University of Minnesota Press.

Fisch, Jörg 1984, *Die europäische Expansion und das Völkerrecht*, Stuttgart: Franz Steiner Verlag.

Fisch, Jörg 1986, 'International Law in the Expansion of Europe', *Law and State: A Biannual Collection of Recent German Contributions*, 34: 7–31.

Fisch, Jörg 2000, 'The Role of International Law in the Territorial Expansion of Europe, 16th–20th Centuries', *ICCLP Review* [publication of the International Center for Comparative Law and Politics], 3, 1: 4–13.

Fisch, Jörg 2001, 'Internationalizing Civilization by Dissolving International Society. The Status of Non-European Territories in Nineteenth-Century International Law' in Geyer, Martin H. and Johannes Paulmann (eds.), *The Mechanics of Internationalism*, Oxford: Oxford University Press.

Fitzmaurice, Gerald 1957, 'The General Principles of International Law Considered from the Standpoint of the Rule of Law', *Recueil des Cours* 92: 70–80.

Fitzmaurice, Gerald 1971, '*Vae Victis* or Woe to the Negotiators! Your Treaty or Our "Interpretation" of it?', *American Journal of International Law*, 65, 2: 358–73.

Fitzpatrick, Peter 2001, *Modernism and the Grounds of Law*, Cambridge: Cambridge University Press.

Fitzpatrick, Peter 2003, '"Gods would be needed . . .": American Empire and the Rule of (International) Law', *Leiden Journal of International Law*, 16, 3: 429–466.

Fitzpatrick, Peter and Alan Hunt 1987, 'Critical Legal Studies: Introduction' in Fitzpatrick, Peter and Alan Hunt (eds.), *Critical Legal Studies*, London: Basil Blackwell.

Flint, J. 1988, 'Chartered Companies and the Transition from Informal Sway to Colonial Rule in Africa', in Förster, Stig et al. (eds.), *Bismarck, Europe and Africa. The Berlin Africa Conference 1884–1885 and the Onset of Partition*, Oxford: Oxford University Press.

Förster, Stig et al. (eds.) 1988, *Bismarck, Europe and Africa. The Berlin Africa Conference 1884–1885 and the Onset of Partition*, Oxford: Oxford University Press.

Franck, Thomas M. 1988, 'Legitimacy in the International System', *American Journal of International Law*, 82, 4: 705–759.

Frankel, Boris 1997, 'Confronting Neoliberal Regimes: The Post-Marxist Embrace of Populism and Realpolitik', *New Left Review*, 226: 57–92.

Friedmann, Wolfgang 1968, 'Interventionism, Liberalism, and Power-Politics: The Unfinished Revolution in International Thinking', *Political Science Quarterly*, 83, 2: 169–189.

Fulton, Thomas Wemyss 1911, *The Sovereignty of the Sea*, London: William Blackwood and Sons.

Furber, Holden 1976, *Rival Empires of Trade in the Orient 1600–1800*, Minneapolis: University of Minnesota Press.

Gathii, James Thuo 1998, 'International Law and Eurocentricity', *European Journal of International Law*, 9, 1: 184–239.

Gattini, Andrea 2002, 'Sense and Quasisense of Schmitt's *Großraum* Theory in International Law – A Rejoinder to Carty's "Carl Schmitt's Critique of Liberal International Legal Order"', *Leiden Journal of International Law*, 15, 1:53–68.

Geertz, Clifford 1973, 'Thick Description: Toward an Interpretive Theory of Culture', in *The Interpretation of Cultures*, New York: Basic Books.

Geyer, Martin H. and Johannes Paulmann 2001, 'Introduction: the Mechanics of Internationalism' in Geyer, Martin H. and Johannes Paulmann (eds.), *The Mechanics of Internationalism*, Oxford: Oxford University Press.

Giddens, Anthony 1985, *A Contemporary Critique of Historical Materialism* Volume 2, *The Nation-State and Violence*, Berkely, CA: University of California Press.

Gill, Stephen 2000, 'The Constitution of Global Capitalism', paper presented at the panel *The Capitalist World, Past and Present* at the International Studies Association Annual Convention, Los Angeles 2000. <www.theglobalsite.ac.uk>.

Gill, Stephen 2003, 'Grand Strategy and World Order: A Neo-Gramscian Perspective', a revised version of a lecture delivered on 20 April 2000 at Yale University.

Glennon, Michael J. 1999, 'The New Interventionism: The Search for a Just International Law', *Foreign Affairs*, 78, 3: 2–7.

Glete, Jan 2001, *War and the State in Early Modern Europe*, London: Routledge.

Global Governance Reform Project 2000, *Reimagining the Future: Towards Democratic Governance*, Melbourne: Politics Department, La Trobe University.

Gong, Gerrit W. 1984, *The Standard of 'Civilization' in International Society*, Oxford: Clarendon Press.

Gosselin, Daniel P. 1998, '*Jus ad Bellum* and the 1983 Grenada Invasion: the Limits of International Law', Department of National Defense (Canada). <http://www.cfcsc.dnd.ca/irc/amsc/amsc1/016.html#n110>

Gottlieb, Gidon 1968, 'The New International Law: Toward the Legitimation of War', *Ethics* 78, 2: 144–147.

Gottschalk, Tikkun A.S. 2003, 'The Realpolitik of Empire', *Journal of Transnational Law and Policy*, 13, 1: 281–303.

Gowan, Peter 1999, 'The Gulf War and Western Liberalism' in, *The Global Gamble: Washington's Faustian Bid for World Dominance*, London: Verso.

Gowan, Peter 2001, 'The Origins of Atlantic Liberalism', *New Left Review*, 8: 150–157.

Gowan, Peter 2003, 'US: UN', *New Left Review*, 24: 1–28.

Gowan, Peter, Leo Panitch and Martin Shaw 2001, 'The State, Globalisation and the New Imperialism: A Roundtable Discussion', *Historical Materialism*, 9: 3–38.

Grabar, V.E. 1990, *The History of International Law in Russia, 1647–1917*, Oxford: Clarendon Press.

Gramsci, Antonio 1971, *The Prison Notebooks*, London: Lawrence and Wishart.

Green, L. and Olive P. Dickason 1989, *The Law of Nations and the New World*, Edmonton: University of Alberta Press.

Green, Peter 2002, '"The Passage from Imperialism to Empire": A Commentary on Empire by Michael Hardt and Antonio Negri', *Historical Materialism*, 10, 1: 29–77.

Greenspan, Morris 1959, *The Modern Law of Land Warfare*, Berkely, CA: University of California Press.

Greenwood, Christopher 1993, 'Customary international law and the First Geneva Protocol of 1977 in the Gulf conflict' in Rowe, Peter (ed.), *The Gulf War 1990–91 in International and English Law*, London: Routledge.

Gregory, Jeanne 1979, 'Sex discrimination, work and the law' in Fine, Bob et al. (eds.), *Capitalism and the Rule of Law*, London: Hutchinson.

Grewe, Wilhelm G. 1984, 'History of the Law of Nations: World War I to World War II' in Bernhardt, Rudolf et al. (eds.) 1995, *Encyclopedia of Public International Law*, Amsterdam: Elsevier.

Grewe, Wilhelm G. (ed.) 1995, *Fontes Historiae Iuris Gentium: Sources Relating to the History of the Law of Nations*, Berlin: Walter de Gruyter.

Grewe, Wilhelm G. 2000, *The Epochs of International Law*, Berlin: Walter de Gruyter.

Grigg-Spall, Ian and Paddy Ireland (eds.) 1992, *The Critical Lawyers' Handbook*, London: Pluto Press.

Grotius, Hugo 2000, *The Freedom of the Seas*, Kitchener, Ontario: Batoche Books.

Grotius, Hugo 2001, *On the Law of War and Peace*, Kitchener, Ontario: Batoche Books.

Grovogui, Siba N'Zatioula 1996, *Sovereigns, Quasi Sovereigns and Africans*, Minneapolis: University of Minnesota Press.

Halberstam, Malvina 1993, 'The Copenhagen Document: Intervention in Support of Democracy', *Harvard International Law Journal*, 34, 1: 165–175.

Hall, W.E. 1884, *A Treatise of International Law* (Second edition), Oxford: Clarendon.

Halle, Louis J. 1974, 'Foreword' in Klein, Robert A. *Sovereign Equality Among States: The History of an Idea*, Toronto: University of Toronto Press.

Halley, Anne 1997, 'Theodor W. Adorno's Dream Transcripts', *The Antioch Review*, 55, 1: 57–74.

Halliday, Fred 1991, 'The Left and the War', *New Statesman and Society*, 8 March 1991: 14–16.

Halliday, Fred 1996, *Islam and the Myth of Confrontation*, London: I.B. Tauris.

Halliday, Fred 1998, 'Colonialism and the Formation of the Modern World: Domination and Resistance', Center for Western European Studies Working Paper No. 1, Kalamazoo, MI: Kalamazoo College.

Hampson, Françoise J. 1993, 'Means and methods of warfare in the conflict in the Gulf' in Rowe, Peter (ed.), *The Gulf War 1990–91 in International and English Law*, London: Routledge.

Hardt, Michael and Antonio Negri 2000, *Empire*, Cambridge, MA: Harvard University Press.

Hargreaves, John D. 1996, *Decolonization in Africa*, London: Longman.

Hargrove, John Lawrence 1991, 'Intervention by Invitation and the Politics of the New World Order', in Damrosch, Lori Fisler and David J. Scheffer (eds.), *Law and Force in the New International Order*, Boulder, Co.: Westview Press.

Harman, Chris 1991, 'State and Capitalism Today', *International Socialism*, 51: 3–54.

Harman, Chris 1998, *Marxism and History*, London: Bookmarks.

Harman, Chris 1999, *A People's History of the World*, London: Bookmarks.

Harris, Douglas C. 2000, 'Review: Laws of the Postcolonial', *Law, Social Justice & Global Development*, 1. <http://elj.warwick.ac.uk/global/issue/2000-1/harris.html>.

Hart, H.L.A. 1961, *The Concept of Law*, Oxford: Oxford University Press.

Hazard, John 1951 (ed.), *Soviet Legal Philosophy*, Cambridge, Mass.: Harvard University Press.

Hazard, John 1979, 'Foreword' in Pashukanis 1980, *Pashukanis: Selected Writings on Marxism and Law*, London: Academic Press.

Head, Michael 2001, 'The Passionate Legal Debates of the Early Years of the Russian Revolution', *Canadian Journal of Law and Jurisprudence*, 14, 1: 3–27.

Head, Michael 2004 (forthcoming), 'The Rise and Fall of a Soviet Jurist: Evgeny Pashukanis and Stalinism', *Canadian Journal of Law and Jurisprudence*, 17, 2.

Heckscher, Eli F. 1994, *Mercantilism* (2 volumes, revised), London: Routledge.

Held, David 1995, *Democracy and the Global Order*, Cambridge: Polity.

Held, David, Anthony McGrew, David Goldblatt and Jonathan Perraton 1999, *Global Transformations*, Cambridge: Polity.

Henkin, Louis 1979, *How Nations Behave: Law and Foreign Policy* (second edition), New York: Praeger.

Hershey, Amos S. 1912, 'History of International Law Since the Peace of Westphalia', *American Journal of International Law*, 6, 1: 30–69.

Heuer, Uwe-Jens and Gregor Schirmer 1998, 'Human Rights Imperialism', *Monthly Review*, 49, 10. <http://www.monthlyreview.org/398heuer.htm>

Higgins, Rosalyn 1968, 'Policy Considerations and the International Judicial Process', *International and Comparative Law Quarterly*, 17.

Higgins, Rosalyn 1969, 'Policy and Impartiality: The Uneasy Relationship in International Law', *International Organisation*, XXIII, 4: 914–31.

Higgins, Rosalyn 1994, *Problems and Process: International Law and How We Use It*, Oxford: Clarendon Press.

Hilton, Rodney (ed.) 1978, *The Transition from Feudalism to Capitalism*, London: Verso.

Hinsley, F.H. 1986, *Sovereignty* (second edition), Cambridge: Cambridge University Press.

Hirsch, Joachim 1978, 'The State Apparatus and Social Reproduction: Elements of a Theory of the Bourgeois State' in Holloway, John and Sol Picciotto (eds.), *State and Capital: A Marxist Debate*, London: Edward Arnold.

Hitchens, Christopher 1990, *Blood, Class and Nostalgia*, London: Vintage.

Hitchens, Christopher 2001, *The Trial of Henry Kissinger*, London: Verso.

Hobbes, Thomas 1981, *Leviathan*, London: Penguin.

Hobsbawm, E.J. 1962, *The Age of Revolution: 1789–1848*, New York: Mentor.

Hobsbawm, E.J. 1975, *The Age of Capital: 1848–1875*, London: Abacus.

Hobsbawm, Eric 1994, *Age of Extremes*, London: Abacus.

Hochschild, Adam 1999, *King Leopold's Ghost*, London: Macmillan.

Holloway, John and Sol Picciotto (eds.) 1978a, *State and Capital: A Marxist Debate*, London: Edward Arnold.

Holloway, John and Sol Picciotto 1978b, 'Introduction: Towards a Materialist Theory of the State' in Holloway, John and Sol Picciotto (eds.), *State and Capital: A Marxist Debate*, London: Edward Arnold.

Holloway, John and Sol Picciotto 1991, 'Capital, Crisis and the State', in Clarke, Simon (ed.), *The State Debate*, London: Macmillan.

Horwitz, Morton 1977, 'The Rule of Law: An Unqualified Human Good?', *Yale Law Journal*, 86: 561.

Hosack, John 1882, *On the Rise and Growth of the Law of Nations*, London: John Murray.

Hsiung, James C. 1997, *Anarchy and Order: The Interplay of Politics and Law in International Relations*, London: Lynne Rienner Publishers.

Huberman, Leo 1936, *Man's Worldly Goods*, New York: Monthly Review Press.

Hueck, Ingo J. 2001, 'The Discipline of the History of International Law – New Trends and Methods on the History of International Law', *Journal of the History of International Law*, 3: 194–217.

Hunt, Alan 1987, 'The Critique of Law: What is "Critical" about Critical Legal Theory?' in Fitzpatrick, Peter and Alan Hunt (eds.), *Critical Legal Studies*, London: Basil Blackwell.

Hutchinson, Allan and Patrick Monahan 1987, 'Democracy and the Rule of Law', in Hutchinson, Allan and Patrick Monahan (eds.), *The Rule of Law: Ideal or Ideology*, Toronto: Carswell.

Hutchison, Terence W. 1988, *Before Adam Smith: The Emergence of Political Economy, 1662–1776*, Oxford: Basil Blackwell.

International Helsinki Federation for Human Rights 2003, *Anti-terrorism Measures, Security and Human Rights: Developments in Europe, Central Asia and North America in the Aftermath of September 11*, Helsinki: IHF.

Ireland, Paddy and Per Laleng (eds.) 1997, *The Critical Lawyers' Handbook 2*, London: Pluto Press 1997.

Jackson, Robert H. 1987, 'Quasi-States, Dual Regimes, and Neoclassical Theory: International Jurisprudence and the Third World', *International Organization*, 41, 4: 519–549.

Jackson, Robert H. 1991, *Quasi-States: Sovereignty, International Relations, and the Third World*, Cambridge: Cambridge University Press.

Janis, Mark W. 1991, 'International Law?', *Harvard International Law Journal*, 32, 2: 363–372.

Jenkins, William Sumner 1935, *Pro-Slavery Thought in the Old South*, Chapel Hill, NC: The University of North Carolina Press.

Jennings, R.Y. 1963, *The Acquisition of Territory in International Law*, Manchester: Manchester University Press.

Jessop, Bob 1990, *State Theory*, University Park, PA: Pennsylvania State University Press.

Jhering, Rudolf von 1924, *Law as a Means to an End*, New York: Macmillan.

af Jochnick, Chris and Roger Normand 1994a, 'The Legitimation of Violence: A Critical History of the Laws of War', *Harvard International Law Review*, 35, 1: 49–95.

af Jochnick, Chris and Roger Normand 1994b, 'The Legitimation of Violence: A Critical Analysis of the Gulf War', *Harvard International Law Review*, 35, 2: 387–416.

Johns, Christina Jacqueline and P. Ward Johnson 1994, *State Crime, the Media, and the Invasion of Panama*, Westport, CT: Praeger.

Johnson, Richard R. 1991, *John Nelson, Merchant Adventure: A Life between Empires*, Oxford: Oxford University Press.

Johnston, W. Ross 1973, *Sovereignty and Protection: A Study of British Jurisdictional Imperialism in the Late Nineteenth Century*, Durham, N.C.: Duke University Press.

Kaldor, Mary 1997, 'Introduction', Kaldor, Mary and Basker Vashee eds., *Restructuring the Global Military Sector. Volume 1: New Wars*, London: Pinter.

Kaldor, Mary 1999, *New and Old Wars*, Cambridge: Polity.

Kalshoven, Frits 1971, *Belligerent Reprisals*, Leiden: A.W. Sijthoff.

Kaplan, Morton A. and Nicholas de B. Katzenbach 1961, *The Political Foundations of International Law*, New York: John Wiley.

Kay, Geoffrey and James Mott 1982, *Political Order and the Law of Labour*, London: Macmillan.

Keach, William 2003, 'International law: Illusion and reality', *International Socialist Review*, 27. <http://isreview.org/issues/27/international_law.shtml>.

Keal, Paul 2003, *European Conquest and the Rights of Indigenous Peoples (The Moral Backwardness of International Society)*, Cambridge: Cambridge University Press.

Kelman, Mark 1987, *A Guide to Critical Legal Studies*, Cambridge, Mass.: Harvard University Press.

Kelsen, Hans 1952, *Principles of International Law*, New York: Holt, Rhinehart and Winston.

Kelsen, Hans 1967, *Pure Theory of Law*, Los Angeles: University of California Press.

Kelsen, Hans 1968, 'The Essence of International Law' in Deutsch, Karl and Stanley Hoffman (eds.), *The Relevance of International Law*, Cambridge, MA: Schenkman.

Kennedy, David W. 1986a, 'Remarks', *American Society of International Law Proceedings*, 80: 161–169.

Kennedy, David 1986b, 'Primitive Legal Scholarship', *Harvard International Law Journal*, 27, 1: 1–98.

Kennedy, David 1987, *International Legal Structures*, Baden-Baden: Nomos.

Kennedy, David 1988, 'A New Stream of International Law Scholarship', *Wisconsin International Law Journal*, 7, 1: 1–49.

Kennedy, David 1989, 'A Rotation in Contemporary Legal Scholarship', in Joerges, Christian and David M. Trubek (eds.), *Critical Legal Thought: An American-German Debate*, Baden-Baden: Nomos.

Kennedy, David 1996, 'International Law and the Nineteenth Century: History of an Illusion', *Nordic Journal of International Law*, 65: 385–420.

Kennedy, David 2002, 'The International Human Rights Movement: Part of the Problem?', *Harvard Human Rights Journal*, 15: 101–125.

Kennedy, David and Chris Tennant 1994, 'New Approaches to International Law: A Bibliography', *Harvard International Law Journal*, 35, 2: 417–60.

Kennedy, Duncan 1979, 'The Structure of Blackstone's Commentaries', *Buffalo Law Review*, 28, 2: 205–382.

Kervegan, Jean-Francois 1999, 'Carl Schmitt and World Unity', in Mouffe, Chantal (ed.), *The Challenge of Carl Schmitt*, London: Verso.

Kimminich, O. 1984, 'History of the Law of Nations: Since World War II' in Bernhardt, Rudolf et al. (eds.) 1995, *Encyclopedia of Public International Law*, Amsterdam: Elsevier.

Kingsbury, Benedict 1998, 'Sovereignty and Inequality', *European Journal of International Law*, 9, 4: 599–625.

Kingsbury, Benedict 2001, 'Reconciling Five Competing Conceptual Structures of Indigenous Peoples' Claims in International and Comparative Law', *New York University Journal of International Law and Politics*, 34, 1: 189–250.

Klein, Robert A. 1974, *Sovereign Equality Among States: The History of an Idea*, Toronto: University of Toronto Press.

Knight, W.S.M. 1925, *The Life and Works of Hugo Grotius*, London: Sweet and Maxwell.

Koechler, Hans 1995, *Democracy and the International Rule of Law*, Vienna: Springer-Verlag.

Kooijmans, P.H. 1964, *The Doctrine of the Legal Equality of States*, Leyden: A.J. Sythoff.

Korff, S.A. 1924, 'An Introduction to the History of International Law', *American Journal of International Law*, 18, 2: 246–259.

Korovin, E.A. 1924, *Mezhdunarodnoe pravo perkhodnogo vremeni*, Moscow.

Koshy, Susan 1999, 'From Cold War to Trade War: Neocolonialism and Human Rights', *Social Text*, 17, 1: 1–32.

Koskenniemi, Martti 1989, *From Apology to Utopia: The Structure of International Legal Argument*, Helsinki: Lakimiesliiton Kustannus.

Koskenniemi, Martti 1995, 'The Police in the Temple – Order, Justice and the UN: A Dialectical View', *European Journal of International Law*, 6, 3: 325–348.

Koskenniemi, Martti 2000a, 'International Law and Imperialism', the Josephine Onoh Memorial Lecture 1999, Hull: Law School, University of Hull.

Koskenniemi, Martti 2000b, 'Carl Schmitt, Hans Morgenthau, and the Image of Law in International Relations', in Byers, Michael (ed.), *The Role of Law in International Politics*, Oxford: Oxford University Press.

Koskenniemi, Martti 2002a, *The Gentle Civilizer of Nations: The Rise and Fall of International Law 1870–1960*, Cambridge: Cambridge University Press.

Koskenniemi, Martti 2002b, 'Book Review: *The Epochs of International Law* by Wilhelm Grewe', *International and Comparative Law Quarterly*, 51, 3: 746–751.

Krasner, Stephen D. 2001a, 'Explaining Variation: Defaults, Coercion, Commitments' in Stephen D. Krasner (ed.), *Problematic Sovereignty: Contested Rules and Political Possibilities*, New York: Columbia University Press.

Krasner, Stephen 2001b, 'Sovereignty', *Foreign Policy*, January 2001.

Kriedte, Peter 1977, 'The Origins, the Agrarian Context, and the Conditions in the World Market' in Kriedte, Peter, Hans Medick and Jürgen Schlumbohm (eds.), *Industrialization Before Industrialization*, Cambridge: Cambridge University Press.

Kunz, Josef L. 1968, *The Changing Law of Nations*, Ohio: Ohio State University Press.

Lachs, Manfred 1987, *The Teacher in International Law*, Dordrecht: Martinus Nijhoff.

Landauer, Carl 2003, 'Book Review: Wilhelm Grewe, *The Epochs of International Law*', *Leiden Journal of International Law*, 16, 1: 191–214.

Lasswell, Harold, Myres S. McDougal and W. Michael Reisman 1968, 'Theories About International Law: Prologue to a Configurative Jurisprudence', *Virginia Journal of International Law*, 8, 2: 188–299.

Lauterpacht, H. 1932, 'The Nature of International Law and General Jurisprudence', *Economica*, 37: 301–20.

Lawrence, T.J. 1910, *The Principles of International Law*, London: Macmillan.

Lawrence, T.J. 1913, 'The Colonies in International Law', in Hearnshaw, F.J.C. (ed.), *King's College Lectures on Colonial Problems*, London: G. Bell & Sons.

Lee, Eric Yong-Joong 2002, 'Early Development of Modern International Law in East Asia – With Special Reference to China, Japan and Korea', *Journal of the History of International Law*, 4: 42–76.

Lenin, V.I. 1939, *Imperialism: The Highest Stage of Capitalism*, New York: International Publishers.

Lenoble, Jacques 1986, 'The Implicit Ideology of Human Rights and its Legal Expression', *Liverpool Law Review*, 8, 2: 153–167.

Levenfeld, Barry 1982, 'Israel's Counter-*Fedayeen* Tactics in Lebanon', *Columbia Journal of Transnational Law*, 21, 1: 1–48.

Levins, Richard and Richard Lewontin 1985, *The Dialectical Biologist*, Cambridge, MA: Harvard University Press.

Lindley, M.F. 1926, *The Acquisition and Government of Backward Territory in International Law*, New York: Longmans.

Linebaugh, Peter and Marcus Rediker 2000, *The Many-Headed Hydra: Sailors, Slaves, Commoners, and the Hidden History of the Revolutionary Atlantic*, London: Verso.

Liu, Lydia H. 1999a, 'The Desire for the Sovereign and the Logic of Reciprocity in the Family of Nations', *Diacritics*, 29, 4: 150–177.

Liu, Lydia H. 1999b, 'Legislating the Universal: The Circulation of International Law in the Nineteenth Century', in Liu, Lydia H. (ed.) *Tokens of Exchange: The Problem of Translation in Global Circulation*, Durham: Duke University Press.

Lloyd, T.O. 1996, *The British Empire, 1558–1995*, Oxford: Oxford University Press.

Lockley, Joseph B. 1938, 'Pan-Americanism and Imperialism', *American Journal of International Law*, 32, 2: 233–243.

Loughlin, Martin 1992, *Public Law and Political Theory*, Oxford: Clarendon Press.

Lukács, Georg 1970, *Lenin: A Study in the Unity of His Thought*, London: New Left Books.

Lukashak, Igor I. 1991, 'The United Nations and Illegitimate Regimes: When to Intervene to Protect Human Rights' in Damrosch, Lori Fisler and David J. Scheffer (eds.), *Law and Force in the New International Order*, Boulder, Co.: Westview Press.

Luxemburg, Rosa 1951, *The Accumulation of Capital*, London: Routledge & Kegan Paul.

Macalister-Smith, Peter and Joachim Schwietzke 1999, 'Literature and Documentary Sources relating to the History of Public International Law: An Annotated Bibliographical Survey', *Journal of the History of International Law*, 1: 136–212.

Malanczuk, Peter 1997, *Akehurst's Modern Introduction to International Law* (seventh revised edition), London: Routledge.

Mallison, W. Thomas and Sally Mallison 1986, *The Palestine Problem in International Law and World Order*, London: Longman.

Malowist, M. 1959, 'The Economic and Social Development of the Baltic Countries from the Fifteenth to the Seventeenth Centuries', *The Economic History Review*, Second series XII, 2: 177–189.

Manas, Jean 1995, 'Beyond Right and Wrong? Thoughts Engendered by a Post-Modernist Critique of the Gulf War', *Harvard International Law Journal*, 36, 1: 245–258.

Manning, Patrick 1990, *Slavery and African Life*, Cambridge: Cambridge University Press.

Manning, William Oke 1875, *Commentaries on the Law of Nations*, London: Macmillan.

Mansell, Wade 1997, 'Pure Law in an Impure World', in Ireland, Paddy and Per Laleng (eds.), *The Critical Lawyers' Handbook 2*, London: Pluto Press.

Marín-Bosch, Miguel 1998, *Votes in the UN General Assembly*, The Hague: Kluwer Law International.

Marks, Susan 2000, *The Riddle of All Constitutions. International Law, Democracy, and the Critique of Ideology*, Oxford: Oxford University Press.

Marks, Susan 2001, 'Big Brother is Bleeping Us – With the Message that Ideology Doesn't Matter', *European Journal of International Law*, 12, 1: 109–123.

Marshall Brown, Philip 1945, 'Imperialism', *American Journal of International Law*, 39, 1: 84–86.

Marx, Karl 1973, *Grundrisse*, London: Penguin.

Marx, Karl 1976, *Capital* Volume 1, London: Penguin.

Marx, Karl 1978, *Capital* Volume 2, London: Penguin.

Marx, Karl 1981, *Capital* Volume 3, London: Penguin.

Marx, Karl and Frederick Engels 1987, *The Communist Manifesto*, New York: Pathfinder.

Masters, Roger 1964, 'World Politics as a Primitive Political System', *World Politics*, XVI, 4: 595–619.

Mattern, Johannes 1928, *Concepts of State, Sovereignty and International Law*, Baltimore: The Johns Hopkins Press.

Matthews, Ken 1993, *The Gulf Conflict and International Relations*, London: Routledge.

McCarthy, Leo 1998, *Justice, the State and International Relations*, London: Macmillan.

McDougal, Myres S. 1952, 'Law and Power', *American Journal of International Law*, 46, 1: 102–14.

McDougal, Myres S. 1953, 'International Law, Power and Policy: A Contemporary Conception', *Recueil des Cours*, 82: 137–258.

McDougal, Myres S. 1955, 'The Realist Theory in Pyrrhic Victory', *American Journal of International Law*, 49, 2: 376–8.

McDougal, Myres S. 1967a, 'The International Law Commission's Draft Articles upon Interpretation: Textuality *Redivivus*', *American Journal of International Law*, 61, 4: 992–1000.

McDougal, Myres S. 1967b, *The Interpretations of Agreements and World Public Order*, New Haven: Yale University Press.

McDougal, Myres S. 1972, 'International Law and Social Science: A Mild Plea in Avoidance', *American Journal of International Law*, 66, 1: 77–81.

McDougal, Myres S., H. Lasswell and W. Michael Reisman 1981, 'The World Constitutive Process of Authoritative Decision' in McDougal, Myres S. and W. Michael Reisman, *International Law Essays*, Mineola, NY: Foundation Press.

McDougal, Myres S. and W. Michael Reisman 1981, *International Law Essays*, Mineola, NY: Foundation Press.

McWhinney, Edward 1984, *United Nations Law Making; Cultural and Ideological Relativsm and International Law Making for an Era of Transition*, New York: Holmes and Meier.

Meron, Theodor 1998, 'Is International Law Moving towards Criminalization?', *European Journal of International Law*, 9, 1: 18–31.

Merritt, Adrian 1980, 'The Nature of Law: A Criticism of E.P. Thompson's *Whigs and Hunters*', *British Journal of Law and Society*, 7, 2: 194.

Meyer, Howard N. 1997, 'When the Pope Rebuked the U.S. at the World Court', American Society of International Law, *UN 21 Interest Group Newsletter*, 15. <http://www.lawschool.cornell.edu/library/asil/15oped.htm>

Michalak, Stanley J. 1980, 'Richard Falk's Future World: A Critique of WOMP-USA', *The Review of Politics*, 42: 3–17.

Middle East Watch 1991, *Needless Deaths in the Gulf War: Civilian Casualties During the Air Campaign and Violations of the Laws of War*, New York: Human Rights Watch.

Miles, Robert 1987, *Capitalism and Unfree Labour – Anomaly or Necessity*, London: Tavistock Publications.

Miliband, Ralph 1973, *The State in Capitalist Society*, London: Quartet.

Miller, Lynn H. 1985, *Global Order: Values and Power in International Relations*, London: Westview Press.

Miller, Jennifer 1990, 'International Intervention – The United States Invasion of Panama', *Harvard International Law Journal*, 31: 633–646.

Mills, Kurt 1998, *Human Rights in the Emerging Global Order: A New Sovereignty?* London: Macmillan.

Mooers, Colin 1991, *The Making of Bourgeois Europe*, London: Verso.

Moore, John Norton 1984, 'Grenada and the international double standard', *American Journal of International Law*, 78, 1: 145–168.

Moore, John Norton 1986, 'The Secret War in Central America and the Future of World Order', *American Journal of International Law*, 80, 1: 43–127.

Moore, John N. 1992, *Crisis in the Gulf: Enforcing the Rule of Law*, New York: Ocean.

Morgenthau, Hans J. 1940, 'Positivism, Functionalism and International Law', *American Journal of International Law*, 34: 260–284.

Morgenthau, Hans J. 1958, *Dilemmas of Politics*, Chicago: University of Chicago Press.

Morgenthau, Hans J. 1967, *Politics Among Nations* (fourth edition), New York: Alfred A. Knopf.

Morgenthau, Hans J. 1981, *In Defense of the National Interest*, New York: Alfred A. Knopf.

Morton, A.L. 1989, *A People's History of England* (second edition), London: Lawrence and Wishart.

Moser, Johann Jacob 1959, *Grundsatze des Volkerrechts: aus "Versuch des neuesten Europäischen Volker-Rechts in Friedens- und Kriegs-Zeiten"*, Frankfurt: Vittorio Klostermann.

Mouffe, Chantal (ed.) 1999, *The Challenge of Carl Schmitt*, London: Verso.

Mullerson, Rein 1991, 'Intervention by Invitation', in Damrosch, Lori Fisler and David J. Scheffer (eds.), *Law and Force in the New International Order*, Boulder, CO: Westview Press.

Nanda, Ved P. 1990, 'The Validity of United States Intervention in Panama Under International Law', *American Journal of International Law*, 84, 2: 494–503.

Neocleous, Mark 1996, 'Friend or Enemy? Reading Schmitt Politically', *Radical Philosophy*, 79: 13–23.

Neff, Stephen C. 2001, 'Book Review: Wilhelm G. Grewe. *The Epochs of International Law*', *Journal of the History of International Law*, 3: 252–254.

Negri, Antonia 1999, *Insurgencies: Constituent Power and the Modern State*, Minneapolis, MN: University of Minnesota Press.

Nesia, Vasuki 2003, 'Placing International Law: White Spaces on a Map', *Leiden Journal of International Law*, 16, 1: 1–35.

Newsinger, John 2001, 'Taiping revolutionary: Augustus Lindley in China', *Race & Class*, 42, 4: 57–72.

Ngantcha, Francis 1990, *The Right of Innocent Passage and the Evolution of the International Law of the Sea*, London: Pinter Publishers.

Nisula, Laura and Katarina Sehm Patomäki 2002, *We, the Peoples of the World Social Forum . . .*, NIGD discussion paper, Helsinki: Network Institute for Global Democratization. <http://www.nigd.org/Discussion%20Papers.html>

Norris, Christopher 1992, *Uncritical Theory*, London: Lawrence & Wishart.

Noyes, C. Reinold 1943, 'Property and Sovereignty', *Journal of Legal and Political Sociology*, 1, 3–4: 72–100.

Nussbaum, Arthur 1947, *A Concise History of the Law of Nations*, New York: Macmillan.

Nys, Erneste 1894, *Les origines du droit international*, Brussels: Castaige.

O'Brien, William V. 1981, *The Conduct of Just and Limited War*, New York: Praeger.

O'Brien, William V. 1991, *Law and Morality in Israel's War with the PLO*, London: Routledge.

Onuma Yasuaki 2000, 'When was the Law of International Society Born? – An Inquiry of the History of International Law from an Intercivilizational Perspective', *Journal of the History of International Law*, 2: 1–66.

Orend, Brian 1998, 'Armed Intervention: Principles and Applications', *The Flinders Journal of History and Politics*, 20: 63–79.

Orford, Anne 1997, 'Locating the International: Military and Monetary Interventions after the Cold War', *Harvard International Law Journal*, 38, 2: 443–485.

Orford, Anne 1999, 'Muscular Humanitarianism: Reading the Narratives of the New Interventionism', *European Journal of International Law*, 10, 4: 679–711.

Orford, Anne 2003, *Reading Humanitarian Intervention. Human Rights and the Use of Force in International Law*, Cambridge: Cambridge University Press.

Orth, Samuel P. 1916, 'Law and Force in International Affairs', *International Journal of Ethics*, 26, 3: 339–346.

Osiander, Andreas 1994, *The States System of Europe, 1640–1990: Peacemaking and the Conditions of International Stability*, Oxford: Oxford University Press.

Owen, Roger, and Sutcliffe, Bob 1972, *Studies in the Theory of Imperialism*, London: Longman.

Oxman, Bernard H., David D. Caron and Charles L.O. Buderi 1983, *Law of the Sea: U.S. Policy Dilemma*, San Francisco: ICS Press.

Padjen, Ivan 1975, *Marxism and Positivism in Soviet Theories on the Foundations of International Law*, LLM thesis, Dalhousie University.

Pakenham, Thomas 1992, *The Scramble for Africa*, London: Abacus.

Palmer, Sarah 1990, *Politics, Shipping and the Repeal of the Navigation Laws*, Manchester: Manchester University Press.

Pashukanis, Evgeny 1978, *Law and Marxism: A General Theory*, London: InkLinks.

Pashukanis, Evgeny 1980a, *The General Theory of Law and Marxism* in Beirne, Piers and Robert Sharlet (eds.) *Pashukanis: Selected Writings on Marxism and Law*, London: Academic Press. <http://www.uiuc.edu/ph/www/p-maggs.pashukanis.htm>.

Pashukanis, Evgeny 1980b, 'International Law' in Beirne, Piers and Robert Sharlet (eds.), *Pashukanis: Selected Writings on Marxism and Law*, London: Academic Press.

Pashukanis, Evgeny 2001, *The General Theory of Law and Marxism*, Somerset, NJ: Transaction Publishers.

Paust, Jordan J. 1979, 'The Concept of Norm: A Consideration of the Jurisprudential Views of Hart, Kelsen and McDougal-Lasswell', *Temple Law Quarterly* 52: 9–49.

Pawlisch, Hans S. 1985, *Sir John Davies and the Conquest of Ireland: A Study in Legal Imperialism*, Cambridge: Cambridge University Press.

Perrotta, Cosimo 1993, 'Early Spanish Mercantilism: the First Analysis of Underdevelopment' in Magnusson, Lars (ed.), *Mercantilist Economics*, Dordrecht: Kluwer Academic Publishers.

Peterson, M.J. 1982, 'Political Use of Recognition: The Influence of the International System', *World Politics*, 34, 3: 324–352.

Picciotto, Sol 1983, 'Jurisdictional Conflicts, International Law and the International State System', *International Journal of the Sociology of Law*, 11: 11–40.

Picciotto, Sol 1988, 'The Control of Transnational Capital and the Democratisation of the International State', *Journal of Law and Society*, 15, 1: 58–76.

Picciotto, Sol 1997, 'International Law: The Legitimation of Power in World Affairs', in Ireland, Paddy and Per Laleng (eds.), *The Critical Lawyers' Handbook 2*, London: Pluto Press.

Picciotto, Sol 1998, 'Globalisaton, Liberalisation, Regulation', paper presented at the conference on Globalisation, the Nation-State and Violence at Sussex University. <http://www.lancs.ac.UK/staff/lwasp/glibreg.pdf>

Piccone, S. and G. Ulmen 1996, 'Introduction to Special Issue on Populism II', *Telos*, 104.

Polat, Necati 1999, 'International Law, the Inherent Instability of the International System, and International Violence', *Oxford Journal of Legal Studies*, 19, 1: 51–70.

Preiser, Wolfgang 1984a, 'History of the Law of Nations: Basic Questions and Principles' in Bernhardt, Rudolf et al. (eds.) 1995, *Encyclopedia of Public International Law*, Amsterdam: Elsevier.

Preiser, Wolfgang 1984b, 'History of the Law of Nations: Ancient Times to 1648' in Bernhardt, Rudolf et al. (eds.) 1995, *Encyclopedia of Public International Law*, Amsterdam: Elsevier.

Purvis, Nigel 1991, 'Critical Legal Studies in Public International Law', *Harvard International Law Journal*, 32, 1: 81–127.

Quinn, Frederick 2000, *The French Overseas Empire*, Westport, CT. Praeger.

Redhead, Steve 1978, 'The Discrete Charm of Bourgeois Law: A Note on Pashukanis', *Critique*, 9: 113–120.

Rees, John 1998, *The Algebra of Revolution. The Dialectic and the Classical Marxist Tradition*, London: Routledge.

Reiman, Jeffrey 1995, 'The Marxian Critique of Criminal Justice' in Caudill, David S. and Steven Jay Gold (eds.), *Radical Philosophy of Law*, New Jersey: Humanities Press.

Reisman, W. Michael 1976, 'African Imperialism', *American Journal of International Law*, 70, 4: 801–802.

Reisman, W. Michael 1994, 'The Raid on Baghdad: Some Reflections on its Lawfulness and Implications', *European Journal of International Law*, 5, 1: 120–133.

Reyna, S.P. 1999, 'The Force of Two Logics: Predatory and Capital Accumulation in the Making of the Great Leviathan, 1415–1763', in Reyna, S.P. and R.E. Downs (eds.), *Deadly Developments. Capitalism, States and War*, Amsterdam: Gordon and Breach.

Riles, Annelise 1995, 'The View from the International Plane: Perspective and Scale in the Architecture of Colonial International Law', *Law and Critique*, VI, 1: 39–54.

Rilling, Rainer 2003, 'American Empire as Will and Idea. The new major strategy of the Bush Administration', Policy Paper 2/2003 of the Rosa Luxemburg Foundation.

Ringmar, Erik 1995, 'The Relevance of International Law: A Hegelian Interpretation of a Peculiar Seventeeth-Century Preoccupation', *Review of International Studies*, 21, 1: 87–105.

Rivkin, David B. 1991, 'Commentary on Aggression and Self-Defense', in Damrosch, Lori Fisler and David J. Scheffer (eds.), *Law and Force in the New International Order*, Boulder, CO: Westview Press.

Robelin, Jean 1994, *La petite fabrique du droit*, Paris: Éditions Kimé.

Roberts, Adam 2002, 'The case for war', *The Guardian*, *G2* section, 17 September 2002.

Rodriguez, Pedro Capó 1921, 'Colonial Representation in the American Empire', *American Journal of International Law*, 15, 4: 530–551.

Roll, Eric 1973, *A History of Economic Thought* (third revised edition), London: Faber & Faber.

Rosenberg, Justin 1994, *The Empire of Civil Society*, London: Verso.

Rostow, Nicholas 1991, 'The International Use of Force After the Cold War', *Harvard International Law Journal*, 32, 2: 411–421.

Rothermund, Dietmar 1981, *Asian Trade and European Expansion in the Age of Mercantilism*, New Delhi: Manohar.

Rowe, Peter, 'Responses to Terror: The New "War"', *Melbourne Journal of International Law*, 3, 2: 301–321.

Rubenfeld, Jed, 'The Two World Orders', *The Wilson Quarterly*, 27,4.

Salter, Michael 1999, 'Neo-Fascist Legal Theory On Trial: An Interpretation of Carl Schmitt's Defence at Nuremberg from the Perspective of Franz Neumann's Critical Theory of Law', *Res Publica*, 5: 161–194.

Samary, Catherine 1995, *Yugoslavia Dismembered*, New York: Monthly Review Press.

Sanborn, Frederic Rockwell 1930, *Origins of the Early English Maritime and Commercial Law*, New York: The Century Company.

Schachter, Oscar 1991, *International Law in Theory and Practice*, Dordrecht: Martinus Nijhoff.

Schindler, Dietrich 2003, 'International Humanitarian Law: Its Remarkable Development and its Persistent Violation', *Journal of the History of International Law*, 5: 165–188.

Schmitt, Carl n.d., 'Space and Greater-Space in International Law', unpublished translation of Carl Schmitt 1940, 'Raum und Grossraum im Vokerrecht', in *Staat, Grossraum, Nomos*.

Schmitt, Carl 1987, 'The Legal World Revolution', *Telos*, 72: 73–89.

Schmitt, Carl 1996, 'The Land Appropriation of a New World', *Telos*, 109: 29–80.

Schmitt, Carl 2003a, *The* Nomos *of the Earth in the International Law of the* Jus Publicum Europaeum, New York: Telos Press.

Schmitt, Carl 2003b, 'Appropriation/Distribution/Production: An Attempt to Determine from *Nomos* the Basic Questions of Every Social and Economic Order' in, *The* Nomos *of the Earth in the International Law of the* Jus Publicum Europaeum, New York: Telos Press.

Schmitt, Carl 2003c, '*Nomos* – *Nahme* – Name' in, *The* Nomos *of the Earth in the International Law of the* Jus Publicum Europaeum, New York: Telos Press.

Schmitt, Carl 2003d, 'The New *Nomos* of the Earth' in, *The* Nomos *of the Earth in the International Law of the* Jus Publicum Europaeum, New York: Telos Press.

Schmoller, Gustav 1967, *The Mercantile System and its Historical Significance: Illustrated Chiefly from Prussian History*, London: Macmillan.

Schröder, Peter 1999, 'The Constitution of the Holy Roman Empire After 1648: Samuel Pufendorf's Assessment in his *Monzambano*', *The Historical Journal*, 42, 4: 961–983.

Schumpeter, J.A. 1951, *Imperialism and Social Classes*, New York: Augustus M. Kelley.

Schwarzenberger, Georg 1952, *Manual of International Law* (third edition), London: Stevens and Sons.

Schwarzenberger, Georg 1967, *A Manual of International Law*, London: Stevens and Sons.

Scott, Shirley V. 1994, 'International Law as Ideology: Theorizing the Relationship Between International law and International Politics', *European Journal of International Law*, 5, 3: 313–325.

Scupin, Hans Ulrich 1984, 'History of the Law of Nations: 1815 to World War I' in Bernhardt, Rudolf et al. (eds.) 1995, *Encyclopedia of Public International Law*, Amsterdam: Elsevier.

Sharlet, Robert 1968, *Pashukanis and the Commodity Exchange Theory of Law, 1924–1930: A Study in Soviet Marxist Legal Thought*, PhD thesis, Indiana University.

Sharlet, Robert, Peter Maggs and Piers Beirne 1990, 'P.I. Stuchka and Soviet Law', in Piers Beirne (ed.), *Revolution in Law*, London: M.E. Sharpe.

Shaw, Malcolm N. 2003, *International Law* (fifth edition), Cambridge: Cambridge University Press.

Shaw, Martin 2000, *Theory of the Global State*, Cambridge: Cambridge University Press.

Shearer, I.A. 1994, *Starke's International Law* (eleventh edition), London: Butterworths.

Sifry, Mica and Christopher Cerf (eds.) 1991, *The Gulf War Reader*, New York: Random House.

Simons, Geoff 1998, *The Scourging of Iraq: Sanctions, Law and Natural Justice* (second edition) London: Macmillan.

Simpson, Gerry 2000, 'The Situation on the International Legal Theory Front: The Power of Rules and the Rule of Power', *European Journal of International Law*, 11, 2: 439–464.

Simpson, A.W. Brian 2001, *Human Rights and the End of Empire: Britain and the Genesis of the European Convention*, Oxford: Oxford University Press.

Sinha, Surya Prakash 1996, *Legal Polycentricity and International Law*, Carolina: Carolina Academic Press.

Sivanandan, A. 1990, *Communities of Resistance*, London: Verso.

Slaughter Burley, Anne-Marie 1993, 'International Law and International Relations Theory: A Dual Agenda', *American Journal of International Law*, 87, 2: 205–239.

Slaughter, Anne-Marie 2003, 'Leading through Law', *The Wilson Quarterly*, 27, 4.

Smith, Tony 2003, 'Globalisation and Capitalist Property Relations: A Critical Assessment of David Held's Cosmopolitan Theory', *Historical Materialism*, 11, 2: 3–35.

Springhall, John 2001, *Decolonization Since 1945*, London: Palgrave.

Steiger, Heinhard 2001, 'From the International Law of Christianity to the International Law of the World Citizen – Reflections on the Formation of the Epochs of the History of International Law', *Journal of the History of International Law*, 3: 180–193.

Stengers, Jean 1969, 'The Congo Free State and the Belgian Congo Before 1914', in Gann, L.H. and Peter Duignan (eds.), *Colonialism in Africa 1870–1960*, Cambridge: Cambridge University Press.

Stone, Julius 1984, *Visions of World Order*, Baltimore: The John Hopkins University Press.

Supple, B.E. 1959, *Commercial Crisis and Change in England 1600–1642*, Cambridge: Cambridge University Press.

Sweezy, Paul 1978, 'A Critique', in Hilton, Rodney (ed.), *The Transition from Feudalism to Capitalism*, London: Verso.

Sylvester, Douglas J. 1999, 'International Law as Sword or Shield? Early American Foreign Policy and the Law of Nations', *New York University Journal of International Law and Politics*, 32, 1: 1–87.

Taiwo, Olufemi 1996, *Legal Naturalism: A Marxist Theory of Law*, Ithaca: Cornell University Press.

Talmon, Stefan 1998, *Recognition of Governments in International Law: With Particular Reference to Governments in Exile*, Oxford: Oxford University Press.

Teschke, Benno 2001, *The Making of the Westphalian States-System: Social Property Relations, Geopolitics and the Myth of 1648*, PhD thesis, LSE.

Teschke, Benno 2003, *The Myth of 1648: Class, Geopolitics and the Making of Modern International Relations*, London: Verso.

Thomas, P.J. 1926, *Mercantilism and the East India Trade*, London: Frank Cass.

Thomson, Janice 1994, *Mercenaries, Pirates, and Sovereigns. State-Building and Extraterritorial Violence in Early Modern Europe*, Princeton, NJ: Princeton University Press.

Thompson, E.P. 1975, *Whigs and Hunters: The Origins of the Black Act*, London: Harmandsworth.

Tilly, Charles 1975, 'Reflections on the History of European State-Making' in Charles Tilly (ed.), *The Formation of National States in Western Europe*, Princeton, NJ: Princeton University Press.

Tilly, Charles 1992, *Coercion, Capital, and European States, AD 990–1990*, Cambridge, MA: Basil Blackwell.

Trakman, Leon E. 1983, *The Law Merchant: The Evolution of Commercial Law*, Littleton, Colorado: Fred B. Rothman & Co.

Travers, David 1993, 'A Chronology of Events' in Rowe, Peter (ed.), *The Gulf War 1990–91 in International and English Law*, London: Routledge.

Trotsky, Leon 1969, *The Permanent Revolution and Results and Prospects*, New York: Pathfinder Press.

Trotsky, Leon 1997, *The History of the Russian Revolution*, London: Pluto Press.

Trotsky, Leon 1998, *Trotsky's Notebooks, 1933–1935. Writings on Lenin, Dialectics, and Evolutionism*, New York: Columbia University Press.

Tuck, Richard 1999, *The Rights of War and Peace: Political Thought and the International Order From Grotius to Kant*, Oxford: Oxford University Press.

Tucker, Robert 1972, 'Reprisals and Self-Defense: The Customary Law', *American Journal of International Law*, 66, 3: 586–96.

Tunkin, Grigory 1975, 'International Law in the International System', *Recueil des Cours*, IV. 3–218.

Tunkin, Grigory 1986, *International Law: A Textbook*, Moscow: Progress Publishers.

Udechuku, E.C. 1978, *Liberation of Dependent Peoples in International Law* (second edition), London: African Publications Bureau.

Ulmen, G.L. 1987, 'American Imperialism and International Law: Carl Schmitt on the US in World Affairs', *Telos*, 72: 43–71.

Ulmen, G.L. 2003, 'Translator's Introduction' in Schmitt, Carl, *The* Nomos *of the Earth in the International Law of the* Jus Publicum Europaeum, New York: Telos Press.

Umozurike, U.O. 1979, *International Law and Colonialism in Africa*, Enugu, Nigeria: Nwamife.

Unger, Roberto 1976, *Law in Modern Society*, New York: The Free Press.

Unger, Roberto 1983, *The Critical Legal Studies Movement*, Cambridge, MA: Harvard University Press.

Vagts, Detlev F. 1990, 'International Law in the Third Reich', *American Journal of International Law*, 84, 3: 661–704.

Vagts, Detlev F. 2001, 'Hegemonic International Law', *American Journal of International Law*, 95, 4: 843–848.

Varga, Csaba 1993, 'Introduction' in Varga, Csaba (ed.), *Marxian Legal Theory*, New York: New York University Press.

Various 2003a, 'Theme II: Security: New Threats and New Strategies', in 'International Symposium on the International Legal Order', *Leiden Journal of International Law*, 16, 4: 873–895.

Various 2003b, 'Theme III: 'Global Governance: Institutions', in 'International Symposium on the International Legal Order', *Leiden Journal of International Law*, 16, 4: 897–913.

Various 2003c, 'Theme IV: 'International Politics and the Role of Law', in 'International Symposium on the International Legal Order', *Leiden Journal of International Law*, 16, 4: 915–927.

Verosta, Stephan 1984, 'History of the Law of Nations: 1648 to 1815' in Bernhardt, Rudolf et al. (eds.) 1995, *Encyclopedia of Public International Law*, Amsterdam: Elsevier.

Verzijl, J.H.W. 1968, *International Law in Historical Perspective* Volume 1, Leyden: Sijthoff.

Victoria, Francisco de 1964, *De Indis et de Iure Belli: Relectiones*, New York: Oceana Publications. <www.constitution.org/victoria/victoria_.htm>.

Virilio, Paul 2000, *Strategy of Deception*, London: Verso.

Viswanatha, S.V. 1925, *International Law in Ancient India*, London: Longmans, Green & Co.

Von Arx, Susan 1997, *An Examination of E.B. Pashukanis's*, General Theory of Law and Marxism, PhD thesis, SUNY.

Walicki, Andrzej 1995, *Marxism and the Leap to the Kingdom of Freedom: The Rise and Fall of the Communist Utopia*, Stanford, CA: Stanford University Press.

Walker, Thomas 1899, *A History of the Law of Nations*, Volume 1, Cambridge: Cambridge University Press.

Walker, Mack 1981, *Johann Jakob Moser and the Holy Roman Empire of the German Nation*, Chapel Hill, NC: University of North Carolina Press.

Walker, Geoffrey de Q. 1988, *The Rule of Law*, Melbourne: Melbourne University Press.

Wallerstein, Immanual 1983, *Historical Capitalism*, London: Verso.

Walzer, Michael 1992, *Just and Unjust Wars* (second edition), New York: Basic Books.

Warren, Bill 1980, *Imperialism: Pioneer of Capitalism*, London: Verso.

Warrington, Ronnie 1980/81, 'Standing Pashukanis on his Head', *Capital and Class*, 12: 102–106.

Warrington, R. 1984, 'Pashukanis and the Commodity Form Theory', *International Journal of the Sociology of Law*, 9.

Wedgwood, Ruth 1991, 'Commentary on Intervention by Invitation', in Damrosch, Lori Fisler and David J. Scheffer (eds.), *Law and Force in the New International Order*, Boulder, CO: Westview Press.

Weiss, Thomas G., David P. Forsythe and Roger A. Coate, *The United Nations and Changing World Politics*, New York: Westview Press.

Weller, Marc 1993, 'The United Nations and the *jus ad bellum*' in Rowe, Peter (ed.), *The Gulf War 1990–91 in International and English Law*, London: Routledge.

Werner, Wouter G. 1999, '"The Unnamed Third": Roberta Kevelson's Legal Semiotics and the Development of International Law', *International Journal for the Semiotics of Law*, 12: 309–331.

Wesseling, H.L. 1997, *Imperialism and Colonialism: Essays on the History of European Expansion*, Westport, CT: Greenwood Press.

Wight, Martin 1966, 'Why is There No International Theory?' in Butterfield, Herbert and Martin Wight (eds.), *Diplomatic Investigations*, London: George Allen & Unwin.

Wilcken, Patrick 1994, *Anthropology, the Intellectuals and the Gulf War*, Cambridge: Prickly Pear Press.

Wild, Payson S. 1938, 'What is the Trouble with International Law?', *The American Political Science Review*, 32, 3: 478–494.

Williams, Eric 1966, *Capitalism and Slavery*, New York: Capricorn Books.

Williams, Eric 1984, *From Columbus to Castro: The History of the Caribbean 1492–1969*, New York: Vintage.

Wood, Ellen 1991, *The Pristine Culture of Capitalism*, London: Verso.

Wood, Ellen 1999, *The Origin of Capitalism*, New York: Monthly Review Press.

Wood, Ellen 2003, *Empire of Capital*, London: Verso.

Wood, Ellen Meiksins and Neal Wood 1997, *A Trumpet of Sedition: Political Theory and the Rise of Capitalism 1509–1688*, London: Pluto Press.

Young, Gary 1978, 'Justice and Capitalist Production', *Canadian Journal of Philosophy*, 3: 421–455.

Young, Oran R. 1972, 'International Law and Social Science: The Contributions of Myres S. McDougal', *American Journal of International Law* 66, 1: 60–76.

Zacklin, Ralph 2000, 'Beyond Kosovo: the United Nations and Humanitarian Intervention', the Josephine Onoh Memorial Lecture 2000, Hull: Law School, University of Hull.

Zemanek, Karl 1999, 'Was Hugo Grotius Really in Favour of the Freedom of the Seas?', *Journal of the History of International Law*, 1: 48–60.

Zinn, Howard 1995, *A People's History of the United States 1492–Present* (revised edition), New York: HarperCollins.

Zoller, Elisabeth 1984, *Peacetime Unilateral Remedies: An Analysis of Countermeasures*, New York: Transnational Publishers.

Index

9/11 Twin Towers attack (2001) 311–2, 314

absolutism 162, 179, 183–4, 187, 190, 201–2
Abyssinia 260
Aceves, William J. 47n
Adewoye, O. 291n
administration 103–4, 106n, 109–13
Adorno, Theodor 131n
Afghanistan 311–2
Africa 241, 248–60, 262–3, 291
  decolonisation of 265
Akehurst, Michael 11n, 12, 24n, 135, 136n, 137n
Alavi, Hamza 229
Alcantara, Oscar L. 4n, 55, 58–9
  on base/superstructure 89
Alexander VI 171
Alexander, Lord 1n
Alexandrowicz, C.H. 167–8, 181, 184
Algeria 218
Allott, Philip 261n
Althusser, Louis 303n
Alvarez, José 311n
America
  'discovery' of 169–78
  – *see* United States
American Declaration of Independence (1776) 233
amity lines 180–3, 207
Anand, R.P. 165, 166n, 168, 211n, 213n
anarchism 47
Anaya, S. James 317n
Anderson, Percy 252
Anderson, Perry 40n, 42, 190, 195–6, 198n, 265n–266n
  on absolutism 202
Anghie, Antony 175n, 183n, 186n–188n, 194n, 225n, 239n, 241n–245n, 247n–248n, 261n, 267n, 270n
  on coercion 246
  on Vitoria 173
apologism 49
Archibugi, Daniele 305n
Arend, Anthony Clark 11n
Aristodemou, Mària 239n
arms economy 219
Arthur, Chris 77n, 97n, 101n, 103n, 138, 200–1
  on Pashukanis 78, 91–2, 119
Artous, Antoine 96
ascending/descending arguments 50–4, 58, 70, 277, 279–80, 284, 289
attack on Iraq (2003) – *see* Iraq, attack on
Aust, Anthony 1n
Austin, John 16, 17n, 34–6
  as denier 18–9
Austria 202
Azikiwe, Ben N. 259

Bailyn, Bernard 232n
Bakan, Abigail B. 94n
Balakrishnan, Gopal 27n–28n
balance of trade 203–4
Banaji, Jairus 94n, 127n
Bangladesh 218
Barber, William J. 230n
Barker, Colin 127, 200n, 218n, 221, 223
Barnett, Randy E. 315n
Barratt Brown, Michael 227n
Barrow, Clyde W. 122n
Bartelson, Jens 188n–189n
base/superstructure 88–91, 95–6
Baxter, John 290n
Beaulac, Stéphane 157n, 179n, 188n
Bederman, David 159
Bedjaoui, Mohammed 302n
Beer, George Louis 180n
Beirne, Piers 75n–77n, 80n, 98n
Belgium 255
Bellinger, Edmund 127n
Bendersky, Joseph 27n
Benner, Erica 29
Bennis, Phyliss 271–2n
Berlin Conference (1884–5) 252–4
Bernitz, Ulf 295n
Bierut 282
Binns, Pete 89–90, 94n, 96n, 99n, 218n
Bismarck 254, 258n
Blackie, Duncan 290n
'blackletter' law 68
Blair, Arthur H. 271n
Blair, Tony 308
Blanke, Bernhard 123n, 125n, 127n–128n
Bloch, Joseph 5n
Blum, Yehuda 143n, 282n
Bodin, Jean 185–8
Bolshevism 21, 239
Borneo 254n
Bosnia-Herzegovina 240n
Bowett, Derek 52n–53n, 143n

Bowring, Bill 303, 304n
Boyle, Francis 20n, 283n
von Braunmühl, Claudia 123
Brazil 218
Brenner, Robert 200
Bresheeth, Haim 272n
Brewer, Anthony 228n
Brewer, John 231n
Brierly, James L. 284n
Briggs, Herbert W. 283n
British Isles 212
Brownlie, Ian 52n
Brugger, Bill 277
Buck, Philip W. 203n
Bukharin, Nikolai 4, 222–3, 228, 261, 273
  on state 292–3
Bull, Hedley 13, 14–5, 26n, 34n, 167, 190n
Bunck, Julie marie 309n
Burn, W.L. 180n
Bush, George W. 272, 279, 311–2
Butkevych, Olga V. 3n, 153n
Butler, Geoffrey 153n
Byers, Micahel 58n

Cain, Maureen 62–3
Calhoun, John Caldwell 127n
Callinicos, Alex 27n, 55n, 88n–89n, 99n, 217n, 219, 226n, 269n, 271n–275n, 287n, 308n, 311n, 312n
  on imperialism 228n
  on 'global governance' 306
  on Great Powers 313
Cambodia 274
Canada 281
Canning, Lord Charles 237
capital logic school – *see* state-derivation theory
capitalism
  as abstract form 217
  imperialism and 273–5, 293
  as juridical 260
  law and 118
  monopoly 227–8
  origins of 214–24
  social capital 107–8
  state and 218–9
Carmichael, C.H.E. 169n
Carty, Anthony 28n, 47n, 48, 225n, 289n, 291n
Casey, Lee A. 311n
Cass, Deborah Z. 47n, 295n
Cassesse, Antonio 307n
Castellino, Joshua 270n
Cerf, Christopher 271n
Charles I 211n
Charles II 220
Charlesworth, Hilary 47n
Chase, Anthony 4–5, 89n
Chayes, Abram 276–7
Cheah, Pheng 303n, 307n
Chimni, B.S. 5n, 6, 9, 22n, 26, 32, 36n, 40n, 42n, 62n, 64–74, 83, 268n
  Falk and 26n, 70–1
  versus Morgenthau 24
China 245–7, 263–4
Chinkin, Christine 1n, 295n
Chomsky, Noam 21n, 237n, 272n, 275–7, 279n, 281, 282n
Christianson, Paul 210n
Churchill, Winston 265
civilisation 242–8, 258
Clark, Ramsey 122n, 272n, 287n
class 65–6
class struggle 99n, 109, 112, 138, 200n, 217, 317
Clinton, Bill 313
CLS (Critical Legal Studies) 5–6, 10n, 25, 46–8, 52, 55–60, 315n, 316, 319n
Coate, Roger A. 302n
Coates. A.J. 279n
Colbert, Jean Baptiste 205–6, 230
Cole, Daniel H. 226n, 316n
Coleman, D.C. 204n
colonialism 7–8, 29, 140, 154n, 169, 174–5, 178, 206–8, 225, 230–5, 264–5
  in Africa 256–7
  ending of 268–9 – *see also* decolonisation
  as variant of imperialism 260
Columbus, Chistopher 171–2, 177
commodity exchange 7, 84–96, 145, 224
commodity-form theory 6–7, 77–9, 109–10, 112, 114–5, 119–20, 141–2, 149, 156, 164, 195, 201, 223–4, 318–9
  international law and 131, 137, 214, 262
Congo Free State 254–6
constructivism 58
content of legal form 83, 140, 158, 162–3
contract 2, 104–7, 126
  Pashukanis on 88
contract theory 105, 110, 213
cosmopolitan democracy 305
Cotterrell, Roger 114
Craig, Paul P. 315n
Craven, Matthew 295n–296n
Crawford, James 1n, 295n
criminalisation 309
Critique du droit 46

Croatia 240
Cromwell, Oliver 205, 220
Crouse, Nellis M. 180n
Cruikshank, Albert 61n
Cuba 71, 276
Curtis, Mark 290n
customary law 72, 78, 242
Cutler, Claire 62, 199n

Davenport, Frances Gardiner 180n–181n
Davidson, Scott 282n
Davies, John 291
Davis, Mike 219
Davis, Ralph 205n
De Pauw, Frans 212n, 214n
decolonisation 81, 114, 260, 264–5
deconstruction 55, 69
Delgamuukw v. British Columbia (1997) 317
democratic governance 305
denial 16–8, 25, 316
 three forms of 17
Denmark 202, 263n
Derrida, Jacques 55, 69
descending argument – *see* ascending/descending argument
Deutsch, Karl 283n
dialectics 5
Dickason, Olive P. 180n
Dickinson, Edwin DeWitt 189n, 191n, 192
Dinstein, Yoram 19, 52, 143n
divine law – *see* law, divine
Dobb, Maurice 200n
domestic analogy 54
domestic law – *see* law, domestic
Dominican Republic 21
Donnelly, Jack 304n
Douglas, William O. 239n, 305n
Drake, Francis 180
dualism 33–4
Dudden, Alexis 263n
Dumbauld, Edward 209n–210n
Dunning, William A. 188n
Dupuy, Pierre-Marie 295n
Dutch East India Company 182

Eagleton, Terry 247n
East India Companies 206–8, 230–1, 234, 240n
Ehrlich, Thomas 281n
Einhorn, Barbara 77
Eldred, Michael 90n
Elias, Taslim Olawale 166n
Encyclopedia of Public International Law 154n
Engels, Friedrich 4–5, 74, 201, 266n
Engelskirchen, Howard 106, 111–2
England 180, 182, 187, 196, 202
 in Africa 251–3
 mercantilism and 204–8
English revolution 189
equality 88, 111, 185–6
 as ideology 194–5
 sovereign 79, 184–6
Espejo-Yaksic, Nicolas 295n
Estreicher, Samuel 1n
Ethiopia 187–8
Eurocentrism 165–7, 175
existentialism 47

Falk, Richard 9, 34n, 36n, 52n, 64, 272n, 274, 277, 282n, 308
 Chimni and 70–1
 as utopian 26
Farley, Lawrence T. 269n
fascism 126
Feinerman, James V. 81n
female labour 111
Fenwick, Charles G. 237n
feudalism 79, 88, 100–1, 106–7, 170, 171
 Bodin on 187–9
 Pashukanis on 130
 Vitoria on 190, 199
Filmer, Robert 189
Fine, Robert 63, 91, 80n, 118n
 on Pashukanis 101
Finkelstein, Norman 272n, 282n
Fisch, Jörg 154n, 176n, 178, 180n–181n, 262n, 292n
Fitzmaurice, Gerald 34, 40n
Fitzpatrick, Peter 147n, 225n, 300–1, 310n
Flint, J. 251n
Foreign Jurisdiction Act (1843) 261–2
form, legal – *see* legal form
formalism 23–4, 32, 34–7, 38–9, 41–2, 60, 79, 83, 126, 219, 231
Forsythe, Dabid P. 302n
Fourteen Points 20–1
Fowler, Michael Ross 309n
France 162–3, 177, 180, 187, 205–6
 in Africa 251–3, 255n
 US and 236–7
Francis II 170
Franck, Thomas M. 283–4
Franco, Generalísimo Francisco 239
Frankel, Boris 28n
free trade 176, 229–31
Freitas, Seraphin de 211–2, 213
French Revolution (1789) 237

Friedmann, Wolfgang 305n
functionalism 118
Furber, Holden 182n–183n, 206n

Gambia 253
Gathii, James Thuo 167n
Geertz, Clifford 59n
George III 233–4
Germany 31
  in Africa 251–3, 255n
Geyer, Martin H. 262n
Giddens, Anthony 222n
Gill, Stephen 318n
Glennon, Michael J. 307n–309n, 313n
Glete, Jan 222n
global governance 305
globalisation 62–3, 229, 306–7
globalism 173, 181n, 200, 209–10
Gold Coast 250, 253, 261
Goldblatt, David 305n
Goldie, George 251
Gong, Gerrit W. 243n–245n, 246, 247n–248n, 263n–264n
Gosselin, Daniel P. 282n
Gottlieb, Gidon 287n
Gottschalk, Tikkun A.S. 296n–297n
Gowan, Peter 54, 131n, 176n, 228n, 280, 290n, 305–7, 311n, 314n
Grabar, V.E. 140n
Gramsci, Antonio 37
Greece 309
Green, L. 180n
Green, Peter 271n
Greenspan, Morris 301n
Greenwood, Christopher 287n
Grenada 143n, 178, 276, 282, 311
Grewe, Wilhelm G. 146n, 153n, 155–6, 158n, 163–4, 170n–172n, 176n, 179–80, 181n–184n, 205n, 208n, 211n, 233n, 235n–236n, 253n–254n, 258n, 265n–266n, 309n
  on absolutism 202
  on Africa 255
  on independence 259
  on monopoly 207
Grief, Nick 1n
Grossraum 29–31
Grotius 10, 26, 32n, 131n, 141, 154n, 157n, 168, 179, 189–91, 193, 195–6, 199, 280
  on freedom of the seas 209–14
Grovogui, Siba N'Zatioula 225n, 251–2, 255, 256n, 257, 259n, 264n, 269–70
  on Jackson 267n
grundnorms 35, 72
GTLM (*The General Theory of Law and Marxism*) – *see under* Pashukanis
Guantanamo Bay 300–1
Gulf War (1990–1) 8, 271–81, 287, 292, 313
Gulf War II (2003) – *see* Iraq, attack on
Gumplowicz, Ludwig 130–1

Haass, Richard 311–2
Habermas, Jürgen 58
Hague
  conference (1899) 288–9
  court of justice 307
Haiti 21, 237
Halberstam, Malvina 308n
Hall, W.E. 264
Halle, Louis 186
Halley, Anne 131n
Halliday, Fred 229, 279n, 287n, 313–4
  defence of Gulf War 272–4, 277–8
Hamas 297
Hampson, Françoise J. 287–8
Hardt, Michael 270–1, 310–11
Hargreaves, John D. 265n
Hargrove, John Lawrence 277n
Harib Fortress 52
Harman, Chris 88n, 90n, 139n, 178n, 200n–201n
  on base/superstructure 96
Harris. Douglas C. 175n
Hart, H.L.A. 14–6
Haynes, Mike 94n
Head, Micahel 75n
Heckscher, Eli F. 204n
Held, David 305n, 306
Henkin, Louis 283n
Heuer, Uwe-Jens 303n
Higgins, Rosalyn 11n, 17–8, 26n, 38, 39–41, 285–6
Hilton, Rodney 200n
Hinsley, F.H. 185n, 188n
Hirsch, Joachim 123n
Hitchens, Christopher 238n, 276
Hitler, Adolf 31
Hittites 158, 160, 162
Hobbes, Thomas 18n, 131n, 189
  Pufendorf and 191
Hobsbawm, E.J. 21n, 237n, 240n 248n–249n, 260n, 265n
Hochschild, Adam 255n
Hoffman, Stanley 283n
Holland 183, 205–6, 209–10, 212–3, 220
Holland, T.E. 9
Holloway, John 63, 122n–123n

Holy Roman Empire 157n, 170–1, 174, 179, 192n, 193
Horwitz, Morton 315n
Hosack, John 154n
Huberman, Leo 230n
Hueck, Ingo J. 154n
Huguenots 188
human rights 78, 302–4, 309–10
  Marx on 93
humanitarian intervention 8, 50, 307–10, 312–3, 313–4
Hunt, Alan 46n–47n
Hurwitz, Agnes 295n
Hussein, Saddam 274, 275n, 277–8
Hutchinson, Allan 315n–316n
Hutchison, Terence W. 230n

idealism 4–5, 18, 36, 54, 81
  and fascism 37
  in Derrida 55n
  in New Stream/CLS critique 59
ideology 72–3
  civilisation and 242–8
  international law and 282–4, 296
  law as 80–2
  imperialism and 7–8, 133, 137–40, 154n, 225–30
imperialism
  British 241
  capitalism and 273–5, 293
  defeats of 237
  ideology and 7–8, 133, 137–40, 154n, 225–230
  international law and 246–7, 270–1, 275, 293
  Lenin on 138–9
  naturalised in law 241–2
  Schmitt and 30–1, 50, 291
  UN and 290
indeterminacy 41, 50, 52, 54–6, 59
  Chimni on 68–71
India 167, 206, 233–5, 240
indigenous peoples 317–8 – *see also* natives
International Court of Justice (ICJ) 276, 282, 297–8
International Law Commission 39
international law
  Africa and 252–60
  American Independence and 234
  as body of rules 13–5, 24, 37–8
  class and 65–6
  as colonialism 168–78
  colonies and 235
  commodity-form theory and 131, 137, 156, 164, 201
  as epiphenomenon 22–3
  force and 286–9
  hegemon and 311
  history of 7, 153–4
  ideology and 282–4, 296
  illegality and 295–6
  imperialism and 8, 225–6, 241, 246, 268–71, 275, 293
  in antiquity 159–64
  Moser and 194
  non-Western 165–9
  normative 3, 23–5 – *see also* norms, *grundnorms*
  Pashukanis on 75–113, 129–32, 160–1
  as policing 140–1, 309–10
  as politics 299–300
  as primitive law 35, 53, 143n
  private/public 2, 137, 199, 319
  as process 281
  as profession 242
  proper 54, 61
  renewed relevance of 1–2
  states and 11–2, 24, 114, 161
  as *status quo* law 314
  theory and 9–11
  Umozurike on 268–9
  US and 275–6, 312
internationalism 21, 131
interpretation 39, 41, 68, 72, 121, 142–4, 285
invisible hand 51
IR (International Relations) 156–7
Iran 283
Iraq 259, 273–81
  attack on (March 2003) 1, 295–6, 298–9, 311
Iroquois 160
Israel 143, 146n, 282, 297–8
Italy 177, 260
ius ad bellum 276, 279, 287
ius cogens 268
ius gentium 130, 170, 175, 193n
ius in bello 287
iusta causa 176

Jackson, Robert H. 267n
Janis, Mark W. 276n
Japan 247, 263–4
Jenkins, William Sumner 127n
Jessop, Bob 119n, 122n, 123
Jhering, Rudolf von 134n
af Jochnik, Chris 288–9
Johns, Christina Jacqueline 281n
Johnson, P. Ward 281n
Johnson, Richard R. 180n

Johnston, W. Ross 243n–245n, 247n–248n, 250n, 252n, 261n–262n
joint-stock companies 107–8
Julius II 171
Jürgens, Ulrich 123n, 125n, 127n–128n
jus – see under *ius*
just cause 175–6
Just War 175–6, 187–8, 211
justice 100

Kaldor, Mary 305n, 310
Kalshoven, Frits 52–3
Kant, Immanuel 148
Kaplan, Morton A. 283n
Kastendiek, Hans 123n, 125n, 127n–128n
Katzenbach, Nicholas de B. 283n
Kay, Geoffrey 104–11
Keach, William 1n
Keal, Paul 317n
Kelman, Mark 46n–47n
Kelsen, Hans 14–5, 34–7, 136n, 166n
  Pashukanis and 79–80
  Purvis on 45n
Kennedy, David 46, 47n, 48, 48n, 131n, 154n, 286n, 295n, 300, 304, 307n
Kennedy, Duncan 46
Kenya 253
Kervegan, Jean-Francois 31n
Kimminich, O. 153n
Kingsbury, Benedict 186n, 313n, 317n
Kirkpatrick, Jeanne 298n
Kissinger, Henry 276, 296
Klein, Robert A. 186n
Knight, W.S.M. 209n
Koechler, Hans 305n
Kooijmans, P.H. 191n–192n, 194n
Korea 253, 264, 276
Korff, S.A. 157–8
Korovin, E.A. 60
Korsch, Karl 91
Koshy, Susan 307n
Koskenniemi, Martti 10, 20n, 23n, 24, 26–7, 28n, 31n, 153n–154n, 155–156n, 225n, 241, 242n, 251n–254n, 255, 258n, 269, 277, 279–80, 282n, 285, 289, 314
  Chimni and 70–1, 74
  on liberalism 49–59
  on McDougal 37
  on UN Charter 266–7
  From Apology to Utopia 48–59
Kosovo 81, 307–8, 313
Krasner, Stephen D. 156n–57n, 301n
Kriedte, Peter 216n
Kubálková, Vendulka 61n
Kunz, Josef L. 21n
Kuwait 277–9, 281
labour 94–5, 105–10
Labour Party (UK) 1
labour theory of value 220
Lachs, Manfred 16–7, 18n, 35n–36n, 169n
Lansing, Robert 21n, 237n
Lasswell, Harold D. 37n, 144n
Latin America 237, 241–42
Lauterpacht, H. 18n
law
  capitalism and 118
  as disguise for force 194–5
  divine 187
  domestic 46
  as ideology 80–2
  interpretation and 39, 41, 68
  law merchant 197–8
  Lenin on 99
  maritime 197, 204–6, 208
  Marx on 77
  Natural, *see* Natural law
  Pashukanis versus 97–101
  politics and 149–50
  pre-capitalist 88–9, 100–1, 130, 169–70, 187–9, 191, 199
  as process 5, 38–9, 41–2, 74
  as progressive 317
  proletarian 99
  public/private 65, 113
  Roman 195–6, 197
  state and 82–3
  withering away of 98–101
'law-ness' 10, 13–6, 84, 103, 280, 297–8
Lawrence, T.J. 154n, 160n, 226n
lawsuit 78, 86, 95
League of Nations 146, 257–8
Lebanon 259
Lee, Eric Yong-Joong 263n
legal form 2, 5, 16, 43, 59, 61
  Cain on 62–3
  categorial 277
  Chimni and 64–8, 73–4
  commodity and 84–96, 141
  Grewe and 164
  Pashukanis on 78–9, 82–96, 118
  Picciotto and 63–4
  social content of 162–3
  universalisation of 268
  violence and 134–7, 150–1, 292–3
Lenin, Vladimir Ilych 4, 21, 90n, 138–9, 222, 273, 292
  on imperialism 226–8
  on law 99
Lenoble, Jacques 303n
Leopold II 255
Levins, Richard 5n

Lewontin, Richard 5n
liberal-cosmopolitanism 305–7, 309, 314, 316
liberalism
CLS on 47–8
Koskenniemi on 49–55
New Stream on 48–9
Lindley, M.F. 208n, 225n
Linebaugh, Peter 205n, 220, 231, 232n
Liu, Lydia H. 175n, 263n
Lloyd, T.O. 180n
Lockley, Joseph 290
Louis XV 162
Lowe, Vaughan 295n
Lugard, Frederick 258
Lukàcs, György 227n
Lukashak, Igor I. 240n
Luxemburg, Rosa 228n

Macalister-Smith, Peter 153n, 159n–160n
Maccoby, Simon 153n
Mackinnon, William 251
Maclean, George 250
Madagascar 247, 253
Madonna 302–3
Maggs, Peter 76, 80n
Malanczuk, Peter 9n, 12, 14, 24n, 32n–33n, 154n, 156n, 185n
on denial 16–8
Mallison, Sally 282n
Mallison, W. Thomas 282n
Malowist, M. 216n
managerialism 194
Manas, Jean 276
mandate system 257–9, 264
Manning, Patrick 232n
Manning, William Oke 154n, 160
Mansell, Wade 282n, 311n
Marín-Bosch, Miguel 265n–266n
maritime law – *see* law, maritime
Marks, Susan 81, 270n, 295n, 296, 299
Marshall Brown, Philip 26n
von Martens 236
Marx Karl 54, 215, 266n, 293
on capitalist production 93–4
on Factory Acts 120, 317
on law 77
on rights 8, 93, 120, 135, 142, 292
Capital Vol 1 112n, 120, 150, 317
Capital Vol 3 199–201
Grundrisse 79
Marxism 3–5
'political' 200n, 217
in Soviet Bloc 60–2
since mid-80s 62–4
materialism 4–5
Matten, Johannes 188n
Matthews, Ken 271n
McCarthy, Leo 14n, 19, 35n
McDougal, Myres S. 5, 9n, 37–43, 50, 64, 74, 121, 144n
Chimni on 68–72
Pashukanis and 141–5
McDougal-Lasswell jurisprudence 37n, 40–2
McGrew, Anthony 305n
Mcwhinney, Edward 129n
mercantilism 7, 97, 168–9, 173–4, 179, 199–200, 202–6, 229–31, 233, 235
capitalism and 200, 214–24
debate over 200
robbery and 133–4
merchant law – *see* law, law merchant
Meron, Theodor 309n
Merritt, Adrian 315n–316n
Meyer, Howard N. 298n
Michalak, Stanley J. 26n
Micronesia 265n
Middle East Watch 272n
Miguel, Dom 239
Miles, Robert 94n
militarism 222–3
Miller, Jennifer 267n, 281n
Mills, Kurt 309
Milovanovic, Dragan 77n
mode of production 62
Monahan, Patrick 315n–316n
monism 33–4
monopoly 206–7, 217, 251
Monroe Doctrine (1923) 21, 237–8
Mooers, Colin 200
Moore, John Norton 277, 282n
morality 2
Austin on 16, 19, 23
Pashukanis on 149–50
Morgenthau, Hans J. 16–7, 45n, 64
McDougal on 38
on realism 19–23
Morocco 247
Morton, A.L. 198n, 231n–232n, 234n–235n, 246n, 248n–249n
Moscovy 187
Moser, Johann Jakob 192–4
Mott, James 104–11
Mouffe, Chantal 27n
Moushabeck, Michael 271–2n
multiculturalism 28n
Muscat 247
myth 59

Namibia 265n
Nanda, Ved P. 281n

national interest 20, 23, 30, 240
- *see also* self-determination
nationalisation 218
nationalism 138, 162–3, 228
natives 174–5, 177, 188, 258, 264n, 317–8
NATO (North Atlantic Treaty Organisation) 81, 307
natural law 32, 175, 191–3, 212, 241–2
Pashukanis on 193
naturalism 32–3, 49
Navigation Acts 204–6, 230
Nazism 27, 31, 155n
Neff, Stephen C. 155n
Negri, Antonio 127n, 270–1, 310–2
neo-colonialism 268–9
Neocleous, Mark 28n
neoliberalism 63–4
NEP (New Economic Policy) 90n
Nesiah, Vasuki 270n
Netherlands – *see* Holland
New Haven school 68
New Stream 46–8, 56–7, 81
Purvis on 58–9
New World 169, 172, 178, 183–4
new world order 63
Newsinger, John 245n
Ngantcha, Francis 213n–214n
Nicaragua vs. US (1986) 282, 298, 317
NIEO (New International Economic Order) 268, 302
Nigeria 253
nihilism 38, 40, 67, 311–2
Nisula, Laura 302n
nomos 28–9
Noriega, Manuel Antonio 281
Normand, Roger 288–9
norms 3, 23–5, 70–2, 74
Pashukanis on 72–3
Norris, Christopher 55n
North America 233–4
Noyes, C. Reinold 190n
Nuremberg Trials 288
Nussbaum, Arthur 11n, 153n, 170n, 174n, 193, 194n–195n, 198n, 211n, 214
nutmeg 282n
Nys, Erneste 153n

O'Brien, William V. 279n, 282n
O'Connell, Maty Ellen 281n
O'Keefe, Roger 295n
obligation 12
oil 272, 278
Onuma, Yasuaki 159n, 162, 163n, 165–6
Opium Wars 245–6
Orend, Brian 307n
Orford, Anne 303, 307–8
Orth, Samuel P. 286n
Osiander, Andreas 157n, 190n
otherness 247–8
Ottomon Empire 243
Owen, Roger 228n
Oxman, Bernard H. 197n

pacifism 209
pacta sunt servanda 72
Paech, Norman 311n
Pakenham, Thomas 255n
Palestine 297–8
Palmer, Sarah 204n
Pan-African Congress 258
Panama 276, 281
Panitch, Leo 228n, 305n–307n, 311n, 314n
Papacy 157n, 170–1, 173–5, 179–80, 211–2
Pashukanis, Evgeny 6–7, 32n, 64, 72–4, 198, 223–4, 292, 318
on ancient law 160
base/superstructure and 89–91, 95–6
on capitalism 260
concedes to Stalinism 76
on customary law 242n
on Grotius 190
on international law 75–113, 129–32, 160–1
late capitalism and 102–7
on law's limits 146–7
McDougal and 141–5
on method 79–80
on natural law 193
on origin of legal subject 286, 289
politics and 117, 122
reputation 75–7
on state 82, 121–32, 138–41
versus law 97–101
violence and 119
A Course on Soviet Law 76
'International Law' (*Encyclopedia* entry) 321–36
'State Law under Socialism' 76, 99
The General Theory of Law and Marxism (*GTLM*) 76, 84–96, 99, 113
Patomäki, Katarina Sehm 302n
Paulmann, Johannes 262n
Paust, Jordan J. 14n–15n, 36n
Pawlisch, Hans S. 291n
Peace of Cateau-Cambrésis (1559) 180
Peace of Madrid (1630) 182
Peace of Westphalia – *see* Treaty of Westphalia

Perle, Richard 311–2
Perraton, Jonathan 305n
Perrotta, Cosmimo 216n
Persia 187–8
Peterson, M.J. 236n, 239n
Petrazhitsky 80n
Petty, William 220
phosphate 257
Picciotto, Sol 63–4, 122n–123n
Piccone, S. 28n
Pierantoni, Riccardo 255n
Plekhanov, Georgi Valentinovich 82–3
Poland 202, 215
Polat, Necati 289n
policing 140–1, 309–10
policy approach 40, 45
Pope – *see under* Papacy, or individual Popes
Portugal 171–2, 206, 209–12, 239, 265
positivism 32–3, 34, 36, 49, 193–4, 197, 236, 241–3, 247
  utopian 35n
postcolonialism 75
postmodernism 55–6, 225n, 247n, 307n
power 19–21, 38, 42
pragmatism 45–6, 69
pre-capitalist law – *see* law, pre-capitalist
Preiser, Wolfgang 153n, 159n
private law – *see* law, public/private
process – *see* law, as process
property 95n–96n, 126
property rights 87, 118, 194–5
protectionism 204
protectorates 253–4, 256
Prussia 202, 263n
public law – *see* law, public/private
Pufendorf, Samuel 191–3, 196, 199
Purvis, Nigel 45n–47n, 48, 49n, 52n, 57n, 58–9

Quinn, Frederick 180n

raya 171–3, 179, 181, 182n
realism 17n, 19–23, 47, 157–8, 277
  McDougal on 38
rebellions 176, 233, 285, 292
recognition 236, 239–40
Redhead, Steve 99n
Rediker, Marcus 205n, 220, 231, 232n
Rees, John 5n
reflexivity 58
Reiman, Jeffrey 118n, 120
Reisman, W. Michael 52, 80n, 144n, 226n
Renaissance 188, 196
reprisals 52–3, 69, 143, 147, 301
respublica Christiana 173, 175, 179
Reyna, S.P. 222n
Rhodes, Cecil 251
Richelieu, Cardinal 182n
rights – *see* human rights; states' rights; property rights
Riles, Annelise 225n
Rilling, Rainer 311n
Ringmar, Erik 283n
Rivkin, David B. 276n, 287n, 311n
robbery 133–4
Robelin, Jean 148n
Roberts, Adam 1n
Rodriguez, Pedro Capó 226
Roll, Eric 230n–231n
Roman law – *see* law, Roman
Roosevelt, Franklin 290n
Rosenberg, Justin 20, 21n–22n, 158, 237n, 260–1
Rosenzweig, Paul 301n
Rostow, Nicholas 276
Rothermar, Dietmar 203n–205n
Rowe, Peter 281n
Royal Navy 231
Rubenfeld, Jed 312n
Rule of Law 23, 57–9, 304–8, 315
  as actually existing 319
rules 13–5, 23, 66–9, 73–4
Russia 239
Russian Reinsurance case 286
Russian Revolution (1917) 21
Ryle, Gilbert 59n

Salter, Michael 31n
  on Schmitt 27n–28n
Samary, Catherine 240n
Sanborn, Frederic Rockwell 198n
sanctions 23, 134–5, 286
Sands, Philippe 295n
Saul, Ben 295n
scepticism 19–20, 23–4
Schachter, Oscar 17
Schindler, Dietrich 307n
Schirmer, Gregor 303n
Schmitt, Carl 50, 155n, 172–3, 174n, 175n–177n, 181n–182n, 193n, 238, 291, 313
  on *nomos* 27–31
Schmoller, Gustav 204n
Schröder, Peter 192n
Schumpeter, J.A. 231n
Schwarzenberger, Georg 2n, 11n, 13, 52n, 154n
Schwietzke, Joachim 153n, 159n–160n
Scotland 187, 206

Scott, Shirley V. 80–2, 284n, 302n
Scupin, Hans Ulrich 153n
Seabury, Samuel 127n
Seattle protest (November 1999) 302n
Selden, John 209, 210–4
self-defence 52–3, 70
self-determination 265, 267–8, 302, 317–8
  Hardt and Negri on 271
self-help 136, 143n, 148
self-interest 51–2, 285
Serbia 307
Seven Years' War 231n
Sharlet, Robert 75n–77n, 80n, 98n
Shaw, Malcolm 1n, 154n, 305n
Shaw, Martin 228n, 305n–307n, 311n, 314n
Shearer, I.A. 11, 12n, 32n–33n, 134–5, 154–5
Shershenevich, Gabriel Feliksovich 85n
Siam 247, 263
Sifry, Mica 271n
Simons, Geoff 272n, 275, 277n, 286n–287n
Simpson, Gerry 9n–10n, 295n–296n, 304n
Sinha, Surya Prakash 167
Sivanandan, A. 273n
Slaughter Burley, Anne Marie 19, 20n, 312n
slavery 94n, 219–20, 232, 248
slavery, uprisings 233
Smith, Adam 230–1
social revolution 318–9
sources 12
South Africa 265n
sovereignty 18–9, 49, 53–4, 142, 184–94, 269
  9/11 and 311–2, 314
  as colonial 175
  human rights and 309
  independence and 258–9
  maritime 213–4
  Pashukanis on 74
  'popular' 189
  as product of capitalism 256
  quasi-sovereignty 248–9
  Rosenberg on 261
space 172, 174, 238
  Grossraum 29–31
Spain 171–2, 174, 177, 180–3, 187, 202, 211–2, 215, 229
  'the Spanish Age' 179, 181
Springhall, John 265n
Stalin 98, 318
state 6, 139–40
  absolutist 201–2
  as agent of international law 317
  ascending/descending power and 50, 54, 58, 70, 277, 279–80, 284, 289
  Bukharin on 292–3
  capitalism and 218–9
  law and 82–3
  maritime 220
  Marx on 54
  mercantilist 203, 207–9, 212
  Miliband on 121–2
  Pashukanis on 82, 121–32, 138–41
  Picciotto on 63
state-derivation theory 121–8
states' rights 194, 280, 305
status 102–3
von Steck, Johann 236
Stengers, Jean 255n
Stephan, Paul B. 1n
Stone, Julius 26n
Stuchka, Petr Ivanovich 75n, 77, 82
superstructure/base – *see* base/superstructure
Supple, B.E. 203n
surplus value 220
Sutcliffe, Bob 228n
Sweden 202
Sweezy, Paul 200, 215
Switzerland 202
Sylvester, Douglas J. 234n
Syria 259

Taiwo, Olufemi 90n
Telos 28n
Tennant, Chris 47n
terrorism 289n, 301
Teschke, Benno 201–2, 203n, 212, 214–24
textiles 216
Thailand – *see* Siam
Thirty Years War 157n
Thomas, P.J. 203n–204n, 206n
Thompson, E.P. 315–6
Thomson, Janice 208
Tilly, Charles 222n
Tobar doctrine (1907) 238
trade unions 108–9
trade, balance of – *see* balance of trade
Trakman, Leon E. 198n
Travers, David 271n
Treaty of London (1827) 308
Treaty of Nanking (1842) 245–6
Treaty of Tordesillas (1494) 171, 181n–182n
Treaty of Westphalia (1648) 132, 156, 179, 190n, 301, 305
Trotsky, Leon 4, 221, 273
Tuck, Richard 131n, 154n, 191n, 210n

Tucker, Robert 52
Tunkin, Grigory 61–2
Turkey 187–8, 218, 243
tyranny 235

Udechuku, E.C. 268n
UK (United Kingdom) 299
Ullman, Walter 50n
Ulmen, G.L. 28n, 291n
Ulpian 54
Umozurike, U.O. 232n, 248n, 252n–253n, 256n–258n, 260n, 264n–266n
  on international law 268–9
UN (United Nations) 52, 71, 114, 151, 185n, 264, 270, 276–7, 289–90, 298, 314
UN Charter 71, 266–7, 281, 306
Unger, Roberto 46, 315n
US (United States) 40, 235, 239, 255, 281–2, 290–1, 298, 300
  foreign policy 240, 279
  as hegemon 311
  human rights and 303
  international law and 312
  apparent violations of international law 275–6
  Woodrow Wilson and 20–1
USSR 60–2, 98n–99n, 318
utopianism 17, 20–1, 36, 49, 57, 64
  Falk and 26

Vagts, Detlev F. 30n, 311n
Varga, Csaba 60n
Vattel 235–6
Verosta, Stephan 153n
Verzijl, J.H.W. 165
Vietnam 71, 274, 276
Vikings 171
violence 8, 126–8, 133–4, 139–41, 148, 287–9, 293, 300
  Kelsen on 35
  legal form and 134–7, 150–1, 292, 318
  Pashukanis on 119
  property and 95n–96n
Virilio, Paul 81
Viswanatha, S.V. 166n
Vitoria 10, 154n, 173–8, 184, 186–8, 190
Von Arx, Susan 75n, 77n, 87, 91, 96n–97n, 101n, 112, 122n
  versus Pashukanis 100–1, 102–4, 110n
Vyshinskii, A.J. 60n

wage labour 219–20
Walicki, Andrzej 90n
Walker, Geoffrey de Q. 304n, 315n, 319n
Walker, Mack 193n
Walker, Thomas 153n, 198n
Wallerstein, Immanual 200
Walzer, Michael 21n
war 70, 136, 147, 221–3, 318
Warren, Bill 273
Warrington 76, 90, 93, 96n
Watson, Adam 167, 190
welfare state 218
Weller, Marc 276
Werner, Wouter G. 156n
Wesseling, H.L. 252n
West Bank 297
Westphalian Treaty – *see* Treaty of Westphalia
Wheaton, Henry 241, 243, 263
Wiess, Thomas G. 302n
Wight, Martin 157–8
Wilcken, Patrick 272–3, 274n
Wild, Payson 314
Wilde, Ralph 295n–296n
Wilhelm I 252
Williams, Eric 180n, 248n
Williamson, Colin 302
Wilson, Woodrow 20, 237n
Wittgenstein, Ludwig 69
Wolff, Christian 193n
Wood, Ellen Meiksins 188n–189n, 195–6, 200n, 221n
Wood, Neal 188n–189n
Woods, Norma 302
working class 120
working day 120
World Social Forum 302n
World War I 146, 222, 227
World War II 265
  Clinton on 313

Yemen 52
Young, Oran R. 37, 40n, 42, 145
Yugoslavia 306–8
Yuval-Davis, Nira 272n

Zacklin, Ralph 307n–308n
Zanzibar 247
Zemanek, Karl 209n, 213n
Zielger, Katja 295n
Zinn, Howard 234n, 237n
Zoller, Elisabeth 52n, 134n